Diagnosing America

Linking Levels of Analysis

Emilio F. Moran, Series Editor

Covering Ground: Common Water Management and the State in the Peruvian Highlands   *David W. Guillet*

The Coca Boom and Rural Social Change in Bolivia
Harry Sanabria

The Social Causes of Environmental Destruction in Latin America
Michael Painter and William H. Durham, editors

Diagnosing America: Anthropology and Public Engagement
Shepard Forman, editor

Diagnosing America

Anthropology and Public Engagement

edited by Shepard Forman

Ann Arbor

THE UNIVERSITY OF MICHIGAN PRESS

1997 1996 1995 1994   4 3 2 1

A CIP catalogue record for this book is available from the British Library.

Library of Congress Cataloging-in-Publication Data

Diagnosing America : anthropology and public engagement / edited by
Shepard Forman.
   p. cm. — (Linking levels of analysis)
   Includes bibliographical references and index.
   ISBN 0-472-10410-1 (alk. paper)
   1. Ethnology—United States. 2. Ethnology—United States—
Methodology. 3. United States—Economic conditions. 4. United
States—Social conditions. 5. United States—Politics and
government. 6. Social prediction—United States. I. Forman,
Shepard, 1938– . II. Series.
E184.A1D43   1994
305.8′.00973—dc20   94-17692
                                                                       CIP

Dedicated to the Memory of
Frank A. Dubinskas

Acknowledgments

Most edited volumes are a compilation of individual contributions. This volume, however, emerged from a carefully constructed collaboration over a two-year period, which is described in the introduction. As Chair of the American Anthropological Association Panel on Disorders of Industrial Societies, which gave rise to this volume, I want to thank the other panelists for their efforts. Each contributed in every sense of that word to each other's work and to the volume as a whole. The volume would have been very different without the benefit of that interactive process. I also want to thank Judith Lisansky of the AAA, Emilio Moran and his copanelists on the Panel on Transformations of Developing Societies, who met in tandem with us, and our rapporteurs, Deborah Winslow, Catherine Ribic, Esther Griswold and James McDonald. A special note of thanks to Anne Woosely and her staff at the Amerind Foundation, Dragoon, Arizona, who graciously hosted our meetings and helped us through our deliberations.

Series Introduction

The series Linking Levels of Analysis focuses on studies that deal with the relationships between local-level systems and larger, more inclusive systems. While we know a great deal about how local and larger systems operate, we know a great deal less about how these levels articulate with each other. It is this kind of research, in all its variety, that Linking Levels of Analysis is designed to publish. Works should contribute to the theoretical understanding of such articulations, create or refine methods appropriate to interlevel analysis, and represent substantive contributions to the social sciences.

The volume before you, *Diagnosing America*, is the product of more than two years of regularly scheduled meetings by an expert panel of anthropologists. They were called together by then President of the American Anthropological Association Roy Rappaport. The meetings were funded by grants from the Wenner-Gren Foundation for Anthropological Research. Shepard Forman was selected to chair the panel's meetings over the two years and charged with editing the volume. By any measure he has done a superb job, in no small part because of the excellence of the contributors. The book fits into this series because it tries to link anthropology's traditional focus on foreign and exotic cultures to the urgent need for these skills to be used in helping ameliorate the problems of contemporary urban industrial America (read U.S.A.). The volume also addresses throughout the ways in which one may link different levels of analysis in trying to diagnose problems and in seeking solutions.

The book has the potential of revolutionizing how future generations of anthropologists think about their objects and subjects of study. The volume as a whole makes innumerable suggestions for future research that will serve anthropology quite well. The chapters demystify the old-time preference of anthropologists and their friends for the exotic, pointing to the no less exotic culture and behavior of the auto assembly plant, the white-collar worker, and the treatment of immigrants at our borders. It focuses on a number of problems—barriers to participation, economic dislocation, poverty, psycho-social stress—and on a number of core

values of American culture—cultural pluralism and democratic participation—that elucidate the dynamic interplay between different political
and economic contexts.

The authors of the various chapters show the intellectual roots of
the discipline, its many myopias, and the many opportunities for research
that only a few have heeded thus far. These lost opportunities are tied
to structures of power in the academy; to the culture of the discipline
that accepted, sometimes reluctantly, its role as the specialist in the exotic;
and an almost pathological reluctance to address policy issues among
the bulk of academic anthropologists. These myopias are shown throughout the volume to be only partial pictures of what the discipline has
been and should be. From the outset, anthropology has been engaged
in issues of great public interest and controversy: race, class, immigration
policy, rural and urban poverty, and the struggle between values of individualism vis-à-vis the common weal.

This volume not only sets a challenge and an agenda for the next
generation of anthropologists, but it informs other social scientists to
the ways in which anthropology speaks with a distinctive voice about
the problems of the contemporary United States of America. In so doing,
the volume serves to re-link anthropology to the other policy sciences
and highlights that one of the contributions that anthropology brings is
its capacity to speak to different temporal and spatial levels of analysis—
the human evolutionary, the historical, the contemporary, the household,
the factory, the town, the nation.

It is my hope that this volume will not only be a major contribution
to our understanding of how to diagnose the problems of American
society and the ways in which to ameliorate them, but that it will inspire
readers to submit their work to the series. Please contact the series editor,
or other members of the editorial board, to discuss your proposed work
and our possible interest in publishing it.

Editor

Emilio F. Moran, Indiana University

Editorial Board

John Bowen, Washington University
Conrad Kottak, University of Michigan
Katherine Newman, Columbia University
Douglas White, University of California, Irvine

Contents

Introduction

Shepard Forman

In 1986, a group of Oxford-based scholars provided the intellectual fire-power to produce a wide-ranging diagnosis of the contemporary United States. *America in Perspective: Major Trends in the U.S. Through the 1990s* was produced by an "interdisciplinary team of economists, lawyers, political and social scientists," under the auspices of Oxford Analytica, a research and consulting firm that specializes in assessing the implications of national and international developments for business. *America in Perspective* was commissioned by three major U.S. corporations (American Express, Bristol-Myers, and Sun Oil) to analyze the United States' future. It is a remarkable volume, not so much for the power of its analysis but for its attempt, in the best tradition of anthropological studies of "culture at a distance," to examine U.S. exceptionalism in light of the major demographic, economic, and social changes buffeting the United States. Concluding that the United States is at a turning point, that its unique endowment of natural resources, energetic and self-reliant people, and vigorous democratic institutions may be diminished, the study reassesses our capacity as a nation to fulfill the American Dream. The study team asks whether the sustaining vision of that dream, "the promise of continuing material advance and therefore of social opportunities for all citizens regardless of class, race or creed" (57) has eroded, taking with it the basic claim to American exceptionalism: freedom *"from the threat of major class divisions and conflict, and hence of the growth of political movements that are fundamentally hostile to the prevailing economic and social order"* (ibid.).

The emphasis on social and political stability aside, *America in Perspective* seeks to identify and reinforce a fundamental set of values that might supercede an unbridled and destructively competitive individualism that has come to characterize economic, social, and political life in the United States today.

Interestingly, it is the underlying belief in the [American] Dream that is being tested here, and with it the notions of justice, equity and ultimately national purpose. This means equity beyond equal opportunity—it means a society where every person has a place and another chance, regardless of his or her position in the marketplace. Americans in the recent past have largely accepted a set of priorities that downgraded these concerns and gave a higher place to economic enterprise, personal fulfillment and competition. But that was not, and is not, the whole story where fundamental American traditions and beliefs are concerned. An underlying desire for equity and fair play, the willingness to put the social health of the wider community ahead of immediate self-interest—these, too, are traditional American values. (368)

And, as if to issue a challenge to American anthropologists to study culture "up close," the volume ends on a ringing note:

We believe that America still has time to choose—a belief reinforced by the paradoxical nature of some of the themes we have identified in the body of this study, including Europeanization versus the resilient American Dream; mystical faith in technology versus pragmatic limits to technocratic life; a self-interested, class-based society versus an equitable and open society; a society more tightly clustered around home-based activity versus pursuit of private interest in a harsh climate of high risk and stress. These paradoxes define the boundaries of the developing pattern of American life and the tone of the coming decade. They imply divergent emphases and therefore choice, on both the institutional level of policy decision and the individual level of action. The choices will depend on which vision reflects the values Americans want to embrace. The choices that are made will determine how Americans live in the next century. (370)

The volume you are about to read, *Diagnosing America: Anthropology and Public Engagement,* seeks to meet the challenge posed by the Oxford Analytica study team, to define clearly in anthropological terms the choices facing U.S. society and, by placing them in bold relief, to suggest a direction consistent with longstanding and fundamental values of cultural pluralism and democratic participation. *Diagnosing America* is written by a group of academic and practicing anthropologists who share a deep concern for the welfare of our society and the condition of all of its members, especially those who historically have suffered race, gender, ethnic and/or class disadvantage. It focuses on a particular set of disorders—barriers to participation; economic dislocation and poverty; psychophysiological stress—and corrective strategies; and seeks to place them within an interpretive framework that elucidates the dynamic of changing orders of values in a complex political and economic context. It also seeks to demonstrate the contribution that anthropology can make to the understanding and possible resolution of serious social issues in the United States. In short, *Diagnosing America* is an outspoken call for a *committed* and *engaged* anthropology, one that expresses a vision of American culture and society rooted in, what we believe to be, strongly held values of cultural pluralism and democratic participation.

The authors of *Diagnosing America* are all members of the panel on Disorder of Industrial Societies, initiated and appointed in January, 1988, by the Executive Committee and President of The American Anthropological Association and charged with exploring ways to revitalize and strengthen anthropology's commitment to the study of social problems and policies in contemporary industrial and postindustrial societies. Although composed of individuals with a wide range of substantive and theoretical interests (ranging from biological to applied anthropology, from cultural to policy analysis), the Panel agreed that its main purpose was to define and demonstrate to the anthropological profession and to diverse publics the value of a distinctly anthropological approach to the study of social disorders and their possible correctives. Funded by the Wenner-Gren Foundation, the Panel met over a two-year period, discussed each member's work, approach, philosophy, motivation for joining the Panel, and objectives. Mindful of the need to delimit a set of tasks that could be accomplished within the two-year period of the Wenner-Gren grant, Panel members agreed to focus attention on the study of the contemporary United States, in the area where each member had done research or analytical work. Moreover, the Panel selected an "umbrella" theme for its work that was felt to be particularly compelling for the 1990s: *disorders of U.S. society that impede the realization of democratic participation and cultural pluralism.*

Our choice is fundamentally value-driven. We begin with the assumption that all individuals and groups should be able to exercise fundamental rights of political and cultural expression, fulfill their aspirations and potential, and secure their physical and economic well-being. We believe that cultural diversity and heterogeneity are a net plus for the nation, and that enabling the full range of its human talent and energy to be productively released, the United States will benefit and prosper in the years to come. We further believe that this vision of human rights is fully consistent with anthropology's basic postulates and teachings but that, for a variety of historical and institutional reasons, the profession is yet to embrace it with regard to the contemporary United States.

With this premise as a starting point, the Panel set itself the twin goals of identifying the constraints—economic, educational, political and cultural—that prevent large numbers of individuals and groups within U.S. society from realizing the American Dream, and "mainstream" anthropologists from addressing them. Initially, we identified racism and ethnic intolerance, low levels of political participation, downward mobility, poverty, stress-related health problems, gender discrimination, and increasing stratification as a critical set of disorders that were amenable to anthropological observation and analysis. Importantly, they also represent obstacles to broad public input in the institutional policy process.

Procedurally, we devoted our first meeting to discussing the general concept of disorder and the meaning of cultural pluralism and democratic participation. We began by examining *disorder* as it has been used both in relation to systems analysis or cybernetics (Rappaport 1979), and in relation to aspects of the human condition (e.g., hunger, poverty, ill health), opting in the end for a looser, but all-embracing definition that incorporates a variety of approaches to the study of complex societies— historical, political economy, social stratification, among them. We focused especially on issues of disadvantage and exclusion as indicative of disorders needing to be remedied, asking ourselves again and again how well our society is doing in responding to the needs of groups of Americans under persistent stress. In particular, we concerned ourselves with the effects of macroeconomic and political processes and forces on the lives and livelihoods of a diverse group of Americans—white- and blue-collar workers, the inner-city poor, Mexican Americans along the border—as they perceive them. While we believe disorders can be defined objectively in systems terms, in many cases the disorders discussed in this volume have been identified by the subjects themselves as impediments to the good life, as obstacles to their realizing their full citizenship in a free, open society where its values, as expressed in law, promise equal opportunity and the free pursuit of happiness for all.

In the end, we narrowed the areas of "disorder research" to what a group with our expertise could reasonably take on. Panelists assigned themselves the "disorder topics" now reflected in this volume's table of contents and prepared a set of discussion papers for a second meeting that examined: (1) the historical development of the disorder (e.g., downward mobility) as a problem of social inquiry; (2) the contributions anthropology has made to the definition and analysis of the issue; (3) the contributions other disciplines have made to understanding the problem; (4) the major gaps and/or missing data needing to be addressed; and (5) the distinctive perspective anthropologists can bring to the description, analysis, and potential correction of the disorder.

We also debated the meaning of cultural pluralism and democratic participation and the utility and appropriateness of defining them as basic values within our society and within anthropology. We agreed that cultural pluralism had two connotations, distributional and normative, and concerned ourselves essentially with the latter, that is with issues regarding the acceptance of diversity and with notions of tolerance, civility, and fair play, and the barriers that stood in the way of their realization. We agreed that these basic values have competed throughout historical time with other (not necessarily inconsistent) tenets of individualism and meritocracy. We began to elaborate a perspective on U.S. society that joined the study of structural, economic, and political processes with an interpretive focus on U.S. culture, concerning ourselves with historical moments, such as the present, when individualism and economism seem to have gained ascendancy to the point of obscuring principles of equity and social justice. These led us inevitably to discussions about access and participation, especially the political processes of empowerment and exclusion. Our subject rapidly moved beyond the study of communities and social groups that could be neatly bounded to questions regarding the relation of individuals and social groups to society as a whole.

Anthropology itself became a major focus of our deliberations, and we had lengthy, sometimes heated, discussions on its historical role and the degree to which it reflected the apparent ambivalence of the society(ies) of which it is a part. In many respects, anthropology has always celebrated diversity. Its subject matter has been the plurality of world cultures, and its methodology one of participant observation—accessing and acting with (and sometimes in behalf of) *other* cultures. Although tainted by its roots in European colonialism and U.S. frontier logic, and reflecting—and occasionally contributing to—many of the biases that beset a hegemonic and ethnocentric world, as well as our own society, generations of anthropologists have demonstrated their commitment to the principles of pluralism and participation through extended field work abroad. They have described the heterogeneity of world populations and sought to give them voice. Many have tried to situate their subjects within dominant national and world structures. While numbers of anthropologists have devoted themselves to studies within the United States, most treat their subjects ethnographically, as socially and culturally contained, and few attempt to contextualize them within a broad macroeconomic, social and political framework.

At the Panel's second and third meetings, members reported their findings on the state of the art in the study of downward mobility and poverty, stress-related disease, workplace crises, the inaccessibility of democratic institutions, the political and economic vortex in which values become ranked and scored, and the individual and political strategies that are employed to cope and, hopefully, restore semblances of order for individuals and groups buffeted by systemic disorders. While the reports took the form of an evolving research agenda, rather than a definitive examination of disorders in U.S. society, we agreed that together they made a suggestive statement that merited publication as a volume.

Diagnosing America is the result of those deliberations. It is an effort to demonstrate in substantive terms what an anthropology of the United States might accomplish. It is not, however, a definitive anthropological account of the social disorders of U.S. society. Rather, this book is intended as one more sign post and as a stimulus to an engaged and public anthropology. It is suggestive of a new and important role for anthropologists in the debates about our nation's future.

To fully apprehend that role, far more is needed than another collection of essays. If anthropologists are to contribute effectively to the study and resolution of contemporary U.S. social problems, they need to consider the complex scope and nature of U.S. society, to surpass the tendency to localism and particularism that characterize the ethnographic method, to master the macroeconomic and political processes that interact and often condition local responses, and to engage with several publics beyond their study subjects and academic audiences. Most especially, anthropologists need to reach out to policy makers and to the broader public. To realize these objectives, the Panel considered the implications of its disorder-research agenda for the discipline, focusing

especially on questions of recruitment, training, and the system of rewards in an anthropology that is defined almost entirely in relation to
the academy. Panel members stressed the need for the profession to
embrace this kind of research, make it part of its self-definition, and
incorporate it into the mainstream of its research activities.

Despite the importance of an engaged anthropology, and despite its
florescence in times past, the profession has failed to encourage and
support policy research in the United States in recent decades. The cost
to anthropology appears to be an increasing peripheralization of the
anthropological perspective in policy debates in the United States and
the discipline's marginalization in the public mind as a source of wisdom
about the society in which we live. The Panel treated these institutional
issues separately, in greater detail, in a statement directed to the profession, which is included as an endpaper to this volume. That statement
discusses the methodological and theoretical implications of an engaged
anthropology for graduate research and training and for the profession
itself. In short, the statement makes a more deliberate case for a new
kind of anthropological engagement in the study of social problems in
the United States, and presses for better means of fulfilling the social
responsibilities we take to be part of the anthropological enterprise.

Most of the chapters in this volume rely on ethnographic data, placed
in a macro, sometimes quantitative, frame of reference. Most are written
from a subject's point of view. Several seek to explicate the policy implications of their research and analysis. All choose sides. Explicitly
addressing the issue of cultural diversity in the United States, James L.
Peacock (chap. 1) identifies a set of "core" U.S. values as defined by
a tradition of "cultural analysis" that extends from Max Weber to Robert
Bellah. Peacock critiques the Weberian legacy in relation to social forces
and life experiences viewed anthropologically, and suggests a more dialectical formulation of American values. In brief, while the values of
individualism and meritocracy persist and remain cogent in U.S. life,
an ethnographic approach reveals great variation among diverse ethnic
and cultural groupings.

In chapter 2, Carol MacLennan argues that participation in the
political process in the United States, while a central democratic value,
is seriously obstructed by institutional and ideological barriers. She examines the ideology of economism and the marketplace, how it has come
to dominate our political thinking and how it limits participation. She
recommends that anthropologists refocus the study of political culture

on the pluralistic nature of U.S. society, including differing notions of democracy, participation, authority and citizenship, and the conditions under which local mass mobilization and political involvement take place. Frank A. Dubinskas, in chapter 3, describes how hierarchical systems of control and management impede worker participation in the workplace and contribute to the decline in U.S. competitiveness and industrial productivity. Drawing on comparative cases from Scandinavia and Japan, and experiments within U.S. industry, he suggests that alternate models of worker-manager relations that incorporate participatory methods of problem-solving as well as the formulation of joint goals can point the way to more productive industrial relations. Outlining the structural and attitudinal changes needed for a resurgence of energy and productivity in the workplace, he notes that the "monochromatic" nature of U.S. management—"White, male, middle-aged and middle-class"—grows ever more distant from the U.S. workforce, increasingly characterized by ethnic, gender, and racial diversity. Anthropology, he argues, can help find, eliminate, and interpret newly emerging systems and relationships and make them accessible as alternative models for action.

Katherine S. Newman's chapter (4) examines some of the social and cultural consequences of deindustrialization, exploring the impacts of economic dislocation on the white-collar middle class, blue-collar workers, and the inner-city poor. Anthropology's contribution to an understanding of this crisis and the response patterns of different classes has thus far been minimal. Hence, the paper develops a research agenda on the local effects of deindustrialization, with particular emphasis on the interpretive dimension of economic disorder.

According to Michael L. Blakey (chap. 5), fear-provoking social experiences invoke a wide range of physiological stress-effects involved in the etiologies of organic diseases. Major stressors of industrial society include the frustration of not achieving socially acceptable goals, disruption of social supports, and a host of economic uncertainties and unpredictabilities. His paper examines the psychophysiological impact of exclusion, marginality, inaccessibility, and discrimination on poor and black people in our otherwise affluent society. Drawing on data from Great Britain as well as studies of immigrant groups, he argues that stress-related disorders are not a reflection of modern life-styles or the cost of acculturation, but a reaction to status and income differentials and societal impediments to achievement.

In chapter 6, Carlos G. Vélez-Ibanez describes a long history of cultural conflict along the U.S.-Mexican border, where Mexicans and Mexican-Americans alike have had to adapt to nearly a century of immigration and labor-policy infringements on traditional family values and interactions. He calls for a review of educational and border policies and questions the basis for scholarly and popular definitions of *minority* and *underclass,* which lump broad groupings of people into passive categories that are constructed by dominant, often misconstrued Anglo perceptions of other peoples' realities. He describes "funds of knowledge," household clustering, and family and community values that are based on reciprocity and mutual trust and that serve as effective coping mechanisms. These values and cultural formations seem to contradict and stand in opposition to dominant national values of individualism, market and instrumental relations, and life as work, which are emphasized and inculcated within U.S. educational institutions.

In the conclusion (chap. 7), Roy A. Rappaport brings the discussion of an "engaged anthropology" home, focusing on the concept of disorder and disorder research, elaborating a theory of "correctives," and describing the synergetic effect that an engaged anthropology can have on theory and practice. In a masterful analysis, Rappaport pulls the anthropological discussion of social problems from the periphery to the core of the discipline. He locates the roots of the marginalization of the anthropological study of social problems in the United States in the history and self-definition of the discipline and its focus on theory and geography. He examines the pluralistic and democratic values that, for the most part, underpin American anthropology and, taking note of proud moments such as the intellectual and public-policy struggle against eugenics, argues for their promulgation. Likening an "engaged anthropology" to Steven Toulmin's post-modern science, Rappaport dismisses the so-called insider-outsider distinction that has hobbled a domestic anthropology, stipulating instead that researchers specify their relationship to their subjects and base their findings in a rich combination of "subjective" and "objective" data that can involve subject and anthropologist jointly in the formulation of correctives for the problems that beset us.

The purpose of this volume is to turn our attention to an anthropology of the United States. That, of course, is not an original undertaking. Generations of anthropologists have used American culture, subcultures, racial and ethnic groups, communities, social deviants, welfare and service institutions, and pop culture as subjects of investigation.

What makes this effort different is its emphasis on large-scale disorders in the contemporary United States, its attempt to situate them in broader social, economic, and political processes (both global and national), to understand them in the terms in which they are experienced by those who most directly suffer their consequences, and to begin to suggest ways in which correctives can be introduced. Furthermore, while individual essays or books may have similar objectives (e.g., Harris 1987), they have been more topical in nature (e.g., Newman 1988, Peacock and Tyson 1989) and depended on more traditional anthropological fieldwork techniques and methods, albeit adapted to more complex settings. In this sense, each of the essays in this volume derives from a similar, more traditional anthropological undertaking, but the individual authors have sought to depart from their data, their analytical frameworks, and the individual interpretation that has marked anthropology in the past, to attempt a collaborative approach to a social and cultural diagnosis of disorders in American society. Over a two-year period, the authors have met, drafted papers that became each other's secondary data, and subjected their interpretations to the reinterpretation and critical analysis of their colleagues. In so doing, we hope to have produced a model of an interactive anthropology more equipped to grapple with complex issues and one that can be emulated, in greater depth, by subsequent (perhaps interdisciplinary) teams of colleagues.

In describing this effort, it is important to note several things the Panel did not do. We clearly did not address all nor necessarily the most salient of social disorders. Racism, gender differentiation, drugs, and poverty, for example, are not examined head-on. This is largely due to the constitution of the Panel—given the experimental nature of our collaboration, we decided to focus on areas of panelist's expertise and strength. Ultimately, we hope that task forces of anthropologists more directly concerned with these other critical areas will emerge to tackle them, along the lines of the American Anthropological Association's task forces on homelessness, AIDS, and famine. Toward that end, the Panel sponsored a plenary session on racism in America at the Association's 1989 Annual Meeting.

We also did not engage in primary research. Nor did we grapple conspicuously with the methodological problems that inhere in the vastness and complexity of the United States. In some ways, disorder research—the definition and analysis of a disorder and the quest for correctives—defined the "community of inquiry." Nonetheless, to supersede the localism and individual interpretation of the solitary field-worker, to make something more of social research than mere descriptive ethnography, we conclude that teams of anthropologists, including members of the affected communities themselves, need to collaborate in carefully designed research efforts. The Panel discussed several possible models for undertaking this kind of work, and hopes that this collection of essays will spark further discussion and experimentation along these lines. Multi-local and regional studies described by Marcus and Fischer (1986) are two such possibilities, although we believe that studies in the United States can be self-contained and that their explicit call for cross-national comparison is unnecessary. Robert Bellah and his colleagues (1985) demonstrated another form of collaborative research, although—from an anthropological perspective—their reliance on survey data from a limited sample poses serious limitations on the depth and range of understanding of values and their meanings. As Peacock points out in this volume, an ethnographic approach is better able to account for ethnic, racial, class, and gender diversity. The emerging American Anthropological Association task forces that seek to join single ethnographers into networks for larger, supralocal comparisons is a promising initiative, although to date these have come together in somewhat ad hoc fashion around mutual on-going research interests rather than in the design and execution of a specific research effort.

One such attempt at a coordinated research strategy, akin to the Panel's concern to understand and act on perceived disorders in the United States, is the recently completed Ford Foundation project on changing relations among newcomers and established residents in communities experiencing a heavy impact of refugees and immigrants. The study, building on earlier work in which anthropologists innovated with team research on the relations of different ethnic groups living in shared neighborhoods and participating in shared institutions (Sanjek 1990), is seeking to understand both the difficulties and possibilities of intergroup relations as they are played out against the backdrop of changing macroeconomic and social processes (Lamphere 1992). With funding from the Ford Foundation, teams, with a common research agenda, were created in six localities in order to be able to generalize beyond the single cases and learn the lessons that might have policy applicability in the fields of ethnic relations, housing, schools, etc. More importantly, perhaps, the study sought to identify the positive sets of interactions that might help to dispel persistent notions of disharmony and job displacement and serve as guides to future immigration policy. To accomplish this larger set of goals, the work of the research teams was overseen by an interdisciplinary national committee that sought to draw out the general implications of each case for national policy. The explicit charge to the national committee was to aggregate the research findings and produce a dissemination strategy that would ensure that the results and recommendations find their way to a public audience capable of acting on them. These goals were accomplished through a final report, *Newcomers and Established Residents in U.S. Communities: Report of the National Board of the Changing Relations Project,* and a film for public television, "America Becoming."

The changing nature of American immigration is only one of the vast and unprecedented social, demographic, and economic changes confronting the United States in the past quarter century. As described in the Population Reference Bureau's 1989 report, *America in the Twenty-First Century: A Demographic Overview,* the face of American society has shifted remarkably in recent years. We are an aging population, and an increasingly diverse one in terms of racial and ethnic composition. In fact, people of color already are in a plurality in many parts of the country, and will comprise more than half the United States' population sometime in the next century. A variety of studies take note of the changing nature of our labor force and of the job market, as women and people of color enter the labor market in great numbers, and as employment opportunities shift from higher-paying manufacturing to lower-paying service-sector jobs. These shifts are reflected in household composition and have come to transform the very definition of the family unit. As Newman notes in her paper in this volume, they are also cause for grave forebodings about income distribution and the ability of American workers to maintain their standard of living in the face of a real slowdown in income growth.

The implications of these changes are extraordinary, and are already being felt in both actual circumstance and in the attitudes and feelings of the American public, as our traditional values of community and equal opportunity appear to be yielding to more individualistic objectives among a "me first" generation. One need only reflect briefly on the statistics on crime and harsher public attitudes regarding the treatment of criminals; on increased racial and ethnic diversity and far less-generous attitudes toward immigration; on the aging of our population and a growing sense of intergenerational conflict as younger workers (increasingly people of color) begin to worry that their social-security payments will be consumed in meeting the needs of the elderly; or on the increasing middle-class struggle to make ends meet and the less-than-charitable attitudes toward the poor. In the words of Harvard economist, and current secretary of labor, Robert Reich, America is undergoing a changing "public philosophy," a gradual shift in social and political attitudes that occasionally come into sharp relief, principally at election time, as evidenced in the unfortunate manipulation of symbols, attitudes, and goals during the presidential election campaign of 1988. According to Reich,

> A public philosophy gives meaning and coherence to what would otherwise seem random phenomena: a starving child, a shuttered factory, a new Russian missile. By "public philosophy" I mean something less rigid and encompassing than an ideology but also less ephemeral than the "public mood." I have in mind a set of assumptions and logical links by which we interpret and integrate social reality. A public philosophy informs our sense of what our society is about, what it is *for.* (1985, 68–69)

This public philosophy is conveyed in what Reich calls "parables," "in the stories we tell one another about the events of the day"—in other words, in the signs, symbols, phrases, and communications that are the stuff of interpretive anthropology.

We believe that anthropologists have a major role to play in both understanding and formulating this public philosophy, in defining "what our society is about, what it is *for.*" The changes that are occurring in American society interact in powerful ways and profoundly influence our daily lives. Moreover, in a society that is increasingly diverse, the impacts vary across a broad range of social, economic, and cultural groupings. Anthropologists can help to understand the impact of these changes on the life chances of diverse populations and can help to reaffirm positive and long-held values of cultural pluralism and democratic participation. These values are not freestanding. As part of an interactive social, economic, political, and cultural system, they inevitably show signs of stress as demographic, economic, and political factors intervene to place pressure on individual lives, causing the kind of attitude shifts that Reich refers to as the "public mood." Occasionally, these stresses reach proportions that appear to threaten the very fabric of society as we know it and wish it to be. However, an equilibrium seems to be reasserted, a balance that is often referred to in common parlance as the great resilience of U.S. Society.

Anthropologists are particularly well placed to sort out the relationship between public attitudes and the ideas and values that constitute the basic assumptions and understandings that give order to our lives. Political attitudes reflect only an immediate response to changing circumstances and their unsettling effects on people's lives. They should not be confused with the underlying understandings that have permitted, throughout our history, values of community and participation to coexist with those of individualism and meritocracy. For if individualism and meritocracy became hallmarks of the United States in the 1980s, the subdued passions of equity, social justice, and community could nonetheless be found. As one example, we can refer to the growth in the poverty rate in the 1980s when a conservative public philosophy emerged, playing values of individualism and self-reliance off against other fundamental U.S. values of a shared sense of community and social justice. Although a conservative administration sought to cut social spending, Americans refused to let cuts go too deep, noting time and again in public surveys and in congressional elections that they believed the poor should continue to be helped. This is the challenge to American anthropology—to understand and lay bare the underlying values and understandings about relations between the generations, between ethnic and racial groups; about work and retirement; about economic and social vulnerability and shared responsibility; in short, to understand and lay bare an anthropological search for meaning *and* action in American life, an effort to reformulate a vibrant statement of key American values and goals that points in the direction of the kind of society in which we care to live.

Two sets of principles—pluralistic and democratic, on the one hand, and stratificatory and exclusionary, on the other—have alternately combined and competed in the course of U.S. history. When they have come together, during the Civil Rights movement, for example, they have been the source of great national strength and pride, "the zenith of American society and culture," in Bellah's terms. When they have competed, as in the last decade, the result has been a divisive, more conflictual social system, one in which the disorders that have and will continue to plague us swell to prominence. These paradoxical tendencies and the choices they pose place our society at a crossroads, and with it American anthropology. We can either live up to the values and ideals of equality and social justice that U.S. society and the discipline have promulgated or declare them to have little more than rhetorical significance, succumbing ourselves to the competing set of individualistic and meritocratic principles that push us, as members of this society, toward stratification and exclusion.

This volume focuses from an anthropological perspective on the disorders that emerge in U.S. society and the correctives that a resilient U.S. society turns up. In that sense, it is both a critical appraisal of the problems inherent in the U.S. system and a celebration of its flexibility and strength. It is our intent to call forth a similar source of flexibility and strength that we know to exist within the profession. As Newman and Rappaport point out in their chapters, there is ample precedence for this in U.S. anthropology. According to Marcus and Fischer (1986, ix), modern anthropology was founded to offer a critique of our own society, to enlighten us about other human possibilities. Margaret Mead pushed this further, of course, believing that analysis of the "other" would shed light on our own society. The question now before us is why not do it directly, why not undertake an ethnography of the United States, and one that goes beyond mere description to clarify the value choices we need to make? Theoretically, the link has long since been made. As Marcus and Fischer point out:

> . . . in American political thought the anthropological concept of relativism was a strong ally of liberal doctrine in the promotion of the value of tolerance and respect for pluralism, against, at one point, such racist doctrines as eugenics and social Darwinism. In the polemics of political debate both inside and outside academia, the relativistic position was sometimes posed in extreme terms. But the stakes were high, and the outcome was critical. Liberalism, including a strong relativist component, triumphed as the explicit ideology of public policy, government, and social morality in America. It became the defining framework for discussions of rights and justice to which groups of all kinds were entitled in a plural society and welfare state. Only now, in the late twentieth century, as the long reign of liberalism comes under attack, are there appearing renewed academic discussions of relativism, both defenses and critiques. (32)

While the influence of anthropology in the realm of social-policy ideas has no doubt been felt, anthropologists have been notably absent in recent years from the important national debates on participation and pluralism. This absence is a result of several factors: a loathing on the part of anthropologists toward perceived "social engineering"; a retreat in the late 1960s to the rapidly expanding coffers of the "Ivory Tower" in the wake of Vietnam, Project Camelot, and other secret military-support operations in which some anthropologists took part; and, where anthropologists did engage on the positive side of the ledger—for example, in field experiments and evaluations related to the War on Poverty—our inability to turn our localized and often microscopic studies into something more than the ethnographic description of culture and behavior. This latter problem, the this-is-how-my-people-do-it syndrome, has permitted the borrowing, and often misappropriation, of anthropological concepts and facts by other social sciences and policy analysts for a variety of uses, with studies in "political culture" (e.g., Verba and Nye) and the "culture of poverty" (e.g., Moynihan) probably the two best-known examples.

While the concept of culture and, more recently, the method of ethnography (widely misunderstood in the other social and policy sciences as the gathering of qualitative data through interviews or surveys), has appeared from time to time in policy analysis and formulation, the field has been taken by economists and, to a lesser extent, political scientists and sociologists with a more macroscopic view of the universe. In fact, the two major reviews of the role of social scientists in the formulation of public policy, Henry Aaron's classic *Politics and the Professors,* and Richard Nathan's more recent *Social Science in Government: Uses and Misuses,* fail to mention anthropology at all. Rather, Nathan describes the major social experiments of the 1960s and 1970s, the negative income-tax and income-maintenance experiments, revenue sharing, and CETA job-training programs as the efforts of economists and a few political scientists and public administrators whom, he notes, designed policy from above with only post hoc attention to the attitudes, beliefs, understandings and behaviors of the "clients" to whom they are targeted. In fact, in describing a set of supported-work demonstrations, Nathan takes note of the disjunction between assumptions underlying the experiments and the national political will. A more holistic approach, one that anthropology could provide, would seek to understand public reactions to major policy interventions, and to join them to the sense of community and participation that underlies them, an effort that Nathan himself attempts with a retrospective analysis of the narrowing of the meaning that came to be attached to the word *workfare*. Still, his principal recommendation is for separate sets of demonstration and evaluation studies. The first would examine the behavioral responses of individuals and groups to specific policy interventions, and the latter would examine the institutional response of schools, agencies, or firms.

In calling for further integration of the social sciences in the study of social policies and for the use of both quantitative and qualitative approaches, Nathan asks for greater reliance on political science to understand the institutional effects and for psychologists to examine attitudinal responses, but he explicates no role for anthropologists. If anthropologists are present in policy research, they are hard at work in some of the demonstration and evaluation research efforts, like so many elves in Santa's workshop, and not called upon to provide a more holistic and interpretive approach to policy formulation and evaluation.

A central question, of course, is what can anthropology provide? What does the special anthropological lens (Peacock 1987) add to the myriad policy studies, social critiques, and cultural assessments provided by economists, policy analysts, political scientists, and other students of American life? To begin, anthropology provides a focus on and commitment to cultural pluralism and diversity. It also provides an analysis grounded in the perspective of the subjects of study (in the case of studies in the United States, this includes the anthropologist as citizen as well as scientist), and it examines and understands events in the totality of an interactive system. Well done, anthropology can provide understanding of the systemic context for change as well as a client's view of social programs.

What anthropologists could contribute to these efforts is an understanding of the vertical integration of such programs if they were able to step back from their involvement as methodologists and field workers and to participate in the design and implementation of policies. It should be possible to integrate demonstration and evaluation research into a more holistic approach, since we know, among other things, that institutional behavior influences the behavior of clients and vice versa. Moreover, it should be possible to bridge the findings of advocacy or client-oriented groups with those examining institutional inputs and outcomes. In short, an anthropological approach to policy would involve community members in the definition and conduct of research, articulate the affected community's analysis of the problem, showcase local people and institutions able to deal with the problem, and help get resources to those people and institutions. Properly undertaken, anthropology could add to the policy sciences what ethnography does best—recording (albeit in the field-worker's rendering) the subjects' own understandings of their place in the social system and the choices they make based on their ideas regarding the alternatives available to them.

A word is necessary about ethnography, both as means and end. To the degree that ethnography is borrowed by the policy sciences, it serves as a means in the hands of others. In anthropology, the question of ethnography as means or end has been wrought with ambiguity. In this context, we see it as a means to define alternatives, or correctives to social disorders, that are rooted in the culture, ideology, and history of the groups and communities we study. Perhaps our effort comes closest to what Marcus and Fischer describe as the merging of ideological and empirical cultural critiques (114–15) in a way that is at once self-critical and critical of the ills of the society that we are experiencing. The one major difference, perhaps, is that we suggest that anthropologists can and should make known their preferences among the alternatives available rather than simply reporting them in ethnographic fashion, the "fundamental descriptive realism" that Marcus and Fischer see as the on-going contribution of anthropology to a contemporary cultural critique of our own society (117). Making choices is essential to the policy process. Choosing not to make them may help to reassert anthropology's scholarly and scientific bona fides at a time of deep self-reflection in the social sciences and humanities, but fails to *engage* the discipline firmly in a commitment to positive social change. This move beyond ethnography—transforming ethnography from an end to a means—is essential if anthropology is to make an active contribution to public life.

Cultural commentary is not, then, the sole purpose of this volume, although each of the authors comment quite purposefully on aspects of U.S. life. What we seek to accomplish is a recognition of the anthropologist as both citizen and ethnographer as well as a forceful engagement of the discipline with contemporary public affairs in the United States. There are two ways in which this can be accomplished, as a critique of intellectual trends in the fashion of Boaz, or like Mead and Benedict, as critics of specific conditions in our society.

An attempt to strike the right balance forces us to consider the differences between political economy with its emphasis on macro trends and applied anthropology, which emphasizes practice. Too often, studies in political economy focus on the impingement of outside forces—the physical environment, the world capitalist system—on dependent and passive populations, a point noted by Ortner in her critique in *Comparative Studies in Society and History* (1984, 142), rather than more correctly depicting the social system of the group in question as having its own history; its own sense of self and identity; its own idea of its place within the larger universe; as well as its own strategies for adjusting, accommodating, incorporating, or rejecting elements of the imposing larger and more dominant system. In this volume, we attempt to incorporate the latter perspective, that is to identify the barriers to participation and cultural pluralism as well as the coping strategies with which people reintroduce some level of order into their lives, livelihoods, and understandings of the world in which they operate. Ethnography can be done in a way that enmeshes historical, political, and economic facts in the perceptions, beliefs, ideas, and attitudes of people at all levels. The idea is to see these as interactive processes rather than as a snapshot of one group's perceived internalization of dominant forces, as Peacock stresses in chapter 1. This is different from a functionalist analysis in which the *system* reorders itself in a way that reintroduces a sufficient degree of harmony or coherence. It suggests instead that part of the complex and multivariant ways in which systems maintain disruptive forces within tolerable bounds includes sets of adaptive strategies employed by affected groups and individuals themselves. Our focusing on these so-called reordering strategies and mechanisms is important for our purposes because they begin to single out ways in which correctives can be identified and built into the system.

Since the focus here is not on the system itself, it is less vulnerable to the kind of radical critique that deems systems analysis as inherently conservative. Rather, it starts from the committed premise that people at all levels of the system are central actors within intersecting spheres, that there are fundamental value principles of pluralism and democratic participation that govern our society, and that these are continually being reasserted in the activities of poor and disadvantaged people. Empowering them to act in their own behalf restates these principles, pushes the system in admirable directions, and places more obligation on the power-holders to respond. Understanding this struggle as well as documenting and encouraging the variety of public and private support mechanisms that not only enable people to cope with adversity but also enable people to work toward their full potential are the most immediate contributions that anthropologists can make.

Diagnosing America places people at the center of anthropological analysis, seeking to understand their place within a broader universe and the forces that shape that relationship. It focuses in on a set of disorders that buffet our collective lives and tries to imagine the possible correctives, both immediate and systemic, that might be introduced or brought to scale. In this sense, we are situated at the center of what Ortner describes as "practice-oriented work" or "practice theory" (146). Our effort is value driven, and we are committed to improving the ways in which social systems distribute their rewards. But we are also interested in elucidating the way in which social systems work in the specific case— in understanding the nature of social disorders and elaborating a theory as well as a practice of corrective action. This is important, because we believe this kind of "disorder research" can bridge theory and practice and, in fact, the former can—if we learn our lessons well—contribute to doing the latter better. This is the essence of an engaged anthropology—one that engages the important social issues of the day and reengages with itself; one that sees anthropology as a part of the system in which it functions. Over the long term, we believe that an anthropology engaged in the critical study of American culture and social structure, and in critical self-appraisal, can revitalize the public voice of the discipline and return anthropology to its central mission: to promote social justice and reaffirm the value of diversity.

REFERENCES

Aaron, Henry. 1978. *Politics and the Professors.* Washington, D.C.: Brookings Institution.

America in the Twenty-First Century: A Demographic Overview. 1989. Washington, D.C.: Population Reference Bureau.

Bach, Robert. 1993. *Changing Relations: Newcomers and Established Residents in U.S. Communities.* New York: Ford Foundation.

Bellah, Robert N., Richard Madsen, William M. Sullivan, Ann Swidlen, and Steven M. Tipton. 1986. *Habits of the Heart: Individualism and Commitment in American Life.* New York: Harper & Row.

Harris, Marvin. 1987. *Why Nothing Works: The Anthropology of Daily Life.* New York: Simon and Schuster.

Lamphere, Louise. 1992. *Structuring Diversity: Ethnographic Perspectives on the New Immigration.* Chicago: University of Chicago Press.

Marcus, George E. and Michael M. J. Fischer. 1986. *Anthropology as Cultural Critique: An Experimental Moment in the Human Sciences.* Chicago: University of Chicago Press.

Moynihan, Daniel Patrick. 1965. *The Negro Family: The Case for National Action.* Washington, D.C.: United States Department of Labor, Office of Policy Planning and Research.

Nathan, Richard P. 1988. *Social Science in Government: Uses and Misuses.* New York: Basic Books.

Newman, Katherine S. 1988. *Falling From Grace: The Experience of Downward Mobility in the American Middle Class.* New York: Free Press.

Ortner, Sherry B. 1984. Theory in Anthropology since the Sixties. *Comparative Studies in Society and History* 26 (January): 126–66.

Peacock, James. 1987. *The Anthropological Lens: Harsh Light, Soft Focus.* Cambridge: Cambridge University Press.

Peacock, James and Ruel W. Tyson. 1989. *Pilgrims of Paradox: Calvinism and Experiences Among Primitive Baptists of the Blue Ridge.* Washington: Smithsonian Institution Press.

Rappaport, Roy. 1979. Adaptive Structure and Its Disorders. In *Ecology, Meaning and Religion.* Richmond, Calif.: North Atlantic Books.

Reich, Robert. 1985. Toward a New Public Philosophy. *Atlantic Monthly* 255 (May): 68–79.

Sanjek, Roger. 1990. *At Work in Homes: Household Workers in World Perspective.* Washington, D.C.: American Anthropological Association.

Verba, Sidney, and Norman H. Nie. 1972. *Participation in America: Political Democracy and Social Equality.* New York: Harper & Row.

Young, David, ed. 1986. *American in Perspective: Major Trends in the United States Through the 1990s.* Oxford Analytica. Boston: Houghton Miflin.

Chapter 1

American Cultural Values: Disorders and Challenges

James L. Peacock

A dominant view of American culture has long been that it is centered around such values as rationality and individualism and is grounded in Enlightenment, Protestant, and Anglo-Saxon traditions. Not only are such values honored by those who celebrate the heritage and worth of America as a culture and a nation, but also a distinguished line of scholarship documents the history and patterning of these values (e.g., Gabriel 1974). Yet both the heritage and the scholarly emphasis are problematical. The spirit of capitalism, revered as the quintessential expression of rational individualism, seems to have lost its mooring in the Protestant ethic or any other ethic as these two images are perverted, by greedy hustlers, from Wall Street to evangelism. Individualism without social responsibility implies disorders ranging from narcissistic solipsism (Bellah et al. 1985; Lasch 1979) to exploitation and bullying of have-nots, which is, in turn, reciprocated by violence. Such disorders call for examination of the so-called core American values and their implications for American society and culture.

Certain current trends also call for the examination of core American values. One such trend is pluralism. America has never been uni-cultural, and the recent influx of Asians, Hispanics, and others challenges the dominance of a core tradition of rationalized individualism rooted in Anglo-Saxon Protestantism. These issues came to light as we celebrated Columbus' discovery of 1492. Do the traditional core values clash with these multiple cultural heritages? If so, how might this clash hamper the participation of noncore groups in U.S. society, especially in its democratic governance?

This chapter addresses these issues by counterposing one dominant approach to defining a core American value system (that stemming from Max Weber and his descendants) to studies and approaches identifiable with anthropology that offer a more pluralistic picture of American culture. The argument is not that the core-value tradition is wrong but that it requires enrichment, some directions of which are suggested through anthropological work. Anthropological analysis, on the other hand, requires systematization in order to frame cultural pluralism and other ethnographic "realities" within the larger U.S. context and in relation to dominant values.

From Max Weber to Robert Bellah: America as a Cultural System

Among the many efforts at defining U.S. culture, one scholarly tradition is distinguished by its coherence and continuity. This is the effort to define the cultural system of the United States as traced from *The Protestant Ethic and the Spirit of Capitalism* by Max Weber (1985) through later Weberian approaches such as *Habits of the Heart* by Robert Bellah et al. (1985).

Weber's key theme is that ideational configurations—religious beliefs, ethical values, even aesthetic forms—have a certain coherence and autonomy that is not entirely explicable or reducible to their social, economic, or political contexts. Such systems of meaning later came to be termed, by U.S. sociologists and anthropologists of the Weberian inspiration, "cultural systems" or just "culture."

Translation of Weber's ideas into the concept of a culture system was primarily the work of Talcott Parsons. Parsons, like Weber, saw human existence as a field of "action." To analyze this action, the analyst must abstract from it patterns and regularities that can be described as systems. One such system is the personality system—the dynamics of the individual self—and another is the social system—the dynamics of the collectivity. A third system, which ordered and gave meaning to the others, is the cultural system, comprised of values, symbols, and beliefs. A fourth system is the environment, which is the setting for the other systems. In anthropology, David Schneider, Clifford Geertz, and others adopted and elaborated this Parsonian notion of the cultural system, privileging it against other, more holistic (but also inchoate) definitions of culture, and highlighting *it,* rather than the social, personality, or environmental systems (Geertz 1973; Parsons 1937, 1951a, 1951b; Schneider 1968). The tradition continues in Robert Bellah's formulation of America as a cultural system in *Habits of the Heart* (Peacock 1988).

To see the United States as a cultural system, then, is not to see America in its entirety, but to abstract from the complexities a pattern— to attempt to formulate guiding meanings (ideas, values, symbols) that tend toward a coherent and autonomous system while, in Parsons' words, "interpenetrating" social life, individual motivation, and environment. This interpretation is important. While the Weberians do see culture as having some autonomy, culture is not viewed as a lifeless abstraction or a purely cognitive construction, but instead as what Turner (1974) calls a "root paradigm"—a framework of deeply grounded beliefs and moral injunctions that embody strong emotion as they confront good and evil, life and death.

What dominant cultural patterns has this Weberian tradition constructed for the United States? Weber himself was primarily interested in America as an expression of a religiously grounded culture, the Protestant ethic, with its associated economic value, the spirit of capitalism. In his 1904 visit to America, during which he carried out a kind of fieldwork, he saw this connection vividly. Visiting his cousins in Mount Airy, North Carolina, Weber asked a man why he was subjecting himself to baptism in a chilly stream. "He plans to open a bank," he was told (Weber 1946, 304). However, in his larger analyses, Weber did not emphasize so much the working relationship between religion and economics as he did the cultural values that underlie both in Anglo-American Calvinist-capitalistic culture. Such values were *instrumental;* that is, all that one did must be efficiently and relentlessly organized toward some end which, religiously speaking, was the glory of God. Such values were religiously and ultimately *individualistic;* it is the individual who is saved or damned for eternity, and no relationship to another human can affect his destiny. Such values were *activist.* In a perverse way, Weber argued, the doctrine of predestination in Calvinism, which logically would seem to engender fatalism, instead spurred a fervent struggle by everyone to prove that he or she was one of those predestined to be of the elect.

These themes of activism, individualism, and instrumentalism resound throughout the writings of the Weberians in regard to America. Talcott Parsons (1982) summed them up as two dominant American values: institutional individualism, and instrumental activism. *Instrumental,* according to Parsons did not mean only a general emphasis on means and methods, it also meant specifically that society was seen as instrumental to other ends. Formerly, he says, these ends were transcendental (e.g., the glory of God); but now it is individual ends that society is seen as properly serving. Constitutionally (in several senses of the word), Americans see the state as serving the individual, rather than the reverse. The addition of the term *institutional* (which means not *institutions* in the narrow sense but *institutionalized*, i.e., established socially) elaborated on a feature that Weber ignored, though his predecessor de Toqueville had highlighted it: the associational character of American life, which Parsons sees as balancing individualism in a non-hierarchical pattern. This American collectivism was also elaborated on, of course, by those who saw the Protestant ethic's individualism on the decline. These elaborations can be seen in David Riesman's (1950) shift from inner-directedness to other-directedness in the forties; in William White's (1956) chronicling of the rise of the organization man in the fifties; and in Reich's *Greening of America,* when a communal, participational sixties counterculture ("Consciousness Three") followed from the creation of a corporate America. While accepting such points, Parsons's term *institutional individualism* affirms Weber's insight—Americans may organize themselves collectively but they do so toward individually defined ends. Americans, also and finally, deploy the state for their pursuit of happiness and other individual goals, rather than the state's claiming their lives for its collective ends. (As elsewhere, Parsons is attempting to formulate the broad tendency in U.S. values over the full span of U.S. history. He is not attempting to consider particular tendencies that vary with eras and regimes, such as some might see as recurrent tendencies for a power elite, or the state, to serve itself more than the citizenry; or for other exploitative processes to override the upholding of core values.)

In formulating these core values, Parsons also makes some general arguments about the place of values in American society and culture:

> We do hold that there is and has been a single well-integrated value system institutionalized in the society which has "evolved" but has not been drastically changed. As such, it must be considered at a high level of generality. The value patterns . . . implicitly or explicitly define the desirable type of society . . . a value system does not describe the concrete state of affairs of the system in which it is institutionalized. . . . (1982, 327)

Core values, then, are held to be core if one looks for them at a high enough level of generality. This is not to deny that there will be variation (implying tension and conflict) between the values and actual behaviors as well as among different values or different groups and persons manifesting those values: "The goals to which the instrumental applies have become those distributively allocated to individual citizens and to subcollectivities..." (1982, 328).

Nor, in the Parsonsian formulation, does recognition of the religious basis of U.S. values presume a simple and unitary equation of doctrine and operant American values. A fundamental fact about America, he emphasizes, is the separation of church and state, which engenders denominational pluralism. Also, American individualism has always emphasized the role of religion in regard to individual life rather than to the collective discipline of the church, as was characteristic in early Calvinism and other religious movements. America shows a "concern with freedom and equality in contrast with the collective discipline of the Calvinistic movements and, what in some respects is a cultural revival and extension of them, Communist versions of socialism" (1982, 328). The American "privatization" of religion, and even a seeming "secularization," does not mean, Parsons emphasizes, that religiously grounded values have ceased to have implications for American society (1982, 330). Here Parsons implies that the loss of specifically religious (doctrinal, ritual) content has not destroyed the values that originally were attached to such content. Owing to the distinctive pattern of American culture, Parsons and Parsonsians caution against applying European theories, such as the Marxist, which inappropriately assume an identity of religion and the state and a division to unitary classes such as proletarian and bourgeois.

A neo-Parsonsian/Weberian argument is continued by Bellah and his associates in *Habits of the Heart*—only through a more empirical analysis resulting in a more critical diagnosis. While affirming the historical significance of cultural traditions like those Weber and Parsons emphasized (Bellah terms them biblical and republican), *Habits of the Heart* finds that these traditions have eroded. The biblical and republican (republican in the larger sense—not with reference to the party) traditions affirmed individualism while grounding it within a framework of social responsibility, but the erosion of this framework leaves behind a kind of individualism that lacks even a language of social values. In the new individualism, the pursuit of happiness, defined as personal success, well-being, and security, has become a goal bereft of perceived relationship to the traditions and groups in terms of which that goal made sense in the culture of an earlier America.

Comparative analysis has always framed the Weberian tradition of the cultural analysis of America. For Weber himself, the Protestant ethic was only a variant within a range of cultural configurations (1972). His studies of Judaism (1952a) endeavored to trace its origins, while his studies of China and India (1952, 1958) attempted to show its distinctiveness as an otherworldly religious ethic that sustained a continuous this-worldly dynamism corroding and reforming all institutions as it disenchanted the world. For Bellah, the individualism of America contrasts implicitly with the collectivism of Japan that he had analyzed earlier (1957) as having its own Protestant ethic, which energizes an intense activism focusing around loyalty to the group rather than around the individual. Other studies in this tradition that did not focus explicitly on the United States could nevertheless be read as implicitly illuminating the analyst's U.S. culture, through discovery of the contrasting values abroad. Clifford Geertz's studies of Bali as radically lacking in the notion of individual (1966), or of the *Religion of Java* (1976) as a variant on Weber's *Religion of China* and *Religion of India,* are further examples of cultural values analyzed as implicit or explicit contrasts to U.S. and Western values.

The Weberian tradition of U.S. cultural analysis overlaps, to a certain degree, with other streams both in anthropology and in other fields. Especially noteworthy is the national character "school" as exemplified by the studies of America by Mead (1943), Gorer (1964), Hsu (1972, 1973), which are similarly holistic and comparative (though with a more psychological than cultural emphasis); the cognitive approach of writers such as Romney and D'Andrade (1964) or Schneider (1968); and the many empirical studies of particular aspects of American life (e.g., Bauman 1983; Foster 1988; V. Harding 1988; Moffat 1989; Perin 1988; Varrenne 1977). Such studies bear out Weberian themes in some ways while showing counterthemes, e.g., communal values in some sectors contrasting with individualistic values in others. While the anthropological studies differ, in ways to be discussed, from the Weberian, they often highlight the same constellation of American cultural themes; individualism, activism, and instrumentalism.

Placing the Weberian Formulation in Context:
System and Life World

The Weberian tradition of American cultural analysis proceeds, as noted, from a certain theoretical framework. Basically, it attempts to abstract the core culture from the totality of American lives. It seeks traditions, such as the Protestant ethic, which seem to have historical grounding and continuity; it defines values that are manifest in the ideals of founding and dominant figures and institutions. In short, through various strategies it searches for unities and continuities within a field that is admittedly in flux and diverse. In these emphases lie the power of the approach and its limitations.

In the remainder of this chapter, this Weberian formulation is critiqued in relation to what might be termed an anthropological view of U.S. life. What is the anthropological view? To characterize that is as difficult as it is to characterize the culture of America (cf., Peacock 1986). Conventionally, the first anthropological trait is that it is comparative, but so is the Weberian formulation. Secondly, it is holistic; so is the Weberian formulation. A third trait is more distinctive of the anthropological approach—participant-observation. Anthropologists, at least sociocultural anthropologists, characteristically if not consistently (cf., D'Andrade), insist on learning about life through participation in it while at the same time observing it. The original Weberian formulation is less based on participant observation than on textual analysis. *Habits of the Heart* brings generalities to life through life interviews. While interviews are highly efficient ways of ascertaining attitudes and can do so at deep levels, one can still consider how participant-observation studies could help contextualize these texts, whether written or oral. It is possible that Bellah's finding of a rampant individualism in American life reflects, in part, his method. The interview abstracts the individual from social life, whereas participant-observation treats group life directly. On one hand, it is suggestive that studies of America that are based on participant-observation have discovered collective values more than have Bellah's studies (Lynd 1959; Morland 1958; Varrenne 1977; Warner 1941–59). On the other hand, some interview-based studies have also revealed communalistic values (Newman 1988).

Holism remains a dominant, if often tacit, value in the anthropological approach. While the Weberian formulation is holistic, it differs from the anthropological in both scale and emphasis. The Weberian focuses on a certain abstracted system—the large-scale, long-term cultural configuration, while the anthropologist-ethnographer locates culture more in concrete and immediate life contexts. In older formulations, these contexts were said to compose whole cultures, not separate from economics or child rearing, but intertwined with them; and the metaphor was often that of fabric—a seamless web. In newer formulations, these contexts are seen as fields of conflicting forces, and the relation of them to culture is less seamless than dialectical. In both approaches, culture is seen as grounded in immediate contexts that are integrated into larger patterns.

Finally, there is comparison. The Weberian formulations are monumentally comparative; the anthropological ones are often more experientially comparative. That is, the Weberian project sets out broad differences in regular relation to other broad differences. The anthropological approach may do this, too, but, following the participant observation emphasis, tends to treat comparison as encounter—to delve sharply at critical points into differences between the analyst's experience in his or her own culture (e.g., U.S.) and his or her experience in another. Such immediate comparisons of experience (which J. Smith (1982) demeaningly and mischievously terms "ethnographic" owing to their anecdotal character) may not be systematic, but they are often sharply suggestive.

Placing the Weberian formulation in anthropological context, we treat two levels of American life: macrotrends that one might term, following Habermas's (1975) "system world"; and the more immediate experiences that he terms "life world." At neither level can we be exhaustive—neither in "covering" the facts on America, nor even in citing the literature; all that is hoped is to be suggestive. I will suggest and illustrate two points: that the kinds of core values formulated by the Weberians are not only *contingent*—dependent on conditions and trends, but also *significant*—pervading and penetrating U.S. life (sometimes in unexpected ways).

Systems and Trends

Many macrosystem trends currently in the United States would seem to challenge and undermine the Protestant ethic. Both scholarly (Wuthnow 1989) and popular accounts (Ostling 1989) plot the diminished salience of the mainline Protestant denominations coupled with the rise of the newer, more fundamentalistic and populist Protestant movements such as Pentecostalism. Associated with this decline is the influx of non-Protestant cultures, such as Hispanic Catholicism, Asian Buddhism, the conversion of some blacks to Islam, and new quasi-religious cults from Scientology to Wicca (see Appel 1983). Many Americans simply become nonreligious; although, by comparison with other Western nations, Americans still stand out as remarkably religious—whether according to various surveys or simple observation. (Compare U.S. churches with the empty churches of Sweden, which are often simply historical monuments, marked with stars to numerically indicate historical touristic importance.) A diminished institutionalization of mainline Protestantism does not prove a diminished salience of Protestant-like values; in fact, as Parsons argues, the values, now freed from institutions, may spread into new spheres, from politics to private experience—a process that may transform but not destroy them.

Economic realities can threaten individualistic activism, though they also can encourage runaway individualism. The gap between rich and poor widens; and the barrier between them rigidifies so that individual initiative, not to mention virtue, is less directly rewarded. Unemployment increases among the poor, but also among the highly placed owing to buy outs and other practices encouraged by the current economy (Newman 1988). The American Dream dims for many as the spirit of capitalism is transformed into a system teetering between irresponsible speculators and stultifying bureaucracy.

The associational aspect of U.S. individualism is threatened as well. Suburbanization corrodes the center city, depriving citizenry of a location historically important as a forum for debate and discussion. Independence Hall is revitalized only as a theme park, and coffee houses serve rebels or faddists rather than opinion-leaders. Electronic media, claiming to fill the vacuum left by the demise of face-to-face participation, may in fact alienate or, worse, manipulate, as our passive listening to a panel, talk-show, or media-groomed politician replaces true participation. Such mass culture is said to breed infantile narcissism as citizenry deprived of citizenship retreat into private indulgence (Calhoun 1988; Slater 1970; Lasch 1979).

The family farm and the small town, historic incubators of American values of individualistic cooperation, are moribund, overrun by mega corporations, suburbs, and exurbs. The family itself, in its nuclear form seen by some studies as engendering Protestant-ethic values of achievement and guilt, rather than shame and affiliation, (Gorer 1964; McClelland 1976; Whiting and Child 1953) is replaced by single-parent households and day-care centers. The changes bestow power, but also responsibilities and tension, on women, who, as single parents, must struggle to support and nurture children while being inadequately supported themselves by society, economy, or the culture. New attitudes concerning gender, sexuality, and socialization, most of which challenge traditions linked to the core cultural values, emerge, but unevenly.

Challenges like this have not lacked response. Fundamentalism in America, in its largely Christian form (paralleling Jewish and Islamic versions of it elsewhere) is one response that affirms not only scripturalism but also traditionalistic values concerning family, gender, and sex. Fundamentalism is not, however, the same as the Protestant ethic. For example, the asceticism and moralism of fundamentalism tend to become ends in themselves rather than means toward more transcendental ends such as service to God or social reform (Peacock 1971). Associated with these tendencies is a rise in conservative politics. Conservatives may affirm some core values, such as individualism and reward of individual effort, but denigrate the value of contribution to the larger society. Violating the core value of individualism in its older, socially responsible form reinforces other trends, such as the separation of rich from poor, of wealthy suburban "enclaves" (Bellah 1985) from needy inner cities.

While most of the trends here noted have been widely discussed, the anthropologist is equipped to perceive also the informal and nascent tendencies that may seem marginal but in fact reveal emerging patterns or underlying contradictions. Kinship bonds, for example, show signs of revitalization as well as evidence of decline. The weakening of the two-parent household, not only weakens family life at one level but also strengthens it at another, bolstering extended family networks of single-parent households. Longer life spans mean that more grandparents, aunts, and uncles are available for extended family support. But such revitalizations are undercut by countertrends, extended-family bases are destroyed when the elderly move to nursing homes or retirement enclaves. At a symbolic level, a renewed interest in extended family is evidenced by renewed interests in "roots," manifested in genealogies and family reunions (Hirsch 1988). But deeper study reminds us of how American identities, grounded in ancestry and kinship, are fragile constructions that are part of a quest for an always-elusive community (Foster 1988). Small discontinuities demand scrutiny: what if boys continue to grow up playing with tinker toys and erector sets while the society deindustrializes, or girls keep playing with dolls as more women enter the workforce?

In assessing any of these trends, the anthropologist necessarily remembers the rest of the world and the historical process of which the

United States is only a piece. Population trends alone are revealing. The United States and other colonies of Europe boasted large population explosions during the eighteenth and nineteenth centuries (Crosby 1986); but East, South, and Southeast Asia will constitute the majority of the world's peoples by the next century. These world trends are reflected in the influx of migrants to the United States, thus spurring pluralism even in comparatively homogeneous regions such as the South (Tindall 1989; Whisnant 1983; Long 1989; Wilson and Ferris 1989). America's diminished place in the world's economy today, compared to even a decade ago, appears not only to reflect the recent selling of America for short-term illusions of prosperity but also to foreshadow future trends as they relate to the core values. What next? A scramble to emulate Japanese culture or the European common market, a reactionary isolation coupled with continuing narcissistic capitalism, some more subtle adjustment or a radical cultural transformation? Whether the United States changes in these directions or not, it is becoming more pluralistic. What are the effects of such trends on U.S. life worlds?

Life Worlds

As the anthropologist moves to get in touch with life worlds, by which Habermas means worlds we experience, what is probably immediately most obvious is the richness of cultural diversity within the United States. Native Americans, Afro-Americans, Hispanics, Asians, Arabs, and Europeans constitute a variety of people that mirrors the entire world. That all of these cultures are located within a single national territory reduces their diversity at certain levels, yet quite radical differences of worldview are apparent at other levels (e.g., Kluckhohn and Leighton 1946; Ortiz 1969; Whorf 1956). While Native American studies were long almost synonymous with U.S. anthropology, some kind of anthropological work with many other cultural groups within the United States can be found—from studies of Chinese in Mississippi (Cohen 1984) to studies of Anglos in Yankee City (Warner 1941–59). Exciting new studies in archaeology, ethnohistory, and physical anthropology reveal new facts about Hispanic, Native American, and Afro-American streams of American history (Blakey 1988; Hudson 1987). These studies offer multiple challenges to the Weberian formulation of core values. The following paragraphs offer a survey of some of these challenges.

Probably the most dramatic challenge to the traditional formulation (one which sometimes, also provides a confirmation of it) comes from studies of tacit culture—the "silent language" expressed through space and time, through metaphors of health and disease, and through the most personal domains of body and psyche, for example. These are at the same time the most distant from abstract values and the deepest expression of them. Anglo-Protestant individualism and instrumentalism may emphasize the distance of one body from another and the directedness of activity along a line (Hall 1959; cf., Johnson (1985), who shows how such ideas are embodied in spatial and temporal arrangements in American schools; and Dubinskas (1988) on time in the work place); but Native American, Afro-American, Hispanic, and Asian cultures may experience time and space differently, at least in some contexts, though conforming to the Anglo values in other contexts (Hall 1959; cf., the more macrocomparative studies of values of American subcultures by Kluckhohn and Strodtbeck (1961); Vogt and Albert (1966) on Texans, Mormons, Hispanics).

Even the deepest levels of body language, of disease, and health ideology express subgroup variation from the dominant values. The Amish have a special form of depression reflecting an oppressive sense of group life (Hostetler 1964); blacks in the South may fear sorcery reflecting particular patterns of kinship relation; Japanese-Americans deploy spiritual healing cults in a distinctively collectivist, kin-focused way in comparison to Anglo-Americans who approach the same cults individualistically (Yamada 1984). Different Caribbean groups in a single city vary widely in medical worldviews (Weidman 1979). A disease like arthritis not only elicits a surprising array of folk remedies (a favorite in one group being lubrication with WD-40 oil) but also expresses tacit political ideologies that, like symptoms, vary with ethnic group (Price 1989). Michael Blakey documents in his chapter (in this volume) a variety of correlations between physiological symptoms and cultural or class membership.

A second challenge comes from studies of social organization. In these also, U.S. cultural groups show patterns not apparent in the dominant culture. Single-head black households, for example, may cooperate in distinctive ways (Stack 1974). Cooperation in Hispanic communities can be more flexible and complex than envisioned in the linear expectations implied by the Protestant ethic's emphasis on the individual career, coupled with independent and mobile nuclear families (see the chapter by Carlos Vélez-Ibanez, p. 193).

Career studies are revealing. At the level of the individual, the core values would predict a linear, instrumentally directed, goal-oriented career as a cultural model for the life history. Such is assumed in the "passages" model (Sheehy 1976) of the midlife crisis; if one expects a career to follow a line, then change is a "crisis." But this model is generalized from a sample of white, urban, northern males (Levinson 1978). Women, according to Catherine Bateson (1989), show quite a different pattern in the life cycle—more flexible and less directed by career than by other demands, such as child rearing or husband's work. Men vary also; the crisis for working-class males is not necessarily job changes, which some do frequently, but can be, in some cases, a religious crisis (Peacock 1984; Peacock and Tyson 1989, 131–49). Variation in modeling of the life cycle is associated with gender patterns of work (Lamphere 1987; Sacks 1984), and kinship, or the like, as well as with symbolic definition.

Aside from subcultural and gender variation from the core values, many domains in American life that are shared by majority and minority groups and by both genders also differ in emphasis from the core values.

The domain of kinship, especially in its domestic nuclear family and nurturing aspects, is often seen as a complement to such core values as instrumentalism. Schneider argues that, whereas the wider American values see culture as conquering nature, kinship is perceived as "natural," as subordinating culture to nature. This ideology is itself cultural, hence subject to challenge (e.g., by feminists who might reject an implied, but not essential, corollary of Schneider's (1968) formulation: that since women are the bulwark of family life, the equation of family and nature relegates women to a natural, rather than a cultural, domain). On the whole, the point is valid: that in American culture the family is widely experienced as a sphere somewhat autonomous from the wider society and is hence guided by values somewhat complementary to those of the wider society. Even where the family may socialize the child in the individualistic achievement values of the wider society, the family is still considered, at least ideally, to be a haven providing relief from such values through placing priority on its own values, such as unconditional love (rather than making affection contingent on instrumental achievement). While the nature of this complementarity between family and society differs according to class and subculture, some kind of complementarity appears widespread.

Ritual life, even in the so-called dominant cultures, including male-centered spheres, is another domain that powerfully shows the continuing presence of values at odds with such core values as instrumentalistic rationalism. Primordial communalism of the kind more recognized by Durkheim than Weber is revealed in Warner's (1941–59) studies of Memorial Day, for example. Hierarchies and ceremonial celebrations of hierarchy are brilliantly described by Rhys Isaacs's (1982) study of Virginia. Stuart Marks's (1991) *Southern Hunting in Black and White* shows quite remarkably how the ritual of hunting displays traditionalist values of hierarchy and gender as men reconstruct their social world through their relations to animals. Frese's (1983) study of symbols of brides and widows shows a remarkable constancy of ritual patterning in a domain apart from the individualistic arena of the wider society. Victor Turner's (1982) writings and exhibits of celebrations, in the United States and elsewhere, show regularities of the life cycle and other rituals that sustain kinship and communal bonds, while F. G. Bailey's (1983) caustic dissections of ritual games played in U.S., as well as in other groups, show other kinds of regularities that complement the core values. These localized studies of ritual contrast suggestively with the national-level analysis of civil religion by Bellah (1985) and others. Such studies show a stable, rather autonomous, sphere of ritual values emphasizing what might be termed "primordial" patterns—communalism, hierarchy, kinship, totemism—maintained in a society professing as its dominant core values instrumentalism and individualism.

Structuralist studies show similar kinds of primordial patterns: stable, structured systems of symbolic patterning in spheres ranging from food and clothing (Sahlins 1976; cf., Kroeber 1923); motels and cafes, sleeping and eating (Peacock 1986); to athletic events (Peacock 1989) and games (Imam-Murni 1991). Such spheres show the same kinds of relations of nature and culture, male and female, high and low statuses that are familiar to anthropologists who study so-called "primitive classification" systems around the world (Lévi-Strauss 1966). They show a ground of U.S. culture that remains salient in daily life and resists incursions of the core values.

Folklorists and anthropologists with folkloristic interests have been particularly effective in documenting primordial and subcultural values not immediately apparent in the core Protestant ethic/Weberian configuration—aesthetic values, for example, and the valuation of tradition itself. John Forrest (1988) discloses an aesthetic tradition behind the pragmatic values of a fishing village. A similar point is illustrated (though not argued) by studies of folk music, arts, and architecture (Abrahams 1970; *Festival of American Folklife* 1988; Glassie, 1968, 1975; Lomax 1978; Patterson 1979; Sutton 1983; Zug 1987). Folkloristic studies show an implicit/methodological emphasis on the aesthetic forms themselves, rather than the cultural values they represent (Alan Lomax [1978] has, however, attempted to explore systematically this relationship for music and dance; Glassie [1975] suggestively treats the relationship between values and architecture; and Conway and Stewart have analyzed lyrics). The folklorists' interest in forms lends itself well to the wealth of performative expression in sound, video, film, and in live performances and festivals, and complements the abstracted cognitive inclination of the sociological formulations of the core values. Folklorists' interest in context tends toward a tracing of the forms to localized politics rather than to broader cultural values (see e.g., David Whisnant 1983). Similarly, a head-on challenge to received wisdom about the dominance of Anglo-Calvinism in American culture comes from Terry Jordan's (1984) study of the log cabin and associated frontier patterns. He argues that the frontier culture derives, not from the Scottish-Calvinistic core, but from Finnish culture and subsequently diffused from the middle-Atlantic states westward.

Regional studies show the distinctiveness of certain regional cultures. The South, for example, displays values distinct from the core values (Reed 1986; Wilson, 1980); and scholars of this region have recently issued a comprehensive encyclopedia documenting its distinctive culture (Wilson and Ferris 1989). (The reverse emphasis, characteristic of the discipline that officially identifies itself as "American Studies," is to treat the peculiarities of New England as representing the whole of U.S. culture—a strategy that reinforces the Weberian definition of U.S. values as essentially Puritan. See the critique by a Japanese historian, Ide (1974) of this bias.) The most suggestive interpretations of American regionalism, at present, are those that reveal interplay between regional particularities and the incursions of national culture. See Walker Percy (1971) and Alice Walker (1983), for example, on the South, and Larry McMurtry (1987) on the Southwest, who depict through fiction the way regions encounter, project, and caricature Americanism.

Studies of folk culture, subcultural variation, ethnicity, ritual, kinship, symbolic structures, and cultural modeling in community and individual experience, then, depict life worlds distinct from the Weberian core-cultural values. On the one hand, a picture emerges of multiple groups and experiences decoupled from, or in dialectic with, a core national culture. In fact, projected against the realities of these varied, localized life worlds, the core values appear abstract and unreal—construct based on generalization, on elite textual sources salient at Monticello or Independence Hall, or on media images manufactured in Hollywood or Manhattan but distant from the contemporary life worlds of many Americans. On the other hand, the core values sometimes manifest themselves at deep levels in symptomologies of disease, in language, in models for the life course, and among groups whose cultural roots may have emphasized contrasting values (see, e.g., Grunkemeyer 1991). Often rebellion and release from the core values manifest these same values; see, for example, Kasson's analysis of Coney Island, which provided "illusion of anarchic freedom and heedless release beneath the underlying reality of control" (1978, 82). In a way that one can appreciate only after riding a roller coaster in a third-world park, the thrills of the U.S. amusement park occur within a firm framework of technology designed to process masses of people efficiently and safely. (Cf., Kasson on the advertisement for the "Loop the Loop," which reassured customers: "The Greatest Sensation of the Age . . . No Danger Whatever," 1978, 82).

A difficulty plagues the anthropological insistence on emphasizing variation from the core values—Native American, Afro-American, Hispanic, regional, etc. The very fact that anthropology has classically defined itself as studying "the other" taints those whom it chooses to study. To become a subject of the anthropologist is to be marginalized. In the case of the so-called ethnic minorities, this marginalization reflects wider views within the society; even to be identified as "ethnic" (or regional, rural, or of a particular gender, age, religion, or whatever) is to be set apart from the mainstream, as when middle Americans naively say, "We don't have an accent."

One solution to the problem of envisioning all minorities as "other" is to define such groups more "objectively" as in demography and geography. But this approach tends to dehumanize while seemingly being tolerant and fair. As Charles Long (1989) and Vincent Harding (1988) note, the blacks are not just a "group" or even a "culture," but they represent a powerful and poignant experience and theme in the American experience, themes such as redemptive suffering, victimization, and the burden of history. A similar point could be made about women, who have developed an enriching countertheme to the dominant male-oriented Calvinistic motif. (It is noteworthy, however, that whereas Weber's texts and figures are almost entirely male, by the time Bellah and his associates

(1985) are writing, major informants are female.) It is not just the groups that need consideration. The interweaving of these themes in the experience of America also needs consideration. Here blacks, Native Americans, and such quasi minorities as women would have a more integral place in the wider experience than some more recent minorities; but size and recency are not the only pertinent factors. The larger point is that, while recognizing diversity, anthropological studies of the United States need to push beyond viewing cultural diversity as a smorgasbord. While celebration of diversity (as in folk festivals and multiple-language teaching) is a necessary step, we need to move also toward understanding the relations among the multiple streams.

Toward Synthesis: Cultural Values, Systems, and
Life Worlds

It may be salutary to emphasize the discontinuities in America: the challenge to core values of macrotrends, the contradictions between core values and life worlds, and the conflictual disorders of American society. A holistic, systematic, and comparative perspective, however, suggests another emphasis. Compared to most nations, America has so far experienced a remarkable political and economic stability. This kind of stability invites a search for cultural continuities framing American life. A synthetic anthropology of America would strive to interrelate subcultural and other kinds of life-world variation, as well as dynamic and conflictful social processes, with whatever core values seem to provide continuity and integration. A few illustrative studies suggest some approaches to this end.

Gwen Neville (1987) argues that Protestantism is distinct from Catholicism in Europe in stressing not pilgrimage—traveling to a sacred center then returning home—but leaving home for good. She traces this general pattern, seemingly reflecting a Protestant individualism, across the Atlantic through the Scotch-Irish migration to the American South, where leaving home becomes balanced by family reunions affirming the arrival and founding of a new community and a new continuity. Here a Protestant individualism and localized collectivism are connected in an interesting dialectic.

James Peacock and Ruel Tyson (1989), and Beverly Patterson (1988), treat Calvinism as it is expressed in the culture of the Primitive Baptists of Appalachia. Here, unlike the Weberian formulation for the mainline culture grounded primarily in New England Puritanism, the dilemmas of predestination for election or damnation are not worked out primarily through striving for success but by a relentlessly paradoxical encounter with the uncertainty itself. The Weberian formulation is found to be salient, but transformed, in this religious/regional subculture's life world that deepens the core values of Calvinism.

Katherine Newman discovers, in *Falling from Grace* (1988), that unemployed, but formerly successful, executives often blame themselves rather than the system for their failure (cf., Claudia Strauss (1988), who traces this in comments by unemployed workers; cf., again Studs Terkel (1970), who finds this attitude among workers in depression days but in present days a tendency to blame others). Here the core value, individualism, expressed as an assumption that one must take responsibility for one's own failure, survives the dismantling of the economic base, and the failure is given a religious overtone—falling from grace.

Many have noted how the new hedonism simply extends the old asceticism into a new arena—taking pleasure seriously. The Protestant ethic, or some analogue (which probably includes the Judeo-Christian tradition generally; cf. Phillip Rieff (1979) on Freud and Judaism), extends moralism to more personal levels. Bellah argues that therapy based on contract theory extends capitalist values into the "depth psychology" of the therapeutic encounter. Consumerism, as analyzed long ago by Thorstein Veblen (1934), shows a parallel to the productive ethic in that individual striving to produce is equalled by striving to consume conspicuously (a trend resurfacing with the Forbes and the Trumps that produces in us an oscillation between fascination and disgust in regard to the display of the rich and famous). Such observations suggest that what appears as a contradiction to core values may in fact show a deeper unity with them.

These last examples suggest some ways that core values are manifest at some levels—locally, personally, and in religious or regional contexts—while being transformed and complemented at others. But what of more violent rejection of such values? What is one to make of the various protest and resistance movements in America? What of the counterculture of the sixties, the civil rights movements, the violence by those discriminated against, the fundamentalist sects, or the extreme right or extreme left political organizations? What of the most destructive disaffection in American history—that of the South during the Civil War, which divided the nation and cost more American lives than any other war?

What of the seeming total alienation of the criminal world—the Mafia, the drug dealers, the underclass (compare values such as "heart"— honor, bravery—among street gangs (Keiser 1979) with core values of instrumentalism, on the one hand, and with the so-called primordial regional and communal values noted earlier on the other)? How should one interpret less violent rebellions, such as minority or regional jokes and toasts that poke fun at dominant values (Deidre Evans-Pritchard 1989; Abrahams 1970)?

Obviously the issue for values-studies is whether these movements and alienated worlds constitute a fundamental contradiction of the core values, or whether they express lower-level contradictions (such as social, political, or economic) while continuing to affirm the core values at some level. For example, associational modes of organization seem to work well with the U.S. kind of instrumental individualism, whereas hierarchical modes are resisted as rigid and authoritarian; the one deviation from the core values is seemingly more drastic than the other. And what is implied for personal identity? A more pluralistic United States implies a pluralistic self, one capable of shifting empathies and roles depending on context and subculture; while the core values suggest a more unitary self. When does such pluralization of self cease to be adaptive and become pathological for the psyche (cf., Lifton 1970)? And when may adaptive flexibility at one level (e.g., the self or subcultural values) become maladaptive at another (e.g., in the need to run the government systematically or to preserve the environment)? Systematic analysis is necessary to work through such relationships, with due attention to dynamism and conflict as well as systematics. Such a goal leads toward anthropological research agendas, some directions of which I suggest in conclusion.

Conclusion

The question of disorder in U.S. society is engaged by attempting to formulate core U.S. values because some such guiding values would seem to be necessary for a system, a nation, or a society to sustain itself with sufficient orderliness to survive (cf., Rappaport 1979; Parsons 1951a and 1951b on "Pattern Maintenance"). One need not be a functionalist or cyberneticist to argue this. Simple pluralism is neither an accurate description of U.S. culture nor, one could argue, functionally adequate for U.S. society. On the other hand, a chauvinistic espousal of core values is abusive, not only because such values are not equally cherished by all, but because the values themselves have their negative underside (Hsu 1972). The issue becomes more complex when one begins to trace out these core values in the varied life worlds of America and to assess the relation of such values to the forces and trends that constitute the United States today. Anthropology is uniquely equipped for such analysis owing to its holism, comparativism, and ethnographic awareness. In fact, anthropological methodologies—attention to wholes, including varying subcultural streams, integrated into total cultures; and observation through participation—resonate with attitudes that enrich the core values of the United States: emphasis on participation by myriads of subcultural life worlds in the democratic U.S. society. Conversely, other features of anthropological methodology, such as a preference for localized, isolated studies of subcultures which may reflect a rugged individualism of sorts, encourage a fragmentary smorgasbord-like view of American culture. Without selling its ethnographic birthright, anthropologists of the United States could move more strongly toward coordinating diversified field studies in relation to each other and to larger issues and macrosystem analyses of America. Anthropologists may resist, on ethical as well as empirical grounds, the unitary thrust of the Weberian formulation of American cultural values, but it challenges them to provide a sufficiently rich, yet still coherent, alternative formulation.

A casual reader may interpret the foregoing as a conventional anthropological effort at challenging a view of the United States as unified through core values by pointing out the diversity of its values. Such a reader might infer further that this analysis of the fact of diversity translates into an ethic of diversity—proclaiming that diversity is good and therefore encouraging it. Neither the interpretation nor the inference are adequate, though they summarize part of the argument.

I do attempt to enrich the core-value model by sketching U.S. diversity, and this sketch could translate into a certain kind of ethic of diversity. While both describing and prescribing cultural diversity are conventional moves for anthropologists to make, they are nonetheless important; they are central to the anthropological calling and responsibility. We are trained to describe the particularities of diverse cultures, and it is our responsibility to do this because nobody else does it very much at all, and those who do, do not do it as well as we. (In saying this, I am aware, of course, of the many criticisms that can be leveled at anthropology—from the left, the right, and the center, and the virtues

claimed by some others who move into "cultural studies"; my claim
stands nonetheless.) Anthropology proceeds in two complementary ways,
by ethnography (intensive study of a particular culture) and the comparative method (extensive analysis of the systematic covariations among
many cultures); their descriptive responsibility entails doing these two
things well. These two descriptive responsibilities tend to lead toward
prescriptive positions, hence engagement. Deepening understanding of
particular cultures tends to lead toward supporting the right of particular
cultures to sustain their identities, especially when those cultures are in
a minority or are otherwise suppressed, threatened, or simply under-
appreciated (this is an ethical correlate of the ethnographic method).
Broadening understanding of the many human cultures in both their
diversity and their systematic regularity tends to lead toward a general
support of diversity (this is the ethical correlate of the comparative
method). The descriptive aspect is elementary and fundamental, while
the prescriptive aspect is something anthropologists tend to do (but do
not necessarily have to do) either as professional anthropologists or as
engaged citizens. For example, I currently serve as chair of the faculty
government at my university and in that capacity I am supporting and
actively participating in an effort to create a black cultural center (ethical
correlate number one: the ethnographic approach) while also advocating
that this center be framed in a wider effort, entailing creating a multicultural curriculum and various modes of communication among cultures
on campus, to enhance understanding and acceptance of cultural diversity generally (ethical correlate number two: the comparative approach).

   Phrasing this engagement process so simply—as Anthro 101 translated into application—misses, of course, the vexed though intriguing
issues entailed in the process. But even if we enrich our statement to
include these, we need to go further still. To simply support diversity
either by ethical correlates number one or number two, or both, is not
enough; worse, it is to invite chaos. Anthropology cannot stop by describing and prescribing diversity for any place, including the United
States. It must go on to describe and prescribe core values. Anthropology
must engage in the creation of core values for the American nation. We
know, of course, that no core value will be sufficient for a nation, whether
judged in terms of some abstract ethical standard or as a consensus;
some paradox or illogic will plague any value, and someone will object
to any value professed because any core value is politically and socially
grounded, hence will always serve some interests more than others. Yet

this difficulty is not sufficient cause to withdraw from the quest for a core value; the quest itself has value, and is part of the process of working together as citizens in an "imagined community" such as America; while, at the same time, without some framework of value, accepted provisionally to be sure but with some degree of commitment, the quest itself is not feasible as a collective project. A further point: Without some kind of core values to unify the whole, preservation of the frame and process necessary to sustain diversity and rights of individual groups would not be possible. Even if we favor diversity and self-determination of cultures as the ultimate good, and even if we challenge any definition of core values as essentialist, oppressive, or whatever, nonetheless we must ultimately favor some kind of core value commitment in order to preserve sufficient order for diversity to flourish. All of this is elementary Durkheim or Hobbes. The question then arises: Who will define the core values of the United States? In the United States, such questions have been left to the politicians and those academics (formerly philosophers and religionists, more recently economists and planners) who are willing to hazard normative formulations. Why should anthropology stay out of this process? Who is better equipped to take account at once of the richness of diversity and the nuanced possibilities for pattern and principle uniting or at least interrelating such diversities?

Finally, then, I stand ethically with the neo-Weberians (such as Bellah, et al.: whom we might term the neocore-value school). Though striving to enrich and problematize their worldview and commitments by enhancing awareness of diversity and of the situational and politicized forces linked to diversity, anthropologists cannot stop short of joining the dialogue (perhaps emerging with renewed vigor under America's new administration and certainly as we move into the twenty-first century) toward formulating core values which at once reach back to historical traditions of America as a nation (constructed, deconstructed, and reconstructed) and forward toward emerging pluralisms. Of course, we want a hundred flowers to bloom and a thousand tongues to sing, but we must seize the task of defining the special architecture of our gardens and the special harmonics of our choirs within which these diversities can flourish. Lacking attention to such structures and values—whether it be the republican and biblical traditions of early America or some other constellation emerging today—nonvalues such as the marketplace or simply anarchy will carry the day. Anthropology is called to join the quest to define our national culture as a diverse and dynamic nonetheless somewhat cohesive and somewhat directed entity.

NOTE

I am deeply grateful to Katherine Newman, Carole Ann McClennan, Shepard Forman, Marilyn Grunkemeyer, Frank Dubinskas, Tim Pettyjohn, and Cecelia Conway for their perceptive critique for a draft of this chapter. I appreciate also suggestive discussions of issues concerning the United States by members of the Panel on Disorder in Industrial Society. Especially will I miss long hikes and warm conversations with Frank Dubinskas. I thank Harihar Bhattarai for help with the bibliography.

REFERENCES

Abrahams, Roger. 1970. *Deep Down in the Jungle: Negro Narrative Folklore from the Streets of Philadelphia*. Chicago: Aldine Publishing.

Appel, Willi. 1983. *Cults in America*. New York: Holt, Rinehart, and Winston.

Bailey, F. G. 1983. *The Tactical Uses of Passion*. Ithaca: Cornell University Press.

Bateson, Catherine. 1989. Weaving Lives. Paper read to the Department of Anthropology, 17 April, at the University of North Carolina, Chapel Hill, North Carolina.

Bauman, Richard. 1983. *Let Your Words Be Few: Symbolism of Speaking and Silence among Seventeenth-century Quakers*. New York: Cambridge University Press.

Bellah, Robert. 1957. *Tokugawa Religion*. Glencoe, Ill.: Free Press.

Bellah, Robert, Richard Madsen, William M. Sullivan, Ann Swidlen, and Steven M. Tipton. 1985. *Habits of the Heart: Individualism and Commitment in American Life*. Berkeley: University of California Press.

Blakey, Michael L. 1988. Social Policy, Economics, and Demographic Change in Nanticake: Moor Ethnic History. *American Journal of Physical Anthropology* 75:493–502.

Calhoun, Craig. 1988. Populist Politics, Communications Media, and Large Scale Societal Integration. *Sociological Theory* 6:219–41.

Cohen, Lucy. 1984. *Chinese in the Post-Civil War South*. Baton Rouge: Louisiana State University Press.

Conway, Cecilia. N.D. *African Banjo Echoes in Appalachia*. Knoxville: University of Tennessee Press. Forthcoming.

Crosby, Alfred W. 1986. *Ecological Imperialism: The Biological Expansion of Europe, 900–1900.* New York: Cambridge University Press.

D'Andrade, Roy. 1984. Cultural Meaning Systems. In *Culture Theory: Essays on Mind, Self, and Emotion,* ed. Richard Schweder and Robert Levine. New York: Cambridge University Press.

Dubinskas, Frank. 1988. *Making Time.* Philadelphia: Temple University Press.

Evans-Pritchard, Deidre. 1989. How "They" See us: Native American Images of Tourists. *Annals of Tourism Research* 16:89–105.

Festival of American Folklife. 1988. Washington, D.C.: Smithsonian Institution Press.

Forrest, John. 1988. *Lord, I'm Coming Home: Everyday Aesthetics in Tidewater North Carolina.* Ithaca: Cornell University Press.

Foster, Stephen William. 1988. *The Past Is Another Country.* Berkeley: University of California Press.

Frese, Pamela R. 1983. The Symbol Complex in American Life Cycle Rituals. Paper presented to the American Anthropological Association, November, Chicago.

Gabriel, Ralph H. 1974. *American Values: Continuity and Change.* Westport, Conn.: Greenwood Press.

Geertz, Clifford. 1966. *Person, Time, and Conduct in Bali: An Essay in Cultural Analysis.* New Haven: Yale University Press.

———. 1973. *Interpretation of Cultures.* New York: Basic Books.

———. 1976. *Religion of Java.* Chicago: University of Chicago Press.

Glassie, Henry. 1968. *Patterns in the Material Folk Culture of the Eastern United States.* Philadelphia: University of Pennsylvania Press.

———. 1975. *Folk Housing in Middle Virginia.* Knoxville: University of Tennessee Press.

Gorer, Geoffrey. 1964. *The American People: A Study in National Character.* New York: Norton.

Grunkemeyer, Marilyn Trent. 1991. A Vietnamese-American Community: An Instance of *Moral Education.* Ph.D. diss., Department of Anthropology, University of North Carolina, Chapel Hill.

Habermas, Jürgen. 1975. *Legitimation Crisis.* Boston: Beacon Press.

Hall, Edward. 1959. *The Silent Language.* Garden City, N.Y.: Doubleday.

Harding, Susan. 1988. The World of the Born-again Telescandals. *Michigan Quarterly* 27, no. 4 (Fall): 525–40.

Harding, Vincent. 1988. Toward a Darkly Radiant Vision of America's Truth. In *Community in America: The Challenge of Habits of the Heart,* ed. Charles Reynolds and Ralph Norman. Berkeley: University of California Press.

Hirsch, John. 1988. At Family Reunions, You Really Can Go Home Again. *New York Times,* 24 August, 15, sec. 3.

Hostetler, John. 1964. Persistence and Change Patterns in Amish Society. *Ethnology* 3:185–98.

Hsu, Francis L. K. 1972. *Psychological Anthropology.* Cambridge, Mass.: Schenkman Publishing.

————. 1973. *Rugged Individualism Reconsidered*. Knoxville: University of Tennessee Press.

Hudson, Charles. 1987. An Unknown South: Spanish Explorers and Southeastern Chiefdoms. In *Visions and Revisions: Ethnohistorical Perspectives on Southern Cultures,* ed. George Saso, III, and William M. Schneider, 6–24. Southern Anthropological Proceedings no. 20. Athens: University of Georgia Press.

Ide, Yoshimitsu. 1974. The Image of the South and West. *American Review* 8:136–50.

Imam-Muhni, Djuhertati. 1991. The Games of Chance in American Culture. Unpublished paper, Department of American Studies, University of Maryland, College Park.

Isaacs, Rhys. 1982. *The Transformation of Virginia 1740–1790*. Chapel Hill: University of North Carolina Press.

Johnson, Norris. 1985. *West Haven: Classroom Culture and Society in a Rural Elementary School.* Chapel Hill: University of North Carolina Press.

Jordan, Terry G. 1984. *American Log Buildings: An Old World Heritage*. Chapel Hill: University of North Carolina Press.

Kasson, John F. 1978. *Amusing the Million*. New York: Hill and Wang.

Keiser, Lincoln. 1979. *The Vice Lords: Warriors of the Streets*. New York: Holt, Rinehart, and Winston.

Kluckhohn, Clyde, and Dorothea Leighton. 1946. *The Navaho*. Cambridge: Harvard University Press.

Kluckhohn, Florence, and Fred Strodtbeck. 1961. *Variations in Value Orientations*. Evanston, Ill.: Row, Peterson.

Kroeber, Alfred. 1923. *Anthropology*. New York: Harcourt and Brace.

Lamphere, Louise. 1987. *From Working Daughters to Working Mothers: Immigrant Women in a New England Industrial Community*. Ithaca: Cornell University Press.

Lasch, Christopher. 1979. *The Culture of Narcissism: American Life in an Age of Diminishing Expectation*. New York: Norton.

Lawrence, Bruce. 1989. *Defenders of God*. New York: Harper and Row.

Levinson, Daniel J. 1978. *Seasons of a Man's Life*. New York: Knopf.

Lévi-Strauss, Claude. 1966. *The Savage Mind*. Chicago: University of Chicago Press.

Lifton, Robert J. 1970. *Boundaries: Psychological Man in Revelation*. New York: Random House.

Lomax, Alan. 1978. *Folk Song Style and Culture*. New Brunswick, N.J.: Transaction Books.

Long, Charles. 1989. Issues in Afro-American and Multicultural Streams. Paper presented at symposium, The Multicultural South, 8 April, at the University of North Carolina, Chapel Hill.

Lynd, Robert S. 1959. *Middle Town: A Study in American Culture*. New York: Harvest Books.

McClelland, David. 1976. *The Achieving Society: With a New Introduction*. New York: Irvington.

McMurtry, Larry. 1987. *Texasville*. New York: Simon and Schuster.

Marks, Stuart. 1991. *Southern Hunting in Black and White*. Princeton: Princeton University Press.

Mead, Margaret. 1943 (c.1942). *And Keep Your Powder Dry: An Anthropologist Looks at America*. New York: Morrow.

Moffatt, Michael. 1989. *Coming of Age in New Jersey: College and American Culture*. New Brunswick, N.J.: Rutgers University Press.

Morland, John Kenneth. 1958. *Millways of Kent*. Chapel Hill: University of North Carolina Press.

Neville, Gwen. 1987. *Kinship and Pilgrimage: Rituals of Reunion in American Protestant Culture*. New York: Oxford University Press.

Newman, Katherine. 1988. *Falling from Grace: The Experience of Downward Mobility in the American Middle Class*. New York: Free Press.

Ortiz, Alfonso. 1969. *The Tewa World: Space, Time, Being, and Becoming in a Pueblo Society*. Chicago: University of Chicago Press.

Ostling, Richard N. 1989. Those Mainline Blues. *Time* May 22, 94–96.

Parsons, Talcott. 1937. *The Structure of Social Action*. New York: McGraw Hill.

———. 1951a. *The Social System*. Glencoe, Ill.: Free Press.

———. 1951b. *Toward a General Theory of Action*. Cambridge: Harvard University Press.

———. 1982. American Values and American Society. In *On Institutions and Social Evolution*. Chicago: University of Chicago Press.

Patterson, Beverly. 1988. Finding a Home in the Church: Primitive Baptist Women. In *Diversity of Gifts: Field Studies in Southern Religion,* ed. Ruel Tyson, James L. Peacock, and Daniel Patterson, 3–78. Urbana: University of Illinois Press.

Patterson, Daniel. 1979. *The Shaker Spirituals*. Princeton: Princeton University Press.

Peacock, James L. 1971. The Southern Protestant Ethic Disease. In *The Not So Solid South,* ed. J. Kenneth Morland, 108–13. Athens: University of Georgia Press.

———. 1984. Religion and the Life History. In *Text, Play, and Story: The Construction and Reconstruction of Self and Society in Social Science,* ed. Edward Bruner, 94–116. Washington, D.C.: American Ethnological Society.

———. 1986. *The Anthropological Lens*. New York: Cambridge University Press.

———. 1988. America as a Cultural System. In *Community in America,* ed. Charles Reynolds and Ralph Norman, 37–46. Berkeley: University of California Press.

———. 1989. Traditionalism and Reform: Constance and Climax in Java and the South. In *Perspectives on the American South,* ed. M. Black and J. S. Reed, 207–15. New York: Gordon Breach.

Peacock, James, and Ruel W. Tyson. 1989. *Pilgrims of Paradox: Calvinism and Experience among Primitive Baptists of the Blue Ridge*. Washington, D.C.: Smithsonian Institution Press.

Percy, Walker. 1971. *Love in the Ruins*. New York: Farrar, Straus, and Giroux.

Perin, Constance. 1988. *Belonging in America: Reading Between the Lines*. Madison: University of Wisconsin Press.

Price, Laurie. 1989. Old Arthur: Models and Metaphors of Arthritis in the Rural South. Paper read to the Department of Anthropology, 1 February, at the University of North Carolina, Chapel Hill.

Rappaport, Roy. 1979. Adaptive Structure and Its Disorders. In *Ecology, Meaning and Religion*. Richmond, Calif.: North Atlantic Books.

Reed, John S. 1986. *The Enduring South*. Chapel Hill: University of North Carolina Press.

Reich, Charles. 1970. *The Greening of America: How the Youth Revolution Is Trying to Make America Livable*. New York: Random House.

Rieff, Philip. 1979. *The Mind of the Moralist Freud*. Chicago: University of Chicago Press.

Riesman, David. 1950. *The Lonely Crowd: A Study of the Changing American Character*. New Haven: Yale University Press.

Romney, A. Kimball, and Roy Goodwin D'Andrade. 1964. Cognitive Aspects of English Kin Terms. *American Anthropologist* 66, no. 3: 146–70.

Sacks, Karen. 1984. *My Troubles Are Going to Have Trouble With Me: Everyday Trials and Triumphs of Women Workers*. New Brunswick, N.J.: Rutgers University Press.

Sahlins, Marshall David. 1976. *Culture and Practical Reason*. Chicago: University of Chicago Press.

Schneider, David. 1968. *American Kinship: A Cultural Account*. Englewood Cliffs, N.J.: Prentice-Hall.

Sheehy, Gail. 1976. *Passages: Predictable Crises of Adult Life*. New York: Dutton.

Slater, Philip Elliol. 1970. *The Pursuit of Loneliness: American Culture at the Breaking Point*. Boston: Beacon Press.

Smith, Jonathan Z. 1982. *Imagining Religion: From Babylon to Jonestown*. Chicago: University of Chicago Press.

Stack, Carol. 1974. *All Our Kin*. New York: Harper & Row.

Strauss, Claudia. 1989. Hegemony and Cognition. Paper read to the Department of Anthropology, 22 February, at the University of North Carolina, Chapel Hill.

Sutton, Joel Brett. 1983. Spirit and Policy in a Black Primitive Baptist Church. Ph.D. diss., University of North Carolina, Chapel Hill.

Terkel, Studs. 1970. *Hard Times: An Oral History of the Great Depression*. New York: Pantheon.

Tindall, George. 1989. Natives and Newcomers: Ethnic Southerners and Southern Ethnics. Paper presented at symposium, The Multicultural South, 8 April, University of North Carolina, Chapel Hill.

Toqueville, Alexis de. 1961. *Democracy in America*. New York: Schocken Books.

Turner, Victor W. 1974. *Dramas, Fields, and Metaphors*. Ithaca: Cornell University Press.

———. 1982. *Celebrations*. Washington, D.C.: Smithsonian Institution Press.

Varrenne, Herve. 1977. *Americans Together: Structural Diversity in a Midwestern Town*. New York: Teachers College Press.

Veblen, Thorstein. 1934. *The Theory of the Leisure Class*. New York: Library.

Vogt, Evon Z., and Ethel M. Albert, eds. 1966. *People of Rimrock: A Study of Values in Five Cultures*. Cambridge: Harvard University Press.

Walker, Alice. 1983. *The Color Purple.* New York: Washington Square Press.

Warner, Lloyd. 1941–59. *Yankee City Series.* 5 vols. New Haven: Yale University Press.

Weber, Max. 1946. *From Max Weber.* Ed. Hans Gerth and C. Wright Mills. New York: Oxford University Press.

———. 1952. *Ancient Judaism.* Trans. and ed. Hans H. Gerth and Don Martindale. Glencoe, Ill.: Free Press.

———. 1952. *Religion of China: Confucianism and Taoism.* Glencoe, Ill.: Free Press.

———. 1958. *Religion of India: The Sociology of Hinduism and Buddhism.* Glencoe, Ill.: Free Press.

———. 1972. *Gesammelte Aufzatze zur Religionssoziologie.* Tübingen: Mohr.

———. 1985. *The Protestant Ethic and the Spirit of Captialism.* New York: Unwin Paperbacks.

Weidman, Hazel. 1979. Profile of an Anthropologist. *Newsletter.* American Anthropological Association 20(10): 6–7 (December).

Whisnant, David. 1983. *All That Is Native and Fine.* Chapel Hill: University of North Carolina Press.

———. 1989. When the Backyard Turns Up on the Front Porch: Thoughts on the Hispanicization of the (old) South. Paper presented at symposium, The Multicultural South, 8 April, at the University of North Carolina, Chapel Hill.

White, William H. 1956. *The Organization Man.* New York: Simon and Schuster.

Whiting, John, and Irvin I. Child. 1953. *Child Training and Personality.* New Haven: Yale University Press.

Whorf, Benjamin Lee. 1956. *Language, Thought, and Reality: Selected Writings.* Cambridge: Technology Press of Massachusetts Institute of Technology.

Wikan, Uni. 1987. Public Grace and Private Fears: Gaiety, Offense, and Sorcery in Northern Bali. *Ethos* 15, no. 4 (December): 337–65.

Wilson, Charles. 1980. *Baptized in Blood: The Religion of the Lost Cause, 1865–1920.* Athens: University of Georgia Press.

———, and William Ferris, eds. 1989. *Encyclopedia of the South.* Chapel Hill: University of North Carolina Press.

Wuthnow, Robert. 1989. Indices of Religious Resurgence in the United States. In *Religious Resurgence,* ed. Richard Antoun and Mary Hegland, 15–34. Syracuse: Syracuse University Press.

Yamada, Yutaka. 1984. Purifying the Living and Purifying the Dead: Narratives of the Religious Experience of Japanese-American and Caucasian Members of the Church of World Messianity, Los Angeles, California. Ph.D. diss., Department of Anthropology, University of North Carolina, Chapel Hill.

Zug, Charles G. 1987. *Turners and Burners: The Folk Potters of North Carolina.* Chapel Hill: University of North Carolina Press.

Chapter 2

Democratic Participation: A View from Anthropology

Carol MacLennan

Over the last decade there has been a resurgence of interest in the United States in the study of democracy, particularly around questions of participation. Evident in the work of sociologists, political scientists, economists, and philosophers is the vision that a healthy society embraces a wide variety of mechanisms by which its citizens have a say in not only the political process beyond the act of voting, but also in the development and use of technologies, the application of science to human problems, and the structure of economic institutions and distribution of goods. A most important concern among social scientists has been to understand why the ideal of democracy in its broadest sense has not been realized in the United States. What are the historical, institutional, and ideological forces that have led to an apparent disinterest in participation, governance, and democratic practice in the United States? Or, is the problem a different one: are there new forms of political participation that go unnoticed? And why?

Twenty-five years ago, political scientists asked similar questions. But their primary concern was with declining voter turnout in elections that rested on a fairly narrow definition of political participation. The problem was the alienated voter; the solution was to reinterest voters in the electoral process—a reflection of the behaviorism of the 1950s and 1960s. Broader discussions about whether democratic practice worked in the United States (and why and why not) were absent.

Today's debates about democracy come after a turbulent period in academe in which the study of power and power structures beginning in the 1960s have deeply influenced the social sciences. Questions in the 1990s about democratic practice now arise out of a concern with ideologically and institutionally blocked efforts of citizens to claim their rights to participation in formal political institutions. The problem is less the voter than those societal forces that impede realization of democratic values, and the response of citizens to this situation.

No one discipline claims territory in this discussion. Truly an inter-disciplinary concern, each field contributes important insights to the study of participation and to analysis of the obstacles that prevent its realization. Anthropology, interestingly, has been largely absent from this discussion. Yet, its contribution could broaden our understanding of U.S. political culture in ways previously unexplored. Anthropology's holism, historical interests, and methods of participant-observation are powerful tools for the analysis of U.S. politics. It is not trapped by the tradition of behavioral analysis (e.g., voting behavior) or institutional studies (e.g., the presidency and Congress) characteristic of political science. Nor is it locked into study of linear decision-making processes that is typical of policy studies.

Because of its ethnographic and pluralistic approach to its subject, anthropology has rich possibilities for exploring how the central values in American political culture are absorbed, resisted, or reformulated in everyday life. Contemporary discussions on political apathy among American citizens, for instance, need not be taken at face value by anthropologists. Participant-observation in political institutions such as federal bureaucracies, Congress, state offices, and even in newspaper publishing might shed light on how notions of apathy are generated by institutionalized actions and then applied to the citizenry. Community research on how citizens participate in (or are excluded from) decision making in many types of activity could explain what really goes on in everyday life.

Particularly ripe for analysis is the role that ideologies play in Amer-ican politics, a subject of potential interest to anthropologists. How do beliefs about free enterprise, the market, property, individualism, etc. affect public policy formation? More importantly, where do these ideas originate? What are the historical and institutional forces that create contemporary notions of political authority, participation, and democ-racy? What beliefs and processes shape the formation of political in-stitutions (bureaucracies), sacred texts (the Constitution), and political practices (regulation)? How do some notions (such as the "free market") come to dominate the political debates? Why are some ideas legitimate and others not? Under what conditions are ideologies internalized and reproduced by individuals? In what situations are these beliefs contested, and what are the structural and/or institutional dimensions of the contest?

This chapter provides a survey of research and thought that is relevant to our concern with democratic participation and the barriers to its realization. Scholars working on the subject of political culture and those engaged in local-level studies of community politics have traditionally written about political participation. However, new thinking on the topic, especially from those who examine the politics of technology, reframes the question in ways that beg for anthropological contributions. Some ethnographers, as described in this chapter, have moved in this direction. Other questions for study are offered.

Political Culture

Political culture might seem the natural starting point for examining the problem of participation. Scholars in this field study the underlying beliefs that affect political action and shape institutional behavior. Yet, traditional research on political culture has been the domain of political science (see Almond and Verba 1963; Pye 1962).

Contemporary political-culture studies do not reflect the significant contributions of anthropology, particularly its pluralist and community perspective. During the early years, research on political culture was significantly influenced by the national culture studies of Benedict (1946), Mead and Metraux (1953), and Gorer (1948). Typically in the social sciences (other than some anthropology) culture was defined as a set of core values. As a result, political-culture studies paid little attention to the pluralist character of industrial societies in their analyses. Differing notions of democracy, participation, authority, and citizenship went unexamined in studies of large nation-states. This led easily into sweeping statements about citizen apathy and it reinforced normative definitions of democratic participation.

As with the national-character studies, the political-culture tradition had a decidedly psychological orientation, with its overriding concern with psychological attitudes and patterns of thought said to characterize the whole society. Mead and like-minded anthropologists sought to explain how attitudes were reproduced in cultures. National character research was based on understanding the patterning of parent-child relations in individual cultures. Culture was learned behavior; therefore the methodology in national-character studies required the studying of socialization.

Political scientists Almond and Verba were influenced by Mead and adopted the concept of culture directly from the national-character studies, indentifying it as "psychological orientation toward social objects." They defined political culture as a "political system internalized in the cognitions, feelings, and evaluations of its population." (1963, 14) Political-culture studies in the 1960s primarily identified and compared political beliefs and attitudes in different national cultures but, unlike the anthropologists, were not concerned with explaining cultural reproduction. Further, this was culture without a pluralist dimension.

While research on national character declined in anthropology, the concept of political culture became quite popular in the field of comparative politics, having a more lasting impact in political science. Interestingly, in a 1979 issue of *Comparative Politics* Elkins and Simeon (1979) discuss at length the continued influence of anthropology (particularly that of Lévi-Strauss, Geertz, and Schneider) on the concept of political culture as "ideational codes" and assumptions of a collectivity.

More important, though, is the current influence of the "political culture" paradigm in policy and proscriptive research that is read widely in academic, government, and corporate circles. Here political culture is used as an explanatory device to account for differences between political societies. David Vogel's research (1986) on environmental politics in the United States and Britain is an example. He analyzes the differences in environmental-policy outcomes in the two countries and attributes the difference to political culture: Americans assume that business and government are political adversaries and cannot cooperate. Social democracies like Britain do not make this assumption; hence, he argues, they manifest dramatically different policy outcomes. Steven Kelman (1981) makes a similar claim for his comparison of worker health and safety programs in the United States and Sweden. Both examine decision-making processes, political maneuvering of interested parties, and public debate in the popular press for their sources of generalizations about political culture. Such research highlights broad cultural trends, identifying distinguishing values that lead to different political practice in each nation. But it does little to describe the contest between differing political structures and ideologies within the larger political culture of any nation, nor can it lead us to answers for the questions about democracy and participation posed at the outset of this chapter.

Community Studies

Some of anthropology's early community studies did address issues of participation. They, too, were drawn toward describing a "political culture"—a set of core values that underlay political activity. But their holistic approach and participant-observation methods led them to more complex and multidimensional descriptions of political life. The focus on behavior and everyday life in communities such as Middletown (Lynd and Lynd 1929; 1937) and Yankee City (Warner 1963) presents us with some interesting observations on American democracy.

Ethnographers of American communities from the 1920s through the 1950s found comparable political themes reverberating throughout their research. They describe a wide disparity between citizen disinterest in local politics and intense interest in national elections. They note the enthusiasm with which citizens embrace national political symbols of freedom (the flag), participation (the vote), equality (the Bill of Rights and the Constitution), and the state (Memorial Day). And they note the lack of citizen interest regarding decisions affecting their communities and states and regarding political participation on these levels. Ethnographers were plagued by the same reliance on voting statistics as were political scientists. Arensberg and Kimball (1965) and West (1945) observed on the one hand that local politics seemed more successful in stimulating apathy and cynicism in citizens than in eliciting participation. On the other hand, the symbols that surfaced during national elections created great enthusiasm, drawing significant attention to the electoral contest.

Research conducted by Robert and Helen Lynd and by W. Lloyd Warner on large American communities explored in depth the paradox of enthusiastic citizen support for democratic principles. They studied rituals and symbolism in communities that were also characterized by citizen apathy and disinterest in political activity and participation. In studies of Middletown and Yankee City/Jonesville they make some attempt to explain the paradox. As we plot an agenda for contemporary anthropologists we should review the conclusions of the Lynds (1929; 1937) and Warner (1949; 1959; 1963).

The Lynds' *Middletown in Transition* (1937) contains a detailed assessment of government and politics. Unlike the first volume, *Middletown,* this study stresses the paradox between democratic symbol and political reality: "There is no area of Middletown's life, save religion, where symbol is more admittedly and patently divorced from reality than in government . . . " (322).

The Lynds painted a disparaging picture of Middletown citizenry during the 1930s depression as uninterested in social problems, as passive onlookers:

> Rather than ponder such things, Middletown prefers either to sloganize or to personalize its problems. And the more the disparities have forced themselves to attention, the more things have seemed "too big" and "out of hand" the more Middletown has inclined to heed the wisdom of sticking to one's private business. . . . (492)

In a pessimistic vein, the Lynds describe patterns of apathetic thinking in Middletown, attempting to explain the paradox of myth vs. reality. They discuss the uneasiness that individuals have in speaking out, in committing to political ideals:

> They believe in "peace, but—." They believe in "fairness to labor, but—." "In freedom of speech, but—." In "democracy, but—." In "freedom of the press, but—." (492)

They describe the citizens' tendency to look to past formulas when faced with troubling signs such as local political corruption. Middletowners assume "the system is fundamentally right and only the persons wrong; the cures must be changes in personal attitudes, not in the institutions themselves" (493).

Throughout this second study of Middletown, the Lynds depict a worldview, a culture that reproduces an apathetic response to the political and societal problems of the depression era in this community. They suggest that Middletowners are unable to conceptualize political reform, and that they look to the individual (rather than the institutions) for blame—an antecedent to the culture of poverty view. "The institutions are there, fixed and final in their major aspects, and the individual must struggle to make them work and to be more worthy of them" (494). This is reinforced by an emphasis on the "instrumental" character of lived life. Middletowners focus on the future of their individual lives— namely "saving," "trying to get somewhere in life"—rather than the quality of the present life. The Lynds argue that this sort of instrumental living places a heavy burden on the reliability of the underlying institutional system. Thus, opportunities for political reform and an increase in political participation were minimal.

In general, *Middletown in Transition* paints a rather dismal picture of an irrational citizenry, governed by impulse and by beliefs in individual salvation, unable to understand the powerful changes in political society required by depression-era events. In the Lynds' view, this thinking provided fertile ground for fascism. In later writing, this pessimism led Robert Lynd toward an advocacy for social planning by professional elites who managed institutional change from above.

Perhaps the most informative treatise on democratic politics and participation is found in W. Lloyd Warner's *Democracy in Jonesville* (1949). It largely reflects the thinking of that period among political scientists and anthropologists. Where the Lynds found "apathy" troublesome, Warner viewed it as functional. He was not troubled with a mishmash of democratic ideals in community life nor with the lack of participation except in annual political rituals. For him, the "ideology of democracy" plays an important role in maintaining the open system of "social" class in America, preventing it from evolving into a castelike system.

Warner acknowledges that "the equalitarian principle expressed in the precepts sacred to our democratic creed are in opposition to the hard facts that press upon the citizens of Jonesville when they experience the secular realities of social class" (296). But he argues that the democratic ideal of equality acts as a counterbalancing force against the power of social hierarchy. Beliefs and rituals that express equality and community instead of hierarchy and individualism are necessary for an open society. His description of Memorial Day rites as celebrations of the dead that draw together diverse, antagonistic groups into a ritual community of equals illustrates the function he attributes to the "ideology of democracy" in American society.

For Warner, then, democratic participation is understood through a lens focused on concerns of equality. Whether participation is real or imagined is of little import, as long as democracy *functions* to maintain a cohesive community undivided by class antagonisms. From this view, there is little motivation to ask what might be the consequences of a society that has limited means for democratic participation.

Sociologists of the 1980s studying working- and middle-class communities describe a similar paradox between steadfast commitment of these Americans to the democratic system and a deep distrust of current political practices. Halle (1948) explains that the working class believes corrupt politicians subvert the system. At the same time, they believe the system itself is not corrupt and they view it positively because, "there is the belief that the system delivers freedom, even if not democracy" (201). As with the Lynds, Halle finds notions of "individualism" dominating the political thought of working people in a working-class, New Jersey community. It seems that citizens value the protections afforded by the political system for individual freedoms over the rights of democratic participation. This is yet another attempt to unravel the paradox of apathy and participation.

In a similar vein, Herbert Gans (1988) describes the ideology of individualism in terms of the middle American's search for personal freedom, thus having implications for the democratic system. In a study of the middle class, he sees resistance to participation in political parties and the rise of single-issue politics as an outgrowth of increased focus on the individual rather than the community, on freedoms rather than participation.

In *Habits of the Heart,* Bellah, et al. (1985) lament the lost language of community and participation that has been replaced by the "individualist vision of politics."

> The limit set by individualism is clear: events that escape the control of individual choice and will cannot coherently be encompassed in a moral calculation. . . . But that means that much, if not most, of the workings of the interdependent American political economy, through which individuals achieve or are assigned their places and relative power in this society, cannot be understood in terms that make coherent moral sense. (204)

Bellah and his colleagues echo the community studies of an earlier era, particulary Middletown, when they locate the problem of participation in the individualist ideologies of citizens. As Peacock notes in this volume, the neo-Weberian orientation in *Habits of the Heart* identifies core values shared by individuals in society but is not sensitive to the pluralist character of the American middle class, which might include contradictory or different values. And so it is easier to identify a one-dimensional cause to the problem: individualist values impede democratic participation.

Further, by resting analysis of American society on "core values" (similar to the political-culture approach), it is difficult for Bellah and other contemporaries to see how additional factors might impede democratic participation. Are there political or social structures that make it difficult for citizens to engage their political system, or discourage them from ever trying? Are there other dominating ideologies (beliefs promoted by powerful interests) that divert public attention away from democratic concerns? The framework provided by the Lynds and their descendants such as Gans, Halle, and Bellah do not give us the opportunity to explore such questions. They highlight an important point: citizens utilize an "individualist" framework to blame politicians, but not the system, for political failures. The language of freedom replaces that of participation. One senses, however, that there is a lot more going on. The insights from anthropology's pluralism are not applied.

Focus on Participation

A different approach to the problem of democratic participation has recently emerged, which breaks away from the tendency to "blame the victim." Scholars from several fields have explored the question of what *constitutes* participation in a democratic society. The traditional definition of "political participation" (such as that in the 1968 *International Encyclopedia of Social Sciences*) is limited to voting and electoral politics. Now the term is used more expansively to include citizen participation in many parts of the political process (regulatory, administrative, and judicial) and worker participation in economic institutions. *Participatory democracy* is the more commonly used descriptor. Phrases such as "citizen participation," "economic justice," and "worker control," have become slogans in the new thinking on participation. Further, inquiries concerned with the causes of political failures and the absence of participation move beyond the citizen to the political system for explanation.

Probably the clearest example of new thinking on the institutional barriers to participation come from those who study the politics of technology. Philosophers (Winner 1986), political historians (Noble 1986), and political analysts (Dickson 1984) argue that technologies of industrial society are leading us toward highly centralized political and social systems that discourage popular control and accountability. The societal choice for large technical systems (e.g., nuclear energy and complex weapons systems) envisioned as solutions to social problems or political dilemmas, they argue, has serious consequences for democratic society. Dominance of scientific and technical experts creates dependent citizens who lack the capability of entering public debate over political decisions (Dickson 1984). Centralization as well as secrecy in decision making characterize decisions, which eventually have major repercussions on communities, the workplace, and daily life. An example would be the recent revelations about safety practices at nuclear-weapons plants such as Rocky Flats, Colorado, where important information concerning public health was intentionally kept from the public. Regulatory agencies (especially federal) are central to political life in the United States. Yet, they seem captive to scientific and technical expertise and to the heavy hand of powerful, nonaccountable agencies such as the Office of Management and Budget in the White House. Commitment to the regulation of technology through statist, rather than decentralized, solutions creates impenetrable government bureaucracies with exclusive power to define the course of events surrounding any controversy (Noble 1986).

Langdon Winner advances the point that "technical things have political qualities . . . they can embody specific forms of power and authority" (1986, 19). This tpye of thinking has been heavily influenced by Lewis Mumford's discussion of the two types of technologies that have existed side by side throughout world history: one system-centered, powerful, unstable, and authoritarian; the other human-centered, resourceful, weak, and democratic.

The significance of this literature, compared to that of political culture, lies in its ability to identify institutional barriers that discourage and even prohibit political participation. It locates the obstacles to participation in the structure and history of power arrangements that are embodied in technologies, administrative powers of government, and dominance of scientific and technical experts over the political process, rather than in citizens. It also shifts the blame away from culture or laziness. While insightful in their analysis of power, these approaches exaggerate structure. One is then led to ask: What role does human action (or reaction) play in a democratic society? These approaches also de-emphasize the plural character of U.S. society and implicitly dismiss the possibility that effective participation may occur outside formal political channels.

Anthropology's Contribution

It is obvious that with a pluralist orientation and ethnographic method anthropology can not only help address these deficiencies, it can do significantly more. Research by anthropologists on the forms of participation, and on access and barriers to democratic participation would be insightful. Research on how different groups respond to exclusion from formal channels of participation would fill important gaps in knowledge. And a historical-anthropological study of power and participation might alter our thinking altogether. Certainly we can move away from the blame-the-victim approach of earlier years that emphasized citizen apathy. By investigating how barriers to participation are erected in specific settings, where they came from, and how they remain powerful obstacles to citizen involvement in political life, anthropologists may help unravel one of the more complex problems of late–twentieth-century America.

Substantive research would be profitable in two areas: (1) in the examination of the barriers that discourage or thwart citizen involvement in political and economic concerns that affect their lives—for instance, how the powerful metaphor of the "marketplace" affects day-to-day decisions, administrative programs, and community debate; and (2) in the local-level response to exclusion from political channels that results in social movements, group acts of resistance, and sometimes development of alternative forms of participation that may effectively challenge the formal system of power.

Barriers to Participation: Institutions and Ideologies

First, what are the real barriers that limit participation in political life? Several avenues of research might prove fruitful: (*a*) research on the administrative power of government to control citizen access to formal channels of power ("studying up," Nader 1972), (*b*) study of how ideologies of the market and of progress dominate (and are internalized) in political and community life, and (*c*) studies of situations where market interests (such as commitment to a particular technology) and other societal interests clash in some form of political conflict.

We might investigate administrative systems of power such as agencies that set standards for environmental protection or for health and safety and how they structure participation. Citizen participation has not been ignored by federal and state law—it is (in principle and in law) a part of the political process. The Administrative Procedures Act, Advisory Committees Act, Freedom of Information Act (FOIA), National Environmental Policy Act (NEPA) all purport to ensure, encourage, and legalize citizen involvement in regulatory decisions. Yet, these laws are ineffective, either because they do not empower citizens at critical points in decision making, or, they in fact, steer citizen participation into ineffective and diversionary channels that leave experts and agencies unchallenged.

The study of administrative reform in the United States is crucial to our understanding of participation. Usually viewed as the domain of political science and public administration, this subject warrants a close look by anthropologists. For instance, I have found in my research on "open government" reforms at the federal level that citizen participation is more often thwarted than served by crucial laws such as the Administrative Procedures Act of 1946, the primary legislation that guarantees citizen access to the regulatory process (MacLennan 1988a). Study of how this act is implemented reveals that while citizen access to federal decision making is a guaranteed right in the day-to-day operation of government, it introduces citizens into the regulatory process at a point far too late to be effective.

Sally Fairfax's research on the hidden problems of the Environmental Impact Statement raises a similar point (1978). These statements, mandated by the National Environmental Policy Act of 1969 (NEPA), she argues, have hindered environmental protection more than they have helped:

> "Litigation under NEPA and preoccupation with the NEPA process truncated preexisting and potentially significant developments in the definition of agency responsibility for environmental protection and citizen involvement in agency deliberative processes." (743)

There is little research to date that explains how administrative barriers are erected and maintained in these government settings, whether they are intentional or not, and why standard nonelectoral modes of participation are not effectively including citizens in political decisions. Anthropologists can evaluate administrative processes, the successes and failures of reforms, and the underlying day-to-day operations of government in a manner that should shed light on whether and/or why citizens are shut out from planning, research, and implementation of federal and state programs that affect their lives and communities. Ethnographic studies of key agencies that often block public participation (such as the Office of Management and Budget) would prove invaluable.

Ideologies that place the market and social-technical progress at the center of the U.S. value system must also be examined. The political and technological controversies that typify community life on the local level (such as sitings of large-scale plants, hazardous waste sites, etc.) are often cast in a symbolic and metaphoric language that promotes the market and progress as twin ingredients to successful conflict resolution and a better society. This needs to be investigated by anthropologists. What is the power of the market metaphor in American life? Its presence in political debates about economic development, deindustrialization, environmental regulation, economic policy, education, and health (to name a few) is a powerful force in labeling which alternatives or solutions are "thinkable" and within the realm of discussion and which are "unthinkable" and outside the realm of discussion (Chomsky 1985).

The market is more than a metaphor, an idea. It is also a structure, a web of relationships that exerts economic power in modern societies. This structure is often reflected in government actions and initiatives. For instance, analytical tools such as cost-benefit assessment (CBA) have proven to be important aspects of a market ideology that effectively limits regulatory initiatives in the health and safety fields (MacLennan 1988b). This decision tool clearly defines legitimate (thinkable) types of information necessary for determining whether or not to regulate technologies or industrial behaviors. CBA has served market interests in government decisions since the 1980s. By placing a monetary value on all costs and benefits of regulations, CBA replaces social with economic criteria for decision making. The case of automotive safety is illustrative: the Congressional mandate to "save lives and reduce injuries," as found in the 1966 Motor Vehicle Safety Act, has effectively been replaced by the requirement that all regulations meet a cost-benefit test (Reagan Executive Order 12291) that is premised on establishing the "value of human life" in order to determine whether the benefits to society are worth the costs to industry.

The market as an "idea-system" in modern American politics serves as a weapon in the clash of social interests. It has the power to bestow meanings that have considerable consequences. This is noted by those who study regulatory conflict over environmental and health and safety policy (Noble 1986; Hays 1987). It is discussed among the most thoughtful political theorists who recognize the structure as well as ideological power of the market. Charles Lindbloom (1984) describes the market as "prison" because of its very real punishing effect in response to reform attempts. Regulatory initiatives that require application of new technologies to products (autos) or production processes (coal-fired power plants) in order to meet societal goals of safety, health, or clean air often bring corporate retaliatory measures in the form of plant closings and layoffs. In such instances, the market serves as a deterrent to social and political reform. This structural power is reinforced by ideologies that may themselves deter reforms by citizen activists. Recall the old industry adage in the early days of the auto-safety movement of the 1960s: "safety doesn't sell." This slogan effectively limited bold actions by the new automotive safety agency during the 1970s and 1980s because government engineers believed that consumer preference was a product of individual choice rather than industry advertising (MacLennan 1988b).

The primacy of the market in regard to public policy planning and implementation is of no surprise to those familiar with democratic theory. C. B. Macphearson (1965) reminds us that market society and its ideology preceded the rise of the liberal-democratic state. In liberal-democratic societies such as the United States, rights and claims of private property historically preceded establishment of democratic rights. It is not co-incidental that capitalism and liberal-democracy go together. As Mac-phearson notes: "Democracy came as the top dressing. It had to accommodate itself to the soil that had already been prepared by the operation of the competitive, individualist, market society..." (5).

More recently, Jennifer Nedelsky (1990) explores how private property affects the American notion of governance and law. She argues that the vision of constitutionalism in the United States developed around distorted and illusory notions of property. As a result, the Constitution neither fosters democratic participation nor does it prevent the power of wealth from undermining democracy (276). The one anthropologist who identifies this type of phenomena in a larger cultural sense is Laura Nader with her concept of "controlling processes" (1987). She writes about an unconscious quality in the exercise of power where structures and ideologies that are taken for granted can control decisions and political outcomes in hidden, quiet ways. An example would be the increasing role of secrecy in democratic governments, as represented by the unquestioned acceptance of a broad definition of "national security" by citizens.

The power of the market as both structure and metaphor is widely recognized in American politics. Yet, we understand little of how it works and, more importantly, whether it is truly internalized by all parts of society. Rappaport (1989) makes a useful distinction between hegemonic and dominant ideas. The market may be a hegemonic idea in federal policy making where it has successfully been internalized and accepted as a legitimate regulator of the policy process. In other political and social sectors of society, however, the market is seen differently. It is an "idea system" that may be merely dominant. That is, it is imposed through the exercise of power, but not necessarily internalized by those on whom it is imposed. This distinction (not developed among political scientists and sociologists who study normative politics or core values) allows for the investigation of resistance to powerful ideas. Such an example is provided in this volume by Vélez-Ibanez who illustrates how U.S.-Mexican households have developed cultural and behavioral practices that have become the core of a cultural identity as a result of binational industrialization. This identity might be viewed as part of an idea system that counters the market ideology of the dominant culture.

Anthropologists are comfortable in the study of local settings— whether communities, government offices, or corporations. They can easily observe the power of a dominant idea, the extent of internalization into everyday thought and community life, and the presence of idea systems that resist the power of the market ideology in community or institutional settings.

From a different angle, the study of the conflict between industry and community groups or social movements would yield important insights into mechanisms of power, barriers to citizen participation and power, and the role played by market ideologies. Research into local-level environmental controversies may prove especially productive. Laying the ground work, historian Samuel Hays (1987) effectively demonstrates that there has been growing competition in U.S. politics between older production values, oriented toward economic development of natural resources, and new consumption (environmental) values that are concerned with the quality of life rather than economic exploitation. As Hays points out, conflicts between groups holding these differing values occur primarily on the local level over environmental and health and safety issues. Newman's (1988) research on Singer company workers also illustrates the conflict of values between workers who value quality and craftsmanship and a company increasingly concerned with efficiency and return on investment over product quality. Singer workers had an elaborate critique of the market values held by their employer. The study of conflicting meanings should provide insight into beliefs and political definitions that counter the dominant culture. Participation may not take the form of involvement in a political process but it may take the form of mental frameworks shared by co-workers that challenge the dominant point of view. From this may spring future political action.

Research by anthropologists on ethnic identity or on technical, environmental, or economic controversy could examine the ways in which the market metaphor and its structural manifestations are operative, whether they dampen (or stimulate) participation, their power over meaning in local political life, and what are the tangible consequences of the market ideology. Such exploration would go a long way toward clarifying the power of and the resistance to other dominant ideologies in American societies—especially the idea of progress, which is closely linked to that of the market.

Local Level Response: Study of Power

Anthropologists would also contribute to our knowledge of participation by examining local-level response to exclusion from, or limited inclusion in, the formal channels of political participation. Traditionally, citizens expect to participate in decisions through the electoral process. But some of the most important decisions concerning community life, public health, and economic development offer limited channels for citizen input. How do different groups respond to this reality. Does opposition to exclusion develop? In what forms?

In an important research contribution, John Gaventa in *Power and Powerlessness* (1980) discusses the roots of quiescence and rebellion in a Central Appalachian community. Following Steven Lukes (1974), Gaventa discusses a three-dimensional system of power in which power and powerlessness are interrelated and mutually reinforcing. A standard notion of power implies the exertion of *A's* power over *B*. Both Lukes and Gaventa argue that the notion of power should be expanded to include both decision making and nondecision making (a second dimension of power). "A decision is a choice among alternative modes of action; a nondecision is a decision that results in suppression or thwarting of a latent or manifest challenge to the values or interests of the decision-maker" (Lukes 1974, 18). As power is wielded in this fashion, there can develop a "mobilization of bias," or barriers (Gaventa) against groups that challenge the dominant values or decision makers. This may reinforce powerlessness and ensure that discontent becomes hidden and contained. For the anthropologist interested in democratic participation (and nonparticipation) this is a useful distinction. It helps unravel the problem of participation outside formal channels of power and may help to explain nonparticipation. A more elusive dimension of power—Gaventa's third dimension—is the means by which symbols, myths, and language shape and determine the "necessities, possibilities, and strategies" of challenge to power in situations of latent conflict (15). Our earlier discussion of how market ideology defines what is appropriate political action and limits the types of political mechanisms available to citizens is an example of this dimension of power.

Gaventa uses the historical and ethnographic method to study issues and nonissues, and participation and nonparticipation in a coal-mining community. Useful areas of research include not only conflict, but latent conflict. Hence, a community-study approach might be most profitable for identifying the latent issues under the surface. Also, the history of a community is crucial to understanding how power is attained and maintained, as well as how rebellion is handled and shaped into quiescence. Community studies, family histories, and a history of political conflict in a region or community might provide evidence of the more elusive nonissues, latent conflicts, and ways in which elites and powerful institutions create powerlessness.

Vélez-Ibanez (1983) looks at a similar issue in his research on a marginalized population in a large Mexican city. He views marginality as economic and political exclusion from the benefits of the national economy and political structure. He attributes the powerlessness of this group to what he terms "rituals of marginality" and "structures of marginalization," not to the behavioral characteristics of the marginalized. Like Gaventa, he attempts to understand which factors create and reinforce a sense of powerlessness and passiveness on the local level. More skillfully than Gaventa, he helps us understand how cultural forces, such as myth and ritual, create an impression of national political and economic integration.

A powerful force in marginalizing large sectors of Mexican society is the central national myth that "everybody in a highly stratified and hierarchical system has equal access to economic resources or is represented politically, regardless of status" (21). This is not too different from widespread beliefs in the United States that promote equal access to economic benefits through education and hard work and promote participation in the political system through the electoral process.

Vélez-Ibanez discovered that political action was always issue-specific.

And, further, issue-oriented politics increased marginalization of the community rather than increasing their integration into the economic and political order. Also interesting is his finding that as political leaders in the community become further entangled in formal political sectors they became more integrated and detached from their community supporters. He discovers that *"individuals,* but not groups become 'integrated,' whereas politically and economically marginalized populations become further victimized . . ." (24). By engaging in institutionalized rituals of marginality expressed by patron-client relationships, political friendships, brokerage, and "favors," these leaders join the formal political sector and become dependent on elites for political support and are thus culturally "delocalized." The local political-action organization experiences a reversal of management. Support from the bottom (local-level participants) gives way to a form of coerced management from nonlocal elites. This leads active, local participants into pessimism and eventual withdrawal. Over time, this becomes an adaptive strategy.

Vélez-Ibanez's ethnography of an urban Mexican political movement provokes research questions that apply to the United States: To what extent do political movements that challenge the established structure exhibit similar features? What political rituals and myths exist on the local level (an update of Lynd's and Warner's findings during mid-century) and how do they impact nontraditional political organizations and initiatives? What purpose is served and who benefits from the discontinuity between the ideal of democracy and the reality of politics?

Vélez-Ibanez's research is relevant to our questions about participation. As does Warner, and to some extent Lynd, Vélez-Ibanez examines the relationship between myth and reality in local political life. Yet, his conclusions are different. The Lynds tended to blame apathy and cynicism on the "instrumental" orientation of Middletowners, which led them to disregard opportunities for political reform. Their conclusions reflect their disappointment in their respondents rather than attempts to understand how apathy originates and is maintained. Warner, a functionalist, views democratic ideologies (which do not match local realities) as a positive aspect of U.S. life. They help maintain an open society and fluidity in the class structure. Warner's description of Memorial Day is one of the "rituals of integration" discussed by Vélez-Ibanez. But Warner is interested in its functional rather than its dysfunctional purpose.

In much the same way, pluralists in political science (Dahl, in his early work, 1961) and sociology (Lipset 1963) have viewed apathy positively in that it functions to ensure a disproportionate participation in the political structure among educated elites. Apathy thus acts as a constraint upon mass movements that are characterized by simplistic views about personal concerns, irrationality, prejudice, and anti-intellectualism (Lipset 1963). Implicit is the belief that elites are supportive of democratic systems while the masses have worrisome antidemocratic tendencies. These assumptions are still prevalent in pluralist theory of today.

Vélez-Ibanez, utilizing ethnography, provides a contrasting view of that which, on the surface, appears to be the same political phenomena: cynicism, political passivity, and withdrawal from organized political structures. His fieldwork provides a corrective to earlier studies of community politics. Where pluralist studies lean toward a view colored by a fear of democracy, Vélez-Ibanez moves below the surface to tease out a more complex picture of local political action and nonaction.

Other anthropologists have examined political movements on the community level in the United States. Susser's work on a movement to save a local firehouse in New York City (1982), and Sacks's (1988) study of Duke University Medical workers' efforts to organize have detailed the success and failures of oppositional political actions. However, interests other than questions of political participation have occupied these researchers. Their research explores a "culture of resistance" theme that emphasizes the informal ties among members of an action group or underclass and how they serve to unite individuals around specific issues. Susser shows how a neighborhood identity among the very poor emerged and strengthened in an effort to save a community building that was symbolic of a shared life among the residents. The politics of poverty (well-organized power wielded by the city vs. the ad-hoc, limited power of the poor) were well illustrated in the struggle to oppose the city's closure of the firehouse. Her research shows how, even in the face of power and ultimate defeat, community and political identity develops as a result of efforts to organize and resist unacceptable decisions from outside the community.

Sacks has extensively documented another organizing effort that ultimately failed. She examines the means by which political activism develops and is nourished through everyday work life, family networks, and a history of mobilization and demobilization of women's social networks. With a historical perspective on this story, Sacks contributes significantly to our understanding of how the less powerful challenge the extensive power of the status quo:

The wellsprings for change lie in people's tasks and interactions—
but these are multileveled, and their quality and texture are seldom
confrontational or radical. If one sits and watches people's work
lives, even where they are most arduous and oppressive, it is rare to
see anyone openly challenging the status quo. But confront they do.
To understand how workers make things *change* requires putting the
day-to-day analysis back in the stream of historical analysis, asking
how the social alternatives may have changed, trying to capture some
of the archeology of workers' cultures. (4)

Her ethnographic and historical review of "work culture" at Duke Medical Center leads her to conclude that while women who were intensely
active politically during the 1979 union organizing drive and later may
have appeared passive after the defeat, were actually working on alternative means to pursuing the goals of improving their work life.

This "resistance" literature serves an important documentary purpose. In ways that only ethnography can enlighten, it describes the
various types of participation that not only do exist but that are also
often missed or misunderstood by social scientists who study political
process and conflict. Sacks's model is particularly important here because
it provides a more complex rendering of the relationship between political
participation and the appearance of quiescence that troubles Gaventa.
However, this type of research does not enable us to answer other questions about the relationship between power and participation that were
identified earlier in this chapter. Reasons for the demoralization or passivity of citizens reported in these studies are not developed in sufficient
detail to improve our understanding of the barriers to participation. In
other words, "resistance" studies inform us of the possibilities and historical dynamics of participation in political processes by people without
access to established power. But we also need to figure out the other
half of the dialectic and determine how powerful institutions and processes limit citizen power—i.e., more attention needs to be given to the
ethnographic study of power itself.

What makes the work of Gaventa and Vélez-Ibanez important models for anthropological research on democratic participation in the United
States is their attention to the *creation* and *maintenance* of powerlessness,
their attention to the workings of power, as well as their descriptions of
local-level response to powerful institutions. Gaventa's "mobilization of
bias" and Vélez-Ibanez's "rituals of marginality" are useful explanatory

tools that attribute that which we often call apathy to a very complex set of factors. They have studied the problem of participation by focusing directly on the *relationship* between the powerful and the powerless, the *mechanisms* by which this relationship is maintained and sometimes altered, and the *forms* through which political interests are expressed on the local level.

Conclusion: Strategy

It seems that a two-part strategy is necessary in order for anthropologists to be able to study democratic participation in the United States. One type of field research could be conducted in powerful institutions that either directly structure participation (federal bureaucracies, local government, courts, and corporations) or play a role in constructing images of participation and apathy (the press, public policy institutes, universities, and social-science professions). What types of structural and ideological contexts affect public policy in areas of intense interest to citizens, such as environment, health, education, and economic policy? Hidden barriers to participation such as the nondecision, ideas about the market and property rights that discourage and limit democratic initiatives, and other dimensions of power can be documented through ethnography. Anthropologists have contributed little to this type of inquiry, but the potential for providing unique and meaningful explanations in this field is great.

Another type of research on the local level could examine the various forms of political action that *do* emerge in opposition to or parallel with established political structures, specifically focusing on the history of these initiatives, their operation, and the impact of powerful political structures on their success or failure. Community studies that explore the relationship between the exercise, structure, and ideologies of power and the modes of participation and response to power beg to be undertaken. Anthropologists such as Vélez-Ibanez and Sacks have made some headway here, but a more complete picture of the relationship among power, powerlessness, and participation needs to be constructed across many types of communities.

Overall, a research strategy should be three-dimensional: vertically, horizontally, and historically integrated. An understanding of participation demands knowledge of the use of power and the response to power (vertical), both historically and in the ethnographic present. The variations in participation and nonparticipation can only be reflected through multisite (horizontal) ethnographic studies. Further, anthropologists must bring their renewed interest in history to bear on the study of power. Democratic institutions, hegemonic ideas, controlling processes, and local-level, citizen responses and political strategies are shaped over time. Application of the historical method sheds light on the ethnographic present, adding explanatory to descriptive interpretation. When we understand where actions and structures originate we can make sense of the social questions that confront us. If anthropologists continue to produce primarily single-site, synchronic studies and avoid vertically integrated, historical studies of power, little will be accomplished.

What confronts us in the 1990s is the irony of modern democracy: the increasing absense of democratic practice in a democratic society. Anthropology has a stake in explaining why this is and how this happened.

REFERENCES

Almond, Gabriel and Sidney Verba, eds. 1963. *The Civic Culture: Political Attitudes and Democracy in Five Nations.* Princeton: Princeton University Press.

Arensberg, Conrad M. and Solon T. Kimball. 1965. *Culture and Community.* New York: Harcourt, Brace & World.

Bellah, Robert, Richard Madsen, William M. Sullivan, Ann Swidlen, and Steven M. Tipton. 1985. *Habits of the Heart: Individualism and Commitment in American Life.* Berkeley: University of California Press.

Benedict, Ruth. 1946. *The Chrysanthemum and the Sword.* Boston: Houghton Mifflin.

Chomsky, Noam. 1985. The Bounds of Thinkable Thought. *The Progressive,* October, 28–31.

Dahl, Robert. 1961. *Who Governs?* New Haven: Yale University Press.

Dickson, David. 1984. *The New Politics of Science.* New York: Pantheon.

Elkins, David J. and Richard Simeon. 1979. A Cause in Search of its Effect, or What does Political Culture Explain? *Comparative Politics.* 11:127–45.

Fairfax, Sally K. 1978. A Disaster in the Environmental Movement. *Science.* 199:743–48.

Gans, Herbert. 1988. *Middle American Individualism: The Future of Liberal Democracy.* New York: Free Press.

Gaventa, John. 1982. *Power and Powerlessness: Quiescence and Rebellion in an Appalachian Valley.* Urbana: University of Illinois Press.

Gorer, G. 1948. *The American People.* New York: Norton.

Halle, David. 1984. *America's Working Man.* Chicago: University of Chicago Press.

Hays, Samuel. 1987. *Beauty, Health, and Permanence: Environmental Politics in the United States 1955–1985.* New York: Cambridge University Press.

International Encyclopedia of the Social Sciences. 1968. Ed. David L. Sills. New York: Macmillan.

Kelman, Steven. 1981. *Regulating America, Regulating Sweden.* Cambridge: MIT Press.

Lindbloom, Charles. 1982. The Market as Prison. *The Journal of Politics* 44:324–36.

Lipset, Seymour Martin. 1963. *Political Man: The Social Bases of Politics.* New York: Basic Books.

Lukes, Steven. 1974. *Power: A Radical View.* London: Macmillan & Co.

Lynd, R. S. and H. M. Lynd. 1929. *Middletown.* New York: Harcourt, Brace & World.

———. 1937. *Middletown in Transition: A Study in Cultural Conflicts.* New York: Harcourt, Brace, & World.

MacLennan, Carol. 1988a. The Democratic Administration of Government. In *The State and Democracy,* ed. M. Levine, C. MacLennan, J. Kushma, and C. Nobb, 49–178. New York: Routledge.

———. 1988b. From Accident to Crash: The Auto Industry and the Politics of Injury. *Medical Anthropology Quarterly* 2(3): 233–50.

Macphearson, C. B. 1965. *A Real World of Democracy.* Oxford: Clarendon Press.

Mead, M. and Metraux, R. 1953. *The Study of Culture at a Distance.* Chicago: University of Chicago Press.

Mumford, Lewis. 1964. "Authoritarian and Democratic Techniques." *Technology and Culture* 5:1–8.

Nader, Laura. 1972. Up the Anthropologist—Perspectives Gained from Studying Up. In *Reinventing Anthropology.* Ed. Dell Hymes. New York: Pantheon.

———. 1987. Controlling Processes. Sir Douglas Robb Lectures, Fall, at the University of Auckland, New Zealand.

Nedelsky, Jennifer. 1990. *Private Property and the Limits of American Constitutionalism.* Chicago: University of Chicago Press.

Newman, Katherine. 1988. *Falling from Grace: The Experience of Downward Mobility in the American Middle Class.* New York: Free Press.

Noble, Charles. 1986. *Liberalism at Work: The Rise and Fall of OSHA.* Philadelphia: Temple University Press.

Pye, Lucian. 1962. *Politics, Personality, and Nation Building.* New Haven: Yale University Press.

Rappaport, Roy. 1989. Personal communication with author.

Sacks, Karen. 1988. *Caring by the Hour: Women, Work, and Organizing at Duke Medical Center.* Urbana: University of Illinois Press.

Susser, Ida. 1982. *Norman Street: Poverty and Politics in an Urban Neighborhood.* New York: Oxford University Press.

Vélez-Ibanez, Carlos. 1983. *Rituals of Marginality: Politics, Process, and Culture*

Change in Urban Central Mexico, 1969–1974. Berkeley: University of California Press.

Vogel, David. 1986. *National Styles of Regulation: Environmental Protection in Great Britain and the United States.* Ithaca: Cornell University Press.

Warner, Lloyd. 1949. *Democracy in Jonesville: A Study in Quality and Inequality.* New York: Harper & Row.

———. 1959. *The Living and the Dead: A Study of the Symbolic Life of Americans.* New Haven: Yale University Press.

———. 1963. *Yankee City.* Abridged ed. New Haven: Yale University Press.

West, James. 1945. *Plainsville, U.S.A.* New York: Columbia University Press.

Winner, Langdon. 1986. *The Whale and the Reactor: A Search for Limits in an Age of High Technology.* Chicago: University of Chicago Press.

Chapter 3

The Heartbeat of Productivity: Hierarchy and Transformation in American Work Relations

Frank A. Dubinskas

American industry in the 1980s seemed like a lumbering behemoth, under siege by nimble, aggressive foreign economies. The first scourge was Japan, then the four "Little Tigers" of Asia: Korea, Taiwan, Singapore, and Hong Kong. Now the united Europe of 1992 looms across the Atlantic as a competitor. The first American response was "They're not playing fair!" Cheap labor was said to give the Asians unfair advantage. With protected domestic markets and inflated prices, they built profits at home and then "bought" market share abroad by dumping goods below cost. How else, we wondered, could upstart Asians beat the American industrial system at its own game?—games we invented like mass-produced automobiles, consumer electronics, and memory chips, or games we dominated like agricultural and construction equipment, or steel making. Even the machine-tool industry, whose computer numerical control (CNC) systems were U.S.-invented, was overtaken by less expensive, superior Japanese imports. The basic tools for making all other manufactured goods—machine tools and electronic controls, were now dominated by offshore competitors (Jaikumar 1986; Winter 1990). At the same time, in the half decade of the early 1980s, we went from being the world's largest creditor nation to the world's biggest debtor. United States industrial productivity continues to stagnate, as "productivity heads into the 1990s at its slowest pace since the 1981–82 recession..." (Cooper and Madigan 1990, 27), capping a continuous four-year slide. By contrast, Japan's comparable producivity growth figure was nearly three times higher.

A critical look at the changes in American industrial strength reveals the fault lines of weakness at home within our own institutions. So where is the root of this change in our competitive position? There are many sources—economic, political, technical, and structural—for our relative decline.[1] One source, however, lies at the heart of all these systems: the social relationships of productive work. The American economy is not driven by a faceless economic "engine" of productivity, but rather by a heartbeat of human energy. This heartbeat of productivity powers the creation of goods, services, and wealth in America; its energy is structured by and channeled through the organizational systems of business, industry, and government. Our contemporary systems of relationships among members of production communities[2] have come under increasing scrutiny and criticism as a fundamental source of industrial ineffectiveness, waste, and damage to American productivity. These relationships constitute a cultural system of managerial practices that no longer serve our social and economic commonweal.

United States industrial and organizational productivity suffers under a stifling blanket of bureaucracy. Mechanistic organization systems cloak the shoulders of managers with disproportionate power and burden the backs of workers and staff with a rigid hierarchy of control. Organizational systems and work processes are sewn into a rigid straitjacket that divides the responsibilities and interests of managers from workers, superiors from subordinates, and functional groups from each other at every level of a hierarchy. Exchange of information and growth of knowledge are blocked while competition and conflict grow rife—or perhaps worse, produce complacency and dull compliance. Its social relations are founded on inequality, foster antagonism, and fester with distrust and disrespect. They create a context conducive to the social divisions of racism and sexism, among others.

Mechanistic principles of authoritarian control are embedded in eighty years of economic success that has blinded many U.S. apologists and managers to their deficiencies. Machine bureaucracies grew out of attempts to rationalize and discipline the chaotic craft-production systems of the nineteenth century, and they were strikingly successful by mid-twentieth century in achieving the goals of increased efficiency and productivity. Rooted in the ideas of Frederick W. Taylor (1911) and fostered by his disciples and descendants, mechanistic organizational systems grew up alongside mass-production manufacturing, pioneered by Henry Ford, and the hierarchical control and coordination systems of the railroads (Chandler 1977). For most of a century, the unparalleled success of the American system of production—mass production for mass markets—

was accompanied by an organization system with detailed analytical subdivision of tasks that relegated all control, coordination, and impetus for change to the top levels of a hierarchic structure. This division of labor and hierarchy of control has become so commonplace that it appears to be the very "natural" state of affairs.

These so-called efficient managerial mechanisms, however, systematically engender divisions and conflict in organizations. These divisions not only impede swift and intelligent responses to a rapidly changing environment, but they also waste the human potential for involvement and improvement (Kolb and Bartunek 1992). There are two fundamental divisions that grow out of industrial hierarchy. The first is between managers and workers across the stratified levels of a structure. The second is between branches of the same organization, divided and separated by rigid walls of bureaucracy and functional specialization (Dubinskas 1988, 1992). These divisions engender separations and conflicts that are destructive of organizational unity and of collective responsibility for company goals. They also provide an easy format for pitting groups of employees against one another by skill, race, gender, or ethnicity in order to consolidate central control. Mechanistic systems have traditionally been based on managerial demands for ultimate control, obedience to authority, and the relegation of only menial, intellectually impoverished tasks to lower-level workers.

Put simply, the predominant cultural patterns of organizational relationships in U.S. business are strangling our ability to grow and compete effectively in a global economy. They have placed a tourniquet on the life-blood of creative human participation. That stricture robs companies of their best, most flexible, and renewable resources: the distinctively human capabilities of employees. These include learning, problem-solving, initiative, and innovation as well as the qualities of human respect and mutual responsibility that knit together the social fabric of an organization with intention and integrity. By contrast, the "divine right of managers" to order, plan, control, and dominate all aspects of subordinates' activities is a social anachronism (Schein 1989).

This chapter has three critical goals. Its first goal is to explore the character and "naturalization" of authoritarian hierarchy as a dominant cultural and social system in U.S. industry. Two ethnographic examples are chosen from the world of high-technology engineering. I choose high-tech engineers (e.g., over factories) because they might otherwise seem to be an exception or an unlikely case for a Taylorist culture.[3] The pervasiveness of the Taylorist culture of managerial practice even in these cutting-edge arenas of work helps establish its ubiquity as an American trope for "organization." Its second goal is to show where and how emergent alternatives to Taylorism are growing up in the American industrial landscape. Drawing on comparisons to Japan and Scandinavia, the outlines of a culture of cooperation, participation, and commitment are drawn. Its third goal is to discuss the role of culture in understanding these new commitment and respect-based systems. A cultural model can help isolate and yet interrelate parameters of change—in ideology, practice, technologies, and commitment—creating an intellectual and practical handle on the dynamics of transformation.

Finally, I suggest an expanded role for anthropologists as analysts and practitioners in the birthing processes of new, collaborative systems of work relations.

Taylorism and the Naturalization of Hierarchy

In the twentieth century, the United States developed a mighty industrial system based on a distinctive mode of production and its accompanying organizational pattern. Over the first three quarters of the century, four transformations took place in a loosely coupled synchrony that appears only in hindsight as a smooth transition. These transformations occur (1) in production systems and the organization of work around machines, (2) in organizational systems and control, as asymmetric relationships create new status and power differences across organizational hierarchies, (3) in relations between managers and workers, including antagonism, conflict, and rebellion; and (4) in technologies of process control in production systems.

This chapter is concerned primarily with only two of the transformations—organizational patterns and their relation to productivity in technical systems. The other subjects, labor-management relations and worker resistance, are extensively treated by labor historians, sociologists, political economists, anthropologists, and management scholars;[4] and I will not treat that body of literature in detail here. The history of the evolution of precision in process control also impinges on the distribution of skills and the free exercise of critical judgment in work (Noble 1977). As such, it also feeds directly into Zuboff's (1988) argument about the "informating" capabilities of new microprocessor-controlled machines.

Latterly, this new environment of electronic information processing and control has become an important fifth transformation (Zuboff 1988).

Entering the last quarter of this century, these interrelated transformations have shaped American work relationships into their common authoritarian, bureaucratic industrial format. Together, they grew into a pervasive social and cultural system of industrial management that is so commonplace that it appears to be the natural character of organizations to us who live in them. The *machine* is the basic model for this organizational system. In his seminal work *Images of Organization* (1986), Gareth Morgan describes the mechanization of industrial life in the factory and office:

> Increasingly, we have learned to use the machine as a metaphor for ourselves and our society, and to mold our world in accordance with mechanical principles. . . .
>
> Consider, for example, the mechanical precision with which many of our institutions are expected to operate. Organizational life is often routinized with the precision of clockwork. People are frequently expected to arrive at work at a given time, perform a predetermined set of activities, rest at appointed hours, then resume their tasks until work is over. In many organizations, one shift of workers replaces another in methodical fashion so that work can continue uninterrupted twenty-four hours a day, every day of the year. Often the work is very mechanical and repetitive. Anyone who has observed work in the mass-production factory, or in any of the large "office factories" processing paper forms such as insurance claims, tax returns, or bank checks, will have noticed the machine-like way in which such organizations operate. They are designed like machines, and their employees are in essence expected to behave as if they were parts of the machines. (20)

The transformation into a mechanical social model is rooted in production systems and the organization of work around machines. It is grounded in the work of Frederick W. Taylor and his "scientific management" (Taylor 1911). Focusing on the individual and the task, Taylor subdivided complex work into infinitely small, simple, and definitively precise tasks. He analyzed and rationalized work to find the "one best way" to perform any individual task. These precisely defined tasks were then recombined into a tightly integrated system of interlocking parts.

Their precision and linkage mimicked the parts of a machine, and Taylor's aim was to make humans work with mechanical efficiency. His system transformed the chaos of a turn-of-the-century factory full of independent craftsmen, each doing complex artisanal work, into a system of closely integrated mini-tasks done by carefully selected, trained, and monitored—but unskilled—workers. Rather than skilled craftsmen controlling expertise, that expertise was now controlled by engineers and adminstered by supervisors.

The "science" in scientific management was the detailed expert examination of work by the very best workers to find the one best way to do a task. Stopwatches and motion-picture cameras were the stock-in-trade of a new legion of professional time-and-motion study observers. Under the tutelage of Frank and Lillian Gilbreth, early Taylor collaborators, these professional consultants pored over tasks from metal work to paper pushing to even housework (Rybczynski 1986, 67–70)! Taylorism's careful observation, measurement, and analysis of manufacturing processes was a key to vast improvements in modern industrial productivity. And like the interchangeable parts of a machine, "Taylorized" industrial workers could be easily replaced. The *social* processes of Taylorist research reflected its extractive rather than collaborative ideology; but they also doomed it to inflexibility. When markets and technologies were relatively stable, great strides in efficiency[5] could be made toward Taylor's one best way; but its human and social costs were great.[6]

A tone was set in Taylor's work that pervades the industrial relations of the next seven decades. In addition to the minute subdivision of tasks, Taylor's followers advocated another drastic separation of functions. All planning, thinking, and control functions should be removed from the purview of workers and delegated exclusively to managers and experts. The separation of head work from hand work was key to the deskilling of industrial work and the aggregation of control and power by managers (Braverman 1974; Noble 1977). Simple, repetitious, precisely defined, and regulated tasks were relegated to workers, whose only contribution was to be their muscle power and their disciplined obedience to the orders of superiors.

Taylor's focus on task detail was complemented on the large scale by the development of mass production manufacturing. Henry Ford was the original master of the art, building the first mechanized auto assembly line in 1911. Production was conceived as one great, interconnected machine, fed with parts and serviced by an army of workers. Assembly was paced by the machine, and tasks were Taylorized in miniscule segments of the assembly process. Just as important, the mechanized chain-drive assembly line made only one kind of product in only one variety and in vast quantity—hence *mass* production. It was what is today called "hard automation": the process machinery is purpose-built and inflexible, designed to serve a large uniform mass market with great volumes of identical products. Both Taylorism and Ford's mass-production system take a mechanistic efficiency-based approach to industrial productivity. And both are strikingly inflexible.

A second parallel historical transformation is in the organizational principles of firms. So-called classical-management theorists made the new twentieth-century manager a planner, controller, and decision maker (Fayol 1949; Gulick and Urwick 1937; Mooney and Riley 1931). Hierarchic control was unified by a chain of command based on a military model of "command and control." People lower in a hierarchy feed information up the chain of command, and decisions [control] come down from above. A person has only one superior, linked to another superior above; and there is a linear and exclusive continuity through links leading to the top. People at the bottom cannot just interact willy-nilly among branches of a hierarchy, but must always act through their superiors up the chain. Here, Taylor's system of subdividing tasks into small pieces begins to map onto the classical school's structured hierarchy. Each branch of a hierarchy is responsible for a different function; and the further out on a branch one climbs, the more specific a task one is responsible for. Finally, at the bottom of the hierarchy are only the most picayune tasks with responsibility only for following procedures.

The divisions among branches create the second great separation in hierarchic systems: different arms or branches of the same organization can only communicate with each other through the head or trunk. Coordination of even the most trivial tasks must (in theory) go up and down the chain of command. As organizations grow larger and more complex, their different parts become yet more separated from one another. Eventually, the parochial interests of functional departments come to dominate over interests of the whole. This leads to grossly ineffective communications and poor responsiveness to a changing environment. It has a darker side, too; the ability to divide and separate people was frequently used by management in a strategy of divide-and-conquer. In the face of antagonistic labor relations, management could consolidate control by fostering internal antagonisms among workers. Crafts and trades were pitted against unskilled workers, whites against blacks, Asians or ethnics against each other, and men against women. Latent racism and sexism could be cynically exploited in a system already based upon separations and barriers.

Why should the ghosts of this outmoded system of control remain to haunt us? The answer lies in the long histories of experience that our current cadres of managers share and in the naturalization of mechanistic organizational practice into a pervasive cultural system of management. Managers and workers alike have learned to expect certain stable characteristics in the system and the human relations it embodies: bosses will boss, and people will follow orders and get paid for it. Organizations will divvy up work into "manageable" pieces; people in each segment worry only about their own narrow responsibilities; and a hierarchy of control will see that everything gets done.

Do these old organizational models still inform American firms entering the last decade of the century? The following two ethnographic examples will illustrate that principles of organization built for mass-production and a mechanistic model of factory management still pervade the thinking and color the actions of contemporary managers. The arguments of business and manufacturing strategists tell us, however, that massive economies of scale in secure and uniform markets are being replaced by high variety and market differentiation and that newly competitive organizations must be flexible to match rapid environmental change. Technologies and organizations alike must be capable of learning and adapting to ever-changing conditions. But flexibility and learning are among precisely those human capabilities that are widely suppressed in Taylorist systems. So, to live on the leading edge of new technologies, one might expect high-technology firms to be first in applying new principles to their own organizational processes. But patterns learned from our industrial past still deeply imbue our industrial culture, even in organizations that are trying with immense effort and goodwill to rise to the human, technological, and competitive challenges of their current environment. The next two cases, from advanced-manufacturing and product-design environments, show that even firms with automated technologies at the cutting edge of industrial transformation are infused with our Taylorist tradition.

The Giant Automated Manufacturing Cell

John Deere & Co. is America's largest manufacturer of heavy agricultural equipment.[7] It enjoys over a century of cordial relations in serving America's farmers, ever since John Deere himself made the first plows that tilled the rich, heavy soils of the Ohio Valley. In 1986, at its Harvester Works in East Moline, Illinois, Deere built forty-eight different types of agricultural combines, the massive, self-propelled leviathans of the grain belt. These mobile grain processing factories are the world's largest commercial machines built by assembly-line production. They cut, winnow, sort and bag the grain, and bale the straw at the same time. Nearly all of the combine is fabricated from raw materials like sheet and tool steel and assembled at the huge Harvester Works on a site over a quarter mile square.

The manufacturing process is essentially a single continuous flow marked by stages, with two separate streams that join at final assembly. Each major stage takes place in its own building. The largest process stream fabricates and assembles the main body of the combines, and the other stream manufactures headers—the front-end assemblies that cut the grain from crops. One kind of product at a time is built for several weeks in a stream, then the plant changes over to another. In 1986, the plant built each combine model for two weeks at a time to produce the year's supply of that model. During one month, *all* parts for the next month's run of four combines were fabricated and stored, waiting for their models' assembly to start. This kind of large lot, flow-through system is typical of traditional mass-production systems. Using traditional equipment, it is very costly in time and labor to stop one product and reconfigure (retool) the plant for the next product; so product changeovers are scheduled as infrequently as possible. The main body stream is the most complex, involving sheet-metal parts fabrication, painting, welding, and assembly. This example focuses on sheet-metal fabrication. The average combine had over one thousand sheet-metal parts, and there were about twelve thousand unique parts for all current models. In 1986–87, Deere engineers had just installed a new computer-automated fabrication "cell" as a pilot project for automating the whole sheet metal "fab" process. Manufacturing cells are usually designed as small, product-focused sets of machines, physically arranged to link manufacturing stages closely. These are usually contrasted to large, flow-through, mass-production systems. Deere, however, modified the product-focused cell concept and transformed it back into an *automated* mass-production system. My aim is to show how the outlines of traditional Taylorist thinking persist even in the face of new automated equipment whose fundamental character could enable a more flexible and smaller-scale approach to manufacturing.

At the cavernous sheet-metal fabrication building, giant coils of sheet steel enter at one end, and finished combine parts exit the other. There is a common sequence to fabricating sheet-metal parts. First, the coil is cut into standard sheets that are stored until needed. To make parts from this stock with traditional equipment, first one cuts a piece of sheet metal into part-sized pieces on a shear; then punches out holes and notches—both regular and irregular shapes—with a punch press; and finally bends flanges and corners of the finished shape on a brake. Machines on the shop floor had been laid out in this sequence since 1977. First were rows of shears, like giant scissors cutting blank sheets into part-sized pieces. Then came forty hydraulic punch presses for cutting holes and notches. These punch presses surround two large tool cribs, where specially shaped cutting tools for each shape and size of hole are stored. At the side of the shop are storage racks for the dies, which match the cutting tools. The punch presses vary from smaller machines to three-storey, multiton monsters, which drive the cutting tool through a metal sheet lying on a die. When Harvester ran full tilt, they created a booming productive cacophony. These presses, with average two hour set-up times, were a bottleneck in making sheet-metal parts. With many different-sized holes in a typical part, the two hour tool change cost over $1300! Following the presses were brakes for bending, flanging, and folding the metal parts. These machines had the next-longest set-up times, at one-half hour on average.

In the summer of 1986, there were 125 machines on the shop floor. The vast majority of these were manually operated and electrically or hydraulically powered; they required manual set-ups of the tools and dies and hand feeding by one or two operators. The first moves to computer-controlled automation came in the late 1970s. Harvester added four numerical control (NC) punches using paper tape, which were later converted to computer numerical control (CNC) using magnetic tape. These punches have turrets of twenty-four tools, and have a much shorter set-up time than manual equipment. Control tapes for the CNC punches, however, were still carried by bicycle from the engineering office, one-quarter mile away, for each new part. In fact, the cost justification for the pilot automated cell was done just on the savings in *tape* making and delivery, since the automated cell included an electronic-data high-way[8] throughout the site.

Harvester's Computer Integrated Manufacturing (CIM) team planned the new automation system. They would eventually design parts on a computer-aided design/engineering (CAD/CAE) system. This system would communicate directly from product designs to machine operating instructions. This data highway could control machine operation, link machines into cells, and help schedule and organize plant-wide production. In early 1986, the CIM team installed two new CNC machines as a flexible manufacturing cell (FMC). This pilot cell would make irregular, flat parts from sheet steel, with eight parts on a typical sheet. Its new Behrens laser punch press replaced five hydraulic presses with their myriad of unique tools and dies. Instead of punching out shapes, the infinitely programmable Behrens cut whatever shape was required with its laser. The second machine was a Fisher CNC shear. It cut apart the pieces still linked after the laser had done most of the shaping. Blank sheets were fed in and final parts were removed and sorted by automated transfer lines. After a six-month pilot period, the computer-run laser cell was making 250 different parts.

This laser had infinite flexible potential; it eliminated the need to build, track, store, and maintain large sets of tools and dies; and it reduced by 80 percent the number of machines needing maintenance. In addition, the laser required almost *no* set-up time, since it automatically aligned the stock sheet, and tracked its own progress in cutting all the required shapes. It could set up for its next part by downloading instructions over the new data highway while it was still cutting the previous part. Furthermore, the machine could be programmed to cut different parts from the same sheet, if desired. One could potentially make parts kits for a single combine, then feed them directly into the assembly flow; and one could alternate kits for different models in any sequence, to build combines in small lots—even lots of one machine. This would enable the fine-tuning of production schedules to meet emerging demand during the short spring sales season. In principle, it didn't matter any longer whether the next part to be made was different from the last. A central rationale for economies of scale necessary in mass production— the cost of set-up time—was completely eliminated. So, with all of this flexibility, how did the engineers prioritize implementation?

Harvester engineers employed the automated cell to cut *one* kind of part at a time from a sheet of standard stock. The parts were nested to fit with minimum scrap; and the laser cut all holes and most outlines of the part, leaving small tabs for the shear to cut. Some sheets held as many as 50 copies of the same small part, all made "at once." These parts were then stored, as before, for the next month's run of combines. Writing software instructions to cut specific parts was very time-consuming, since parts specifications had to be translated "by hand" from paper onto the CAD/CAE system for machine instructions for the laser. To get maximum use out of the laser's flexible capabilities, Deere engineers needed to write algorithms which would allow *more than one kind* of part to be cut on a sheet; and that would multiply the complexity of the software. The engineers knew that mixing different parts on a single sheet would confer an important advantage in lot-size reduction and scheduling flexibility, but they had to balance this project against other pressing software development needs. Fitting diverse, complex parts on a single sheet had ramifications for the organization of production, depending on how the parts were grouped. It would also affect the plant's overall CIM software architecture: what kind of information was going where. In the end, they chose to focus on the top-down, plant-wide architectural integration first, rather than the refinement of the local, cell-based production flexibility.

Over the next years, Harvester planned to replace three-quarters of their equipment with CNC machines. By 1987 for instance, four new Behrens lasers would replace nineteen standard presses and shears. The machines were to be in three functional cutting cells, each containing just two very large laser punch presses with shears. Bend brakes would be in adjacent cells. These automated cells were planned as generic, functional groupings, through which any set of parts could be routed. Essentially, Harvester was replacing old, inflexible machines with new automated ones; but they were organizing the deployment of equipment in exactly the same massive flow-through functional sequence they were familiar with. They planned to convert the fab plant into one huge automated cell before considering any of the advantages of diversity and flexibility to be gained from having clusters of machines (cells) making a variety of parts at once. Until the whole installation was complete, attention would be focused on getting everything to work together, rather than on bringing small cells up to speed making the diversity of parts of which they were capable. They were planning a centralized system for "automating" the existing process flow: mass production with large lot sizes. The flexible option of building a constantly changing mix of products was to be put off while old mechanico-electrical equipment was replaced by new computer-driven machines. The result gains some quality and efficiency from automation, but it ignores or postpones the benefits that stem from considering the underlying assumptions behind highly flexible, automated-manufacturing processes.

This planning sequence represents the deeply ingrained and generationally replicated cultural patterns of Taylorism and mass production in the everyday worlds of even the most progressive engineering managers. In deference to John Deere's engineers and managers, I do not argue that they do not or cannot understand the potential flexibility of cell-based automation. Rather, I argue that the systematic patterns of thought, embodied in everyday practice, which have been created in nearly a century of American business, push these kinds of well-understood patterns of practice to the fore. The key to my argument lies in the laser's abolition of the need for large lot sizes. Autonomous cells could be making a wide variety of products at once. This potentially huge advantage in the market from flexibility is put aside, however, while work proceeds on integrating every machine into a single flow-through system. Rather than refining the capabilities of individual cells, the large scale systems integration—the natural goal of mass production—is sought first. It is the very naturalness of this traditional scheme as a cultural system that imbues it with the power to shape the deployment of even the most advanced technological systems.

Automating the Design Process: Factory Model or Custom Shop?

We often think of product design as the realm of art, a bastion of creativity, innovation, and craft and a bulwark against the onslaught of mechanization. But in art as well as industry, elegant execution within the constraints of a medium, the strictures of a canon, or the dictates of a style also measures aesthetic accomplishment.[9] Integrated circuit design—the placement and connection of features on a silicon chip— once bore much of this craftwork character. Working with pencil on mylar, chip layout engineers and drafters drew a large-scale replica of the silicon surface. They brought craftwork expertise as well as analytic knowledge to bear on grouping and spacing features—transistors—as well as how to connect them. Final drawings were actually part of the manufacturing process: they were photographed and reduced to make "masks," which define features on each layer of a chip. Chips had far fewer features than today, yet designing a large chip was still time-consuming and messy.

By the 1980s, however, a series of transformations took place in the silicon-design process. First, computers replaced paper and pencil, as computer-aided design (CAD) tools made it possible to create designs on a computer screen. A generation of drafters who had made precision drawings from the sketches of design engineers disappeared. The work was consolidated upward into the hands of engineers at their terminals. These engineers, however, still embodied both analytical and craftwork knowledge for optimal layout of silicon features.[10]

As chips became smaller and features denser, designing by hand—even with CAD tools—became prohibitively complex, costly, and time-consuming. As microchip use proliferated, demand for the scarce silicon-design engineers soared far beyond their numbers. Using unaided human engineering skills, it would take almost *two years* to design a chip with five thousand "gates" (logic features). But by 1990, new microprocessors were being designed with a *million* gates; and the difficulty of the design task increases *geometrically* with the number of gates! The demand for special-purpose chips, especially, has soared; and each special purpose requires a new design. Unlike standard logic components or memory chips that are mass-produced, these are "application specific integrated circuits" or ASICs. ASICs are now ubiquitous, controlling everything from watches to VCRs to cameras to cars. VLSI Technology, Inc. (VTI) is in the ASIC design and fabrication business.

The tool that made cheap ASICs possible is the "silicon compiler." A silicon compiler is software for automating circuit layout and placement on silicon. VTI's silicon compiler was designed to let customer engineers who plan circuit functionality—the "what does it do" logic of a chip—create their own *physical* chip layout. Working from an electrical schematic, a logic diagram, or a standard-parts list, customers could now define the physical layout of a chip to achieve the functions they wanted. A tape-deck maker, for instance, comes to VTI and says: "I want a chip to provide all the control functions for my product." In essence, the VTI software converts the logic circuits to physical transistors, simulates their functions to check for logical consistency, automatically "places" the elements in space-efficient clusters on the chip, and decides how to connect (route) them with metal pathways to form the integrated circuit. A design that took eighteen to twenty-four months in 1981 could be finished in ten to twelve weeks by 1985 using a silicon compiler, an order of magnitude improvement.

Despite automation, VTI engineers still play a large role in chip design. Initial decisions must be made to partition chip logic into functional blocks and to arrange these blocks on the chip surface. Then the silicon compiler can work in several modes, from hand placement to complete automation. Each succeeding mode implies less human intervention. In the "custom" mode, the design engineer places and routes features completely "by hand," using software like a CAD drafting tool but making all decisions herself. Moving to more automation, the designer can place features on the chip by hand, but let the software connect them. Also, there are predesigned "standard features"—chunks of logic with standard functionality called cells that duplicate off-the-shelf components. Cells are stored in a software library; and the designer can call them up and place them in any design. In addition, VTI has "megacells" in its library: multithousand-gate modules of functionality, like color TV controls. These, too, can be recombined in ever larger-scale integrated circuits. ("VLSI," from the company's name, stands for "very large scale integration.") Megacells are the offspring of customer designs, where VTI has kept the rights to reuse the design later. Finally, the system can run in a completely automated mode, placing and routing features without engineering intervention.

With all this flexibility, how should VTI organize the design process; and how should human expertise be deployed? One alternative embodied the same principles of mass production and Taylorism that dominate our commonsense cultural models for industrial order. The VTI design operations manager proposed a "design factory," applying traditional manufacturing "efficiency" to the design process. The efficiency and cost saving would be gained by subdividing the engineers' tasks. As it was, VTI engineers often worked closely with customer engineers to partition and refine systems, adding valuable insight to the chip-layout process. They interacted with customers to explore, define, and modify functional specs as well as to create the best design layout for them. VTI's silicon designers were highly capable at negotiating the important trade-offs that must be made in partitioning among cost, chip speed, chip size, and testability; and these exploratory processes also created new knowledge about customer applications for VTI.

The design manager wanted to separate out certan simpler tasks and assign them to low level technicians rather than engineers. Technicians could work three shifts entering data from customer specs into compiler software. Valuable and costly engineering contact could be reduced and restricted to "design" problems only. VTI engineers wouldn't be wasted on data entry or on monitoring automated functions of the software like testing, simulations, and rule-checking. Design work would be divided into "more manageable" units and extend greater managerial control over human and software resources. This control would make it faster and cheaper to mass-produce designs from an already-existing data-base of logic cells and megacells. This was a high volume, low cost model for industrial efficiency. The manager spoke in a familiar Taylorist rhetoric of division of labor, rationalization, separation of unskilled work from skilled engineering, and centralization of control.

However, this Taylorist tendency could have big consequences for long-term growth of the business. Growth, for VTI, lies in new customers and new kinds of circuits to build on silicon. Reducing the interaction between VTI's designers and customers' engineers also reduces the contacts through which new and better design ideas emerge to serve a customer's special needs. For instance, implementation or testing cannot always be left to technicians. The whole integrated process of designing and then simulating a design's functionality in the software is one of experimentation and learning. Trying ideas in software is far cheaper than making a chip to test it. Chips will suit their purposes best if the joint expertise of customers and VTI designers is continuously brought to bear throughout the design process. Deeper exploration with customers has two consequences: (1) better designs and greater customer satisfaction and (2) new knowledge of product domains for VTI. The first outcome solidifies a customer base, and the second is the platform of intellectual capital for continued growth and expansion into new markets. A Taylorizing system cuts off this growth potential and eventually even narrows the quality dimension for existing customers.

Even in the crucible of high-tech design, principles of mechanization dominate managerial discourse. The natural response to complexity has consistently kept to this central tendency: divide up tasks and control from the top. At Deere and VTI, Taylorist approaches to automation limit both business opportunities and productivity gains, while they also ignore or stifle the creative, collaborative potential of human synergy with new technologies. New automating technologies *could* be deployed to free people from physical or intellectual drudgery to exercise more discretionary judgment and creativity. But we are embedded in a managerial culture that is determined to use these automated systems to extend managerial control, to keep related tasks and functions separated from one another, and to keep decisions isolated from the daily practice of work.

The Consequences of Untempered Power

This culture is a system of institutionalized authoritarian social relationships that have evolved toward greater and greater separation of managers from workers. This separation has been accompanied by antagonisms and conflicts that arise from its denial of fundamental human capabilities and desires. A general consequence of the process is a deep embedding of adversarial relations between managers and workers. Narrow and inflexible task assignments are met by a lack of initiative on the shop floor. Managers who are distant from daily work because of status (and experience) have a poor understanding of the intimate detail of process issues and data; and their ignorance leads to slow problem solving, poor decisions, costly change implementation, and a glacial pace of improvement. Neither managers nor workers, in the extreme case, are really committed to improvement, to learning, or to any sense of collective responsibility. The consequences are high manufacturing costs, low quality output, and the development of wastefully inflexible systems of production—even in highly automated environments.

The human consequences are as dismal as the implications for productivity. Dissatisfied employees neither give nor get respect. Forcing people to the lowest common denominators of human capacity through simplifying automation *forces* people to act dumb. It kills cooperation, even when a changing environment calls for more collaboration and unity. But the classic response of hierarchical authority to economic threats is often a self-reinforcing cycle of yet harsher top-down control (Lawrence and Lorsch 1967), more conflict and deprivation, and no real long-term improvements.[11]

The ultimate paragons of separation are senior U.S. executives, some of whom have risen to new heights of imperial status and powers of managerial authority:

> Pharaoh in all his glory would have envied today's CEOs (Chief Executive Officers) their perquisites and ever-sweetening pay. Too busy having lived the cosseted life, America's managerial elite have lost touch with the humble employee. Workers' faith in top management is collapsing. CEOs who don't come down from the heights are in for trouble. (Farnham 1989, cover)

Relations between employer and employee are not good, and at an especially dicey moment. Just when top management wants everyone to begin swaying to a faster, more productive beat, employees are loath to dance. . . . CEOs say, "we're a team, we're all in this together, rah, rah, rah." But employees look at the difference between their pay and the CEO's. They see top management's perks—oak dining rooms and heated garages vs. cafeterias for the hourly guys and parking spaces half a mile from the plant. And they wonder: "Is this togetherness?" (56)

When CEOs like Lee Iacocca take $25 million from Chrysler over three years of *declining* returns to shareholders and layoffs for employees from 1979–89, it is hard to argue that line workers making nearly five hundred times less should give their whole-hearted cooperation (Byrne, Grover, and Hof 1990). This great gulf of wealth and gap of trust can poison attempts to build new forms of collaborative relationships (Crystal 1991a; 1991b). By comparison, at the nadir of the 1973 oil crisis that nearly sank Mazda Motors, its new president, Yoshiki Yamasaki made only about ten times more than the lowest-paid Mazda employee. In interviews, he explains that management took cuts in pay; but workers were not asked to. Nor were workers laid off; they were redeployed to sell cars (Japan's Manufacturing Miracle 1984; Pascale and Rohlen 1988). Yet in America, the managerial prerogatives of status and wealth are taken as a fact of our industrial culture; they seem naturalized into our expectations about hierarchy. While President Bush's January 1992 trip to Japan with U.S. auto industry CEOs sparked a new criticism of their wealth excesses (Abramson and Chipello 1991), it will take sea-changes in these patterns of managerial practice to break out of the self-reinforcing cycles of estrangement and antagonism. Taylorist "cultures of separation" (Bellah et al. 1985) and control are destructive of productivity and of its very heartbeat—the committed power of working intellect.

Alternatives to Hierarchy: Cultures of Cooperation

In contrast to the dominant model of authoritarian managerial culture, however, there are also deep countercurrents in American culture and society that challenge the exclusivity of hierarchic control as a model for organizational practice. These include a key symbolic nexus of America's public political culture: democracy and egalitarian participation. This political right to participatory control is linked to the culture of individualism (Bellah et al. 1985); and American participatory democracy is explored further by MacLennan in this volume or Montgomery (1979).[12] Systems of democratic participation, distributed or decentralized control, and local empowerment are classic symbols of our native political culture. They are expressed in the politics and sociality of small towns and neighborhoods, religious congregations, voluntary civic and charitable associations, sporting clubs, as well as some trade unions and ethnic associations, to name just a few. However, inside work organizations, egalitarianism and participation or principles of "workplace democracy" have but rarely flowered in the United States. Breaching the "Berlin wall" that separates the worlds of work from our broader society is not impossible, though, as examples from both American and Scandinavian organizations illustrate.

As well as a brake on industrial productivity, Taylorist organizational culture also constrains our native human propensities to sociality. These fundamental human capabilities underlie cooperative action and democratic participation (Blakey, in this volume) and they *can* engender a culture of shared responsibility and shared fate—an American "culture of coherence" (Bellah et al. 1985). Core American cultural patterns encompass the alternative model of a communitarian ethos of cooperation and collaboration (Peacock, in this volume), including our pervasive image of "teamwork." Looking for these key symbols of collaboration in organizational cultures uncovers an ethos of "shared purpose and shared fate" linked to mutual respect and responsibility that can be found in both foreign (especially Japanese [Rohlen 1974; Morita 1986]) and American examples. Both of these movements—toward collaboration and toward democratic participation—emphasize fundamentally human, social aspects of organizational life, in contrast to Taylor's rationalized machine image.

The second broad aim of this paper is to bring to the surface some alternative models of industrial organization from at home and abroad and, finally, to suggest a role for anthropology in promoting them. Workplace participation movements, quality circles, "empowerment," team building, and the like are still uncommon in American firms; and many implementation attempts have failed (Hoerr 1989). There is also a growing backlash among trade unionists against management-sponsored team-building programs, which are sometimes seen as a mask for speed-up (Grenier 1988; Parker and Slaughter 1988). My aim is not to argue with the critics, but rather to bring to light possibilities and positive cases that may presage a new movement toward change. At the same time, even a minority of successful democratizing or collaborative examples indicate cracks in any hegemonic model of social processes, such that alternative forms may grow up and even flourish. The following discussion is not a comprehensive survey of changes, but rather a beacon from a cultural perspective on alternative patterns of organizational collaboration.

In identifying cultural patterns, the human, flexible, self-organizing, and "growable" aspects of organizations (Morgan 1986; Ulrich and Probst 1984) are crucial for meeting the economic and social challenges of the next decades. Central to this process is "employee involvement" or "EI" as it is known in the management literature. In its various transformations, EI is the contemporary surrogate in the 1990s for cooperation and participation across divisions of hierarchy (*Productivity* 1990; *JHRA* 1988; Walton 1985). Criticism of bureaucracy and hierarchy is widespread in the business press and the management academy, not to mention in labor sociology, political economy, and the anthropology of work. Relations across vertical and horizontal barriers of hierarchic systems are commonly discussed either from the point of view of managers or from a contrasting one of working communities. Few studies, however, treat manager-worker relationships as an interdependent system. Fewer still consider them from the perspective of culture; as *meaning* systems as well as social systems, enacted through patterned work processes and interpreted and validated through a shared history of experience.

In debates over managerial styles and attributes of leadership, or over worker motivation or resistance, there is a tendency for those with the best vantage point for interpreting one side of the relationship to be strikingly less well informed about the other. But managers and workers, leaders and followers, or coparticipants of different statuses—however the group is construed—*cannot* exist without each other. Leadership implies followers, and vice versa. They interact in ways that are historically shaped, culturally patterned, politically charged, and played out in the context of a shifting economic environment (Dubinskas 1983; Schein 1985). As a system, responsibility for the ways people are (and are to each other), and for the outcomes of their actions, is shared by both parties. It is a joint social construction, but with a strong imbalance of power.

Alternatives have always existed, but a recent resurgence of interest has brought a few cases to broader public attention. Examples of alternative workplace relations from Japan and from Scandinavia are introduced in this chapter, not as paragons or models to be slavishly emulated but as other places noticed for what we may learn from their experience. The contextual peculiarities of these examples have both resonances and dissonances with the American industrial environment. There are also new experiments in the United States that are building systems on mutual respect, teamwork, and an ethos of shared responsibility and fate. Here, anthropology has largely missed an opportunity to make a contribution in an area where it has a distinctive competence. The study of culture and social practice in organizational life, particularly in Japan, is an area where anthropological research was a source of important changes in the thinking of business practitioners and academics.

Cultures of Hierarchical Cooperation: Japan

The business press became interested in both Japan and "culture" in the late 1970s, as newly competitive, high-quality, low-cost products from Japan flooded U.S. markets. Culture embodied the essence of difference; and early studies of Japanese companies located their success in group solidarity, mutual respect (including respect both up *and down* a status hierarchy), and shared responsibility for success across all levels of the firm. Tom Rohlen's (1974) ethnographic study of social life and culture in a Japanese bank, and the sociologist Robert Cole's (1971) studies of work in Japan lie at the bibliographic heart of most subsequent explorations of Japanese business culture; and part of their enduring value lay in linking culture as "thought" and as practice. Ouchi (1981) and Pascale and Athos (1981) contrasted American and Japanese firms to draw lessons about effective management, as did a legion of subsequent business writers. Ouchi, for instance, identified trust, subtlety, and intimacy in organizational relationships as keys to productivity.

A new business literature grew up on "organizational culture"—how to mend, mold, and custom make culture in your American company. While they emphasized new relationships among employees and managers, most business writers focused on "values" as a substitute for a richer anthropological concept of culture. With simple suggestions, thin examples, and a kind of pop anthropology to shore it up, this vein of work flourished briefly, then declined by mid-decade (Barley, Meyer, and Gash 1988). While a few academics from other fields (e.g., Schein 1985; Frost et al. 1985) pursued detailed or theoretically motivated studies on culture and management, anthropologists largely ignored it (Baba 1986; Holzberg and Giovannini 1981; Pennbridge 1985).

Simultaneously, a parallel current arose focusing on Japanese manufacturing practices, rather than culture per se. The now familiar alphabet soup of quality and productivity improvement measures: JIT, TQC, SPC, MRP, CAD/CAM, CIM,* and others were introduced as engineering principles to be understood as *technical* rather than social or cultural in character. Books by Taiichi Ohno (1978; 1988), the architect of Toyota's widely lauded manufacturing system, and books and tours by Shigeo Shingo (1985; 1986), the industrial engineering guru of waste reduction, introduced these ideas to an engineering audience in the United States. Their methods were initially interpreted by Americans as rational, analytical "efficiency" tools for increasing productivity. The difficulties that U.S. firms had making these systems work, though, were tied to a fundamental misunderstanding of the *social* aspects of Japan's manufacturing system, including workforce engagement or participation. American managers focused too narrowly on the *mechanics* of efficiency, and ignored the holistic and social aspects of technology strategy and implementation (Skinner 1986). Our culturally ingrained Taylorist sense of how to manage contributed to this blindness. Central ingredients of Japanese manufacturing management, missing in the U.S. technocrat's view, are employee involvement in all aspects of productivity improvement and a broader understanding of technical systems by all employees.

Central to high-performance Japanese production systems is active engagement of *all* employees, contributing their intellectual powers and their moral commitment as well as their physical effort. Knowledge building and participation are key (Schonberger 1982). For instance, among top Japanese firms, Canon stands out both in product design (EOS cameras, the Personal Copier, and laser printer engines) and in manufacturing. In the *Canon Production System* (*JMA* 1987), they describe their continuous improvement program as tying advances in efficiency and waste reduction to "the creative involvement of the total workforce." Masaaki Imai, a productivity expert with extensive United States and

---

*These stand for: Just-in-Time (inventory management), Total Quality Control, Statistical Process Control, Material Requirements Planning, Computer-Aided-Design/Computer-Aided Manufacturing, and Computer Integrated Manufacturing.

Japanese experience, discusses *kaizen* (continuous improvement) as a system of

> ... process-oriented management [focusing on] discipline, time man-agement, skill development, participation and involvement, morale, and communication. In short, such a manager is people-oriented ... [*kaizen* strategy] should be extended to everyone, top management, middle management, supervisors, and workers on the shop floor. (1986, 21)

By the later 1980s, this emphasis on involvement of all levels and a return to social and cultural issues is also reflected in the American "manu-facturing renaissance" literature (Ciampa 1988; Clark 1988; Hayes and Wheelwright 1984; Schonberger 1982, 1986; Walton 1985).

In the Japanese examples, active commitment to the good of the whole by all members is matched by mutual responsibility of the firm to its members. Akio Morita, President of Sony Corp., for instance, expresses the relationship as familylike:

> The most important mission for a Japanese manager is to develop a healthy relationship with his employees, to create a familylike feeling within the corporation, a feeling that employees and managers share the same fate. Those companies that are most successful in Japan are those that have managed to create a shared sense of fate among all employees.... (1986, 144)

Americans often associate this shared fate with a commitment to lifetime employment in Japan. As many scholars have noted, lifetime (or long-term) employment is only for men, not women; and it is prac-ticed only in the first tier or largest employers—about 40 percent of all workers. Lifetime employment is also not a Japanese industrial *tradition,* but rather was imposed by the liberal economic technicians of the post-WWII American occupation.[13] But Morita places responsibility for stim-ulating employee engagement directly in the hands of management: "It is management's responsibility to keep challenging each employee to do important work that he [sic] will find satisfying and to work within the [company] family." (1986, 210) Just how much Japanese management owes to Japanese culture as a whole is controversial; but Japanese social scientists argue that a sense of community or group relatedness cuts across all aspects of Japanese life and self-identity (Doi 1988; Nakane 1970; Sano 1983). Company loyalty is only one facet of group identification; and companies often explicitly include the welfare of local communities, the nation, and humanity in their codes and philosophies.

With the metaphoric link to family comes an automatic respect for authority and age that Americans might see as too paternalistic and hierarchical. For instance, discipline is prominent among the *kaizen* principles listed by Imai, and respect for authority infuses the values of Matsushita Electric Co: "national service through industry . . . fairness . . . harmony and cooperation . . . struggle for betterment [*kaizen*] . . . courtesy and humility . . . adjustment and assimilation [and] . . . gratitude" (Pascale and Athos 1981, 75). Morgan (1986) argues that hierarchy and harmony coexist in Japanese organizations in a way inimical to American individualist culture:

> Hierarchy in a Japanese corporation is as much a system of mutual service as one of top-down control. . . . there seem to be different relations between subordination and self-respect in Japan. In many Western countries individualistic culture leads us to seek and gain self-respect by competing with others, or against the wider "system," thus emphasizing our uniqueness or separateness. In Japan, on the other hand, cultural conditions allow workers to achieve self-respect through service *within* the system, even though there may be many aspects of the system which they find distasteful. (116)

In Japan, respect is a reciprocal relationship, with continuing expectations on both sides (Sano 1983 [on Kimura 1973]), and without the sense of lowered self-esteem that Americans ascribe to low status.

Americans, on the other hand, want respect to be *earned* by individuals, regardless of status. We are unlikely to lend automatic respect to a boss—or an employee—without proof in their actions. The Japanese culture of respect relationships, widely reinforced by managerial action, contributes to willing collaboration across vertical levels of hierarchy and to considering the shared fate of the organization ahead of the needs of the individual. Americans, on the other hand, are more consistently distrustful of the authority ascribed to managers (often with good reason); and we expect to be rewarded individually (and proprotionately) for our contributions to the whole.[14] American individualism's "culture of separation" (Bellah et al. 1985), combined with a Taylorist culture's emphasis on division, means that building a sense of shared fate requires more managerial effort in the United States.

Whatever difficulties an American firm might have in emulating Japanese principles, insight into the social relations of Japanese work, at least, provides the kernel of understanding that things can be different. While Japanese group exercises, uniforms, and formal acts of respect like bowing may seem too alien for American workers; flat organizational hierarchies, smaller pay gaps, and vastly enriched internal communications in Japanese companies soften the rough edges of authority for their employees.[15] The general principles of mutual respect and cooperation, however, can take many forms in different contexts. We can examine some of these further by first turning to an American example with close links to Japan: New United Motors Manufacturing Co., Inc. (NUMMI), the joint autobuilding venture of General Motors and Toyota.

Egalitarian Cooperation: America and Japan Together

NUMMI was a learning experiment by both General Motors and Toyota. GM wanted to learn about Japanese manufacturing through involvement with its premier practitioner. Toyota wanted to learn to manage an American workforce. In 1984, they reopened a shuttered GM plant in Fremont, California together; and NUMMI began recruiting workers to build Chevy Novas—or Toyota Corollas. While NUMMI was a separate legal entity, Toyota provided its plant managers. Toyota also designed the car and laid out the plant for production. General Motors supervisors were mostly incorporated for shorter periods of time to learn from their Japanese counterparts.

Brown and Reich (1989) discuss the successes of this plant and compare it both to its GM predecessor in Fremont and to a contemporary GM plant in Van Nuys, California with "traditional" labor-management relations. To set the stage, GM knew that Toyota had more than a $1,000 per vehicle average advantage in production costs; and Toyota's average vehicle quality was more than twice as good as General Motor's. The NUMMI plant has met or exceeded General Motors' expectations for productivity. NUMMI exceeded its Fremont predecessor's productivity by 50 percent, making it the *best* of GM's plants; and it equalled its sister plant that was building Corollas in Takaoka City, Japan. Quality has soared as defects have plummeted, and Nova owners reported the highest satisfaction among all GM customers. With a work force recruited largely from the same militant union members as the old GM plant, NUMMI cooperated with the United Auto Workers in a radical reorganization of work relations in the plant.

Brown and Reich argue that work teams and cooperative labor-management relations are key to NUMMI's productivity. They studied and discounted two strong competing explanations: the crisis of plant closure and screening out opposition in recruitment. Acknowledging other factors, their conclusions still point to changed circumstances in the social organization of work and the dismantling of traditional hierarchies.

> The key to NUMMI's success is the application of the team concept to reorganize production in the context of union-management cooperation.... it is the change in worker involvement and motivation and the completely different relationship between management and the union that are most impressive.
>
> Employee involvement through teams results in improvements such as reductions in the number of steps needed to accomplish a specific task, or modifications to ease the task.... These improvements occur because workers are interested in making improvements and because management actively solicits and encourages them. (32)

Like Morita's observation earlier in this chapter, management efforts and employee enthusiasm combine to create a reciprocal system of commitment. Operating changes at NUMMI include the drastic reduction of job categories, from over one hundred in some GM plants to only *one* production grade. This allows crosstraining and variety in work, undercutting the Taylorist dictum of infinite, specialized division of labor. Similarly, several layers or managers have been removed, reducing the distance from top to bottom. Engineering needs are also reduced, because workers now help set production standards and scheduling. NUMMI provides continuous skill training; and jobs are assigned on the basis of skill and need, with seniority only as a tiebreaker.

Many former prerogatives of management have devolved to production teams, and other issues are negotiated jointly with management. The process of building trust and respect was entered into cautiously and tentatively by both sides. By emphasizing cooperation and flexibility as a goal on both sides, NUMMI has grown into not only a highly productive environment but also one with a spirit of collaboration and shared fate uncommon in traditional American industry. Many aspects of Japanese hierarchical relations have been modified for American culture at NUMMI, with an emphasis on egalitarian symbols and action. Interaction is more casual across status lines, dress is less formal (but still uniform), and workers share cafeterias with managers. Parker and Slaughter (1988), however, argue that this hybrid Japanese management system is really just a disguise for speed-up, a kind of retro-Taylorism in chic clothing. NUMMI management *and* unions disagree. They say the ability to stop assembly at any time without penalty helps alleviate or eliminate the causes of stress on the line. They work easier and smarter as well as faster. Speed-up would be more relevant if relations were antagonistic, but a joint commitment to cooperation and productivity ameliorates what an outsider might see as oppressive.

A sister GM plant in Van Nuys, California, contrasts strongly with NUMMI. Long rounds of labor strife and discontent prevented attempts to build a team-based production system. There were no benefits in cost reductions, productivity and quality suffered, and the plant was shuttered in 1991. Brown and Reich note that job security was key to the Van Nuys failure. General Motors used layoffs to adjust for capacity and demand. With frequent layoffs and no commitment to security, Van Nuys workers clung to seniority and job classifications. Training was limited to generic team-building skills but was not linked to practical work on the assembly line. Van Nuys workers fought the team concept where promotions and assignments were tied to skills and production needs. They would lose the security of seniority, and they had never received any real technical training. By contrast, at NUMMI workers had only a good-faith guarantee that job security was a top priority; but this principle was outlined in the union contract. Trust was gradually built over time by consistent managerial action. NUMMI workers also saw an ongoing commitment to skill building through technical-skills training and job rotation, necessary prerequisites to rejecting a traditional seniority system of job assignments.

In the end, both management and labor at NUMMI took risks to start their new relationship, and the risks seem to have paid off. Productivity and quality are up, management costs are lower, and worker satisfaction indices are high. At the core of this success is a rebuilt culture of work relations and an ideology of collaboration for the common good. It is coupled with specific management actions in security, skill building, and devolution of control on the line. It is also clear from the Van Nuys comparison that management must take the first and biggest steps toward change—that their hearts, too, are really in the new ways of work—before workers will believe that they are seriously committed.

Culture and Cooperation in U.S. Teamwork

General Motors' Saturn Project is an attempt to build team-based, collaborative work relations independent of a Japanese partner. Saturn is especially interesting because its parent is otherwise known for a massive bureaucracy, rigid functional divisions, and Taylorized factory work systems. While academic studies are lacking, Saturn is widely covered in the business press; and their seven-year, planning-team process itself is instructive. The views of union and management leaders converge in an image of cooperation that is grounded in specific rules, agreements, and practices (Lewandowski and O'Toole 1990; Teece 1990). Like NUMMI, it is a "greenfield" site—a new plant in Spring Hill, Tennessee, with a work force carefully recruited from other GM sites. The keystone of Saturn's plan is their 1985 UAW-management agreement. A core team of ninety-nine GM and UAW members made up a work-and-technology planning group that visited forty-nine GM plants and sixty other sites around the world.

> We believe that all people want to be involved in decisions that affect them, care about their jobs, take pride in themselves and in their contributions and want to share in the success of their effort. By creating an atmosphere of mutual trust and respect, recognizing and utilizing individual expertise and knowledge in innovative ways, providing the technologies and education for each individual, we will enjoy a successful relationship and a sense of belonging to an integrated business system capable of achieving our common goals which insures security for our people and success for our business and communities. (Lewandowski and O'Toole 1990, 4)

This cooperative ethos adds a particularly American twist to teamwork. Saturn has a comprehensive agreement on a conflict-resolution process, including a formal, rule-based system for consensus decision making. Unlike most Japanese *ringi* decision-making systems, Saturn's is not confined to managers, but applies to all employees and covers a broad range of issues in the factory. It is designed to create open information flows, build consensus, and guarantee 100 percent commitment to implementation. In contrast to a taken-for-granted group commitment, Saturn's U.S. style of building solidarity is a set of legalistic rules and a focus on individuals' rights in the system. These are designed to buttress company values with guarantees of appropriate practice.

Workers are also involved in matching technologies to work-force skills. There is no push to "leapfrog" Japanese productivity by throwing high technology at the plant. Saturn core members selected and developed new production technologies and equipment. Among them were a moving platform for vehicle assembly, a "lost foam" casting technology, and transmission-testing equipment. Worker input to technology choices are unusual in the United States (but not in Scandinavia), because these are usually the sole prerogatives of managers or engineers. Saturn's aim was to choose technologies that would be productive *in the hands of the users*.

For instance, assemblers usually walk and work on a moving car on a traditional assembly line. Each does a tiny task, and there are many work stations strung out along the line. If a problem arises, there is no time to correct small mistakes. Workers are pressed to match the mechanized line speed; quality suffers; and the work is stressful and boring. The Saturn team decided to seek other solutions. They considered and rejected small-team assembly on free-standing movable platforms—Automated Guided Vehicles (AGVs) pioneered in Scandinavia. Although AGVs yielded high-quality results, its computer controls were complex and costly. Saturn's other top choice was a "skillet" system—a moving wooden platform where workers stand while they build the vehicle. They no longer have to move while working, since workers and the vehicle move together. When work is done, assemblers get off and walk back to start the next car. Innovative savings came from turning vehicles sideways, saving 40 percent of skillet space and reducing the line length. Two years of field investigations and a seven-day marathon meeting led to the skillet choice over AGVs. As part of the agreement to make technology decisions by consensus, the skillet system was chosen in open negotiations among managers, engineers, and workers. Despite the long lead time, there was now a core of people from all levels of the process who understood the technology and were strongly committed to a successful implementation.[16]

Saturn speaks of changing attitudes as well as practices. The plant has intensive training programs both in teamwork and technical skills, committing 5 percent of paid time to learning. But the practical results of technology teams are the "proof in the pudding" that individualist American workers need in order to feel that an ideology of mutual respect and trust is real. Ideology, practice, and the technical content of work are embodied in the skillet team's results.

Both General Motors and its critics acknowledge many institutional barriers to teamwork. There is a huge, change-resistant bureaucracy in General Motors; the company has three times more layers of management than Toyota: twenty-one versus seven; and General Motors still shutters plants and lays off workers while handing out big executive bonuses (Crystal 1991a, 1991b). "To take a company that has 800,000 people worldwide and try to change the culture, that's kind of like trying to parallel-park the Queen Mary" (Teece 1990, 62). Also, the factory teamwork model doesn't address issues of collaboration across the whole firm (Dubinskas 1989). The key Saturn metaphor is "team" and "teamwork cooperation," but teams can be as mechanistic and centralized as professional football or as fluid and dynamic as soccer (Brooks 1976; Imai, Nonaka, and Takeuchi 1985; Nonaka 1988). "Teamwork" is a multivocal symbol, and its important meaning differences are context dependent. Finally, it is unclear how the long-term relationship between Saturn's managerial hierarchy (flatter though it is) and the shop-floor teams will work. By 1991, they have already abrogated a profit-and-risk-sharing clause in the original agreement. All of these issues will affect the success the new work-force relationship.

While Saturn is not the only GM plant to innovate, General Motors looks to it as a model for other older plants, just as NUMMI was for it.

> GM's joint venture with Toyota . . . proved that a change in labor-managment relations could do more for productivity and quality. Technology takes a back seat to labor-management issues at Saturn. Says LeFauve [President of Saturn Corp.]: 'When people come and say, 'How did you do that?' we'll say we did it through people.' (Teece 1990, 58)

Saturn is a highly visible symbol of transformative change. It has the potential, because of its scale and visibility [and $5 + billion cost], to affect the way people far from Spring Hill see the value in new forms of industrial cooperation. Saturn is far better known than a legion of excellent American manufacturers, like the Baldridge award winners and others, who have taken to heart the principles of building knowledge, respect, and trust through cooperation. One only has to follow the business press or peruse a volume like Schonberger's (1986) *World Class Manufacturing,* with four score U.S. sites that embody new forms of employee involvement in productivity building.

Empowerment and Democratic Participation

Despite the emphasis on participation, cooperation, trust, and (sometimes) empowerment in these short American examples, the notion of "democracy" per se has not been central to the ideology or practice of this transformation in work relationships. We must look to Scandinavia for most examples that are consciously driven by the principle that a democratic society must embody democracy in its workplace relations. Sweden and Norway have special conditions that foster industrial democracy: strong but flexible trade unions, a history of social-democratic governments, and a supportive legal infrastructure. Socio-technical-systems approaches to participative integration of work and technology were widely explored (Emery and Thorsrud 1976; Mumford 1987; Trist and Bamforth 1951). From that base, more radical approaches to involving workers in the development of production technologies and computer-design tools have emerged. While this chapter is too short to explore these, two sources introduce a range of cutting-edge work: *Computers and Democracy—A Scandinavian Challenge* (1987) by G. Bjerknes, P. Ehn and M. Kyng eds. and *Work-Oriented Design of Computer Artifacts* (1989) by Pelle Ehn. One common theme is the spreading of democratic participation from the implementation phase back into the actual design of technical artifacts. Another is a respect for human skills and expertise and the need to preserve and enhance those skills in designing and using tools (rather than automating work and deskilling workers). A third principle is that the *social* relations of knowledge use are key to good technology designs and policies.

The focus of these studies is often on relations between engineers and workers—often highly skilled workers. The principles, however, have been developed and articulated in many different contexts. Including technologies as "actors" in a system of social relations (Latour 1987) is crucial to developing better ways of understanding the transformation of modern work. With their emphasis on engaged research, detailed field study, and practical applications, the praxis of these Scandinavian social scientists provides a good model for building anthropological engagement as well.

Flexibility and Pluralist Cultures or Taylor's "One Best Way"?

Examples of industrial democracy abroad or participatory cooperation at home cannot mask the fact that these successes are islands in a sea of traditional management. Less than 10 percent of U.S. firms employ autonomous work groups or team-based employee involvement, despite striking productivity gains when they are instituted (Hoerr 1989). Why are demonstrably valuable ideas left untouched?

One reason is the long-naturalized Taylorist principles of management. Top executives as well as the legion of middle managers who emulate them are socialized in this "culture of Taylorism";[17] and their opposite numbers in the workforce—employees, workers, direct labor, the working class, and the middle class—likewise expect that system from management. And workers have often responded with withdrawal, antagonism, or rebellion to the strictures of authoritarian systems, in self-reinforcing cycles of conflict.

That there is only one best way to do anything is a central Taylorist premise. Taylor used systematic analysis to define and refine any task into the one best way to do it. This method was then enshrined in standard operating procedures (SOPs) and mandated to workers as iron-clad rules. Work processes were specified in minute detail, and no deviation was allowed. The aim was perfect efficiency. The result was complete inflexibility. But both workers and technolgies must be flexible to achieve productivity improvements (Adler 1988; Safizadeh 1991). Taylor's one best way fosters narrow solutions, adherence to tradition, and stasis. However, in a universe of rapid and sometimes hostile change, there is a pressing need for radical flexibility. Today's decisions do not need to cut out poor options (variety reduction) as much as they need discovery and exploration of the widest possible range of choices. An organization's internal-control systems must match the complexity of its environment in order to achieve a new (if transient) homeostasis. This requires variety *amplification* in ideas and experience for decision makers (Imai, Nonaka, and Takeuchi 1985; Nonaka 1988; 1990).

But top ranks of American management are overwhelmingly monochrome—white, male, middle-aged, and middle-class. Their social worlds lack the fruitful dissonance of other voices. Their accustomed way has always worked, through two great wars and the post-war expansion; and theirs has been a remarkably unified voice for traditional systems of mechanistic efficiency—driven authority (Skinner 1986). Theirs was the one best way; and they expect, in principle, that there is a single authoritatively right system. The convergence of the worship of scientism— Taylor's scientific management—together with a presumed hierarchy of knowledge and authority has yielded a remarkably stable and potentially hermetic system of ideology and practice (Zuboff 1988).

Among the pernicious effects of this hegemony are the persistence of institutionalized racism and sexism. Its very pervasiveness is used to falsely validate ideologies of racial or gender superiority under the guise of social Darwinism (Gould 1981; Blakey, in this volume). This leaves managers, workers, and change agents on the horns of a dilemma. It seems to require a major transformation to move the parties away from their venerable, but now vulnerable, positions. The American motivators for transformational change almost *always* seem to be shocks or crises of external origin (Beer and Walton 1987), even if the groundwork for disaster was laid by poor management for years before.

This practical dilemma is matched by a dilemma implied in my cultural modelling. On the one hand, I argue that Taylorist managerial systems endure because they have become our common-sense culture of management. This implies that it is intractable because it is deeply ingrained or naturalized. On the other hand, I argue that counter-examples suggest new cultures of management are growing up in the cracks of the old system. How is this consistent with a cultural model of managerial practice?

Clifford Geertz describes common sense as a cultural system: "[a] relatively organized body of considered thought" that denies any systematic character and "affirm[s] that its tenets are immediate deliverances of experience, not deliberated reflections on it" (1983, 75). Taylorist principles may have begun as systematic, rational theories; and the principles of mass-production in manufacturing and classical theory in organizations were likewise inscribed in systematic treatises. But their systematic rules are rarely any longer explicit for most of the managers and workers whose actions are guided by them. These principles ubiquitously imbue managerial practice with a sense of everyday rightness and natural orderliness. Managers act with Taylorist common sense, "judiciously, intelligently, perceptively, reflectively . . . and [they are] capable of coping with everyday problems in an everyday way with some effectiveness'' (76). The Taylorist guide is no longer a set of formal rules, but has shifted to the intellectual background.

Taylorist culture was taught, implemented, imposed, refined, and otherwise impregnated into the body of American management by a legion of dedicated professional practitioners and pedagogues. Not just an intellectual movement, Taylorism was a methodology of practice habituated by years of so-called scientific attention to work processes and administrative structures. Professional schools of management arose to teach managers the new principles and to supplement industrial engineers in spreading Taylorism. Gradually, too, it became harder to rise from the shop floor to managerial positions without a formal degree. Then advances in managerial theory relegated its Taylorist progenitors to the back of the bibliography, as more sophisticated (and in some cases, more humane) schools arose. But by the 1960s, yet more rationalizing and control-oriented disciplines grew up, like decision science, operations research, and information theory. Hierarchic control systems were built into the taken-for-granted demands for stability, consistency, reliability, and repeatability that characterized management in the post-World War II era. Sometimes a conscious ideology and almost always an unarticulated but coherent pattern of principles, Taylorism was constituted out of everyday practice, reiterated, and naturalized in precisely the same sense that Geertz (1973) uses when he characterizes how a religious worldview becomes compelling to believers. Religious—substitute *Taylorist*—principles appear "as the imposed conditions of life implicit in a world with a particular structure, as mere common sense given the unalterable shape of reality" (90). These principles extend even beyond traditional Taylorist bureaucracies into the realms of the newest technologies of design and manufacturing, as the John Deere and VLSI Technologies examples illustrate.

If the key to the unspoken pervasiveness of Taylorism is praxis, then praxis is also a key to the viability of contemporary counterexamples. The practical construction of meaning—through changed work, attitudes, and administrative practices—is also key to reformulating cultural patterns in transformed organizations. Collaborative systems require both a visionary ideology and practices to support them. If Taylorism was naturalized over decades, with trial and error, refinement and change in itself, we can anticipate that new organizational relationships will require a comparable social effort. NUMMI and Van Nuys are instructive. Both began with an ideology of cooperation, promoted by management. At NUMMI, however, careful attention was paid to the rules, procedures, benefits, and incentives to cooperation. Security was protected, symbols of hierarchy were reduced, control of work processes (like line stoppage) were placed in the hands of workers, and management delivered on its promises for skills training. Despite a similar ideology, none of these were put into practice at Van Nuys. Changing *practices,* guided by a vision of a collaborative, participatory work environment, eventually changed the "outlook," interpretive regime, ethos, or culture of work relations at NUMMI.

Cultural systems are coherent patterns of understanding built from the reciprocal relationships among (1) knowledge or beliefs: the shared conceptual understandings of what or how things are; (2) patterns of practice: both the models for doing and the model-guided, habituated actions of everyday practice; (3) tools and artifacts: the means and ends of practical action; and (4) patterns of affect that embody the compelling force of culturally appropriate models. The relationship between ideology and practice is especially crucial to understanding assent and then involvement at NUMMI. Culture is never just an intellectual or cognitive category, but rather one that is intimately tied to how people do things—praxis, and what they do them with—tools and technologies. Cultural patterns are both models *of* reality and also models *for* acting in the world (Geertz 1973). A monastic rule for prayer and fasting and a company's manual of standard operating procedures (SOPs) are similarly guides to right (if not always righteous) conduct. Conversely, the daily process of acting according to the guides makes the world envisioned in those guides both believable and compelling. The continuous reiteration of everyday practice habituates us to the coherence and validity of this reality.

Without new methods and rules for practice to support teamwork and collaboration, initiative and participation, changes in the culture of work relations cannot survive. The failure of collaborative praxis doomed the Van Nuys attempts. Changes in praxis must also go beyond generic team building to touch the technical core of how people work. At NUMMI, skill building was pursued along two tracks: social skills for teamwork and technical skills that enabled workers to intervene in and improve their work processes. The technical half was absent at Van Nuys. Leaving technology out of a program for change rules out of court that overwhelming preponderance of workday practices where tasks and technologies are inseparably linked. Including technologies and skills makes the ideology of new work relations concrete. It also builds a platform of skills and confidence that empowers workers to take advantage of new self-controlling or self-managing opportunities. That lesson is borne out strongly in the Scandinavian experience with workplace democracy and empowerment (Bjerknes, Ehn, and Kyng 1987; Ehn 1988; Emery and Thorsrud 1976). By contrast in the Saturn example, without an explicit ideology of democratization, the assembly skillet system exemplifies technological empowerment and process control by workers. "Practical knowledge building" or "employee involvement" may serve the same roles in America as an ideology of practice that "workplace democracy" has in Scandinavia.

Finally, the normalization of these relationships and a sense of commitment to them is illustrated by a NUMMI worker initiative. When sales of Chevy Novas began to drop in the late 1980s, workers funded their own advertising campaign to boost sales by touting vehicle quality. This theme of high commitment to product quality has been borrowed in contemporary ads for the new Saturn vehicles.

While affect, technology, practice, and vision are all interrelated aspects of work culture, practical changes in work processes are probably the easiest to handle for initiating the change process. A vision of new relations is a necessary (but not rigid) guide; but simple, practical changes in the everyday rules of work are where proof of commitment must be constituted. New cooperative relations take on meaning through concrete practices. Since management initially has the most control, it is management who must take the first steps toward change. Also, to achieve quality and productivity goals, the technical issues integral to work must be part of the new changes.

In terms of the culture model, while all aspects of a cultural system must change, there is more leverage for change at the level of concrete practices. If practice is given an ideological frame of collaboration, respect, and participation; and the technical issues significant to quality and productivity results are engaged; then there is a chance that people will not only follow but also believe and commit to the new changes. I say "a chance" because this discussion is entirely in the realm of the cultural modelling of the process. As the Van Nuys example shows, and many other failed attempts could testify, a host of historical contingencies can intervene to produce other outcomes. Among these are the well-deserved skepticism of workers toward management, who have treated them as an expendable source of raw labor for so long. Another is exigencies of markets over which local plants and workers have little influence, or where decisions of distant directors or competitors make a whole production system irrecoverably obsolete. The Supreme Court, in a case under current review, may even decide that U.S. labor law, under the guise of protecting workers from "company unions," makes most cooperative work arrangements illegal.

Nevertheless, the emergence of new forms of collaboration implies new opportunities for change. What *internal* dynamics can prime the pump for transformation, absent a pending disaster? A detailed answer is beyond the scope of my chapter, but the outlines of a program can be sketched:

Enhanced participation and employee involvement, which entails empowerment;

Reskilling jobs, rotating assignments, and building the knowledge and expertise base in the workforce, which enables real participation and empowerment;

New technologies designed with users and for implementation. These empower people (at all levels) to control the complexity of new environments by enhancing human skills and enabling critical judgment at the local level;

Valuing difference and variety amplification in human resources—both in hiring and promotion. These give voice to new and challenging issues while providing more potential solutions to match complex new environments;

Combining variety, participation, skills, and technical empowerment redistributes knowledge-based power within the organization and undermines hierarchical authority.

None of this will happen without a new catalysis of knowledge, experience, threat, or crisis and a new willingness to experiment, take risks, and reach toward uncommon goals. As anthropologists, we have valuable experience and knowledge to add if we too are willing to take the risk of engagement.

A New Role for Anthropology

No simple rubric encompasses all of the changes in U.S. industry. However, new research on workplace relations, which combines attention to processual detail with 'systemic wisdom' is needed (Bateson 1972). New cooperative relationships and flexible structures are emerging out of our economic crisis; and process-focused ethnographic research can track and interpret unfolding action better than static data or post-hoc analysis. Culture theory also provides a model for multidimential analysis as well as for synthetic generalizations like "Taylorism as a cultural system." Finding, illuminating, and interpreting the newly valuable and changing systems and relationships, though, is only a first step. Making them accessible as alternative models for action, and then participating in their adoption is an expanding challenge for anthropologists.[18]

There is intellectual room for engagement, because only a paucity of ethnographic detail addresses the relationships as whole systems, rather than as the experience of one level or group within the system. Investigating the detail of social practice in firms reveals the symmetries and disjunctions between ideology and daily action, the role of the unspoken principles of power and influence in shaping outcomes, and the translation of skills into concrete actions and products. There is room, especially, for a deeper exploration of the interpretive dimensions of organizational life. In the face of rational reductionists, it is necessary to discover how significant actors and groups negotiate understanding, because it is these cultural constructions upon which they base actions. Finally, a historical sense of cultural patterns and change is needed, including recognition of the tension between their tenacity versus their interpretive malleability in rapidly changing organizational environments.

Besides intellectual space, there is political room for intervention in change processes. Wulff and Fiske (1987) and Trotter (1988), for instance, provide introductions to contemporary engagement in more traditionally applied anthropology domains; while Giovannini and Rosansky (1990) discuss the roles, value, and difficulties of organizational or management consultancy and its relationship to anthropological theory and practice. The latter also discuss how to enter this arena of practical work. Many representatives of all sides in the power array in organizations are keenly interested in understanding their past failures and future prospects. There are new opportunities to address issues of authority, responsibility, respect, and control not just with economic competitiveness in mind, but also for the principles of mutuality, ethical action, cooperation, democratization, and empowerment. These principles are increasingly seen not just as moral or political ends extraneous to business aims, but as social necessities of revitalized organizational life.

Among practicing mangers, the naturalization of hierarchy is so ubiquitous that extraordinary efforts—from the ground up as well as the top down—are necessary to effect change. Economic and social crises may stimulate a broader public and managerial recognition of the need for change, but it will take the ranks of many committed professionals and practitioners working as change agents in the everyday trenches of companies to affect real change. If anthropologists have a strong desire to aid in the reformation of American society, new opportunities abound to deploy our empirical tools and our holistic and synthetic approaches. With a critical stance toward our culture and society, we can create new knowledge and apply it to changing social relationships at the heart of American economic life. Instead of being a distant observer of continued demoralization and decline, anthropology can become a more central player in the reshaping of the human relations of productive life—and be close to the heartbeat of a renewed America.

NOTES

This paper is part of a collaborative effort of the Panel on Disorders of Industrial Society to read, critique, and reformulate our arguments over a two-year period of meetings. I owe a debt of gratitude to the whole Panel: Shepard Forman who guided the process to completion, Michael Blakey, Carol MacLennan, Kathy Newman, James Peacock, Roy Rappaport, Carlos Vélez-Ibañez, and Alvin Wolfe. Thanks to Judith Lisansky of AAA Progams, Emilio Moran, Panel rapporteurs Deborah Winslow, Cathy Ribic, Esther Griswold, and Jim McDonald for their comments, as well as to the anonymous reviewers of the University of Michigan Press; and thanks to Laura Goode for research assistance, and Anna Hargreaves for editorial comments. Anne Woosely and the Amerind Foundation of Dragoon, Arizona, made us very welcome for our meetings; and the School of American Research in Santa Fe, New Mexico, has provided me a gracious haven for completing this work as an NEH Resident Scholar.

1. These include the cost of capital, the U.S. savings rate, closed markets in Japan, Japanese leadership in process technologies, culture, and work ethics, among others.

2. I prefer *production community* over *firm* or *organization* because it is often necessary to draw wider system boundaries to capture the scope of relevant participants. Extraorganizational entities might include suppliers and customers, professional communities, local communities; and relevant scales might also be far smaller than an organization, for instance one plant, a work cell, a project/ product team, a department, an interest group or committee, etc.

3. Here I use *Taylorism* as a common gloss for the loosely linked complex

of managerial relations and practices stemming from Taylor and his disciples, classical management theorists, and mass-production principles together.

4. Many works cross the category boundaries. Braverman's (1974) work, in particular, has been influential in debate about inherent tendencies of capitalist systems to substitute "dead labor" (in the form of capital embodied in machinery) for living labor. The transformation of work relations in conjunction with new technologies is part of an ongoing dialog among political economists on class, power, and productivity in America (e.g., Burawoy 1979; Edwards 1979; Edwards, Reich, and Weiskopf 1986; Greiner 1988; Gutman 1976, 1987; Montgomery 1979; Noble 1977; Zimbalist 1979). An extended discussion of these (mostly) political-economy approaches and their relation to anthropology, however, lies outside the scope of this chapter.

5. An alternative model from the early years of American industry is outlined by Clark and Hayes (1988), who discuss the constant interaction of science and craft in the work of certain European immigrant entrepreneurs in U.S. manufacturing. Their application of scientific methods to process improvements was based on a collaborative rather than an extractive relationship with craft workers, and the results—particularly in the development of wartime industry in WWII—were impressive.

6. Any discussion of Taylor, his theories, and their influence or evolution in American managerial history is bound to be controversial. Here, I discuss only some of his original principles (Taylor 1911). His work was a foundation for central ideas of manufacturing management during the formative years of American industrial growth; and his ideas were widely applied elsewhere in business, including office work. Taylor's critics (see footnote 4 above) and other exegetes are legion (e.g., Giedion 1969; Hounshell 1984; Littler 1978; Nelson 1975, 1980). Some of my discussion of Taylorism and its influence in American industry is drawn, in addition, from management literature, especially the "manufacturing renaissance" movement (Clark, Hayes, and Lorenz 1985; Hayes and Wheelwright 1984; Hayes, Wheelwright, and Clark 1988; Jaikumar 1986; Skinner 1986). In the discussion that follows, I will let the example of "manufacturing" stand for the much broader scope of Taylorism's influences in working life.

7. This description is derived and modified from a field-based teaching case, "Deere & Company: CIM Planning at the Harvester Works" (Dubinskas 1987), which was researched and written by the author and published by the Harvard Business School. All materials herein are in the public domain.

8. This was the first U.S. installation of a system using the Manufacturing Automation Protocol or "MAP," jointly developed by major American manufacturers and automation equipment suppliers to help standardize the interfaces and interactions among disparate kinds of computer-controlled equipment in factories.

9. This description is derived and modified from a field-based teaching case, "VLSI Technology, Inc. (A): Automating ASIC Design" (Dubinskas 1986), which was researched and written by the author and published by the Harvard Business School. All materials herein are in the public domain.

10. Braverman (1974) and Noble (1977) focus on the disappearance of human skills into machines. See also Zuboff (1988) for the distinction between "action-

oriented skills" and "intellective skills." Experienced silicon designers have a craftwork familiarity with their tools, while they also have access to systematic intellective models of the knowledge domain—the interaction of features on the chips they design. A CAD drafter simply places parts mechanically from an engineer's sketch.

11. This chain of reasoning is argued on a macro scale by a legion of writers from within the managerial academy, especially the authors in the "manufacturing renaissance" movement. [See also footnote 4.] Zuboff (1988) approaches the issue from both a systematic (macro) scale and from the perspective of social and psychological dynamics. Braverman (1974), Noble (1977), and others likewise criticize from a political-economy perspective.

12. See also European commentators like Emery and Thorsrud (1976) on Scandinavia or Bate and Mangham's (1981) ethnographic study in Britain.

13. A comparable percentage of Americans have de facto lifetime employment guaranteed through seniority systems (Thurow 1985, 6).

14. It is interesting to note that the whole body of literature on individual motivation in business academia is peculiar to the United States. It is not a subject of much interest in European academia, and it is virtually absent from Japanese scholarship. It is not much of an issue in areas where the emphasis in practice has been focused on groups.

15. The oppressive side of Japanese industrial productivity is examined by Kamata (1982) in his first-hand accounts of Toyota's race to become a world-class manufacturer in the 1970s. It is also important to consider the role of Japan's recent history, particularly World War II, the occupation, labor strife of the late 1940s and early 1950s, and the suppression of radical unions in setting the tone for todays' relatively cooperative relationships.

16. A downside of this consensus process is its very long time frame. Saturn argues that the trade-off in usability is worth it. A second problem is that technological advances may be driven down to the lowest common denominator in the design team. How are rapid improvements in process technology to be introduced and implemented? Saturn argues that if they can't use it, it doesn't do them any good. Incremental improvement has also been the path to Japanese excellence in manufacturing, but this still begs the question of how to introduce radically new process technologies.

17. See footnote 3 above.

18. The history and ethos of anthropological engagement with these issues is discussed in Wolfe (in this volume) and Richardson 1979. Additional recent sources on industrial anthropology include Holzberg and Giovanini 1981, Pennbridge 1985, and Baba 1986.

REFERENCES

Abramson, Jill and Christopher J. Chipello. 1991. Compensation Gap: High Pay of CEOs Travelling with Bush Touches a Nerve in Asia. *Wall Street Journal,* Dec. 30, A1, A8.

Adler, Paul S. 1988. Managing Flexible Automation. *California Management Review* 30(3): 34–56.

Baba, Marietta L. 1986. Business and Industrial Anthropology: An Overview. *National Association for the Practice of Anthropology (NAPA) Bulletin* No. 2.

Barley, Stephen R., Gordon Meyer, and Debra Gash. 1988. Cultures of Culture: Academics, Practitioners and the Pragmatics of Normative Control. *Administrative Science Quarterly* 33: 24–60.

Bate, Paul and Iain Mangham. 1981. *Exploring Participation.* New York: John Wiley and Sons.

Bateson, Gregory. 1972. *Steps to an Ecology of Mind.* New York: Ballantine.

Beer, Michael and Anna E. Walton. 1987. Organization Change and Development. *Annual Review of Psychology* 38:339–67.

Bellah, Robert N., Richard Madsen, William M. Sullivan, Ann Swidlen, and Steven M. Tipton. 1985. *Habits of the Heart: Individualism and Commitment in American Life.* Berkeley: University of California Press.

Bjerknes, G. P. Ehn and M. Kyng, eds. 1987. *Computers and Democracy: A Scandinavian Challenge.* Avebury, U.K.: Aldershot.

Braverman, H. 1974. *Labor and Monopoly Capital.* New York: Monthly Review Press.

Brooks, Frederick P. 1976. *The Mythical Man-month.* Reading, Mass.: Addison-Wesley.

Brown, Clair and Michael Reich. 1989. When Does Cooperation Work? A Look at NUMMI and GM-Van Nuys. *California Management Review* 31(4): 26–44.

Burawoy, Michael. 1979. *Manufacturing Consent: Changes in the Labor Process under Monopoly Capitalism.* Chicago: University of Chicago Press.

Byrne, John A., Ronald Grover, and Robert D. Hof. 1990. Pay Stubs of the Rich and Corporate. *Business Week* May 7, 56–64.

Chandler, Alfred D. 1977. *The Visible Hand: The Managerial Revolution in American Business.* Cambridge: Harvard University Press.

Ciampa, Dan. 1988. *Manufacturing's New Mandate: The Tools for Leadership.* New York: John Wiley and Sons.

Clark, Kim B. and Robert H. Hays. 1988. Recapturing America's Manufacturing Heritage. *California Management Review* 30:9–33.

Clark, Kim B., Robert H. Hayes, and Christopher Lorenz, eds. 1985. *The Uneasy Alliance: Managing the Productivity-Technology Dilemma.* Boston: Harvard Business School Press.

Cole, Robert E. 1971. *Japanese Blue Collar: The Changing Tradition.* Berkeley: University of California Press.

Cooper, James and Kathleen Madigan. 1990. Business Outlook: Desperately Seeking a Dose of Productivity. *Business Week* Feb. 19, 27–28.

Crystal, Graef S. 1991a. *In Search of Excess: The Overcompensation of American Executives.* New York: Norton.

———. 1991b. Why CEO Compensation Is So High. *California Management Review* 34(1): 9–29.

Doi, Takeo. 1988. Dependency in Human Relationships. In *Inside the Japanese*

System: Readings on Contemporary Society and Political Economy, ed. D. I. Okimoto and T. P. Rohlen, 20–25. Stanford: Stanford University Press.

Dubinskas, Frank A. 1983. Leaders and Followers: Cultural Pattern and Political Symbolism in Yugoslavia. *Anthropological Quarterly* 56:95–97.

———. 1986. VLSI Technologies, Inc. (A): Automating ASIC Design. Case no. 9-686-128. Boston: Harvard Business School.

———. 1987. John Deere & Co: CIM Planning at the Harvester Works. Case no. 9-687-093. Boston: Harvard Business School.

———. 1988. Janus Organizations: Scientists and Managers in Genetic Engineering Firms. In *Making Time: Ethnographies of High Technology Organizations,* ed. F. Dubinskas, 170–232. Philadelphia: Temple University Press.

———. 1989. *Managing Complexity: Cooperation and Integration in the RA90 Project.* Product Marketing and Strategic Programs. Marlboro, Mass.: Digital Equipment Corp.

———. 1992. Culture and Conflict: The Cultural Roots of Discord. In *Hidden Conflict in Organizations: Uncovering Behind-the-Scenes Disputes,* ed. D. Kolb and J. Bartunek, 188–209. Newbury Park, Calif.: Sage Publications.

Edwards, Richard. 1979. *Contested Terrain: The Transformation of the Workplace in the Twentieth Century.* New York: Basic Books.

Edwards, Richard, Michael Reich, and Thomas E. Weiskopf. 1986. *The Capitalist System: A Radical Analysis of American Society.* Englewood Cliffs, N.J.: Prentice-Hall.

Ehn, Pelle. 1988. *Work-oriented Design of Computer Artifacts.* Stockholm, Sweden: Arbetslivscentrum.

Emery, Fred and Einar Thorsrud. 1976. *Democracy at Work: The Report of the Norwegian Industrial Democracy Program.* Leiden, the Netherlands: Martinus Nijhof.

Farnham, Alan 1989. The Trust Gap. *Fortune* Dec. 4, 56–78.

Fayol, H. 1949. *General and Industrial Management.* London, Pitman.

Frost, P. J., L. F. Moore, M. R. Louis, C. C. Lundberg, and J. Martin. 1985. *Organizational Culture.* Newbury Park, Calif.: Sage Publications.

Geertz, Clifford. 1973. Religion as a Cultural System. In *The Interpretation of Cultures,* ed. C. Geertz, 87–125. New York: Basic Books.

———. 1983. Common Sense as a Cultural System. In *Local Knowledge: Further Essays in Interpretive Anthropology,* ed. C. Geertz, 73–93. New York: Basic Books.

Giedion, Siegfried. 1969. *Mechanization Takes Command.* New York: Norton.

Giovannini, Maureen J. and Lynne M. H. Rosansky. 1990. *Anthropology and Management Consulting: Forging a New Alliance. National Association for the Practice of Anthropology (NAPA) Bulletin,* No. 9.

Gould, Stephen Jay. 1981. *The Mismeasure of Man.* New York: Norton.

Grenier, Guillermo J. 1988. *Inhuman Relations: Quality Circles and Anti-unionism in American Industry.* Philadelphia: Temple University Press.

Gulick, L. and L. Urwick, eds. 1937. *Papers in the Science of Administration.* New York: Institute of Public Administration, Columbia University.

Gutman, Herbert G. 1976. *Work, Culture, and Society in Industrializing*

America: Essays in American Working-Class and Social History. New York: Knopf.

———. 1987. *Power and Culture: Essays on the American Working Class.* New York: Pantheon.

Hayes, Robert H. and Steven Wheelwright. 1984. *Restoring our Competitive Edge: Competing Through Manufacturing.* New York: John Wiley & Sons.

Hayes, Robert H., Steven Wheelwright, and Kim B. Clark. 1988. *Dynamic Manufacturing: Creating the Learning Organization.* New York: Free Press.

Hoerr, John. 1989. The Payoff from Teamwork. *Business Week,* July 10, 56–62.

Holzberg, Carol and Maureen J. Giovannini. 1981. Reappraising New Directions. *Annual Review of Anthropology* 10:317–60.

Hounshell, David. 1984. *From the American System to Mass Production, 1800–1932.* Baltimore: Johns Hopkins University Press.

Imai, Ken-ichi, Ikujiro Nonaka, and Hirotaka Takeuchi. 1985. Managing the New Product Development Process: How Japanese Companies Learn and Unlearn. In *The Uneasy Alliance: Managing the Productivity - Technology Dilemma,* ed. K. B. Clark, R. H. Hayes, and C. Lorenz, 337–75. Boston: Harvard Business School Press.

Imai, Masaaki. 1986. *Kaizen (Ky'zen): The Key to Japan's Competitive Success.* New York: Random House.

Jaikumar, Ramchandran. 1986. Postindustrial Manufacturing. *Harvard Business Review* 64(6): 69–76.

Japan's Manufacturing Miracle. 1984. San Francisco: California Newsreel. Film.

JHRA [Japan Human Relations Association]. 1988. *The Idea Book: Improvement Through TEI (Total Employee Involvement).* Cambridge, Mass.: Productivity Press.

JMA [Japan Management Association]. 1987. *Canon Production System: Creative Involvement of the Total Workforce.* Cambridge, Mass: Productivity Press.

Kamata, S. 1982. *Japan in the Passing Lane.* New York: Pantheon.

Kimura, B. 1973. *Hito to Hito tono Aida: Seishin Byorigakuteki Nihonron* [Between a person and another: psychopathological "theory" of Japanese]. Tokyo: Kobundo.

Kolb, Deborah M. and Jean M. Bartunek, eds. 1992. *Hidden Conflict in Organizations: Uncovering Behind-the-Scenes Disputes.* Newbury Park, Calif: Sage Publications.

Latour, Bruno. 1987. *Science in Action: How to Follow Scientists and Engineers through Society.* Cambridge: Harvard University Press.

Lawrence, Paul and Jay W. Lorsch. 1967. *Organization and Environment.* Boston: Harvard Business School Press.

Lewandowski, Jim and Jack O'Toole. 1990. Forming the Future and Marriages of People and Technology at Saturn. Paper presented at the conference: Technology and the Future of Work, March at Stanford University.

Little, Craig R. 1978. Understanding Taylorism. *British Journal of Sociology* 29:185–207.

Montgomery, David. 1979. *Workers' Control in America: Studies in the History of Work, Technology, and Labor Struggles.* New York: Cambridge University Press.

Mooney, J. C. and A. P. Reiley. *Onward Industry.* New York: Harper & Row.

Morgan, Gareth. 1986. *Images of Organization.* Newbury Park, Calif. Sage Publications.

Morita, Akio. 1986. *Made in Japan: Akio Morita and Sony.* New York: Dutton.

Mumford, E. 1987. Sociotechnical System Design: Evolving Theory and Practice. In *Computers and Democracy: A Scandinavian Challenge,* ed. G. P. Bjerknes and M. Kyng. Avebury, U.K.: Aldershot.

Nakane, Chie. 1970. *Japanese Society.* Berkeley: University of California Press.

Nelson, Daniel. 1975. *Managers and Workers: Origins of the New Factory System in the U.S., 1880-1920.* Madison: University of Wisconsin Press.

———. 1980. *Frederick W. Taylor and the Rise of Scientific Management.* Madison: University of Wisconsin Press.

Noble, David F. 1977. *America by Design: Science, Technology, and the Rise of Corporate Capitalism.* New York: Knopf.

Nonaka, Ikujiro. 1988. Creating Organizational Order out of Chaos. *California Management Review* 30(3): 57-73.

———. 1990. Redundant, Overlapping Organization: A Japanese Approach to Managing the Innovation Process. *California Management Review* 32(3): 27-38.

Ohno, Taiichi. [1978] 1988. *Toyota Production System.* Tokyo: Diamond Publishing, Cambridge, Mass.: Productivity Press.

———. 1988. *Workplace Management.* Cambridge, Mass.: Productivity Press.

Ouchi, William G. 1981. *Theory Z: How American Business can meet the Japanese Challenge.* Reading, Mass.: Addison-Wesley.

Parker, Mike and Jane Slaughter. 1988. Management by Stress. *Technology Review* 91:37-44.

Pascale, Richard T. and Anthony G. Athos. 1981. *The Art of Japanese Management: Applications for American Executives.* New York: Simon and Schuster.

Pascale, Richard T. and Thomas P. Rohlen. 1988. The Mazda Turnaround. In *Inside the Japanese System: Readings on Contemporary Society and Political Economy,* ed. D. I. Okomoto and T. P. Rohlen, 149-69. Stanford: Stanford University Press.

Pennbridge, Julia N. 1985. *Industrial Anthropology: A Selected Annotated Bibliography.* Society for Applied Anthropology Monograph Series, No. 14. Washington, D.C.: Society for Applied Anthropology.

Productivity. 1990. [catalog] Cambridge, Mass.: Productivity Press.

Richardson, F. L. W. 1979. Social Interaction and Industrial Productivity. In *The Uses of Anthropology,* ed. W. Goldschmidt, 79-99, Special Publication No. 11. Washington, D.C.: American Anthropological Association.

Rohlen, Thomas P. 1974. *For Harmony and Strength: Japanese White-collar Organization in Anthropological Perspective.* Berkeley: University of California Press.

Rybczynski, Witold. 1986. *Home: A Short History of an Idea.* New York: Viking Penguin.

Safizadeh, M. Hossein. 1991. The Case of Workgroups in Manufacturing Operations. *California Management Review* 33(4): 61–82.

Sano, Toshiyuki. 1983. The Effect of Culture on the Development of Scientific Theory: Imanishi and Darwin. Working paper, Department of Anthropology, Stanford University, Stanford.

Schein, Edgar H. 1985. *Organizational Culture and Leadership.* San Francisco: Jossey-Bass.

———. 1989. Reassessing the Divine Rights of Managers. *Sloan Management Review* 30(2): 63–68.

Schonberger, Richard J. 1982. *Japanese Manufacturing Techniques: Nine Hidden Lessons in Simplicity.* New York: Free Press.

———. 1986. *World Class Manufacturing: The Lessons of Simplicity Applied.* New York: Free Press.

Shingo, Shigeo. 1985. *A Revolution in Manufacturing: The SMED System.* Cambridge, Mass.: Productivity Press.

———. 1986. *Zero Quality Control: Source Inspection and the Poka-yoke System.* Cambridge, Mass.: Productivity Press.

Skinner, Wickham. 1986. The Productivity Paradox. *Harvard Business Review* 64(4): 55–59.

Taylor, Frederick W. 1911. *The Principles of Scientific Management.* New York: Norton.

Teece, James B. 1990. Here Comes GM's Saturn. *Business Week,* April 9, 56–62.

Thurow, Lester C., ed. 1985. *The Management Challenge: Japanese Views.* Cambridge, Mass.: M.I.T. Press.

Trist, E. L. and K. Bamforth. 1951. Social and Psychological Consequences of the Longell Method of Coal-getting. *Human Relations* 4:3–38.

Trotter, Robert T., ed. 1988. *Anthropology for Tomorrow: Creating Practitioner-Oriented Applied Anthropology Programs.* Special Publication Series, No. 24. Washington, D.C.: American Anthropological Association.

Ulrich, Hans and Gilbert J. B. Probst, eds. 1984. *Self-Organization and Management of Social Systems.* Berlin: Springer-Verlag.

Walton, Richard. 1985. From Control to Commitment: Transforming Workforce Management in the United States. In *The Uneasy Alliance: Managing the Productivity-Technology Dilemma,* ed. K. B. Clark, R. H. Hayes, and C. Lorenz, 237–65. Boston: Harvard Business School Press.

Winter, Ralph E. 1990. Foreign Ownership Trend is Growing among Machine Tool Makers in U.S. *Wall Street Journal,* Jan. 8.

Wulff, Robert M. and Shirley Fiske, eds. 1987. *Anthropological Praxis: Translating knowledge into Action.* Boulder, Colo.: Westview Press.

Zimbalist, Andrew, ed. 1979. *Case Studies on the Labor Process.* New York: Monthly Review Press.

Zuboff, Shoshana. 1988. *In the Age of the Smart Machine: The Future of Work and Power.* New York: Basics Books.

Chapter 4

Deindustrialization, Poverty, and Downward Mobility: Toward an Anthropology of Economic Disorder

Katherine S. Newman

Since the birth of world-systems analysis and underdevelopment theory, anthropologists have played a central role in chronicling the devastating impact of global economic change on the peoples of the third world. The replacement of diverse subsistence economies by narrowly based, extractive industry or mono-crop agriculture has created tremendous upheaval as native populations become increasingly dependent on unpredictable market fluctuations. Our central focus has been the human toll of macroeconomic change on local peoples: declining political autonomy, an upsurge in rural-to-urban migration, increasing impoverishment, and malnutrition. This tragic litany is, by now, well known and well documented.

These problems, which have reached crisis proportions in many non-Western societies, wear a third-world face in most of the anthropological literature. We are accustomed to thinking of economic dislocation as a dilemma of the "other." Yet the social consequences of industrial upheaval are not confined to distant shores. Inside the capitalist West, a sea change has taken place that is producing massive internal economic dislocation. A host of familiar social problems, ranging from the decay of inner cities and the rise in homelessness, to the abandonment of company towns by the industries that have been their bedrock for the past century, dominate the news in the U.S. press.[1] They are symptomatic of a fundamental transformation in our economic infrastructure that has left thousands of poor, working-class, and middle-class families at a loss to control the circumstances of their lives (see especially Hopper 1985, Lamphere 1987, Nash 1989, Newman 1985, 1988). These personal traumas are symptomatic of disorder on a large scale.

There can be little question that economic disarray constitutes a serious impediment to democratic participation. The unsettling, disorganizing impact of deindustrialization as it is manifested in the continuing problems of poverty and downward mobility create major barriers to meaningful participation in the political arena. Families struggling to contend with the burdens of inadequate housing, dangerous streets, financial insecurity, educational disadvantage, occupational dislocation, and discrimination are likely to be preoccupied with the task of survival. Their claims to a fair share of the country's resources and their capacity to articulate their own concerns and perspectives in the realm of public policy is often usurped by the prior need to provide for themselves and their children. To the extent that a solid foundation remains out of reach for the poor, and has increasingly slipped away from the middle and working classes in the United States, the conditions for genuine participation in the public arena are eroding.

Why has economic insecurity and occupational disorganization grown in recent decades and how can anthropology shed new light on the consequences of these disorders? Although anthropologists have contributed to the study of economic turmoil in recent years, the topic remains largely the purview of economists, quantitatively oriented sociologists, urban planners, and demographers.[2] Where anthropology was a critical force in studies of urban poverty in the 1960s and 1970s, providing a necessary corrective to studies based entirely on survey and census data, its presence has diminished and the more quantitative fields have become the dominant intellectual force in poverty studies. Hence, the not-so-hidden agenda of this chapter is to sketch the contours of a research program that would enhance anthropological scholarship on the social and cultural consequences of economic dislocation.

One important starting point may be found in the literature on deindustrialization, a thesis developed by liberal economists to describe changes in the postwar economy of the United States. It provides us with a macrolevel framework within which to locate the local-level ethnographic studies anthropologists are best known for. Using this perspective as a starting point, this chapter goes on to examine the particular forms of dislocation that deindustrialization has visited on the poor, the blue-collar working class, and the white-collar middle class. For each group I then consider: (1) What is missing from the social-scientific picture in each of these class contexts? What is not yet known? and (2) What would a distinctly anthropological approach to these unknowns entail? How can we contribute to the social scientific enterprise in this domain in ways that are complementary to efforts underway among colleagues in sister disciplines?

The Deindustrialization Paradigm

The unprecedented wave of industrial-plant shutdowns in the 1970s and 1980s attracted the attention of a wide variety of labor economists and industrial sociologists. Conservatives among them argued that the downturn was simply another swing in the business cycle, a term used to describe the episodic ups and downs considered natural, normal features of capitalist systems. If anything else was to blame for U.S. economic doldrums, conservatives suggested that unproductive and "overpriced" labor was primarily at fault. Union demands were understood to be the root cause of the flight of manufacturing overseas where wages are lower.

Liberal economists took issue with this view and began to look for new paradigms to describe the post-war development of the U.S. economy. Two well-known scholars on the political left, Barry Bluestone and Bennett Harrison, took issue with the business-as-usual explanation, and argued instead that a fundamental change in the country's economic structure was underway. Their much-debated book, *The Deindustrialization of America*, united the demise of the country's manufacturing sector with the movement of industry overseas and the spectacular increase in corporate mergers, and in so doing articulated a new and darker vision of the country's economic predicament:

> Underlying the high rates of unemployment, the sluggish growth in the domestic economy, and the failure to successfully compete in the international market is the deindustrialization of America. By deindustrialization is meant a widespread, systematic disinvestment in the nation's basic productive capacity. . . . Capital . . . has been diverted from productive investment in our basic national industries into unproductive speculation, mergers and acquisitions, and foreign investment. Left behind are shuttered factories, displaced workers, and a newly emerging group of ghost towns. (Bluestone and Harrison 1982, 6)

Bluestone and Harrison indicted American corporations for systematically stripping even those plants that were demonstrably profitable in order to "milk" the "cash cows," shift resources either into the acquisition of other companies or the construction of factories in areas with nonunion labor, while capitalizing on provisions of the tax code that encourage huge write-offs. Deindustrialization was most pronounced in the rustbelt zones of the Northeast and Midwest, yet Bluestone and Harrison showed that nearly half the jobs lost to plant shutdowns during the 1970s had occurred in the "sunbelt" states of the South and West (Ibid, 10). Hence the trend could not be dismissed as a regional problem; instead, it was diagnosed as a nationwide headache.

Sociological and policy research based on the Bluestone-Harrison approach has focused on the catastrophic macroeffects of industrial decline, utilizing survey data that pinpoints the ripple effects of plant shutdowns including (1) a sharp decline in the health of tertiary and supplier industries that can no longer depend on the missing factories as sources of demand for their products and services; (2) rapidly increasing unemployment whose duration lengthens as an area becomes economically depressed; (3) the loss of tax revenues, which generates a decline in the quality and quantity of public services (schools, hospitals, roads, etc.); and (4) a rising demand for social and medical services related to increased stress stemming from unemployment including psychological distress, alcoholism, and high blood pressure (Bluestone and Harrison 1982; Buss and Redburn 1983).

Localities struggle to contend with these social and fiscal burdens by cutting public expenditures, which in turn renders city, county, and state employees vulnerable to unemployment just when their services are most in demand. At the same time, enterprising officials begin to solicit new industry to fill the gap in the local economy. With their collective backs against the wall, communities compete against each other to attract new corporations by providing tax breaks or promises to construct new sewer lines in the hopes of beating out localities offering less. Apart from the fiscal burden this places on local residents, the vulnerability of economically depressed communities leaves them in a weak position to demand much in return: They risk losing business investment if they try to exact industry promises to stay put.

The spectre of industrial decline does not tell the "whole story" of deindustrialization.[3] There is a growth side to the saga as well, represented by booming growth in the service sector. Indeed, job creation in the 1980s and 1990s is largely (though not entirely) a function of increasing demand for services ranging from fast food to banking, from child care to nursing-home attendants. In addition, the past decade saw a growth in high-tech industries, though they also experienced periods of contraction as overseas competition bit into American market shares. In most of these growth areas, however, the wage structure has been unfavorable. A small number of well-paying, professional jobs, has been swamped by minimum-wage positions. More than half of the eight million (net) new jobs created in the United States between 1979 and 1984 paid less than $7,000 per year (in 1984 dollars). While many of these were part-time jobs (another growth area of dubious value), more than 20 percent of the year-round, full-time jobs created during this period paid no more than $7,000 (Bluestone and Harrison 1987; Newman 1988, 31).

Hence workers displaced by deindustrialization, new entrants to the labor market (young people and women), and the increasing number of elderly returning to the employment scene to supplement retirement, are finding the available opportunities limited with respect to the income they provide. Moreover, service-sector employment often fails to offer the benefits (health insurance, retirement provisions, etc.) routinely expected of "good" jobs. Increasingly we are seeing the macrolevel consequence of "pyramidal" job growth—which features small numbers of good jobs compared to large numbers of bad jobs—in the form of rising income inequality. The distribution of national income is becoming increasingly polarized, with a significant number of households (largely dual-income, white-collar families) moving upscale, and an even larger number moving down into poverty and the lower class (Bluestone and Harrison 1987; Ehrenreich 1989). The image of U.S. society splitting into the legions of the haves and the have-nots is increasingly coming to pass.

The economic effects of deindustrialization add up to an assault on the standard of living and social security of most working Americans. Yet their concrete impact on class and occupational groups in the United States varies considerably, for each community confronts economic hardship with different resources in the form of skills, work histories, educational credentials, financial cushions, and cultural supports. For the anthropologist, these variations are essential contextual facts defining structural conditions that frame local subcultures. We must therefore consider some of the major configurations of deindustrialization as they impact differentially on the "underclass," the blue-collar working class, and the managerial-professional middle class.

Deindustrialization and the Plight of the Urban Poor

The study of poverty and the social structure of poor communities has a long history stretching back to the Progressive Era and the muckraking efforts of liberal reformers.[4] Shocking accounts of Chicago slums and New York tenements were instrumental in the passage of legislation designed to regulate, though not eradicate, poverty through limitations on working hours, control of working conditions, the development of public health measures, the passage of housing legislation, and the limitations placed on child labor (Wilson and Aponte 1987, 165). Succeeding the progressive journalists and social critics were the earliest representatives of "Chicago school" social ecology, who attempted to provide a sociological analysis of poverty through a conceptual understanding of urban social structure. Poverty was situated in its social context by understanding its peculiar features as outcomes of urban density, distance from a social center, and the like. Whatever the limitations of the social-ecology perspective, it was noteworthy for the ways in which it shifted the analysis from the view that poverty is caused by internal, individual character flaws, to the notion that its causes are social.

The sociological argument provided an intellectual legacy that was reinforced by studies of the poor, inspired by the civil-rights movement and funded by Lyndon Johnson's war on poverty. *The Other America,* Michael Harrington's (1962) dramatic account of lives dominated by hopelessness, hunger, and squalid living conditions in the midst of American affluence, stimulated the nation's conscience and inspired a decade's worth of demographic studies of the poor. As Wilson and Aponte (1987, 168) point out, these studies were oriented toward analyzing the composition of the poverty population. The quantitative studies revealed that: (1) poverty had shifted from being largely a rural phenomenon to a problem concentrated in the cities; (2) the absolute numbers of poor people fell from World War I through the 1960s, but then began to climb sharply; (3) although whites still represented the largest group within the population classified as poor, minorities were increasingly overrepresented (compared to their numbers in the population as a whole).

This latter point gave way to the now famous (or infamous) studies of Moynihan and others who began to investigate the relationship between minority status and poverty, with special emphasis on the social structure of the black family. This debate is well known in the anthropological community and therefore need not be reviewed here.[5] Suffice it to say that the ethnographic approach to the study of poverty left its most powerful and enduring mark during this period. Anthropologists such as Elliot Liebow, Ulf Hannerz, and Carol Stack picked up where their earlier counterparts (e.g., Powdermaker, Dollard etc.) left off, and entered the foray over the culture of poverty. The debate through the mid-1970s (which some would argue is still a central public-policy preoccupation) revolved around the question of "transmission": how to account for the apparent existence of a persistently poor population. For Moynihan et al., who were persuaded by the culture of poverty perspective, the answer lay in the structure of the black family. For critics of this view, including most anthropologists, the truth was to be found in the persistence of structural barriers to employment, stable housing, and decent schooling that each generation of poor, black families faced anew.

The "transmission debate" continues to dominate the literature of the 1980s and 1990s but with important new twists that, for the first time, link the macroeconomic findings on deindustrialization with more traditional concerns regarding the deterioration of economic conditions in the inner cities. A number of policy scientists and sociologists—most notably John Kasarda and William Julius Wilson—have begun to argue (1) that the plight of urban minorities has worsened dramatically since the 1960s and (2) that rapid and catastrophic changes in the living conditions of black and hispanic families can best be understood in terms of the differential impact of plant shutdowns and service-industry growth. Debate over the impact of family structure on persistent poverty continues. Yet instead of being cast as the prime mover in the perpetuation of social problems in minority communities, family instability is seen as a pathological outcome of structural flaws in our postindustrial economy. The political conclusion to be drawn from this shift in perspective is clear: Programs designed to increase family stability (e.g., teenage-pregnancy prevention, delinquency intervention, etc.) will have little effect absent a Marshall plan for full employment.[6] The main culprit in the story of poverty—particularly, but not exclusively, minority poverty—is defined in terms of the pernicious effects of deindustrialization.

The Truly Disadvantaged is arguably the most important statement on minority poverty in the last decade. It has been the focus of an extraordinary amount of attention in policy circles, think tanks, and foundations responsible for research funding. For the most part, *The Truly Disadvantaged* proceeds without the benefit of participant-observation, drawing instead on macrolevel data gathered from the census and from survey data generated by panel studies. Although the ethnographic approach is strikingly absent from this book,[7] the analysis dwells at length on patterns of social interaction and isolation in urban ghettos and the pernicious impact of concentrated poverty on youth aspirations, community social structure, and the instability of religious and commercial institutions. Absent an anthropological foundation, some of the book's conclusions strike the qualitative social scientist as speculative, while others seem incontrovertible contributions to our understanding of the economic context of poverty.

Above all, however, the arguments and claims in the book underline the critical importances of bringing anthropology back into the debates on urban poverty to which it contributed in important ways in the 1960s and 1970s. To do so, we must begin by reviewing the structural evidence of deindustrialization and economic decline among poor minorities and then shift to the more controversial elements of this new perspective on poverty that need to be tested against findings drawn from qualitative research.

The deindustrialization perspective advanced by Bluestone and Harrison documents the dramatic loss of manufacturing industries and hence blue-collar employment since World War II, which has accelerated rapidly since the late 1960s. Millions of wholesale, retail, and manufacturing jobs have been wiped out and have not been replaced by growth in the service sector. Kasarda (1988, 168) notes that the impact of this transformation has altered the employment base of virtually all U.S. cities:

Manufacturing dispersed to the suburbs, exurbs, nonmetropolitan areas, and abroad. Warehousing activities relocated to more regionally accessible beltways and interstate highways. Retail establishments followed their suburbanizing clientele and relocated in peripheral shopping centers and malls. The urban exodus of the middle class further diminished the number of blue-collar service jobs such as domestic workers, gas station attendants, and delivery personnel.

This does not mean, of course, that cities suffered overall employment losses. On the contrary, they saw spectacular gains in other economic sectors:

Between 1953–1985, New York City lost over 600,000 jobs in manufacturing. During this same period, white collar service industries grew by nearly 800,000 jobs. (Kasarda 1988, 169).

While the net effects of the transition to an "information and administrative control" based economy may have been positive, the impact of this change on urban minorities has been devastating. Entry-level jobs for the low-skilled disappeared by the thousands and unemployment for experienced blue-collar workers grew steadily. Skilled-service jobs demand educational credentials that decaying inner cities have not provided for minority children. Hence, those economic sectors in which blacks, especially black men, have been overrepresented (especially blue-collar manufacturing) were hardest hit. Urban employment opportunities surged ahead in fields in which, historically at least, blacks have been underrepresented.

Those growth sectors that might have provided employment opportunities for minorities, especially teenagers seeking a foothold in the labor market, moved to distant suburban communities that were, for all practical purposes, inaccessible to inner-city workers.[8] Ironically, declining birth rates among the white middle class has translated into labor shortages in service industries that cater to these outlying communities. The much-heralded surge in service employment, then, represented no solution to those trapped in urban poverty. Instead, Kasarda argues, we have ended up with a complete "mismatch"[9]: the inner-city labor force is displaced, unable to move into the expanding service sector, and physically "trapped" by prohibitively high housing costs in outlying communities where jobs are going begging.

In *The Truly Disadvantaged,* William Julius Wilson (1987, 39) advances Kasarda's argument by considering the consequences of this mismatch for those seemingly trapped in persistent poverty:

> Urban minorities have been particularly vulnerable to structural economic changes, such as the shift from goods-producing to service-producing industries, the increasing polarization of the labor market into low-wage and high-wage sectors, technological innovations, and the relocation of manufacturing industries out of the central cities.

The mismatch that results is reflected in higher unemployment rates for central-city blacks, increasing levels of labor force "dropouts," and the persistence of high, black unemployment even in the face of economic recovery in many northern cities. Particularly disadvantaged in this scenario are young black men seeking entry to the labor market: their jobless rates have jumped up sharply since 1969 in the large central cities of the Northeast and Midwest (Wilson 1987, 41). Only 58 percent of all black, young-adult males (sixteen to twenty-four) were employed in 1984, "[revealing] a problem of joblessness for young black men that has reached catastrophic proportions" (Ibid, 43).

Why were black men especially affected by plant shutdowns in the 1970s? There are several related reasons that underscore the importance of linking the deindustrialization debate to the plight of urban minority families: (1) manufacturing industries represent a major source of black employment in the twentieth century; (2) manufacturers are more sensitive to economic downturns than other sectors; and (3) within these industries, low-wage workers and newly hired workers—both of which are disproportionately black—are at highest risk for layoffs and job losses (Wilson 1987, 45).[10]

These macroeconomic facts are hardly in dispute, and they form an important foundation for studies of inner-city poverty. The central question is, however, what follows from these facts in terms of the social structure of poor communities and the life chances of their inhabitants? Wilson (1987, 46) argues that one profound effect was an increasing concentration of poor people in urban poverty zones. He suggests that blacks who were economically successful and therefore able to afford better housing and schooling for their children, fled the inner cities along with their white counterparts who make up the "working class suburbs."[11] Those left behind in the ghettos were the most disadvantaged, the most vulnerable to the economic disarray caused by deindustrialization. As the general condition of the country's economy slipped, both the numbers of poor and their concentration in the inner city grew by an astounding rate:

> Although the total population in [New York, Chicago, Los Angeles, Philadelphia, and Detroit] decreased by 9 percent between 1970 and 1980, the poverty population increased by 22 percent. Furthermore the population living in poverty areas grew by 40 percent overall, by 69 percent in high-poverty areas . . . and by a staggering 161 percent in extreme-poverty areas. It should be emphasized that these incredible changes took place within just 10 years. (Wilson 1987, 46)

It is this population, trapped in increasingly deteriorating conditions in the major urban areas, that forms the backbone of what Wilson has called the "underclass," a mainly minority group that he argues is caught in a web of persistent poverty.

From my perspective, the most important contribution of Wilson's work is his insistence that scholars give due weight to the changing "economic class structure of ghetto neighborhoods." To fully appreciate his policy perspective, however, one must analyze closely what Wilson suggests the social consequences of this change have been, for here we find the elements of controversy for which he has been criticized and which, I would argue, can only be settled through the field methods of anthropology. *The Truly Disadvantaged* points out that the more mixed, economic class structure of ghetto communities prior to the 1960s—a mix created by segregation—supported a social structure defined by "vertical integration of different income groups" (Ibid, 49). Middle-class, professional black families from the 1940s to the 1960s, who might have had the resources to move out of the inner city, were prevented from doing so by restrictive housing policies and racial antagonism. The same was true, Wilson notes, for working-class blacks. Hence inner-city communities were class heterogeneous.

Successful legal challenges to housing discrimination opened opportunities for suburban flight to these more affluent segments of the black community. Those who could, fled from the inner city (along with their white counterparts), while those who lacked the resources to join the exodus were "left behind" to suffer the ravages of deindustrialization. We have already noted these consequences in terms of rising unemployment. It remains to show what other problems followed from these compositional and economic facts.

Much of *The Truly Disadvantaged* is devoted to hammering home some unpleasant findings on indicators of social dislocation in ghetto areas. Statistics on rising rates of crime, skyrocketing rates of joblessness, an extraordinary increase in out-of-wedlock births, female-headed households, and "welfare dependency" over generations show a very sharp contrast between the post-war period of 1940–1970 and the era of deindustrialization that commenced in the early 1970s (see Wilson 1987, 20–62). Conservative thinkers (e.g., Charles Murray in his controversial volume, *Losing Ground* [1984]), have argued that these indicators are proof of the failure, indeed the exacerbating tendency, of social-welfare programs initiated during the Great Society era of Lyndon Johnson and perpetuated by Democratic administrations thereafter.

Wilson convincingly demonstrates the fallacy of this view, mainly by showing a sharp decline in the real economic value of federal aid to the poor in the 1970s. Nonetheless he insists that liberal policy scientists face up to the rapid deterioration of conditions in the ghettos and seek to identify the causes of persistent poverty. Rather than blame government intervention, as Murray does, Wilson argues that lack of economic opportunity—primarily steady work for minority men—created a shortage of "marriageable males" in the black community (defined as those employed), and encouraged the formation of single parent, female-headed households. Young, single mothers and their families are at serious risk for poverty, owing both to child-care problems and limited labor-market opportunities for women. This in turn places extraordinary burdens on children, who are increasingly born to families under extreme stress, struggling to cope with poverty. Their educational options are limited, both by the failure of city administrations to invest in local ghetto schools and by what Wilson sees as the cultural failure of the very poor to support educational attainment as a way out.

Finally, *The Truly Disadvantaged* suggests that the flight of the working and middle classes from ghetto communities across the nation created a hermetically sealed underclass in which "the chances are overwhelming that children will seldom interact on a sustained basis with people who are employed or with families that have a steady breadwinner" (Ibid, 57). Wilson sees this class isolation as having two primary consequences: (1) it destroys opportunities for networking, personal contact with those who might be able to help with job prospects and (2) it promotes fatalism in children who cannot sustain aspirations for educational success, job prospects, or family stability and leaves them open to recruitment for criminality or welfare dependency.

Wilson denies any similarity between his viewpoint and either the classic formulation of the culture of poverty (à la Oscar Lewis) or its neoconservative incarnate in the 1980s (e.g., Murray). For proponents of the latter view, the culprit in persistent poverty is a flawed culture that is transmitted through the generations, economic opportunity notwithstanding, and the solution is draconian: Cut government benefits and let the strong survive through their own efforts. For Wilson, shifting the focus to class-based isolation yields a strikingly different picture: The features of failure attributed to the culture of poverty are a direct outgrowth of structural failures in the economy, primarily the inability of the postindustrial economy to generate decent, secure jobs for inner city black men. The solution lies neither in Band Aid efforts to engineer a new subculture nor in government cuts, but in a Marshall plan for full employment.

I dwell here on *The Truly Disadvantaged* both because it represents the most important recent challenge to theories of poverty and because the arguments it contains cry out for ethnographic inquiry of a kind that has been noticeably absent from the anthropological scene in recent decades. To formulate an agenda for a renewed anthropology of urban poverty, we must therefore consider what the central controversial elements of this new thesis on poverty are and then ask how ethnographic investigation can shed light on them. There are two main areas of controversy in my view, each with many subcomponents: (1) is Wilson's description of the past accurate and, if so, was it responsible for the comparatively better conditions of life in inner city minority communities in the years 1945–70? and (2) is Wilson's description of the social structure (or lack thereof) of the urban underclass accurate for the present period? The first is a historical inquiry for which the classic anthropological texts of the 1960s provide some important findings. The second demands a new anthropological research agenda focused on social conditions in the ghetto.

The Truly Disadvantaged attributes much of the comparatively stronger social structure of minority communities in the past to the fact that their composition was class heterogeneous. He argues that in the old days (post-World War II), middle-class professionals and steadily employed, working-class families combined with institutions such as the church to provide a backbone of stability for ghetto communities. They contributed essential services in their localities—medical, legal, educational—and their relative prosperity insured an effective demand for commerce (grocery stores, shoe stores, hardware stores, etc.) that in turn served as a source of service employment. Most of all, however, Wilson suggests that the class composition of the inner-city black community provided role models: examples of success that were worthy of emulation and that, he believes, stimulated those less fortunate to aspire to educational and occupational success.

The ethnographic record compiled in the 1960s by anthropologists working in the urban black community paints a different picture. Hannerz's (1969) classic, *Soulside,* notes the existence of various class segents in the black enclaves of Washington D.C. However, he goes to some length to show that physical proximity does not promote close social interaction. The "mainstreamers," nuclear families who are homeowners, are socially separated from the "swingers" and express their disdain for those who are economically less advantaged. The ghetto Hannerz describes is internally segregated by class where residence is concerned, with the boundaries between those who are better off and those who are poor demarked as "no man's land" or as zones of conflict-ridden interaction. Liebow's (1967) often-cited study of marginally employed black men, *Tally's Corner,* protrays a social group almost entirely cut off from the working and middle classes within their own community, and at least as likely to draw their aspirations from media images of a distant white world as from fellow minorities who have succeeded.

One might be tempted to argue that this is an example drawn from the past, while Wilson's work reflects the increasing class isolation of contemporary inner-city neighborhoods. Readers of Eli Anderson's (1991) ethnographic work will recognize, however, that sharp class conflict remains a persistent feature of life in urban centers particularly where gentrifying haves rub shoulders uncomfortably with increasingly impoverished have-nots. Anderson's fascinating book, *Streetwise,* documents the friction and fear that characterizes relations between poor African-Americans and their middle-class neighbors (both black and white) in city centers where residential groups that diverge sharply in income and lifestyle live side by side.

In short, while the ethnographic record substantiates Wilson's statistical portrait of class heterogeneity in urban minority communities of the past, it is not entirely clear that this "mix" had the social consequences he posits. Residential diversity did not lend itself to the kind of social interaction Wilson argues was the foundation of appropriate role models, networking contacts, and the like. The ethnographic materials we have at hand do not provide great support to a portrait of postwar ghettos as characterized by cross-class social contact of the kind that Wilson argues is essential to educational and occupational mobility for the truly disadvantaged.[12]

The second critical point to be made about his model revolves around the contemporary class composition of urban minority communities. I cannot dispute his census data on the increasing concentration of the poor into extreme poverty zones. This would indeed seem to confirm his point that the gap between the haves and have-nots has grown as a consequence of deindustrialization and that the have-nots are increasingly squeezed into run-down urban areas.

This "concentration" finding says nothing (or at least nothing conclusive) about the existence of social institutions such as the church, which journalistic evidence would suggest is still a thriving force in black communities. Sunday mornings in poor black communities in New York City find large numbers of adults and children dressed up, walking to church. The statistics on residential composition also tell us nothing about social interaction, even though Wilson infers a great deal from them vis-à-vis questions of childhood socialization, networks, and role models. I do not know where the black business owners of central Harlem live, but it is evident to even a casual observer that they continue to do business along its main commercial throroughfares. Whether the degree of interaction between classes in black neighborhoods is greater or lesser than it was in the 1945–70 period is unclear. However, if class isolation is to be understood as a major social force leading to an upswing in persistent poverty—and there are reasons to question this thesis—the quality and character of cross-class interaction must be understood in far greater detail than compositional statistics can reveal. This alone suggests a need for renewed interest in fieldwork in the black community.

The influence of cultural relativism on studies of poverty populations has been pronounced in anthropology. The notion that one should not measure or evaluate the social practices of one group against some universal, or more likely class-bound, yardstick is an underlying theme in much of what has been written about the urban poor. This perspective is most pronounced, for example, in Carol Stack's (1974) classic, *All Our Kin,* where she argues convincingly that it is a mistake to assume that households and families are coterminous, or that the absence of husbands translates into the absence of males in black families. She points out that "the Flats" is structured by a different, but no less coherent, set of social bonds that distributes responsibilities for child-rearing across households that include both actual and fictive kin. The importance of her perspective in light of Wilson's argument is two-fold. First, it underlines the necessity of fieldwork for understanding any and all aspects of social structure. None of her findings would have been evident from a statistical portrait of residence, educational attainment, crime, or out-of-wedlock motherhood.

Second, Stack's work (in keeping with much of the other ethnographic research on the urban poor), would lead readers of *The Truly Disadvantaged* to question either the definition of the "underclass" or the extent to which its membership should be regarded as pathological.[13]

The underclass is defined mainly by income. However, in discussing the "tangle of pathology in the inner city," Wilson points to indices of black crime, teenage pregnancy, female-headed families, welfare dependency, and low educational attainment, and appears to define the underclass in terms of these variables. I have little trouble defining crime as a pathology. But to place career criminals and female-headed families side by side, as if incumbents of these categories are on equal footing in the category of the underclass strikes me as a questionable prelude to a morality play that few anthropologists would subscribe to. That such families are at increased risk for poverty is clear enough: The pathology in question is one of poverty, rather than family structure per se. This "neutral" designation has surely been applied to the spectacular rise of single-parent families and out-of-wedlock births among whites, who are also at risk for downward mobility, but who are less likely to be condemned as pathological social forms.

Nonetheless, anthropologists should be alert to Wilson's insistence that conditions of life have deteriorated in the inner city. Occupational prospects for young men and women in the poverty zones have declined sharply, given the twin disasters of deindustrialization and federal abandonment of income support programs. Wilson's point, that the social science community cannot walk away from this disaster and leave conservatives to blame the victim is well taken. However, this still leaves social scientists and policy makers of a more liberal persuasion with the burden of pinpointing the midrange social structures that link macrolevel economic decline to individual behavior, pathological or otherwise.

Moreover, the notion that the presence of success stories in the ghettos of the past and their absence in the present is responsible for cross-generational poverty identified in *The Truly Disadvantaged,* strikes me as speculative at best. Margaret Thatcher's Britain has brought about the existence, in the space of little more than a decade, of a thoroughly disenfranchised generation of white English youth who are now cresting into their late twenties and early thirties having never held a job (McDermott 1985; Massey and Meegan 1982). Astounding increases in the rates of out-of-wedlock births have been recorded for this cohort, who are the sons and daughters of stably employed working-class whites now faced with the prospect of supporting adult children for the foreseeable future. More than fifty percent of the babies born in the northern city of Manchester in 1991 were children of unwed parents. Lambeth, Nottingham, Southwark, and Liverpool all record illegitimate pregnancy rates of 45–47 percent for the same year (Manchester Guardian 1991). School dropouts with no likely prospects for employment in Britain constitute a first-generation underclass and a taste of what deindustrialization on a massive scale looks like. Crime rates have gone up and the riots that spread throughout urban Britain in the early 1980s are evidence of social dislocation on a grand scale.[14] These people are not lacking in role models: Their own parents are living proof of the tangible rewards of stable employment. This has not saved them from replicating patterns of behavior that in the United States we link to social dislocation in the urban ghettos (including the spread of heroin abuse). What this comparison should tell us is that the presence of role models, or concrete examples of success do little, if anything, to shape the social behavior of adolescents. If they are locked out of the labor market and cannot make progress, social dislocation will follow.

Clearly there is a critical need for a new generation of qualitative, comparative studies of urban poverty. The contributions for which anthropology is best known—particularly *Tally's Corner, Soulside,* and *All our Kin*—predate the major structural changes that Wilson so effectively details in his discussion of deindustrialization and inner-city dislocation. Do the marginal employment prospects Liebow points to as the source of sustenance for street-corner men still exist? Or have the transportation problems he cites as major barriers to permanent employment only worsened with the flight of industry from the central cities? Have the mainstreamers of *Soulside* fled the Washington ghetto, leaving only swingers behind, or are some inner-city areas characterized by class heterogenous, but socially antagonistic groups as Anderson's (1991) work suggests? Are the survival strategies Carol Stack so clearly describes—fictive kin networks, swapping, child sharing, and resource dispersal—still operative in the Flats? Or did those very strategies depend on economic resources, meager and fragile as they were, that are no longer in place? Much of what anthropology has to say on these issues is based on evidence gathered before the storm of deindustrialization hit the inner cities of the United States.

These "structural" questions, which speak to the social organization of the family, the impact of demography and economy on the black community, and survival strategies are urgent. Yet, as the ascendance of the interpretive perspective in contemporary anthropology reminds us, they are but a part of a larger cultural picture. Economic facts and forces do not escape the "webs of significance" elaborated by Geertz

(1973) that give them form and meaning in the lives of ghetto dwellers. The data on which the "new" analysis of poverty is based comes almost entirely from survey research sources that cannot provide a portrait of inner-city cultures. Cultural analysis is the province of symbolic ethnographers, who have the conceptual tools to examine the structures of meaning that inform the lives of those in poverty.

Were cultural anthropologists to focus attention on these issues, there is no shortage of important problems their perspective would illuminate. Racism, to take but one example, would surely figure in any cultural anthropology of the contemporary urban scene. Wilson (1987) goes to some length to show that racial antagonism cannot account for the rapid decline in living conditions in the inner cities since, compared to earlier periods, the post-1970s period created a comparatively favorable climate vis-à-vis housing, access to education, and employment discrimination. The conditions that beset inner-city minorities have worsened dramatically even as social attitudes were legally restrained. His view, that racism is not a compelling explanatory factor in the intensification of social disorder in the ghettos, has been challenged and criticized by scholars who point to continuing evidence of discrimination in domains ranging from health care to employment. Mercer Sullivan's (1989, 61) research, documents the fact that Brooklyn factories import workers from external communities rather than hire local Hispanic and African-American youth who live in the immediate vicinity. Are these findings typical, and if so, what does this tell us about the persistent significance of racial bias in explaining patterns of employment in poor neighborhoods?

Whatever the truth of these competing claims, I would argue that an interpretive, informant-centered anthropology of the black community in the inner city cannot avoid the spectre of racism. Minority resentment of bigotry, of lack of opportunity, of the institutional dominance of whites in commerce, of the criminal-justice system, of social-welfare agencies, and of a host of other spheres has been building to crisis levels in recent years. It has been amply documented in popular culture (e.g., Spike Lee's film, *Do the Right Thing*) and by some anthropologists who have been particularly interested in ethnic conflict (e.g., Sheehan 1985). An exclusive focus on structural issues is not likely to shed much light on this bitter aspect of contemporary black culture. Yet it can hardly be denied that voices are rising in minority enclaves that speak of their communities as oppressed by the power of outsiders. How does this frame of reference shape the understandings members of the underclass have of their fate? Statistics cannot provide a nuanced answer to this question. Cultural anthropology has a vital role to play in searching for it. Indeed, experience teaches that policy initiatives that fail to incorporate the "target" community's understanding of its own values and culture are not likely to be successful.

Anthropology must reclaim the center stage by adding to the examples of ethnographic engagement noted here and put its shoulder to the wheel to do more. Only when such an anthropological war on povery is launched—with due attention to geographical differences, variations in the industrial patterns of different cities, and sensitivity to local characteristics ranging from education to labor markets—will we be able to understand how the macrophenomenon of deindustrialization has shaped the social lives of the truly disadvantaged.

Blue-Collar Dislocation and Downward Mobility

The destructive side of deindustrialization is nowhere more visible than in the spectacle of shuttered factories and manufacturing ghost towns. From the northeastern steel mills to the midwestern auto plants, hundreds of businesses collapsed and millions of blue-collar jobs have disappeared over the past two decades. Manual workers accustomed to stable, well-paid jobs, have been forced into long-term unemployment (Bensman and Lynch 1987). Over half the experienced workers officially classified as "displaced" between 1981 and 1986 were blue-collar men and women (Newman 1988, 26).[15] Those still working have suffered devastating wage losses. The most recent government figures indicate that between 1979 and 1987, the real earnings of the least-educated sectors of the work force fell between 9 and 15 percent (Blackburn, Bloom, and Freeman 1989). This is indicative of the declining clout of unions and the weakened bargaining power of blue-collar labor in the face of deindustrialization.

I have already indicated some of the structural consequences of this dislocation on American communities dominated by single industries and large plants: falling tax bases, forced migration of the work force, declining services, increasing stress on those left behind. The connection between these dimensions of social dislocation and family violence (child abuse, battered wives) has not gone unnoticed in the medical and psychiatric communities, particularly among researchers interested in high blood pressure, cardiac stress, and related diseases. As Michael Blakey notes in his contribution to this volume, there is more for anthropologists to do in addressing the relationship between economic disorder and physiological manifestations of stress.[16]

For the social anthropologist, a host of unanswered questions remains about the ways in which deindustrialization reshapes working-class communities and family life. The impact of long-term unemployment and forced migration, to name only two related topics directly connected to deindustrialization, are both under researched. One is practically forced back to the Great Depression to find substantial sociological literature on these topics. There is much we can contribute to a contemporary study of blue collar downward mobility through local studies of plant shutdowns.[17] How do families adjust their relations with kinsmen and neighbors in the wake of job dislocation? What kinds of support networks exist to cushion the blows? Do these networks differ in communities that are economically diverse versus those that are dependent on single industries? How do gender roles shift in the wake of a new-found reliance on the remaining earners in the household? For how long do work-based social relationships last in the wake of a plant shutdown? These, and many other questions, can only be effectively addressed through a fieldwork methodology and, unfortunately, there is no shortage of communites in which such studies could be conducted.

For the cultural anthropologist, the intersection of deindustrialization and the meaning systems of blue-collar communities provides a new setting within which to apply the methods and insights of symbolic anthropology. Some work has been done on the ways in which structural economic failure has generated a cultural critique of a deindustrialized America. In particular, anthropological studies have shown that plant failures can occasion critical reflections on the "abandonment of tradition," a reading of economic tragedy as moral collapse (see Dudley 1994; Newman 1985; 1988). Here, again, however, there are many important questions we have yet to answer: What is the relationship between deindustrialization and identity? How do workers who have spent their entire working lives in the confines of one factory conceptualize the collapse of the economic infrastructure that defines their lives? Symbols of enduring significance inhere in industries and factories that have defined the nature of collective life in American towns from Detroit to Pittsburgh for the better part of the last century. These economic realities have an interpretive side, and, in the wake of a massive shift in resources away from the old steel towns and center of auto manufacturing, it behooves the engaged cultural anthropologist to ask how this change is symbolically manifested.

Labor economists and sociologists can give us the macropicture of deindustrialization, the statistical contours of occupational dislocation, income loss, and patterns of disinvestment. This data is critical as a contextual background for a social and cultural anthropology of blue-collar life in the 1990s. It is incumbent on anthropologists to read beyond the boundaries of our own discipline in order to be conversant in the economic facts that underpin community studies. But a complete understanding of what deindustrialization (and reindustrialization) means in the lives of blue-collar people depends on an ethnographic method to which anthropology is positioned to contribute.

White-Collar Downward Mobility

The classic portraits of deindustrialization focus on blue-collar, rust-belt communities, which is why many Americans (academics, laymen, and policy makers alike) are under the mistaken impression that the problem is class-specific and concentrated only in certain geographical regions. However, because the flip side of plant shutdowns is a concentration of capital in the form of business mergers, thousands of white-collar middle managers have found themselves standing on the unemployment lines alongside their blue-collar brethren. Indeed, over the past decade or so the number of mergers has tripled, and pink slips have flowed freely in the management ranks of the insurance, banking, brokerage, shipping, retail sales, and manufacturing industries. The United States Bureau of Labor Statistics figures show that for 1981–1986, 37 percent of the country's five million experienced displaced workers were in the managerial, professional, technical, sales, and administrative support categories. Nearly half of the displaced managers in this group had to go outside the managerial and professional occupations in order to find new jobs (Newman 1988, 43). Clearly any comprehensive understanding of downward mobility must encompass the lives of those at the top of the occupational pyramid as well as those at the bottom.

While many of these skilled, educated, long-time managers find themselves permanently unemployed, the majority do find new jobs. However, in common with the stoppage experienced by their blue-collar counterparts, these new jobs are likely to pay less, provide fewer opportunities for advancement, and subject the newly hired manager to the insecurity of being "last hired" and therefore "first fired" when belt tightening hits their industry. Even well-qualified employees with many years experience and enviable track records find themselves pushed down the occupational ladder. This is especially true for white-collar workers who are older, members of minority groups, or women—all three groups find themselves pounding the pavement longer and coming up with less in the way of replacement positions than their younger, white, male counterparts.

Anthropological research on the phenomenon of white-collar displacement is, to put it in the most flattering light, in its infancy. The world of industry and corporate bureaucracies has been the province of sociologists ever since C. Wright Mills wrote his famous analysis in *White Collar*. Nonetheless, there is a place for the ethnographic method (as Rosabeth Kanter has shown in her pathbreaking work, *Men and Women of the Corporation*). Beyond this, there is also an important place for the kind of cultural analysis that is seldom practiced by sociologists (whose interests focus more on aspects of corporate social structure). We must recognize that white-collar workers live in a symbolic world, that they, too, construct meaning out of their jobs and their misfortunes, and that it is here—perhaps more than elsewhere along the occupational spectrum—that "Americanists" will find important material on the ideological configurations of the contemporary United States.

My own research suggests that white-collar settings foster the view that "meritocratic individualism" defines self-worth and explains the fortunes of particular men and women (Newman 1988). As a moral value and a guiding principle, meritocracy begins from the perspective that the fate of an individual is under his or her own control. There is little place in this symbolic world for the economic forces of deindustrialization, the ups and downs of industry, or the behavior of the Federal Reserve Bank. These "contextual" facts are known, but they fade in importance next to the agency of individual effort where managerial workers are concerned.[18]

The general perspective of meritocracy is wedded to the view that occupation measures the internal, moral worth of an indivudual—that one's job is an accurate barometer of his or her intelligence, skills, capacity, and deservedness. Such a view breaks the category of "the deserving" into a loosely defined hierarchy of ranks and status positions, each more laudible than the next. As long as any given individual is seen as moving up this ladder, meritocratic individualism accords the manager respect and praise. The opposite trajectory—a move down the ladder— is nearly unthinkable, and surely to be condemned as a sign of failure. Failure, in turn, is conceptualized as a badge of shame, a signal of internal flaws that have surfaced in the form of a measurable drop in social and occupational status. Meritocratic individualism is harsh in its condemnation of those who have become downwardly mobile, seeing in their fate none of the structural conditions that might be beyond individual control, and placing blame squarely on the shoulders of the victim.

As these brief remarks suggest, the problem of managerial downward mobility has both an economic and a symbolic face. Anthropologists must rely on the good offices of other disciplines to provide us with the macropicture. Yet when it comes to understanding what such a large-scale transition in our economy means in the lives of real people, the tools of the interpretive analyst are indispensible. We cannot come to an understanding of the damage deindustrialization has done without paying close attention to the symbolic dimension. When approached in this way, we reinforce the view that economic facts are "lived" through cultural filters. Sometimes those filters can act to bolster the self-esteem and sense of personal worth of individuals in crisis.[19] At other moments, culture intervenes to render moral judgement and crush the spirit of the downwardly mobile. Understanding this texture, and the variation in experience it produces, is an important part of the anthropologist's task where downward mobility is concerned. The surface of this problem has barely been touched by ethnographic hands.

Conclusion

Deindustrialization is a broad, systematic process that has had a profound transformative impact on the domestic economy of the United States. Its effects are manifested in distinctive ways for groups and communities that are positioned differently across a national occupational and income spectrum. For the very poor, deindustrialization has had the consequence of removing entry-level positions from their reach, creating a mismatch between those desperately in need of jobs in the inner cities and jobs going begging in outlying suburbs. The results of the mismatch are evident in the rising levels of minority youth unemployment, and the devastating impact of economic instability on inner-cities families.

For the blue-collar worker, deindustrialization has meant the breakdown of a social contract that bound employees to paternalistic companies for generations, an end to the economic stability that has underwritten home ownership, and an end to long-term security. It has introduced blue-collar families to lurking fear of the future, a sense of helplessnesss, and a profound skepticism of the American dream. Communities have been abandoned by industries that were built out of the sweat of manual labor, severing the symbolic identity of company towns, and the material base of their survival, from the industries that put them on the map.

White-collar managers have not escaped the clutches of the business cycle, as their jobs have been gobbled up in a tidal wave of mergers and hostile takeovers. They must confront the prospect of scarcity and insecurity, even though they have played by the rules of deferred gratification and credentialism. They ask, and their children ask, what rules are there then? If this approved recipe of pursuing a higher education, working one's way up the corporate ladder, ends this way, then what is the proper message to convey to future generations? The answers are sculpted not out of thin air, but out of the cultural materials that simultaneously bind Americans together and separate them into distinctive groups.

As anthropologists, we need to understand the macrocontours of deindustrialization, poverty, and downward mobility and then take up the task we are best at: investigating the survival strategies of different communities locked in crisis. This single economic process has multiple outcomes, landing as it does on the heads of those who bring a variety of cultural perspectives and structural supports to the task of survival. Statistics and surveys cannot answer these questions: anthropological methods can. If anthropology is to reengage itself with the questions that are of uppermost policy concern in the contemporary United States, it will need to make a public commitment to take these issues up where the discipline left off in the days of the war on poverty.

Anthropologists committed to the rights of individuals, families, and communities to determine their own futures and participate in the policy decisions that impact upon their lives can do a great deal to further this goal by focusing on the consequences of economic disorder. For absent a secure livelihood, most people lack the time, energy, and power to make themselves heard in the decision-making process. One fundamental prerequisite of a meaningful democracy is a solid economic foundation that frees its members from constant worry over occupational security and financial instability. Deindustrialization poses a serious threat to democratic participation because it undermines the economic and occupational foundations upon which the poor, blue-collar workers, and the managerial middle class depend. It remains the anthropologist's task to understand what this powerful, disorganizing force means in the everyday lives of the communities we study.

NOTES

1. See Hopper (1985) for an excellent article that links the problems of urban homelessness to general trends of deindustrialization and gentrification reviewed in this chapter.

2. Recent anthropological contributions to the study of economic disorder include di Leonardo (1985), Nash (1989), Newman (1988; 1985), Fernandez-Kelly (1984), and Fernandez-Kelly and Garcia (1985) among others.

3. See Fernandez-Kelly and Garcia (1985) for a vivid example of reindustrialization in the lives of Mexican and Cuban women in the garment trade in Los Angeles and Miami counties. They make a convincing case that industrial growth in the present period often translates into low-paying, oppressive work.

4. This brief review of past literature on poverty draws heavily on a very useful appendix in Wilson's *The Truly Disadvantaged* (1987, 165–87). For further details, the reader is referred to this "state of the art" review of the literature on urban poverty.

5. See Valentine (1968) for an important anthropological critique of the culture of poverty perspective.

6. There are, of course, other political conclusions involved. One advanced by Wilson (1987) is that politicians must develop broader support for government programs by making them universal rather than race or class-specific. He argues that by targeting low-income and minority groups as prime recipients of aid, Congress set the stage for alienation and antagonism on the part of the middle class that was only too ready to support budget cuts when economic pressures mounted.

7. Wilson and his University of Chicago colleague in Anthropology, Raymond Smith, are at work on an ethnographic study of the same neighborhoods that are portrayed through survey data in *The Truly Disadvantaged*. However, this material has yet to be published.

8. Christopher Jencks (1988) has argued that the mismatch hypothesis cannot account entirely for the fortunes of black men, since those who live in suburban areas appear to fare no better than their urban counterparts in the employment market. He is more inclined to pin the blame on generally high levels of unemployment that have always had a differentially negative effect on minorities. Other studies however seem to show that black women who move to suburban communities do noticeably better in terms of employment.

9. Kasarda (1988, 188) defines a mismatch as follows: "A discordant distribution of labor qualifications vis-à-vis the qualifications required for available jobs at a particular point in time. Mismatch has both nonspatial (nationwide) and spatially specific (community) aspects. The nonspatial aspect results from transformations in the overall economy from an industrial to a postindustrial base and the corresponding shrinking demands for traditional blue-collar labor. . . . [Community] specific mismatches emerge in those areas in which transformations in local employment bases occur faster than their local labor can adapt, either through retraining or relocation."

10. Of course blacks were hardly alone in suffering the consequences of deindustrialization. Wage rates across the country fell in the years following the OPEC price increases that pushed inflation and unemployment up and forced the United States into one of its worst periods of economic contraction. As the economist Frank Levy (1987) has shown, only the impressive increases in the proportions of two-income families prevented massive downward mobility in the face of declining wages after 1973.

11. See Halle (1984) and Gans (1988) for a discussion of the origin and composition of these blue-collar home-owning suburbs.

12. A far more likely explanation for the comparative lower levels of poverty, single-parent families, crime, juvenile delinquency, educational success, and other indices of social stability in the past is to be found in Wilson's own economically driven argument. The 1945–70 period was, in general, a time of industrial growth that provided ever-increasing wage levels and employment opportunities. While minorities never benefited from this boom period as much as whites did, the expansion of manufacturing industries had a clear impact on their fortunes.

13. Herbert Gans (1989) has raised this point in his critique of Wilson's work.

14. These riots were interracial in character, with class and age creating the social glue between participants.

15. Blue-collar workers are here defined to include production, craft, and repair personnel as well as operators, fabricators, and laborers.

16. For a thorough review of the sociological literature on the physical consequences of occupational stress, see Kaufman (1982) or O'Brien (1986).

17. Newman 1985.

18. See Newman (1988, ch. 3) for further elaboration of these ideas.

19. See Newman (1986; 1988) for discussions of downwardly mobile air-traffic controllers who were able to draw on cultural imagery to bolster their battered spirits.

REFERENCES

Anderson, E. 1991. *Streetwise*. Chicago: University of Chicago Press.
Bensman, D. and R. Lynch. 1987. *Rusted Dreams: Hard Times in a Steel Community*. Berkeley: University of California Press.

Blackburn, M., D. Bloom, and R. Freeman. 1989. Research Working Paper No. 3186. Washington D.C.: National Bureau of Economic Research (November).

Blakey, M. 1994. Psychophysiological Stress and Disorders in Industrial Society. In *Diagnosing America*. Ed. S. Foreman. Ann Arbor: University of Michigan Press.

Bluestone, B. and B. Harrison. 1982. *The Deindustrialization of America*. New York: Basic Books.

————. 1984. Is Deindustrialization a Myth? Capital Mobility versus Absorptive Capacity in the U.S. Economy. *Annals of the American Academy of Political and Social Sciences* 475: 39–51 (September).

————. 1987. *The Great U-Turn*. New York: Basic Books.

Buss, T. and F. Redburn. 1983. *Mass Unemployment: Plant Closings and Community Mental Health*. Newbury Park, Calif.: Sage Publications.

di Leonardo, M. 1985. Deindustrialization as a Folk Model. *Urban Anthropology* 14:237–58.

Dudley, K. 1994. *The End of the Line*. Chicago: University of Chicago Press.

Ehrenreich, B. 1989. *Fear of Falling: The Inner Life of the Middle Class*. New York: Pantheon.

Fernandez-Kelly, M. 1984. *For We Are Sold, I and My People*. Albany: State University of New York Press.

Fernandez-Kelly, M. and A. Garcia. 1985. The Making of an Underground Economy: Hispanic Women, Home Work and the Advanced Capitalist State. *Urban Anthropology* 14:59–90.

Forces in Society, and Reaganism Helped Dig Deeper Hole for Poor. 1989. *New York Times,* July 6, 1.

Gans, H. 1988. *Middle American Individualism*. New York: Free Press.

————. 1989. *A Critique of the Concept of the Underclass*. Paper delivered at the Center for American Culture Studies, Columbia University, New York.

Geertz, C. 1973. *The Interpretation of Cultures*. New York: Basic Books.

Halle, D. 1984. *America's Working Man*. Chicago: University of Chicago Press.

Hannerz, U. 1969. *Soulside*. New York: Columbia University Press.

Harrington, M. 1962. *The Other America: Poverty in the United States*. New York: MacMillan.

Hopper, K., E. Susser, and S. Conover. 1985. Economies of Makeshift: Deindustrialization and Homelessness in New York City. *Urban Anthropology* 14 (1):183–236.

Jencks, C. 1988. Deadly Neighborhoods. *The New Republic* 198:23–32 (June).

Kasarda, J. 1988. Jobs, Migration, and Emerging Urban Mismatches. In *Urban Change and Poverty,* ed. M. McGeary and L. Lynn, 148–98. Washington D.C.: National Academy of Sciences Press.

Kaufman, H. 1982. *Professionals in Search of Work*. New York: John Wiley & Sons.

Lamphere, L. 1987. *From Working Daughters to Working Mothers: Immigrant Women in a New England Industrial Community*. Ithaca: Cornell University Press.

Liebow, E. 1967. *Tally's Corner*. Boston: Little, Brown and Co.

Levy, F. 1987. *Dollars and Dreams*. New York: Russell Sage Foundation.

More Babies Born out of Wedlock. 1991. *Manchester Guardian,* December 18, 4.

Massey, D. and R. Meegan. 1982. *The Anatomy of Job Loss*. London: Methuen.

McDermott, K. 1985. All Dressed Up and Nowhere to Go: Youth Unemployment and State Policy in Britain *Urban Anthropology* 14:91–108.

Murray, C. 1984. *Losing Ground*. New York: Basic Books.

Nash, J. 1989. *From Tank Town to High Tech: The Clash of Community and Industrial Cycles*. Albany: State University of New York Press.

Nash, J. and M. P. Fernandez-Kelly. 1983. *Women, Men and the International Division of Labor*. Albany: State University of New York Press.

Newman, K. 1985. Declining Fortunes: Anthropological Perspectives on Deindustrialization. *Urban Anthropology* 14 (1–3): special issue.

———. 1988. *Falling From Grace: The Experience of Downward Mobility in the American Middle Class*. New York: Free Press.

O'Brien, G. 1986. *Psychology of Work and Unemployment*. New York: John Wiley & Sons.

Sasson, S. 1988. *The Mobility of Labor and Capital*. New York: Cambridge University Press.

Sheehan, B. 1986. *The Boston School Integration Dispute*. New York: Columbia University Press.

Stack, C. 1975. *All Our Kin*. New York: Harper & Row.

Sullivan, M. 1989. *Getting Paid*. Ithaca, N.Y.: Cornell University Press.

Valentine, C. 1972. *Culture and Poverty*. Chicago: University of Chicago Press.

Wilson, W. 1987. *The Truly Disadvantaged*. Chicago: University of Chicago Press.

Wilson, W. and R. Aponte. 1987. Urban Poverty: A State of the Art Review. Appendix to *The Truly Disadvantaged,* 163–87. Chicago, University of Chicago Press.

Chapter 5

Psychophysiological Stress and Disorders of Industrial Society: A Critical Theoretical Formulation for Biocultural Research

Michael L. Blakey

The purpose of this chapter is to consider the use of psychophysiological stress measurements for gauging disorder in industrial societies. Its goal is to formulate a critical biocultural theory of stress, which is capable of revealing the impact of political and economic forces on human biology and health. This endeavor requires a critical examination and reformulation of extant theories of psychophysiological stress that not only reveals their political and economic influences but also positions the reformulation critically.

This chapter speaks principally to those who study human biology and health and whose theories are historically rooted in an uncritical emphasis of natural history that limits their understanding of the biology of industrial societies (Blakey 1987). The corrective being suggested here requires a greater integration of biology with the social sciences and humanistic epistemology, focusing on the psychophysiological effects of social inequity, and appealing to a broader range of social and behavioral scientists.

The author knows that he brings a unique set of social experiences and assumptions to this kind of epistemological exploration. Among these are participation in Afro-American society and an anthropological background (exemplified by historic perspectives of Douglass 1854; Cobb 1939, and as described by Drake 1980) that emphasizes the role of social conditions in regard to human variations, and criticizes theories that view causality in the opposite direction. Similar perspectives drawn from the more widely known Marxist and Boasian traditions have also been important influences. Ashley Montagu's work in social biology (Montagu 1955) presages some key aspects of this theory. A desire to end the societal conditions that bring about human inequity and to create a fairer society has also motivated this effort.

Medically defined, a disorder is a derangement or abnormality of function; a morbid physical or mental state. Intuitively, biological systems represent a basic level at which societal morbidity or disorder can be measured. Just as pathological symptoms in a constituent organ represent systemic disorders in the organism as a whole, human biological disorder may accompany relationships among the individual organisms that comprise a society. The integrity of physiological systems is inextricably tied to the sociocultural relations on which they depend, especially in highly social species like ours. The extent to which changes in sociocultural systems cause dysfunction or destruction of vital biological systems is one dimension of disorder in a biocultural system.

Biological indicators of biocultural disorder are relatively easy to measure and compare across cultures. The vital physiological needs of human beings are about the same, while sociocultural systems meet (or fail to meet) those needs in various ways *and* to varied degrees.

Figure 1 shows basic human physiological needs as they were described by Malinowski (1944) and revised by Montagu (1955). Walter Cannon argued in the 1930s that organisms are explicable as a homeostatic system, and though they are flexible systems they operate within definite functional parameters. Organisms must satisfy physical needs and the substances and environments suitable for that purpose are limited. It is normal for an organism to adapt by experiencing the heterostasis that signals physiological deprivation, by satisfying their needs, and by then returning to a homeostatic state or phase. Prolonged heterostasis results in physical disorder, dysfunction, and death. Heterostasis, both normal and pathological, is synonymous with the term *stress* as used below.

The sociocultural systems on which humans depend to meet their basic needs are at once adaptations and environments. Disorder is manifested to the extent that a sociocultural system fails to provide adequately structured relations for the attainment of the needs of its members.

Some societies and sectors of society have more restricted access to resources than do others. Potential for frustration or fulfillment varies among social groups and societal strata. Constituent individuals must make choices for balancing the full range of needs, and for some individuals

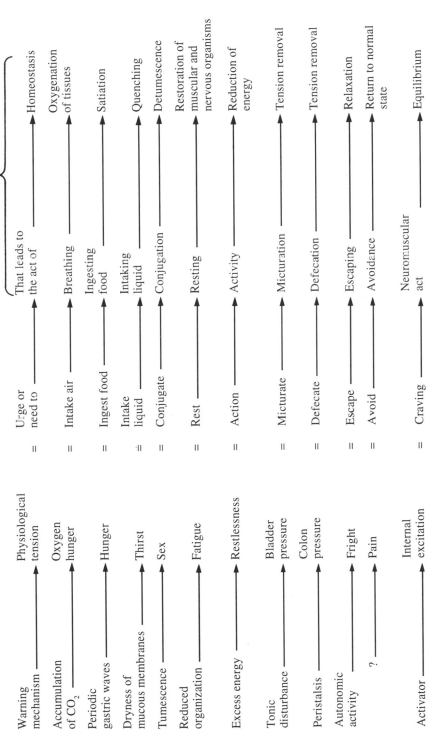

	Physiological tension		Urge or need to	That leads to the act of		Satisfaction
Warning mechanism	→	=			→	Homeostasis
Accumulation of CO_2	→ Oxygen hunger	=	Intake air	→ Breathing	→	Oxygenation of tissues
Periodic gastric waves	→ Hunger	=	Ingest food	→ Ingesting food	→	Satiation
Dryness of mucous membranes	→ Thirst	=	Intake liquid	→ Intaking liquid	→	Quenching
Tumescence	→ Sex	=	Conjugate	→ Conjugation	→	Detumescence
Reduced organization	→ Fatigue	=	Rest	→ Resting	→	Restoration of muscular and nervous organisms
Excess energy	→ Restlessness	=	Action	→ Activity	→	Reduction of energy
Tonic disturbance	→ Bladder pressure	=	Micturate	→ Micturation	→	Tension removal
Peristalsis	→ Colon pressure	=	Defecate	→ Defecation	→	Tension removal
Autonomic activity	→ Fright	=	Escape	→ Escaping	→	Relaxation
?	→ Pain	=	Avoid	→ Avoidance	→	Return to normal state
Activator	→ Internal excitation	=	Craving	→ Neuromuscular act	→	Equilibrium

Fig. 1. Montagu's homeostatic model of basic human needs and the processes by which needs are satisfied. This model is an elaboration on the schema of Malinowski (1944) and Cannon (1932).

these may be so limited that some will be met at the expense of others. Biological systems may begin to break down because of poor nutrition, disease, work, and physical-environmental stressors. Rates of morbidity and premature mortality ultimately reflect to a considerable degree the cumulative biological effects of the disorders of social systems.

Biological anthropologists have begun to use a broad range of skeletal, demographic, and physiological indicators of stress to appraise the adaptation of sociocultural and ecological systems for present and past human populations (Goodman et al. 1988). Bioarchaeological analyses, for example, have shown that the evolution of agriculture and the state often greatly increased nutritional and infectious disease stresses in comparison to hunting and gathering societies (Cohen and Armelagos 1984).

Biohistorical studies (skeletal and demographic) of one industrial society, the United States, have begun to show patterns of morbidity and mortality related to the socioeconomic conditions of African Americans in slavery and as rural and urban workers during the nineteenth and early-twentieth centuries (Corruccini et al. 1985; Rose and Hartnady 1991; Rathbun 1987; Blakey 1988; Rankin-Hill 1990). Skeletal stress indicators epitomize the infraspecific and interspecific comparability of these measures of the physical quality of life. For example, enamel hypoplasia (defective dental enamel resulting from systemic disease and nutritional stresses in childhood) has shown up in many archaeological, historical, and clinical studies. African American slaves, as well as both black and white poor working populations, exhibit frequencies of enamel hypoplasia that are among the highest recorded in human history (Lamphere 1990). These data can be compared directly, even with archaic Homo sapiens (Ogilvie et al. 1989).

For industrial populations taken as a whole, malnutrition and infectious diseases have historically given way to a proportionate increase in chronic diseases; many of which have a substantial psychosocial etiology. Comparisons of living hunter-gatherer, agricultural, and industrial societies show the highest cardiovascular effects of psychological stress to be in the latter (Eyer and Sterling 1977). Psychophysiologically mediated disorders may be of particular and increasing relevance to biomedical research in the industrial and postindustrial world. I believe the etiology of stress-related disease is best understood as an effect of social alienation.

Ashley Montagu (1955) describes both basic and *"acquired"* needs (fig. 2), including the need for secure, affective, and effective social re-

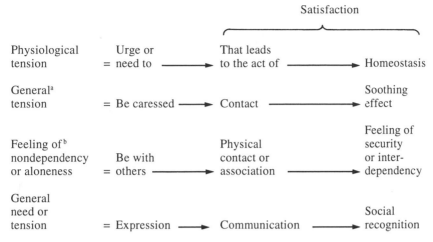

Fig. 2.   Montagu's homeostatic model of the "acquired" social needs. The tactile contingencies (*a*) are primary during infancy, while the affiliative needs (*b*) represent an abstraction of tactile and all other major social goals.

lationships. The adequacy of these social relationships regulates the homeostatic responses of the psychophysiological system discussed in this chapter. The measurement of psychophysiological activity makes it possible to gauge biologically the adequacy of social and psychological resources. Although it is important to consider the effects of an industrial society's failure to meet basic physiological requirements (including the maintenance of adequate nutritional, thermal, and respiratory conditions all of which may be compromised by poverty and pollution), I have chosen here to focus on the social and psychological, the most complex and socially sensitive biological indicator of disorder.

Stress, Sociality, and Disease

Psychophysiological stress is manifested in a broad yet distinctive range of psychosocial and physiological behaviors. The most stereotypical effects of stress include (*a*) the affective psychological states of anxiety and depression and (*b*) hormonal and neurotransmitter activity associated with such psychological states, including elevated secretion of ACTH, adrenal catecholamines and steroids, along with depressed testosterone secretion, and serotonin and endorphin activity (fig. 3).

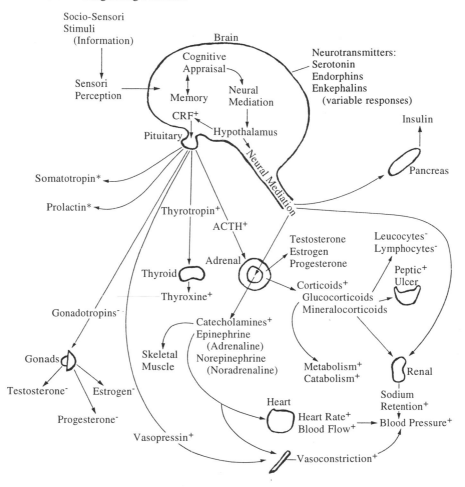

Fig. 3. The human psychophysiological system. The stereotypical cascade of neuroendocrine effects of social stress and related physiological and health effects. A negative sign indicates a reduction in levels, a positive sign indicates increased levels, and an acute increase with subsequent reduction is indicated by an asterisk.

When stressful stimuli occur, a general pattern of effects follows, beginning with a perception of threat, and leading to the stimulation of the hypothalamus. The hypothalamus releases CRF(H), (corticotropin releasing factor or hormone), which stimulates the pituitary glands to release ACTH, (adrenocorticotrophic hormone), into the blood stream.

ACTH causes a cascade-like stimulation of hormonal axes or glands, including the adrenal cortex, which releases corticoids—gluccocorticoid and mineralocorticoid—during stress. Gluccocorticoids are closely associated with immune suppressing effects, while mineralocorticoids cause retention of sodium and fluid, thus contributing to elevated blood pressure. At the same time, the hypothalamus sends neural signals to the adrenal medulla, which releases the catecholamines—epinephrine (adrenaline) and norepinephrine (noradrenaline). These hormones mediate the most obvious excitory effects of stress, including muscle tension and cardiovascular changes involved in the elevation of blood pressure. Simultaneously, neurotransmitters associated with feelings of calmness, satisfaction, gratification, euphoria, or painlessness (prominently including serotonin and beta-endorphin) are for various reasons restricted in their ability to bind at their receptor sites. All of this chemical activity is complexly associated with affective behavior.

Medical reports from Britain and the United States suggest that prolonged and frequent stress is to some extent involved in the majority of physical illnesses (Blythe 1973). This chapter focuses on two of the most clear-cut and dangerous consequences of excessive stress—cardiovascular and immunological disorders and their associated affective states.

Careful experimental research on laboratory animals has shown that psychophysiological stress dramatically suppresses the replication of white blood cells that are responsible for immune responses to infectious disease (Riley 1981). Claman (1988) has reviewed a broad and impressive range of immune inhibitory effects of psychophysiological stress based on human and nonhuman experimentation. The relationship between stressful life events and organic disease has been clearly demonstrated (see Kiecolt-Glazer and Glazer 1988 for review). Human experiments have also shown that stress causes sodium and fluid retention that precipitates an elevation in blood pressure (Light et al. 1983). Survey data (Eyer and Sterling 1977) and clinical data (Trowell 1981) suggest that the origins of hypertension can be found in an industrial society while an age-related increase in blood pressure can be found in industrial and (to a lesser extent) rural agrarian societies. Blood pressure problems do not exist among hunter-gathers. An industrial society, then, contributes significantly to the pathogenic effects of unrelieved psychophysiological stress.[1]

Psychophysiological stress, like other physiological stresses, can be understood using a homeostatic model (fig. 4). But rather than the biotic and physical environment, psychophysiological stress is a heterostatic response to the perception of inadequacies of the *social* environment.

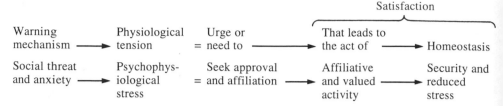

Fig. 4. Macromodel: the relationship between the psychophysiological system and social needs. The relationship between warning, need, action, and physiological homeostasis in accordance with the general scheme of Montagu (1955).

Increasingly, it appears that the inadequacies involved are best understood in relationship to the affective requirements of social mammals.

The stressors that effect these responses are *cognitively perceived* social and environmental conditions or events. A person's perceived inability to predict or control conditions or events leads one to perceive an element of *threat* and distinguishes the psychological stressor from other, nonstressful events. Cognitive specificity in the perception of psychophysiological stressors is demonstrably a more accurate explanation of stressful effect than is Selye's general adaptation syndrome (Lazarus 1975; Lazarus and Opton 1966; Mason et al. 1976).[2] If conditions or events constitute threat of harm to social relationships, then they constitute social or psychosocial stressors. I will be concerned in this chapter with the psychophysiological effects of *social* stressors.

Human Fight or Flight Stress Reassessed

Interpretive models of social stress have a social history that reveals political ties and epistemological shortcomings relative to their alternatives. Attempts to formulate theory without a critical analysis impede understanding of masked past biases and thus both facilitate their reproduction and undermine the effort to transcend them and their paradigms. Historical criticism allows one to learn from the observable cultural construction of scientific ideas (as opposed to more strictly philosophical approaches to deconstruction). In the following analyses of the "fight or flight" and "modernization" models, a critical reexamination contributes to a new construction or formulation of theory.

When Walter Cannon first described psychophysiological stress (Cannon 1963, first edition 1932), he located its physiological effects among the most important adaptations in human evolution.

The key to these marvelous transformations of the body is found in relating them to the natural accompaniments of fear and rage [resulting from contests for dominance]. . . . All these (physiological) changes are directly serviceable in the violent display of energy . . . for innumerable generations our ancestors had to meet the exigencies of existence by physical effort, perhaps in putting forth their utmost strength. The struggle for existence is a nerve and muscle struggle.

This early framing of a fight-or-flight response, stresses the aspects of energy mobilization, strength, and endurance that the psychophysiological response enhances during conflict. The Hobbesian notion of an early human society in which every man was against every man (also embodied in Malthusian and Spencerian ideas) was dominant during Cannon's time. Psychophysiological stress was seen as a configuration of physiological changes that gave an individual a surge of energy for escape or attack—in adaptive response to circumstances. Salient circumstantial elements could include natural physical hazards or the organisms with whom one competed for rank or mates, members of other groups competing for territorial dominance, or predators whom one fought or fled in order to survive. In the early twentieth century (and presently in Wilsonian sociobiology) life-or-death competition for social dominance, mates, and survival had been stressed as the main selective force and stimulus of progressive evolution. Indeed, the perception of stress as a special burden of competitive corporate executives is related to these evolutionary notions. Thus, Lenart Levi (1971) could explain that the stress of modern life derives from an antiquated physiological mechanism for agonistic (fight or flight) display that is poorly adapted to the civilized and restrained society in which we now find ourselves. He argued that we cannot cope with the stresses of industrial life through the display of aggressive energy as we once did, but that the hostility intrinsic to humankind is suppressed to the point where it causes damage in a fast-paced, rapidly changing, yet civilized society. McClean's triune brain model (1958; 1968) shares the assumption that an anatomically distinct paleomammalian seat of emotion (the limbic system), *causes* fear and aggressiveness. Our biological adaptations thus conflict with our civilization, which serves, imperfectly, to subordinate our primordial instinct to fight or flee whenever fear is sensed.

While energy mobilization for fight or flight does appear to be an adaptive property of the psychophysiological system, I argue that this is not its specific nature. Psychophysiological stress is a *general* fear response that has long been as adaptive for social as for physical fears. Understanding its socially adaptive and maladaptive significance provides a more cogent understanding of the current causes of stress-related disorders than does its conceptualization as a primordial system adapted for physical responses to agonistic situations.

The psychophysiological system has not evolved for aggressive/competitive interactions alone but also for affective/cooperative interactions. The ills of stress (obviously the effects of maladaptation) are the result of constraints that civilization has imposed on the latter adaptive needs. If the physiological stress response is outdated, it is not because it is difficult to cope aggressively. Rather, it is because the lack of secure social and affective relationships like those characterizing most of our evolution as hunter-gatherers has made it difficult to cope. This paints a very different picture of human adaptation from that on which the fight-or-flight concept was framed.

A contemporary understanding of hominid evoluton and the hunter-gatherer way of life is supportive of something more like a *social maintenance* stress paradigm than fight or flight. Hominids are a physically vulnerable and deeply interdependent social species and cooperation is key. Competition and hostility are minimized among hunter-gatherers. Lancaster and Lancaster (1983) argue from an analysis of primate energetics that food *sharing* was more essential to hominid adaptation than was competition. That view follows on Lovejoy's (1981) while moderating that author's overemphasis on male hunting in early hominid society. J. Desmond Clark (1970) pointed to the fact that the paleoanthropological and early archaeological record is characterized by site types and tool assemblages for the exploitaton and sharing of food. Clark (1970, 64–67) contrasts his view with Robert Audrey's (1961) (and possibly, Raymond Dart's [1959]) early guess that the broken animal bones associated with early African hominids must have been weapons of war and interpersonal strife (also see the critique of Montagu 1976).

Audrey's and Dart's perspectives were contemporaneous with Cannon's and Selye's framing of the fight-or-flight paradigm, and the sway of Hobbsean notions that would eventually lead to Audrey's concept of humankind as the spawn of killer apes or a similar characterization in Konrad Lorenz's "Das Sogenannte Bose" published in 1966 as *On Aggression*. It does not seem irrelevant that both Cannon's and Lorenz's writings closely followed their personal experiences in the midst of war.

Indeed, Jane Goodall (Goodall et al. 1979) has shown that a group of our nearest hominoid relatives, the chimpanzee, while engaging in group combat for one brief period in the course of nearly twenty years of study, were for the most part peaceful, accommodating, and profoundly sensitive to their own social relationships. What is more, very little competitiveness, status differentiation, or warfare exists among living hunter-gatherers, even those living on scarce desert (Lee and Devore 1976) or arctic resources (Balikci 1970).

The changes in relationships between neurological systems that have made the limbic system (McClean's "paleomammalian" brain) other than the "seat of aggression" must also be considered. It may well be that the limbic system in general and the amygdala in particular, evolved from early mammalian and premammalian structures that closely resembled them in form, yet primarily served as a fight-or-flight adaptation. Our complex learning and rational processes emerged with the evolution of what McClean (1968) calls the "neomammalian" brain, or cerebral cortex. There seems to have been a simple fallacy of Cartesian reductionism in which the earlier-evolved structure is attributed with (1) structural autonomy, (2) immutable functional continuity, and (3) the ability to take precedence over subsequently evolved structures (such as the cerebral cortex), even if only rarely and with difficulty (as in the emergence of aggressiveness). Not only can it be argued that cognition strongly *influences* the neural and chemical responses taking place in the limbic and endocrine systems (note the pathway of effects in figure 3), but these systems have been functionally altered—are new systems—because of their integration within a brain that is on a whole different from their predecessors' brain. Humans cannot survive with a "paleomammalian brain" alone.

The human brain is a unique and integrated system. It is not part rodent or lizard, but entirely hominid. The whole of this brain is not only different from the sum of its parts, but its parts are different *as parts* from what they would be if they were isolated wholes, by virtue of their integration within the unique relationships of a new system. We now have a brain that functions for the social life to which hominids have evolved and that is responsive to the conditions set forth by its biological and cultural evolution. Richard Lewontin and his colleagues (Levins and Lewontin 1985; Lewontin et al. 1984) have made good use of this contrast between dialectical and deterministic biology in their writings.

The difference between fight or flight vs. cooperation or death (as the sociality maintenance model might be characterized) is very important for the development of a methodology, appropriate for understanding the social etiology of stress in industrial societies. If suppressed hostility is shown to be the main stress component of the type A personality or shown to be in the etiology of hypertension in African-American men (Harburg et al. 1973), is it that the beast within black men is unable to contend with a civil world; or is it that *all* humans are socially sensitive organisms, frustrated and enraged by the inaccessibility and unpredictability of social gratification and security in what, for *some,* must be a beastly world? Much of today's interpersonal violence can most possibly be accounted for by the failure of social structures and cultural values to provide adequate means to satisfy the needs that they themselves specify for a sense of social effectiveness (influence), recognition, and affection.

Looking back on the evolutionary scenarios of the first third of the twentieth century, it becomes clear that the competitive, socially irresponsible, laissez-faire attitudes engendered by a culture of capitalism were imposed on a primitive past to which these, our baser instincts, were attributed. Today the evidence of that past points toward an opposite conclusion, that humanity is best adapted to a more cooperative and supportive social environment than prevails in the industrial world, and that the "beast" conceived *in* the industrial world and extrapolated to earlier human evolution actually exists in that industrial world rather than in biological vestiges of an imagined past. In this light it seems that sociality and civilization (in its current state) may be in conflict rather than in concordance, and that psychophysiological stress reflects that dissonance. Most importantly, if this is the case, causes and solutions are to be sought in the organization of society rather than in biological remedies. Thus, we arrive at another important feature of a critical approach: it is possible to hold human biology up to society as its mirror, equally showing in biology the social disorders whose amelioration would improve a people's health.

Social Etiology of Stress

A clearer etiology emerges from what we now know about the major social causes of stress and disease in industrial society. Exit or social-separation events have been shown to be the most severe and negative stressors known. These events undermine an individual's sense of control over his or her environment (Paykel 1973; Schroufe 1979) and in the presence of vulnerability factors (such as a low sense of mastery or control, childhood separations, unemployment, and attempting to raise several children alone [Brown and Harris 1978]), separation events are the most likely of all stressors to lead to clinical depression.

Social-separation events (or exit events) are also prominent among the stress factors that comprise social instability status (SIS) and are indicated by high rates of separation and divorce, migration, and institutionalization of family members. These factors were furthermore positively correlated with elevated blood pressure in the Detroit studies conducted by Earnest Harburg and his associates (1978a, 1978b), and are correlated with variation in stroke mortality (related to hypertension) in James' and Klienbaum's study of rural North Carolina. Unemployment (based on the SIS rating) can also be considered an exit event that typically results in the loss of affective *and* instrumental social relationships that in turn lead to social-role and economic limitations that restrict further social network engagement. High SIS is generally associated with low socioeconomic status (SES), revealing the impact of the economy on social and psychophysiological well-being. Livingstone and colleagues (1991) show that blood pressures in a large African American survey are lowest in those who have the strongest group affiliations (including churches and informal groups) as well as access to supportive others. Gary and associates (1989) point out that depression has a social etiology similar to the social etiology of high blood pressure, and both studies correlate the effects of high stress with low income and unemployment.

Conversely, social support appears to be the most effective buffer (the opposite of vulnerability factors) to the ill effects of stressors. "Confidants" (persons in whom one can trust, to whom one can reveal personal loss, and from whom one can acquire emotional support) help facilitate one's ability to cope by reinforcing the sense of self worth, social acceptance, and control (Brown and Harris, 1978). They satisfy one's need to know that they "are not alone" in a time of crisis. Absence of support increases one's vulnerability to stress—elevating the stressfulness of life events and the likelihood of clinical, psychological, and physical symptoms. Some researchers have even begun to view the quality of support as the main predictor of stress effects, rather than the "life events" or the stressors themselves. Researchers have increasingly emphasized the role of poor social supports in the etiology of stress-related psychological and organic disorders (Dohrenwend and Dohrenwend 1984; Goodman 1984; Gore 1984; Livingstone 1991).

If poor social supports and life events involving unwanted social disengagements are most strongly associated with psychophysiological heterostasis (stress)—while support and coherent, gratifying, and empowering social relationships are commonly associated with the homeostatic nonstressful state—our view of organic systems changes. The psychophysiological system is better understood as a homeostatic system for the regulation and maintenance of human sociality (the tendency to be attracted to and exist together with members of one's own species) than for aggression and competitiveness. Humans modulate from the perception (and consequent physiological effects) of being highly stressed to the perception and neuroendocrinological effects of calm; from anxiety or depression to a sense of security and mastery; from social alienation to social support; from heterostasis to homeostasis to heterostasis, and so forth. Most humans (and perhaps other socially sensitive mammals) probably undergo these fluctuations frequently during social intercourse as they continuously monitor their social relationships. As with any other homeostatic physiological system, the most adaptive behaviors involve short-term heterostasis within a benign range of fluctuation, leading to effective environmental interactions that rapidly reestablish homeostasis.

Simply put, acutely perceived threats of social disengagement (including such things as expressions of disapproval or threat of ostracism) or short-term exits (such as temporary maternal separations) create a physiological tension that helps motivate social reengagement (attachment behavior, or behaviors that enhance one's chances of desired social interactions, e.g., more appropriate role behavior, status enhancement, or socializing with friends). This system then becomes part of the glue that binds society.

In human society access to social resources is achieved by means of symbolic communication (including both language and the use of material symbols) of one's social value or affiliations in accord with the norms, roles, and values of particular cultures (Schachter, 1959 has commented on the perceived relationship between an individual's existing and future social affiliations). Another way of expressing this is that social support (broadly defined) is not randomly distributed but is customarily reciprocal when one performs favorably in the terms of his or her culture. Montagner and co-workers (1978) found that adrenal hormones associated with stress were negatively correlated with the quality of social support and social status among French school children. Steklis and Raleigh (1984) show similar findings in monkeys. Experimental alterations in social status also altered support (grooming).

In this respect the psychophysiological system also motivates learning, whether enculturative or acculturative. In this sense, culture can be understood as the inventory of symbolic means of communicting and modifying one's relationships with others, relationships that are at once social, psychological, and physiological. When gratified, one is socially secure and homeostasis has been achieved. If admonished or threatened with alienation, heterostasis motivates behavioral modification. In these respects, *transient* stress is adaptive.

We may conclude that psychophysiological stress has both adaptive and maladaptive effects. Stress is adaptive when an individual is alerted to its social insecurity or the threat of alienation from the social group or significant others on whom it depends for its existence. Coping may be precultural as in the lost-baby cries of all primate young who become separated from their care giver and need reassurances of social support. That support may also be conveyed by the care giver through precultural, tactile communication that involves the provision of bodily warmth through an embrace, or rocking (whether given deliberately in cradled arms or casually by carrying the child). The similarity of these responses to the intrauterine environment, it is plausible to suggest, communicates the familiar, predictable, and secure, to the infant. The psychophysiological effects of anxiety are relieved, the child has coped, and the stress response has been adaptive. The work of the Harlowes (1965), and of Montagu (1955) support this view.

Later in development, human children seek reassurances of social support through enculturated means. They "perform" according to the cultural expectations, first of parents and subsequently of an expanding sociocultural context that includes their peers, their community and the institutional groups with which they affiliate. Although there is a remarkable cross-cultural unity in what are considered appropriate social behaviors (such as economic productivity and sociocultural reproduction), precise specifications of the behaviors are culturally determined and often culturally varied. A child's role in educational, or ritual performance elicits socially gratifying responses from others. Social others may continue to express and/or provide that gratification through tactile means, or through the symbolic communication of praise through language, gifts, or passage to new and rewarding social affiliations and roles. On the other hand, there may be ostracism or rejection expressed through corporal punishment, isolation of the child, or symbolic expressions of disapproval. To the extent that children receive reassurances of social support and social gratification, they sense their social effectiveness and security. Psychophysiological tension is relieved, the child has coped, and the stress response has been adapted. Not only has their performance been socially cooperative but they have also learned; and both the socialized and the socializers will be gratified at their mutual success in reproducing their familiar/predictable or desired culture.

Continuous societal rejection or ambiguity in response to these attachment behaviors (broadly defined) causes prolonged stress, a poor sense of environmental mastery, and affective disorder in children (Rutter 1972). Vulnerability to later stresses may also be increased by the development of a "cognitive set" in which an individual perceives him/ herself to be less able to cope with or control the social challenges of adulthood. Those challenges become more threatening and stressful by virtue of these perceptions of control. The tendency to give up, increases as the individual assesses his or her inability to cope and the risk of clinical depression is increased (Brown and Harris 1978). Seligman (1975) uses the term *learned helplessness* to describe analogous development of affective behaviors and organic symptoms of stress in experimental animals.

This social-psychological-physiological process continues to modulate throughout one's social life. At its most adaptive or homeostatic, it motivates learning, productivity, and cooperation. The stress effects of anxiety—elevated ACTH, adrenal catecholamines and steroids—are brief. At its least adaptive or most heterostatic, this process entails social alienation, an emergent sense of hopelessness and helplessness, prolonged or frequent psychophysiological arousal, and ultimately psychological and organic disease. *Long-term* heterostasis is associated with a perception of powerlessness, an inability to cope, and physiological wear and tear. The inability to cope and relieve stress by achieving and maintaining socially gratifying roles, identities, and social relationships, is essential to the etiology of pathogenic stress or, in Selye's terminology, distress.

The roles and identities that individuals aspire to vary from one culture to another. We see that once the particular values of a society are entered into the stress equation, the motivational and pathogenic aspects of stress develop similarly across cultures. The following section is a reassessment of the stress effects of cultural change based on the theory formulated here. The social ambiguities of acculturation enter into the etiology of distressed communities. Also important, however, are the particular limitations placed on the acquisition of secure and satisfactory social status conditioned by the cultural values and economic structure generated by Western industrial captialism, within which most cultural groups have become integrated.

Stress, "Modernization," and Inequity

An extreme form of stress pathology (i.e., shock) is manifested in cases of "magical death" in Australia that is the result of ostracism and social separation (more like social death) in response to improprieties or inadequacics in role and ritual performances. Eastwell (1982) has described the culture-specific "life-events" associated with the fear of sorcery and social death (fig. 5). Rivers (1922) first explained "Vodoo death" as part of a "giving up" syndrome resulting from the ambiguities in appropriate behavior, social separations, a consequent "meaninglessness of life" due to colonization, Western acculturation, and coerced labor. Vodoo or magical death represents a formalized expression of the social, psychological, and physiological consequences of social misconduct.

The case of widespread depression among Mornington Islanders off the Australian coast is similar to River's observations of the effects of colonization and cultural change. Ecological perturbation and colonial law increasingly prevented men from performing important roles (food producer, warrior, and polygamous husband); thus leading to widespread depressive illness (Cawte 1979). This example illustrates how the imposition of social restrictions on whole populations starkly limited their ability to cope. We are left with the question: What of the effects of unemployment on role performance in New York or London where employment constitutes one of the most fundamental grounds of social worth and influence?

Modernization studies show similar effects of affective disorder, social disruption, and alcoholism among Native Americans and others caught between the destruction of their traditional values and their experience of discrimination and poverty within the broader industrial society into which they are incorporated at the bottom rung (Spindler 1977). Stress effects are especially pronounced among unskilled and semiskilled occupational strata, whatever their cultural background (Eyer and Sterling 1977).

Psychophysiological stress studies of modernization have produced

Life Event Precipitating Fear of Sorcery Syndrome	Number of Patients
Sudden death of close clan relative	8
Serious illness of close clan relative	5
Disputes over acquisition of second and third wives	5
Promiscuity with married women	5
Life-threatening accident to patient (motor vehicle, electric shock, lightning strike)	3
Dispute with wife's lover	2
Promiscuity of sons	1
Murder of opponent in interclan spear fight	1
Unwitting desecration of ceremony ground	1
Ceremonial "mistakes" by father	1
Severe physical illness	1
Tribal healers accused of causing deaths	2
Unknown (precipitants not investigated)	4
	39

Fig. 5. Eastwell's description of life events perceived as evidence of sorcery and precipitating "voodoo death" in Australia. Most of these events contain prominent elements of social disruption, separation (exit events), loss, and threat to sociocultural goals and status, similar to severe events involved in the etiology of depression in Western cultural contexts.

results consistent with those expected from the approach described here, but explain them differently. American Samoans migrating from rural agrarian communities to engage in the urban labor-wage economy, show an increase in blood pressures (McGarvey and Baker 1979). Harburg and associates (1982) and Ward (1983) show similar changes in blood pressures in several Pacific-island populations undergoing industrialization and rural-urban migrations. The classic study by Scotch (1963) showed a similar trend for urban vs. rural South-African blacks. And Brown (1981; 1982) showed an increase in catecholamine excretion in a sample of urban Filipino-Americans in Hawaii when compared with rural Filipino-American counterparts. The "transitional group," those with the poorest English-language skills, educational attainment, and other indices of "acculturation" were the most physiologically aroused of the urban groups. Brown found lower catecholamine levels in those who were successfully acculturated and were participating in a middle-class lifestyle.

Modernization theory characterizes these rural groups as adapted to a traditional life-style. The urban wage-laboring groups have been viewed as being in transition—undergoing acculturation and unable to participate fully in their new culture. Transitional acculturation is treated as a stressor because it constitutes dramatic change and a heterostatic point in the process of modernization, complete adjustment to which is presumed inevitable. While this explanation is consistent with the expectation of a high level of stress under conditions of ambiguous social cues, I argue that taking economic factors into consideration, it is likely that large segments of these populations will *continue* to be excessively stressed, not because of their inability to acculturate or fully participate in an urban-industrial society, but because they integrate and participate *fully* in the lowest socioeconomic strata where they, like the indigenous population, will continue to live under the least secure and least socially gratifying conditions that such societies present.

Two erroneous assumptions have impeded our understanding of this phenomenon: (1) that physiological homeostasis in an organism is analogous to the acculturation of populations and (2) that acculturation (modernization) and acquisition of middle-class membership (upward socioeconomic mobility) are equivalent. Although the first assumption is most closely associated with the biological anthropologist's view and the second with the sociocultural anthropologist's view, they are closely related epistemologically, and are ideologically similar. The following reassessment of these assumptions reveals the economic dimensions of stress in industrial society.

The problem with the first assumption is that psychophysiological stress differences in migrant populations categorized by the extent of their exposure to new conditions of modernization, (differences in indices of acculturation) are approached as though they represent effects occurring at different points in time *to a single organism* or homeostatic physiological system. In fact, each category (such as traditional, transitional, or acculturated) contains a distinguishable group of distinct organisms. Some undergo persistent psychophysiological heterostasis and rapid onset of psychological and physiological disorder and high morbidity and mortality. Others remain relatively homeostatic with more attenuated periods of heterostatic flux and lower disease risk.

Over time, some members of the former highly stressed group will acculturate, modernize, and (more importantly) achieve social and economic mobility, in effect becoming like the latter group. Others will remain in the same social stratum under similar conditions throughout their lives, as will most of their immediate descendants. Neither these classes nor the individuals who comprise them can be said to undergo adaptation in the sense that a single, acclimatizing organism does.

Furthermore, whether or not these particular individuals or groups move from one social stratum to another seems no more important than the structural persistence of these strata. Large populations, whoever they are and wherever they come from, are *continuously* exposed to the stressful conditions of the lowest strata so long as the larger political-economic system maintains its structural integrity. An exploited working class and surplus labor define and maintain the capitalist mode of production. A less-stressed elite profits from low wages paid workers on the one hand and close association of consumerism and social status that motivates spending on the other.

Regarding the second false assumption, the concepts of both acculturation and modernization confound cultural and economic-class attributes. A leading medical anthropology text indicates that modernization means "emulating the lifestyle of people—colonists, soldiers, diplomats, the urban elite who have material goods, leisure, and privilege" (McElroy and Townsend 1989, 343–44). Successful acculturation in a Westernized industrial capitalist society (i.e., modernization) is also described as synonymous with acquiring a middle-class lifestyle in which traditional and transitional individuals have yet to participate fully (Brown 1982; Spindler 1977). The stresses of acculturation and modernization are in larger measure stresses of frustrated aspirations for class mobility. Furthermore, the connotations of the term *modernization* confound mobility with inevitable social and technological progress, which in turn falsely suggests the inevitability of class mobility. The ideological content of these concepts is profound (MacClennon in this volume addresses several related aspects). Rather than attributing stress to the inaccessibility of upward economic mobility and economic security in class stratified societies, stress is attributed to the oppressed's resistance to the acquisition of, or lack of participation in, modern culture. A recent reassessment of the salience of the explanatory power of modernization adheres to this ideology nonetheless, where "lifestyle stress" is viewed as a result of a "discrepancy between economic resources and a modern lifestyle (color television, stereo, vacation travel, newspaper reading).

> Dressler and his associates (1987) found that it was not modernization itself but modernizing beyond one's means that affected blood pressure. (McElroy and Townsend 1989, 344)

If one were to explain the stress-related high blood pressures of economically disadvantaged blacks and whites in the United States (Harburg et al. 1978a; 1978b; James and Klienbaum 1976) in the same terms as for the Brazilians discussed above, the obfuscation of the stresses of class inequity by modernization language would become obvious. The empirical results of the quoted study (Dressler 1987) are consistent with the expected association between social inequity and stress, while its language and interpretation neutralize any social criticism those results might have suggested. "Modernizing beyond one's means" is an epistemologically and politically distinct alternative to characterizing such populations as *striving for a socioeconomic status that is for the most part unattainable due to the exploitative character of capitalist class relations.* Parenthetically, these conceptualizations of cultural dissonance are also analogous to explaining the ill effects of stress as a result of personal dissonance between one's aggressive, primitive impulses and the social constraints of civilization that Cannon, Levi, and McClean articulated.

These errors are all the more troubling when one considers that, historically, the term *traditional* has often been used as a euphemism for *primitive* and *savage;* and that *modernization* has meant *Westernization,* which has in turn been understood as synonymous with *civilization.* Early in this century, anthropolgists questioned the non-European's ability to adapt to civilization; an ability often equated with economic success. The Boasians, however, believed acculturation could (and probably would) be total (Blakey 1987). Interestingly, these influences preface modern syntheses of biological and cultural anthropological theory that attribute stress to a population's difficulty in adjusting to modern life, while disguising structured social and economic inequity as variations in "cultural" attainment.

The cultural embeddedness of this line of reasoning is clear. Euro-Americans (far more than Afro-Americans, for example) usually deny that significant structured barriers interfere with upward socioeconomic mobility. While this view is consistent with their individualism (see Peacock in this volume, ch. 1) and the legitimating ideology of freedom, meritocracy, and equality, it is at odds with material facts (Jaynes and Williams 1989, 113–60).

Modern industrial societies are not equally stressful for all. Stress in immigrant groups will be better understood when the stresses of the particular social stratum or class into which they integrate are considered as a distinct problem of industrial society. Yet most modernization studies conducted by physical anthropologists are concerned wth "human adaptability" and ignore socioeconomic variation as though it were contaminating statistical noise. Similarly, sociocultural and medical anthropologists tend to emphasize cultural change rather than intrasocietal economic inequity.

Studies of sedentary industrialized populations show that the frequencies of stressful life-events, social instability variables, and vulnerability factors (mentioned previously) are negatively correlated with socioeconomic status in Britain (Blakey 1985; Brown and Harris 1978) and the United States (Eyer and Sterling 1977; Harburg et al. 1978; James and Klienbaum 1976). Also correlated with income and these stressors are rates of crying relative to laughter (Inkles 1970), psychiatric disorder (Fried 1969), clinical depression (Brown and Harris 1978), stroke mortality (James and Klienbaum 1976), elevated blood pressure and hypertension (Harburg et al. 1978a; 1978b), sleep latency, anxiety, depressed mood, and low self esteem (Blakey 1985). Furthermore, since 1900 economic cycles or modulating rates of unemployment in the United States have been mimicked precisely by rates of suicide and ulcer deaths (Eyer and Sterling 1977). Liem and Liem (1979) have shown the socially disruptive and depressive effects of unemployment.

What I am suggesting is that psychophysiological stress also corresponds largely to status and income variation because the means of social gratification and perceived security in an industrial, capitalist society are most frustrated for the poorest populations. Not only are individuals motivated (often directly by advertising agencies) to seek material symbols of the bourgeoisie as both means and reassurances of their access to social support, but successful performance of other culturally derived roles such as father, mother, wife, husband, man, and woman is powerfully influenced by one's economic means.

What is more, these are societies that create surplus labor in order to sustain industrial profits. Unemployment denies individuals the ability to achieve most of the basic material requirements for acceptable role performance, identity, or acquisition of the material symbols of social status. The ability to elicit gratifying social relationships is strictly limited by the inability to work, even for low wages.

At worst, the threats of economic insecurity are fully realized by homeless and malnourished populations. Their physical, nutritional and disease stresses are compounded by the cognitive perception of their insecure status. While psychiatric and physical illness has put many at risk of unemployment and homelessness, the reverse is also obviously true.

One's position in the economy affects the risk or frequency of such profound social insecurity. For example, semiskilled and unskilled laborers experience the lowest employment security. Immigrant and nonwhite workers find themselves disproportionately within these least stable economic strata with few governmental protections for temporary and illegal workers.

The following study uses variables suggested by the sociality maintenance model, in an industrial society (Britain) with many strong parallels with the United States. It emphasizes that, while immigrant populations are involved, much of their stress results from class barriers and racial discrimination similar to that experienced by sedentary populations.

The London Stress Study

A survey was conducted in a sample ward in Brent Borough, London to test whether or not there is a substantial sense of hopelessness among the working class, particularly the black working class and whether measurable stress effects are associated with perceptions of social and economic control. One hundred and thirty questionnaires were distributed by a random door-to-door survey of households, producing a 50 percent return rate.

The Brent ward where the primary data for this study were obtained is similar to communities Gwaltney (1981) calls "core black culture" in an Afro-American context. It has relatively large West Indian and Asian populations, is highly urbanized, and predominated by skilled and semi-skilled workers. Although the unemployment rate is high, it has a relatively large proportion of private-home ownership (Shepherd et al. 1974). It is not as mean a place as poorer multiethnic communities in East and South London, or the cavernous, concrete estate-housing complexes visible in the adjacent ward. I spent six months in Brent during the winter and spring of 1980.

The household survey and interviews were primarily concerned with stressors and in highlighting difficulties that may convey a less-than-comprehensive depiction of this community's way of life. These data, however, may accurately reflect part of the real and pervasively darker side of one of the better places where black Londoners live. I was often struck by the droning expression of woundedness, loss, and sometimes, desperation underlying their outward pleasantness and hospitality. One could often sense an admixture of courage and despair in peoples' attitudes.

In this analysis, the sample of Brent blacks and whites, combined, is divided into high- and low-helplessness groups (table 1). The high helplessness sample consists of those who reported they had "often" felt "helpless to improve finances, . . . relations at work . . . or . . . social life" during the preceding six months. To feel such helplessness seems remarkably severe. The low helplessness sample "never" or "rarely" felt powerless to enhance or control these broadly articulating means of social fulfillment.

Helplessness is significantly ($p < .02$) correlated with the frequency of feelings of anxiety and tension, depression, recurrent worries, and the length of time required to fall asleep at night (sleep latency). There is a stronger association between sleep latency and worries (mean hours of 1.5 and 0.35 in the "often" and "never" or "rarely" worries groups, respectively). Helplessness also correlates with the incidence of stress-related illnesses (see WHO report, *Acta Psychsomatica* in Blythe 1973).

In addition to psychological state and health, several social factors were related to helplessness. The proportion who reported high helplessness differed by ethnic group. Asians, $n = 4$, and blacks, $n = 20$, reported the highest responses, followed by the English, $n = 22$, and then the Irish, $n = 9$ (table 2). This order reflects the income levels of the ethnic groups studied (English people living in this community were among the lowest income groups for whites in England generally). As shown in table 1, income and helplessness are negatively correlated.

TABLE 1.   Social Factors and Stress Effects in Relation to Hopelessness/ Helplessness Self-Reports

Self-Report	High Helplessness			Low Helplessness		
	N	(n)%	s.d.	N	(n)%	s.d.
Anxiety and tension**	23	(14) 61%	—	28	(7) 25%	—
Depression***	27	(12) 44%	—	22	(2) 9%	—
Recurrent worrying thoughts****	16[a]	(10) 62%	—	28[a]	(3) 10%	—
Sleep latency in hours****	16[a]	.87	.67	19[a]	.25	.16
Self-esteem score****	28	8.14	3.53	20	12.05	2.60
Income in pounds*	11	3,829	957	14	4,658	142
Divorce and separation	11	(7) 64%	—	11	(4) 36%	—
Married	21	(10) 48%	—	21	(11) 52%	—
Two or more stress-related illnesses***	27	(17) 64%	—	22	(3) 14%	—
Two or more other diseases***	27	(15) 55%	—	22	(4) 18%	—
Stress-related illnesses per person	27	1.74	1.42	22	.50	1.02
Migraine	27	(7)	—	22	(5)	—
Hypertension	27	(5)	—	22	(5)	—
Nervous disorder or breakdown	27	(5)	—	22	(1)	—

Source: Self-esteem scale from: Rosenberge, ML and RG Simmons (1973) Black and White Self-Esteem: The urban school child. New York: Arnold and Rose Publishers.

Note: $*p = .05$, $**p = .02$, $***p = .01$, $****p = .005$, using single tailed χ^2 or t-test where appropriate
[a]excludes Asians (who have exceedingly high average worry and sleep latency scores)

The negative correlation between perceived helplessness and self esteem ($p < .005$) is supportive of the assumption that socioeconomic goal frustration strongly influences the sense of social worth, covarying with stress effects. Further support for the association between self-esteem and stress surfaced in the series of interviews and discussions with people in the community. One person believed that "stress is inferior complex" while others associated stress with devaluation by employers and members

TABLE 2.   Ethnicity in Relation to Perceived Helplessness

	High Helplessness		Low Helplessness	
Asian	100%	($n = 4$)	none	
West Indian (Black British)	60	($n = 12$)	40	($n = 8$)
English	48	($n = 10$)	52	($n = 12$)
Irish	33	($n = 3$)	67	($n = 6$)

of the community. The most stressed, according to neighbors, were those who were often concerned with their failure to "keep up with the Joneses" in cars, clothing, property, and other objects of value. Unsocial behavior (noticeably minimized interaction with neighbors) or petty expressions of social competition were often associated.

These differences are a result of the economic differentiation and decline common to all British ethnic groups. Excessive economic inequity and immobility in the black community, resulting in the highest stress levels, derives from past and persisting discrimination (Moore 1975; Runnymeade Trust 1980).

Racism, Socioeconomic Frustration, and Stress in Britain

Racial discrimination disproportionately relegates blacks and other oppressed minorities to the most unstable and least mobile strata in such industrial capitalist nations as the United States and Britain, and in addition, discrimination resulting from racial stereotyping introduces its own peculiar dimension of unpredictability to the perceptions of social performance and rewards.

Three primary characteristics of a stressor or threat pertain to racist encounters: (1) the element of unpredictability or lack of control over (2) the apparent potential harm to (3) a basic need or meaningful goal. The expected positive relationship between work effort and reward is to some extent negated by the stereotypes that employers, for example, introduce in the evaluation of employees. The expression of racism and the imposition of stereotype at once communicates that the worker has less predictable control over the appraisal of the quality of his or her work and consequent rewards, that he or she is not socially accepted, and is, therefore, at risk of not achieving important social and economic goals within that or any related context. They have little control over who they "are" to the other. Interviews of blacks in the London Stress Study showed that persons were aware of these aspects of racism at all ages throughout the life cycle (Blakey 1985). Sutherland and Harrell (1986–87) revealed psychophysiological stress responses in Afro-Americans resulting from subtle experimental racist encounters. As would be expected, those blacks who were least prepared and who least expected to encounter racism experienced the highest psychophysiological responses.

The attitudes and behaviors of those white British who control social and economic resources are important components of the social environment of blacks, and during the present economic crisis social relations with and among blacks are affected by the stress and frustration experienced by whites.

It appears that the dimensions of white racism had steadily worsened in Britain. Studies in the 1960s and early 1970s showed that between 33 and 15 percent of whites were relatively free of prejudice but that suddenly in 1973, 25 percent were very hostile toward other racial groups (Bagley et al. 1979; Marsh 1976).

While stress effects vary according to social and economic status under stable conditions, economic recession precipitates a process of stress displacement downwardly in terms of structured economic and social stratification (Bagley et al. 1979; Jahoda 1961). Rising racism exacerbates that displacement in a way that ostensibly favors whites, yet which (as racist and anti-immigrant scapegoating) obscures recognition and fails to address the real causes of economic hardship and its beneficiaries among a continuously profiting ownership class. In the London Stress Study interviews showed that displacement occurs, not only along class and ethnic lines, but in terms of gender and age as well (Blakey 1985).

Racism in the Contemporary United States

Extensive survey data on the United States for the period between World War II and the early 1980s points to similar problems. Inconsistencies emerged between the majority view of Euro-Americans favorable toward the "principle" of racial equality, and a much smaller minority view toward actual "implementation" of public programs to produce equity in jobs, schools, and housing. This National Research Council report (Jaynes and Williams 1989) cogently explains these differences as resulting from a belief (shown most prominently among Euro-Americans) that the individual's behavior, and not social factors such as class barriers and racial discrimination, is the root cause of inequality. Only racist explanations, therefore, are likely to account for the social and economic differences among so-called racial groups from the Euro-American perspective. But sanctions against overt racism have caused racist perspectives to become implicit rather than explicit among most Americans. Like scapegoating in Britian, the worst victims of economic inequity are blamed for their condition, consistent with present political efforts to dismantle the welfare system and correctives for discrimination that include affirmative-action programs in the United States.

Most Afro-Americans responded that both personal and broader social processes contributed to social inequity. Furthermore, 41 percent of African Americans in a national survey during 1979–80 felt that whites "want to keep blacks down," 33–32 percent felt that equally qualified blacks "almost never" can get as good a job or make as much money as whites, and only 7 percent felt that most white people can be trusted, with substantial ambivalence about whether progress is being made (Jaynes and Williams 1989, 118–49). Indeed, a carefully controlled experiment in Chicago and the District of Columbia in 1991 showed that Afro-American men were discriminated against, solely on the basis of race, three times as often as have whites when applying for entry-level jobs (Turner et al. 1991). Sociologist, William Julius Wilson's analysis of the black underclass (see Newman's chapter in this volume), while pointing to some of the important structural economic factors, fails to address adequately the significance of white racism as a continuing deterrent to Afro-American mobility. Racism and its economic effects continues to plague the United States, although it is disguised by principals of racial equality that are more prevalently expressed today than in the past. Euro-American *denial* of racism may constitute racism's most pervasive form because it leads to both racist explanations of inequality and obstruction to the dismantling of institutional discrimination.

The problem of stress-related disorder may not be one of modern life-styles or entirely one of cultural change, but of particular social relationships of industrial societies that create prolonged social frustration, insecurity, and alienation for large masses of the world's population. These are people who are psychophysiologically motivated to seek secure and gratifying social relationships (a condition to which our species is best adapted), but who encounter an often adversarial society over which they may have reason to perceive they have little control and in which many must swim against powerful social and economic currents, too often achieving too little from which to sense the personal effectiveness and status fulfillment needed to feel secure (fig. 6)

Adaptation, Cultural Coping, and Political Struggle

The apparent conflicts between biological and cultural systems present challenges to the structural integrity of each. Human psychophysiology appears to be undergoing stress sufficiently maladaptive to destroy the structural integrity of organs and organ systems, including impairment of psychobehavioral function and social adaptation in some individuals, disproportionately represented among different social groups. Obviously, structural change is resulting from the tensions created by the contradictions between social and psychophysiological systems. Three possible outcomes of those contradictions are discussed next.

We might consider three possible futures. The conflict between biological and cultural integrities resulting from psychophysiological stress could lead to (1) the maintenance of a particular sociocultural (political-economic) structure, or system at the expense of the integrity of particular organic structures, or systems; (2) the maintenance of both structures or; (3) the maintenance of organic structures at the expense of a particular sociocultural structure. These three contingencies are the consequences of evolutionary adaptation, cultural coping, and social revolution, respectively.

Evolutionary Adaptation

The first possibility is one that requires sufficient genetic variation in individual psychophysiological responsiveness to allow for Darwinian selection and organic evolution. Previous research has been unable to show a genetic link to variation in psychophysiological response. The obvious immensity of the plasticity of this system also makes it very unlikely that selection will take place. These concerns notwithstanding, selective pressures would be exerted on lower social strata more strongly than among the social elite, leading to populations that are more or less psychophysiologically comfortable with a high degree of social alienation and distress. Given the relationship between the adaptive or transient stress effects and motivational systems, however, the best adapted populations to distress should also become the least able to learn, the least productive, and the least cooperative. The differences in sociality in these groups would doubtlessly bring about even greater barriers to interbreeding, contributing in the long run to speciation. The social costs and conflicts inherent in the existence of such an asocial and fearless hominid species would, it seems, bring about the destruction of any human social system with which we are familiar. I think Arthur Miller put it well in *The Misfits* when he wrote that, "If it wasn't for the nervous people in the world, we'd all be eating each other." The fact that low socioeconomic status groups experience the highest organic disorder from biocultural stress, demonstrates that such adaptation has not taken place through selection.

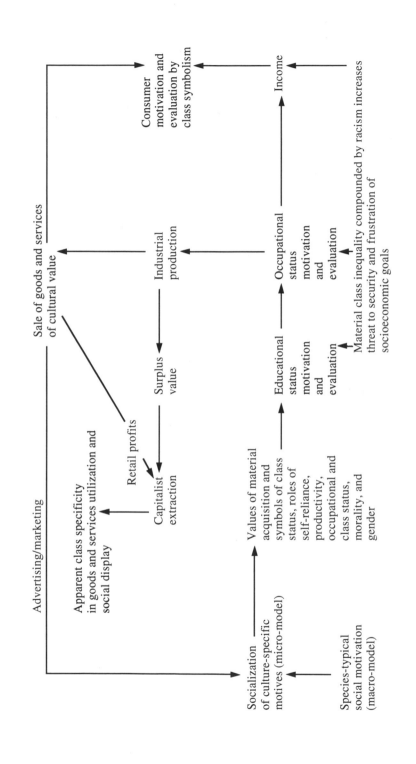

Fig. 6. The capitalist mode and relations of production effecting cultural evaluation and stress. The basic species-typical motivation to enact approved behavior in order to achieve social gratification, influence, and security is interpreted through socialization as a culture-bound set of valued goals and roles. Evaluation by ascription to these consensual, materialistic values (in the Western case) is limited by the sociomaterial differences engendered in class and racist relations. Profit accrues to capitalists by extracting surplus value from depressed wages and maximizing the price of consumer goods and services (status-laden symbols) constituting major social goals for workers. The simple association between material acquisitions and elevated class, status, and social approval, both empirically and through advertising, constitutes much of the socialization by which workers are motivated to train, labor, and consume in the maintenance of the mode of production. While that benefits the capitalist class with respect to profits, the inegalitarian relations of production (class and ethnic exploitation) deters the worker's access to class goals, and ultimately tends to frustrate their evaluative activity and the realization of effective sociality.

Specific physiological stress effects might be considered for selection. For example, genetic differences in the immune system's sensitivity to cognitive stress would have obvious evolutionary significance. An adaptive advantage would be conferred on organisms that are least compromised. On a macroevolutionary scale where such differences appear to exist, humans, monkeys, sheep, and Guinea pigs are resistant to steroid-induced lymphocyte lysis in vitro, while rabbits, rats, and mice are lumped among sensitive mammalian species (Claman 1988). The large amount of variation among the species that share relative resistance with humankind is not suggestive of intraspecific variation of substantial magnitude. Nonetheless, in order for increased resistance to be selected, massive loss of life must occur for many generations to come; hardly an adaptive strategy attractive to civilized people.

Cultural Coping
Another possibility involves accommodations that, more than other options, maintain the genetic integrity of human biology as well as the inegalitarian structure of industrial society as currently constituted. Cultural means of coping also create their own societal tensions and conflicts, and these are usually not capable of social structural transformation. For example, the use of drugs and alcohol in distressed communities "fools" the brain by substituting exogenous chemical analogues for some of the endogenous chemicals (neurotransmitters) that evoke a sense of calm and satisfaction or that dampen one's awareness of dissatisfaction and physical pain (including the endorphins and serotonin).

The illegal trade in narcotics also provides a segment of the dispossessed communities with the means of achieving employment, economic mobility, and the material symbols of status and acceptability otherwise unavailable to them. Yet the costs to these communities and the broader society are great enough to lead to what appears to be the acceleration of intrasocietal tensions, conflict, and growing mortality. An international network of elite entrepreneurs and growers and the street criminals they supply seem to benefit in the terms of some of the goals and values of capitalist societies, and the placating effect of the trade on the societal underbelly might have a functional-homeostatic effect that favors the maintenance of the societal status quo, the integrity of the mode of production. The associated increase in crime, however, elevates societal instability and mortality. Lusane (1991) has revealed the impact of the drug trade on Afro-American and Third World communities, and the involvement of major U.S. political and economic organizations.

Choosing to increase clinical distribution of drugs would simply legalize and centralize profit making, and like ending Prohibition, a legally drugged society might also show a reduction in street crime. It would not, however, change the fact of socioeconomic inequity, and would probably deepen it by reducing the resistance that the stress of social dissatisfaction often creates.

Other, seemingly more benign examples of cultural coping can be found in the development of cultural or "revitalization" movements, such as the Rastafari, under highly stressful conditions. The Rastafari, who can be found in low-income, urban, black communities in Europe, the United States, and the Caribbean, seek to disarticulate from the materialism of industrial societies and connect to alternative social values, through which they attempt to rebuild social cohesion, individual self-assuredness, and (Messianic) hope for the future against the pressures of unemployment, underemployment, and racist insults (Barrett 1977; Blakey 1985; Nettleford 1972). In the London Study, Rastafari was the leading cultural alternative for black youth who had given up on the unrewarding way of life that had brought about their parents' sense of hopelessness. (In the United States, however, stylistic elements of Rastafari appear to have been incorporated by many bound up in the drug trade.)

Close parallels can be shown between this cultural response and a number of conservative cultural movements (the Cargo Cult, Ghost Dance, Ku Klux Klan, and some Christian, Jewish, and Islamic fundamentalists) in the wake of colonial conquest and acculturation or long-term frustration of social and economic mobility. The sense of social value, security, and hope for the future is derived from spiritual authority in the absense of predictable or favorable secular means. Ritually induced trance states (along with the use of drugs in some of these groups) appear to stimulate the release of "endogenous opiates" that relieve or disguise anxiety (Prince 1982). "Opiate of the masses," indeed, these movements both incorporate and resist the values of the surrounding society.

> The capitalist is I shepard. I shall always be in wants. He maketh I to be down on sidewalks. He leadeth I beside insanitary water. He tormenteth I soul . . . (Rastafari Sufferer's Prayer).

Adherents to these cultural movements may or may not continue to participate in the reproduction of the working class and the maintenance of the integrity of the political-economic system. They often provide a relief valve for both the individual and economic system alike. But revitalization movements identify a race, class, and/or economic system as the source of their distress. They may attempt to bring about social change if not by warfare, by refusing to participate in that system's production and reproduction; thus creating an alternative way of life (my interpretation of Spindler 1977).

The growing Afrocentric movement in the United States, currently seeking to create a reformulated "African" ritual, educational, and value system, in order to save a threatened generation of Afro-American youth, has many parallels in cultural movements such as the Rastafari. In each example there is an attempt to disarticulate from the inherently frustrating and demeaning values of a materialistic and white supremacist order, while creating a more cohesive and gratifying society.

These examples are aspects of more comprehensive systems of cultural coping that are familiar to us, that are meant to enhance human sociality and to reduce anxiety. Indeed, the maintenance and reformulation of *ethnic identity* itself is often influenced by adverse social conditions to which its members respond collectively in order to preserve or create an alternative value system and worldview, cohesive intragroup social relations, and both individual and collective strategies for dealing with discriminatory and demeaning external societies.

Familial and other social networks serve to reinforce ethnicity while giving support to individuals. Velez's discussion of U.S. Mexicans (in this volume) speaks to the coordinate roles of households and the social networks among them in maintaining ethnic coherence and reproducing practical knowledge against adverse external forces. Extended African-American kinship networks also reflect that group's historical influences, constitute definitive features of ethnicity, and provide social support for those whose access to the resources of the broader society are limited (Sudarkasa 1988). The Christian church has long been a major institution in Afro-America for social and emotional support. Research that proves blood pressure reduction in association with church membership has been discussed previously (Livingstone et al., 1991).

The stress effects of racism were discussed earlier in this chapter. The rise of racism, furthermore, relates to group affiliation and the enhancement of identity in a "white people's" counterpart to the other cultural movements that have been the subject of the present discussion. It should therefore be no surprise that cyclical economic downturns in such societies are accompanied by a rise in racial nationalist movements such as the Ku Klux Klan and "Skinheads" similar to revitalization movements among "nonwhites." These racist movements are consistent with a continuing belief in the existence of an economic meritocracy and individual self-worth, despite observable economic barriers. Someone else, though not societal organization itself, must be to blame.

Some evidence suggests that whites in the United States make exclusive claims to national identity rather than to an ethnic category (Blakey 1990; Gwaltney 1980, 5)—major difference from minority or colonized groups. In fact politically dominant ethnic movements may take on the dimensions of national political parties such as Britain's National Front, or succeed in dominating the state apparatus as in prewar Germany and postwar South Africa. When such revitalization or cultural-nationalist movements assume political power, the displacement of stress to poor and minority communities becomes a matter of public policy. The rollback of civil rights and an upward redistribution of wealth by the Republican party in the United States during the Reagan and Bush administrations must be seen as a collective effort to cope that elevates psychophysiological stress among others.

Newman's observations (in this volume) of deindustrialization and downward economic mobility in the United States must be viewed as a precipitator of both stress and massive efforts to cope, as defined by the North American cultural context. Whether or not coping succeeds, the effects described intuitively do not suggest conflict among equally empowered social groups but rather a process of stress displacement from dominating toward subordinated groups whether in class, racial, ethnic, gender, or age-status categories. Consider the observation that periods of economic recovery in the Euro-American population typically occur in concert with rising unemployment in the African-American population (Hill 1978).

As members of organized groups, however subordinated, individuals can assert a level of influence over societal conditions common to them by disarticulating from broader, alienating values. These cultures provide an alternative frame of reference in which to place one's identity and to evaluate one's social status. All these factors allow for and create oppositions between systems of thought and action (not necessitating an individual's marginalization, deviance, and exacerbated alienation).

Social Revolution

A third alternative is to alter the structure of the broader social system to adapt to human psychophysiological requirements, bringing about a more equitable distribution of access to secure and gratifying social relations. That, too, would require structural change in the mode of production from one that requires class differentiation and surplus labor and that promotes discrimination, to one that does not. In order to reduce the high stress of poorer communities, such a system would need to make food, housing, clothing, education, and health care (that people need and worry about not having) predictably accessible. It should similarly provide the material and cultural bases for satisfactory role performance and the means of self-fulfillment from which the perceptions of security and social satisfaction are derived. That is not likely to be achieved if goods, services, and productive, culturally valued, and influential roles are made inaccessible to large segments of the populace. While socialist societies have not provided for many of these "needs," capitalist society is structurally *incapable* of doing so. Class differentiation and unemployment are essential to profit making.

Maladjustment of societal organization to the psychophysiological needs of its constituent organisms encourages the transformation of social systems (as described in the first two alternatives). Yet, an initial intelligent transformation of the social system that reduces stress disorder constitutes the most biologically conservative procedure over the long run.

The creative sociocultural movements described above are also partly involved in cultural maintenance, and partly in cultural change. Biocultural research can monitor the biological efficacy of the sociocultural experiments constituting the human struggle for a more secure and satisfying life. Obviously, intelligent structural modification of the social environment to enhance human adaptation should involve anthropological research with that specific goal in mind. No endeavor is more essentially human than seeking ways to a more secure future.[3]

Methodological Recommendations

What this conceptualization of the etiology of stress informs about methodology is that emphasis should be placed on social stressors involved in alienation, including class and racism, social-status differentiation, social and economic insecurity, social instability and separation, role and goal frustration, losses to identity and self-esteem, and the psycho-physiological stresses flowing from them.

Anthropology, if it will grapple with its epistemological and ideo-logical blinders, seems especially, and perhaps uniquely, well equipped for research that integrates social, cultural, biological, and medical as-pects of stress. When biological anthropologists turn to the security of natural-science theory, they may also be turning away from the key methodology for understanding the stresses of industrial life. The theory and method for analyzing these stressors is largely economic, sociolog-ical, cultural, and psychological and requires the human biologist to work with social and behavioral scientists. Simply to infuse bioanthro-pological research with concepts borrowed from modernization and ac-culturation studies, while stereotypically anthropological, falls short of what is needed. It is incredible to dismiss the cognitive, sociological, and economic dimensions of stress etiology as beyond our disciplinary pur-view, beneath our presumed rigor, or as just plain too complex. The patterns of resource distribution within industrial societies are compre-hensive causes of most preventable and treatable health problems, and deserve our utmost attention.[4]

NOTES

1. While obesity constitutes an important contributor to elevated blood pressure, the studies cited above show stress effects when weights are controlled. Sodium intake, while capable of elevating blood pressures, has been shown to be less in Afro-Americans than in Euro-Americans who have lower blood pres-sures (Frisancho et al. 1984). Attempts to attribute greater sodium retention to hypothetical evolutionary differences in African descent groups (Wilson and Grim 1991) have not satisfactorily controlled for environmental (psychophysiological) effects on the renal system (Light et al. 1983). Nor have these evolutionary just-so stories on which those hypotheses are based been compelling (Jackson 1991), but best reflect an uncritical tendency to assume the existence of genetic deter-minants. Hutchinson and Crawford (1981) found no relationship between blood pressure and African admixture in Caribbean blacks based on serological genetic markers. Studies in the United States showed that darker pigmentation (especially in low SES samples) was associated with higher blood pressures (Harburg et al. 1978a; 1978b; Klag et al. 1991). That trend, however, was best explained by stress effects of discrimination and consequent socioeconomic differences effecting the Afro-American poor. While the blood groups studied by Hutchinson adequately

measure genetic admixture, pigmentation differences (a partial but far less adequate admixture measure) also represent visible, social "markers" related to status.

2. Hans Selye (1976), perhaps the most familiar proponent of the fight-or-flight concept, followed immediately on Cannon's lead with a more generalized model. His General Adaptation Syndrome (or GAS) likens the stress responses to a combative struggle in which there is an initial phase of "alarm," a second phase of "resistance," and (if this is unsuccessful in bringing adaptation about) a final phase of "exhaustion." The idea that these physiological behaviors are responsive to the full range of human stressors (biotic, abiotic, and sociocultural) is problematic for two main reasons. First, over the long run nutritional and disease stresses are exacerbated, not ameliorated, by psychophysiological responses, questioning whether the stress response is in fact a generally adaptive syndrome. While an exhaustion phase is brought to account for such maladaptive effects within the GAS conceptualization, much of the endocrine activity and related physiological effects (such as immune compromise) have continuous activity patterns that bear little resemblance to a tripartite scheme. Secondly, the stress responses have been shown not to be influenced directly by nonpsychological stimuli. Only the *perception* of threatening conditions acts as an environmental stimulus causing ACTH, corticoid, and catecholamine secretions (Lazarus 1966; Lazarus 1975; Mason 1976). The GAS is more specifically a cognitively mediated response system with characteristic effects that are both adaptive and maladaptive, and is not consistent with an armed defense of the body against all that would invade it.

3. The cultural manifestations of mass coping discussed in the preceding section can be partly understood as the interaction between homeostatic and dialectical processes. Homeostatic models help in understanding fluctuations within the limits of a system's structural integrity. They may also be useful for showing how loss of integrity in one system (structural change) serves to reestablish the integrity of another. Rappaport's comments on evolutionary change seem relevant here:

> [S]tructural transformations in some subsystems made it possible to maintain more basic aspects of the system unchanged. This proposes that one of the fundamental questions to ask about any evolutionary change is "What does this change maintain unchanged?" To translate the matter . . . into informational terms, changes in the descriptions of substructures may preserve unchanged the truth value of more fundamental propositions concerning the system in the face of changes in conditions threatening to falsify them (Rappaport 1988, 6).

The relationship characterized as that of "subsystems" to "more basic aspects of systems" and "descriptions of substructures" to "more fundamental propositions concerning the system" is an important one of definition, hierarchy, and judgement. The extraction of a decaying tooth (substructure) to prevent systemic infection is easily adaptive for the maintenance of the organism (system).

It would be very difficult to justify under any rationale, the maintenance of this clearly defined substructure at the expense of the whole organism. But the removal of the entire dentition may simultaneously constitute the eminent destruction of the organism in which it represents only a structure of the digestive subsystem.

Similar judgments can be made for social systems. Capital punishment for example involves a clear judgment about the nature of system ("the social good") and subsystem (the individual life), while the debate over its "morality" suggests the difficulty in making this judgment because of the interdependence of the regard held for the integrity of human life and human society. When one considers the conflicts between the maintenance of social and biological systems, we are met face-to-face with a determination as to whether social organization is subordinate to the structural integrity of human organisms, or whether it is the structural integrity of human organisms that is subordinate to that of the social organization. Such a judgment is made no easier when one realizes that both biology and culture evolve, and that the ability to do so is fundamental to their survivals and extinctions. It is also entirely reasonable that no such hierarchy between biology and culture exists, that they are dialectically unified yet separate systems, so that any value judgment about which system is the more important is arbitrary and has consequences for both systems. It becomes difficult, then, to argue for the primacy of the maintenance of either system. Yet, I have argued that the survival and well-being of populations of organisms can represent the adaptive efficacy of social or cultural systems. In whatever way one views the primacy of systems, pathological effects of psychophysiological stress demonstrate *biocultural* disorder.

We know that systems and their structures are maintained *and* change in the natural course of their interactions. A dialectical approach can help clarify the changing relationships between structures such as those examined here. While homeostasis may well characterize the means by which the integrity of systems is maintained, other principles are needed to help explain those conflicts between systems that lead to structural change. Transformations via conflict between interpenetrating systems is what I take dialectical process to mean in this case. The conflict with which we are most concerned is between biological and social systems, although the changing relationships among biological systems are also usefully understood dialectically (Levins and Lewontin 1985). Efforts to achieve homeostasis in one system influence structural alterations as well as structural reinforcement of all engaged systems. One could say, that some aspects or systems change in order for others to remain unchanged. In so doing, however, the unchanged system has also been altered as a consequence of its articulation with newly changed systems.

4. I should gratefully thank R. Brooke Thomas and Johnnetta B. Cole for their help with the ideas of this paper, though I have no reason to believe that they are in full agreement with them. I should also thank Alan Goodman for suggesting some important references, and the Panel on Disorders of Industrial Societies for three years of productive exchanges in the Arizona desert. I am indebted to Elizabeth Anionwu, Hannibal Candicore, Andrew Salky, and the Brent Community for help with the London study.

REFERENCES

Ardrey, R. 1961. *African Genesis*. New York: Atheneum.

Bagley, C., G. Verma, K. Mallick, and L. Young. 1979. *Personality, Self-Esteem, and Prejudice*. West Meade: Saxon House, England.

Balikci, A. 1970. *The Netsilik Eskimo*. New York: Natural History Press.

Barrett, L. E. 1977. *The Rastafarians: The Dreadlocks of Jamaica*. Kingston: Songsters Heinemann.

Blakey, M. L. 1985. *Stress, Social Inequality, and Culture Change: An Anthropological Approach to Human Psychophysiology*. Ph.D. Diss., University of Massachusetts-Amherst.

———. 1987. Skull Doctors: Intrinsic Social and Political Bias in the History of American Physical Anthropology. *Critique of Anthropology* 7:7–34.

———. 1988. Social Policy, Economics, and Demographic Change in Nanticoke-Moor Ethnohistory. *American Journal of Physical Anthropology* 75:493–502.

———. 1990. American Nationality and Ethnicity in the Depicted Past. In *The Politics of the Past,* ed. P. Gathercole and D. Lowenthal. London: Unwin Hyman.

Blythe, P. 1973. *Disease Stress*. London: Arthur Parker.

Brown, D. E. 1981. General Stress in Anthropological Fieldwork. *American Anthropologist* 83:74–92.

———. 1982. Physiological Stress and Culture Change in a Group of Filipino-Americans: A Preliminary Investigation. *Annals of Human Biology* 9:553–63.

Brown, G. W. and T. Harris. 1978. *Social Origins of Depression: A Study of Psychiatric Disorder in Women*. New York: Free Press.

Cannon, W. B. 1963. *The Wisdom of the Body*. New York: Norton.

Cawte, J. 1978. Gross Stress in Small Islands: A Study in Macropsychiatry. In *Extinction and Survival in Human Populations,* ed. J. D. Laughlin and D. A. Brady, 95–121. New York: Columbia University Press.

Claman, H. N. 1988. Corticosteroids and the Immune Response. In *Mechanisms of Physical and Emotional Stress,* ed. G. P. Chrousos, D. L. Loriaux, and P. W. Gold, 203–208. New York: Plenum Press.

Clark, J. D. 1970. *The Prehistory of Africa*. New York: Praeger.

Cobb, W. M. 1939. The Negro as a Biological Element in the American Population. *Journal of Negro Education* 8:336–48.

Cohen, M. N. and G. J. Armelagos, eds. 1984. *Paleopathology at The Origins of Agriculture*. New York: Academic Press.

Corruccini, R. S., J. Handler, and K. Jacobi. 1985. Chronological Distribution of Enamel Hypoplasias and Weaning in a Caribbean Slave Population. *Human Biology* 57:699–711.

Dart, R. (with D. Craig). 1959. *Adventures with the Missing Link*. New York: Harper and Brothers.

Dohrenwend, B. S. and B. P. Dohrenwend, eds. 1984. *Stressful Life Events in Their Contexts*. New Brunswick, N.J.: Rutgers University Press.

Douglass, F. [1854] 1950. The Claims of the Negro Ethnologically Considered. In *The Life and Writings of Frederick Douglass,* ed. P. S. Foner. New York: International Publishers.

Drake, S. C. 1980. Anthropology and the Black Experience. *The Black Scholar* 11:2–31.

Dressler, W. W., J. E. Dos Santos, P. N. Gallagher, Jr., and F. E. Viteri. 1987. Arterial Blood Pressure and Modern Brazil. *American Anthropologist* 89:398–409.

Eastwell, H. D. 1982. Voodoo Death and the Mechanism of Dispatch of the Dying in East Arnheim, Australia. *American Anthropologist* 84:5–18.

Eyer, J. and P. Sterling. 1977. Stress Related Mortality and Social Organization. *Review of Radical Political Economy* 9:1–44.

Fried, M. 1969. Social Differences in Mental Health. In *Poverty and Health,* ed. J. Kosa, A. Antonovsky, and I. K. Zola, 113–67. Cambridge: Harvard University Press.

Frisancho, A. R., W. R. Leonard, and L. A. Bollettino. 1984. Blood Pressure in Blacks and Whites and Its Relationship to Dietary Sodium and Potassium Intake. *Journal of Chronic Disease* 34:128–32.

Gary, L. E., D. R. Brown, N. G. Milburn, F. Ahmed, and J. Booth. 1989. Depression in Black American Adults: Findings from the Norfolk Area Health Study. Final Report for the Institute for Urbans Affairs and Research, Howard University, Washington, D.C.

Goodall, J., A. Bandora, E. Bergmann, C. Busse, H. Matama, E. Mpongo, A. Pierce, and D. Riss. 1979. Intercommunity Interactions in the Chimpanzee Population of the Gome National Park. In *The Great Apes,* ed. D. A. Hamburg and E. R. McCown, 13–54. Menlo Park, N.J.: Benjamin/Commings.

Goodman, A. H. 1984. The Epidemiology of Social Coping Strategies During Temporary Systems Change: Two Studies of First Year Undergraduates. Ph.D. Diss., University of Massachusetts-Amherst.

Goodman, A. H., R. B. Thomas, A. C. Swedlund, and G. J. Armelagos. 1988. Biocultural Perspectives on Stress in Prehistoric, Historical, and Contemporary Population Research. *Yearbook of Physical Anthropology* 31:169–202.

Gwaltney, J. L. 1980. *Drylongso: A Self-Portrait of Black America.* New York: Random House.

Harburg, E., J. Erfurt, and L. Hausenstein. 1973. Socioecological Stress, Suppressed Hostility, Skin Color, and Black-White Male Blood Pressure. *Psychosomatic Medicine* 35:276–96.

Harburg, E., L. Glieberman, and P. Roper. 1978a. Skin Color, Ethnicity, and Blood Pressure 1: Detroit Blacks. *American Journal of Public Health* 68:1177–83.

Harburg, E., L. Glieberman, F. Ozgoren. 1978b. Skin Color, Ethnicity, and Blood Pressure 2: Detroit Whites. *American Journal of Public Health* 68:1184–88.

Harburg E., L. Glieberman, and V. Harburg. 1982. Blood Pressure and Skin Color: Maupiti, French Polynesia. *Human Biology* 54:283–98.

Harlowe, H. F. and M. K. Harlowe. 1965. The Affectional Systems. In *Behavior of Nonhuman Primates.* Vol. 2, ed. A. D. Schrier, H. F. Harlowe, and F. Stolluitz, 288–334. New York: Academic Press.

Hill, R. 1978. The Illusion of Black Progress. *The Black Scholar* 10:18–24.

Hutchinson, J. and M. H. Crawford. 1981. Genetic Determinants of Blood Pressure Level among the Black Caribs of St. Vincent. *Human Biology* 53:453–66.

Inkles, A. 1970. Class and Happiness. In *Readings on Social Stratification,* ed. M. Tumin, 180–85. Englewood Cliffs, N.J.: Prentice-Hall.

Jackson, F. L. C. 1991. An Evolutionary Perspective on Salt, Hypertension, and Genetic Variability. *Hypertension* 17:129–32 (supplement).

Jahoda, M. 1961. *Race Relations and Mental Health.* New York: UNESCO.

James, S. A. and D. G. Kleinbaum. 1976. Socioecologic Stress and Hypertension Related Mortality Rates in North Carolina. *American Journal of Public Health* 66:354–433.

Jaynes, G. D. and R. M. Williams, Jr. 1989. *A Common Destiny: Blacks and American Society.* Washington, D.C.: National Academy Press.

Kiecott-Glaser, J. K. and R. Glaser. 1988. Psychological Influences on Immunity: Making Sense of the Relationship between Stressful Life Events and Health. In *Mechanisms of Physical and Emotional Stress,* ed. C. P. Chrousos, D. L. Loriaux, and P. W. Gold, 237–50. New York: Plenum Press.

Klag, M. J., P. K. Whelton, J. Coresh, C. E. Grim, and L. Kuller. 1991. The Association of Skin Color with Blood Pressure in U.S. Blacks with Low Socioeconomic Status. *JAMA* 265:599–602.

Lancaster, J. B. and C. S. Lancaster. 1983. Parental Investment: The Hominid Adaptation. In *How Humans Adapt: A Biocultural Odyssey,* ed. D. J. Ortner. Washington, D.C.: Smithsonian Institution Press.

Lazarus, R. S. 1975. A Cognitively Oriented Psychologist Looks at Biofeedback. *American Psychologist* 30:553–61.

Lazarus, R. S. and E. M. Opton. 1966. The Study of Psychological Stress: A Study of Theoretical Formulations and Experimental Findings. In *Anxiety and Behavior,* ed. C. D. Spielburge. New York: Academic Press.

Lee, R. B. and I. Devore. 1976. *Kalahari Hunter-Gatherers.* Cambridge: Harvard University Press.

Levi, L. 1971. *Society, Stress, and Disease.* New York: Oxford.

Lamphere, K. M. 1990. Frequency and Distribution of Enamel Hypoplasias in an Historic Skeletal Sample. *American Journal of Physical Anthropology.* 81:35–44.

Levins, R. and R. Lewontin. 1985. *Dialectical Biologist.* Cambridge: Harvard University Press.

Lewontin, R. C., S. Rose, and L. J. Kamin. 1984. *Not In Our Genes: Biology, Ideology, and Human Nature.* New York: Pantheon.

Liem, G. R. and J. H. Liem. 1979. Social Support and Stress: Some General Issues and their Application to the Problem of Unemployment. In *Mental Health and the Economy,* ed. L. A. Forman and J. P. Gordus, 347–77. Detroit: Upjohn Institute for Employment Research.

Light, K. C., J. F. Koepke, and P. T. Obrist. 1983. Psychological Stress Induces Sodium and Fluid Retention in Men at High Risk for Hypertension. *Science* 220:429–31.

Livingstone, I. L., D. M. Levine, and R. D. Moore, 1991. Social Integration and Black Intraracial Variation in Blood Pressure. *Ethnicity and Disease* 1:135–49.

Lovejoy, C. O. 1981. The Origin of Man. *Science* 211:341–50.

Malinowski, B. 1944. *A Scientific Theory of Culture and Other Essays.* Chapel Hill: University of North Carolina Press.

Marsh, A. 1976. Who Hates Blacks? *New Society* 23:649–52.

Mason, J. W., J. T. Maher, L. H. Hartley et al. 1976. Selectivity in Corticosteroid and Catecholamine Responses to Various Natural Stimuli. In *Psychopathology of Human Adaptation,* ed. G. Serban, 147–71. New York: Plenum.

McClean, P. D. 1958. The Limbic System with Respect to Self-Preservation and Preservation of the Species. *Journal of Nervous and Mental Disorders* 127. 1–11.

———. 1968. Alternative Neural Pathways to Violence. In *Alternatives to Violence: A Stimulus to Dialogue.* New York: Time-Life Books.

McElroy, A. and P. K. Townsend. 1989. *Medical Anthropology in Ecological Perspective.* Boulder: Westview Press.

McGarvey, S., and P. T. Baker. 1979. The Effects of Modernization on Samoan Blood Pressures. *Human Biology* 51:461–79.

Montagner, H., J. C. Henry, M. Lombardot et al. 1978. Circadian and Weekly Rhythms in Corticosteroid Excretion Levels of Children as Indicators of Adaptation to Social Adaptation. In *Human Behavior and Adaptation,* ed. N. B. Jones and V. Reynolds, 209–66. London: Taylor Francis.

Montagu, A. 1976. *The Nature of Human Aggression.* Oxford: Oxford University Press.

Montagu, M. F. A. 1955. *The Direction of Human Development: Biological and Social Bases.* New York: Harper Brothers.

Moore, R. 1975. *Racism and Black Resistance in Britain.* London: Pluto Press.

Nettleford, R. M. 1972. *Identity, Race, and Protest in Jamaica.* New York: Morrow.

Ogilvie, M. D., P. K. Curram, and E. Tinkause. 1989. Incidence and Patterning of Dental Enamel Hypoplasia among Neandertals. *American Journal of Physical Anthropology* 79:25–42.

Paykel, E. S. 1973. Life Events and Acute Depression. In *Separation and Depression: Clinical and Research Aspects,* ed. J. P. Scott and E. C. Seney, 215–36. Washington, D.C.: AAAS Publication No. 94.

Prince, R. 1982. The Endorphins: A Review for Psychological Anthropologists. *Ethos* 10:299–302.

Rankin-Hill, L. 1990. *Afro-American Biohistory: Theoretical and Methodological Considerations.* Ph.D. diss., Department of Anthropology, University of Massachusetts-Amherst.

Rappaport, R. A. 1988. Logos, Liturgy and the Evolution of Humanity. Paper presented at the International Congress of Anthropological and Ethnological Sciences, July, Zagreb, Yugoslavia.

Rathbun, T. 1987. Health and Disease in a South Carolina Plantation: 1840–1870. *American Journal of Physical Anthropology* 74:239–53.

Riley, V. 1981. Psychoneuroendocrine Influences on Immunocompetence and Neoplasia. *Science* 212:1100–109.

Rivers, W. H. R. 1922. *Essays on the Depopulation of Melanesia.* Cambridge: Cambridge University Press.

Rose, J. C. and P. Hartnady. 1991. Interpretation of Infectious Skeletal Lesions from a Historic Afro-American Cemetery. In *Human Paleopathology: Current Synthesis and Future Options,* ed. D. J. Ortner and A. C. Aufderheide, 119–27. Washington, D.C.: Smithsonian Institution Press.

Runnymeade Trust and Radical Statistics Group. 1980. *Britain's Black Population.* London: Heinemann.

Rutter, M. 1972. *Maternal Deprivation Reassessed.* Middlesex: Penguin.

Schachter, S. 1959. *The Psychology of Affiliation: Experimental Studies of the Sources of Gregariousness.* Stanford: Stanford University Press.

Schroufe, L. E. 1979. The Coherence of Individual Development: Early Care, Attachment, and Subsequent Developmental Issues. *American Psychologist* 34:834–41.

Scotch, N. A. 1963. Sociocultural Factors in the Epidemiology of Zulu Hypertension. *American Journal of Public Health* 53:1205–14.

Seligman, M. E. P. 1975. *Helplessness: On Depression, Development, and Death.* San Francisco: Freeman.

Selye, H. 1976. *Stress in Health and Disease.* Boston: Butterworths.

Shepherd, J. J., J. Westway, and T. Lee. 1974. *A Social Atlas of London.* Clarendon: Oxford Press.

Spindler, L. S. 1977. *Culture Change and Modernization.* New York: Holt, Reinhart, and Winston.

Steklis, H. D. and M. J. Raleigh. 1984. The Evolution of Social Bonds: The Contribution of Neural Mechanisms. Paper presented at the American Association of Physical Anthropologists Annual Meetings, Philadelphia.

Sudarkasa, N. 1988. African and Afro-American Family Structure. In *Anthropology for the Nineties,* ed. J. B. Cole, 182–210. New York: Free Press.

Sutherland, M. E. and J. P. Harrell. 1986–87. Individual Differences in Physiological Responses to Fearful, Racially Noxious and Neutral Imagery. *Imagination, Cognition, and Personality* 6:133–50.

Trowell, H. C. 1981. Hypertension, Obesity, Diabetes Mellitus, and Coronary Heart Disease. In *Western Diseases: Emergence and Prevention,* ed. H. C. Trowell and D. P. Burkitt, 3–32. Cambridge: Harvard University Press.

Turner, M., M. Fix, and R. Struyk. 1991. *Opportunities Denied, Opportunities Diminished.* Washington, D.C.: Urban Institute.

Ward, R. H. 1983. Genetic and Sociocultural Components of High Blood Pressure. *American Journal of Physical Anthropology* 62:91–105.

Wilson, T. W. and C. E. Grim. 1991. Biohistory of Slavery and Blood Pressure Differences in Blacks Today: A Hypothesis. *Hypertension* 17:122–28 (supplement).

Chapter 6

Plural Strategies of Survival and Cultural Formation in U.S.-Mexican Households in a Region of Dynamic Transformation: The U.S.-Mexico Borderlands

Carlos G. Vélez-Ibanez

The United States and Mexico border region has been an arena of conflict, struggle, massive population movements, and technological innovation. Native Americans, Spaniards, Mexicans, and Anglo-Americans have fought one another and a harsh physical environment in order to establish hegemony over labor, land, water, and production. Such dynamic circumstances have created conditions of structural, cultural, and social pluralism[1] among competing ethnic groups and between nations in the borderlands region. As a consequence, stratified systems of advantage and disadvantage have emerged within and among populations as well as between nations. Such stratification influences the types of household strategies that the region's constituent populations use to cope with differences of income, opportunity, status, political influence, and regional ethnicity. As an unintended consequence, such strategies may become part of highly functional, implicit cultural systems to be used by generations, regardless of their initial selective advantage, eventually becoming transformed in the process.[2]

Central to this discussion is the manner in which U.S.-Mexican[3] households in the region have created a series of kinship-based social and economic coping mechanisms and strategies to mitigate the effects of structural and social pluralism and the economic and political conditions of the border region. This chapter will also illustrate how such strategies and mechanisms become situated within the social and cultural platforms[4] that contextualize the emergence of future generations. Such

193

emergence, of course, is conditional, based on existing empirical contexts that support it as well as with the success with which households control their labor and productivity.

This work will detail how U.S.-Mexican households struggle for ideological, linguistic, and material control. The emphasis is that the historical forces of binational industrialization and accompanying immigration policies since the late nineteenth century have contributed to the rise of U.S.-Mexican ethnicity, to the formation of binational families, to the creation of densely clustered U.S.-Mexican households, and to cultural and behavioral practices that have become part of the implicit core of regional U.S.-Mexican cultural identity.

As well, I will explain that educational forces and practices mitigate against such cultural identity and that alternative policies should be considered. I will also question border policies and theoretical assumptions regarding "minoritization," or "underclass" explanations, as well as examine their premises.

As a study of U.S.-Mexican household clusters will demonstrate, each generation must struggle against different forces, yet the defense that emerges for the most part seems to be invariant—human creativity coupled with an enormous ability to mobilize and expand social relations. The negative or positive outcome of such struggles specifically depend on the social health of household clusters and their ability to maintain both security and identity.

The Struggle for Household Hegemony

The struggle for U.S.-Mexican household control in the border region began in the late nineteenth century when various types of large-scale, industrially organized technologies[5] created a two thousand-mile political border comprised of 52 million persons in ten border[6] states. Half of that population lives within a four hundred-mile-wide belt bissected by the border (Martinez, 1988). The population of the six Mexican border states has increased threefold since 1950 while that of the four U.S. border states has increased from twenty million in 1950 to forty-two million in 1980. This growth has been the result of uncontrolled industrialization on both sides of the border, created by a series of symbiotic economic and technological relations in manufacturing, processing, industrial agriculture, and labor exchange, as well as in twin plants development.[7] Such relations in the border region strongly shape the conditions of Mexican household formation as well as its cultural and social response in the United States. A "border subeconomy" has been organized by the internationalization of production and the exchange of populations (Moore 1988, 16), and from the perspective adopted here, strongly influences U.S.-Mexican household development.

United States border policy also influences the manner in which Mexican households on both sides of the border cope with changing economic and political fortunes. Whether yesterday's Mexican national becomes today's U.S. citizen is very much dependent on the economic health of the region since border immigration policy toward Mexicans of the region is driven by economic conditions. As will be shown, even ethnicity and its attending political implications among Mexicans in the Southwest is probably of very recent origin and largely a production of post-Depression border policies.

Cultural and Ideological Household Struggles

Such dynamic conditions impact U.S.-Mexican households culturally and ideologically,[8] since it is within the household that economic and political forces struggle for control of its labor and energy.[9] As Wolf (1988, 108) points out, "by treating kin relations precisely as a battleground in which cultural contexts are fought out, we may gain a more sophisticated understanding of how 'indigenous peoples' may so often survive and cope in political and economic environments hostile to their continued identity."

The position adopted here is that the struggle over household labor and production is not an aftermath of "industrial disorder" or economic crisis, but a constant—part of the normal operating procedure of appropriation that all complex systems of extraction seek to establish regardless of their purported ideology.[10] At the household level, the main struggle of the members is to defend themselves against the repeated attempts by the state and/or the "market" to exert complete control over their labor and productive capacities. This attempted control is inherent in complex industrial and advanced technological systems; local households respond culturally, socially, and at times politically.[11] The border region is a highly charged and dynamic arena in which new versions of labor and energy-extracting technologies are developed. In concert with such development, a constant struggle emerges within U.S.-Mexican households over control of values and attitudes in regard to work, family, and self. For working-class and middle-class Mexican house-hold the struggle focuses on avoiding indebtedness and tempering the acquisition of what Jules Henry (1963, 13) has termed *driveness,* the push for achievement, competitiveness, profit, and mobility. In the middle-class Mexican household, the push toward driveness creates a struggle over cultural reference, a conflict over historical and cultural identity, and a resistance against the loss of children to consumptive and self-absorbed attitudes.

But since labor markets are basically segmented, a selective movement toward greater specialization also emerges for households. Such specialization cuts off historical information that is the basis for subsistence, so households often try to cope with the loss of technical and survival knowledge that I have termed *funds of knowledge.* These are the nuts and bolts of information inherited by households from past generations and experience. Such loss transforms the Mexican household, from a relatively self-sufficient unit that is interdependent with others in the exchange of skills and information, to one dependent on the market-place for whatever household needs that may arise. Kin and friendship reduces in density and multiplicity.[12]

The U.S.-Mexican working-class household is often required to support additional kin and friendship relations both within the household and without; to maintain ritual and dense social relations; and to mobilize cooperation, reciprocity, and interdependence with others. Such action occurs while the household is bombarded with electronic, occupational, and interpersonal messages as to the efficacy of greater consumption, the acquisition of consumer goods, and the importance of individualism and self-gratification. While most working-class Mexican households maintain a broad and diverse repertoire of skills, information, and relationships, they seem to be selected toward greater specialization as they join primary labor markets.

U.S.-Mexican Households: Structural and Class Characteristics

Such a struggle[13] can be understood by the fact that most Mexican households are supported by working-class occupations. Only 22.5 percent of the Mexican labor force in the Southwest is in upper white-collar and upper blue-collar occupations; the largest percentage (75 percent) is concentrated in the secondary and tertiary labor sectors; low white-collar

(21.3 percent), low blue-collar (32.5 percent), service (15.5 percent), and a small portion as farm workers (5.8 percent).[14]

Such occupational participation is reflected in per-capita income. The ratio of Mexican to non-Hispanic white per-capita income is .55, and of mean household income is .78.[15] Therefore, individuals in Mexican households earn slightly more than half as much income as Anglos, and at the mean household level, Mexican households earned three-fourths as much income as did the Anglo households.[16]

Approximately one in five households are in poverty, but it is also true that three have working-class income that is largely derived from employment by several household members and/or members having two jobs, all of whom use scarce resources in innovative and creative ways. Also more Mexican households contain more adults than do non-Hispanic white households, and thus, there are more earners per household.[17] This advantage, however, is offset by a larger number of children per household, greater unemployment than among the non-Hispanic white population, and, probably for the first ten years of a household cycle, intermittent unemployment.[18] One in five households are also largely part of the primary labor sector in income, stability, and security of employment.[19] Thus, there is a significant percentage of middle-class households for whom scarcity is not the result of a primary struggle but rather indebtedness due to ease of credit.

Yet if only income and wealth of households are used as indicators of household stability, little is understood of Mexican's historical resistance to such structural conditions. The general household strategy has been to struggle for cultural and social survival in the face of political and economic policies designed to homogenize the population culturally and to separate its members physically from their points of origin.

The Emergence of U.S.-Mexican Culture and Ethnicity

Before 1929, the north and south movement of persons between border communities was relatively uninterrupted. Cross-border families were in fact common, with portions of large extended kin networks residing on both sides.[20] It still is not uncommon for children to attend elementary and secondary schools in the United States while their parents reside in a Mexican border town or city. Such cross-border kinship systems, as Heyman (1989, 7) points out, were really "a series of bilaterally related households and networks scattered between similar types of neighborhoods on both sides of the border."

Yet after 1929, the cross-border character of Mexican families was somewhat interrupted by the massive repatriation and deportation policies and practices of the 1930s. And as Heyman (1989, 1) points out, the new legal context of visa regulation instituted during the heyday of the repatriation period[21] "caused the differentiation of documented and undocumented entrants, and divided Mexican from Mexican-American kin in a manner not seen in the period before 1929."

After 1929, legal citizenship became the hallmark of cultural identity rather than cultural context. For many Mexicans born in the United States, immigration restrictions on Mexican kin created a "they"/"us" differentiation and interrupted the easy flow of kin between extended cross-border familial systems. As American schools under the guise of "Americanization" programs,[22] relegated the Spanish language to a secondary position and denigrated its use, self-denial processes set in. Some U.S. Mexicans began to change their names, anglicize their surnames, and internalize self-hatred and self-depreciation.[23]

Such differentiation was accentuated historically by systematic deportation, repatriation, and voluntary departure processes during "Operation Wetback" in 1954,[24] and recent immigration sweeps such as "Operation Jobs" in 1982. In the present, the Simpson-Rodino Immigration Reform and Control Act (IRCA) passed in 1986, was created to reduce undocumented immigration. It has had no striking impact on the labor sectors of which Mexican undocumented workers are a part.[25] In fact, what it has done is to guarantee permanent settlement of Mexican migrants through legalization and has increased the flow of individual workers and families back and forth to the United States with newly acquired legality.[26]

Yet, a certain consequence is that the IRCA has created further division between eligible and noneligible Mexicans. Even within the same extended familial network the legalization of one family member sharply contrasts with the illegality of others. Together with accompanying immigration sweeps of Mexican workers that seem to coincide with immigration "reform" bills such as the IRCA, further emphasis is made between the "foreignness" of the Mexican population in Mexico and that of the U.S.[27] Such demographic and political splitting between Mexico-born and U.S.-born Mexicans establishes the cultural basis for the creation of an ethnic U.S. Mexican, and the denial of cultural continuity between separate populations.

However, many U.S. Mexicans resisted and refused to be erased culturally, and more important, socially within households and extended kin. Spanish in fact has remained important to many; today in Tucson, Arizona, fully 84 percent of the Mexican population speaks both English and Spanish, and mostly or only Spanish at home.[28] In fact, many U.S. Mexicans became bilingual through familial visitations to Mexico or through parents' sending acculturating children to family in a Mexican border state to attend elementary school during the summer. For the most part, U.S.-Mexican households, in spite of strong pressures in opposition, did maintain some functionality in language, but cultural integrity is largely a consequence of social exchange rather than adherence to language. For the most part, then, border policy coupled with school "Americanization" programs in the twentieth century set into motion acculturative and assimilational processes that were simultaneously accepted by some U.S.-Mexican households but withstood by most in a largely unconscious manner due to the reality of economic scarcity.

Border Balanced Households

Historically such resistance and variation of response have not been distributed in the same manner throughout the border region; the closer to the border, the stronger the probability that a border bicultural identity will emerge. I have long known of the existence of a particular form of family not discussed in the literature until Heyman (1989) termed it the *border balanced* household. This type of household balances its source of income from the United States with its social residency in Mexico. Made possible by the green card that allows Mexicans to work in the United States, the border-balanced household takes advantage of access to dollars that are spent in Mexico on housing, services, foodstuffs, and repairs. Culturally, most members of the balanced household are functional bilinguals, participate in recreational activities on both sides of the border, and attend schools on both sides of the border (through the sixth grade in Mexico and junior high school and high school in the United States). It is highly likely that intermarriage with U.S.-born Mexicans will be the result of balanced households. The ease with which members of such households move between cultural contexts in the United States and Mexico is truly impressive.

An associated phenomenon that arises in both the border balanced and in the cross-border clustered[29] households (to be discussed), is what may be termed generational "hopscotching," in which one or more members of a given household are born in Mexico and others are born in the United States. Or one generation may be born in the United States, a second in Mexico, and a third in the United States. Such hopscotching has both negative and positive consequences for members of a given household but, in general, the phenomenon legally provides an advantage in the access to personal or institutional resources on either side of the U.S.-Mexican border.

The Cross-Border Clustered Households of Tucson, Arizona

One important type of variant[30] further removed from the border is that familial clustering of households or extension of families beyond the nucleated household increases with each succeeding generation. I have termed these *cross-border clustered* households because 77.1 percent of our sample have relatives in Mexico and a significant proportion (61 percent) organize their extended kin relations in the United States in a clustered-household arrangement of dense bilateral kin and maintain kin ties with their Mexican relatives.[31] Studies (Keefe et al. 1978; Keefe 1979, 360; Keefe et al. 1979; Griswold del Castillo 1984, 129–32) have shown that regardless of class, Mexican extended families in the United States become more extensive and stronger with generational advancement, acculturation, and socioeconomic mobility. Although an assimilationist perspective would indicate that the opposite should be true, this has not been the case. In fact, Sena-Rivera (1980, 75) suggests that the "modified extended family" in the United States is more the norm than are nuclear families. The former, he suggests, is characterized by a series of nuclear families bound together with a strong emphasis on maintaining extended-family, interactional-communication bonds. However, in the Mexican case, we have found our sample to be strongly bigenerational and tri-generational but without the attending authoritarianism associated with such familial forms (Litwak 1960, 9n).

Even though our sample was composed of 74 percent U.S.-born residents and was largely working class, this pattern of extension in clustered households was significant and extended with each succeeding generation. Such extended familial networks cross borders, and class, are dynamic in composition, and increase in following generations. Keefe et al. (1979, 146–47) and others (Arce 1982; Ramirez 1980, 2) point out that first-generation Mexicans generally have established extended family networks in the United States. Such networks become highly elaborated in the second and third generations and are actively maintained through frequent visiting and the exchange of mutual aid. Even acculturation, as measured by language scales, seems to strengthen extension. In fact, extended familism is greatest among those who are likely to be English speakers. In addition, the higher the economic and educational status of the household, the higher the extended familial integration. These findings are supported by preliminary findings in a national study[32] that revealed that the clustered-residential households I will describe for Tucson, Arizona, were more common among U.S.-born Mexicans than among Mexican immigrants or Anglos.

Of theoretical interest, given these findings, are the parameters that are likely to make ethnic culture a fruitful analytical and descriptive category. If language as a cultural marker is neither necessary nor sufficient, then the density, duration, and multiplicity of relations define ethnic culture. We might surmise that the basis of ethnicity lies in the qualitative differences in social relations between populations rather than only in language or custom.

This finding of a relation between a preference for English and familial extension is not borne out by our study. In fact, Spanish in some combination with English is the preferred language within our sample. The results from our study of Mexican/Hispanic households in Tucson, Arizona, show that though the nuclear family is not the primary locality for social life, it is in that setting that *confianza* (mutual trust) is most likely to emerge.[33] Like Keefe (1979), and Keefe and Padilla (1987), we have found that the U.S.-Mexican populations operate within a cluster of kin relationships connected to other local households as well as to households across the Arizona-Sonora border. Our data in Tucson, Arizona, show that over 61 percent of our sample have localized kin groups made up of a number of related households involved in extended social and economic exchange relations.

Usually focused on a "core" household of active and largely employed middle-aged-to-older adults, the peripheral households carry out their life cycles very much in relation to a centrally located grandparent or parent. The core and peripheral households create social "density" from the fact that members of such networks are kin and in their daily lives add layers of relationships based on other contexts. The person to whom one is cousin is also the person with whom one exchanges labor assistance, has a fictive kinship relation of *compadrazgo* (cogodparenthood), shares in recreational activities and visitations, participates in religious and calendric activities, and in many instances may live nearby. That cousin will either recruit or be recruited by a network member to work in the same business or occupation.

Such networks function differently depending on the situation, so that whichever one of their many functions dominates in a particular instance depends on the circumstances of the people involved. In the recruitment process mentioned above, our findings indicate that such networks function not only as a reliable defensive arrangement against the indeterminacy and uncertainty of changing circumstances but also to "penetrate" the single strands of employee and employer relations and entangle them within the multiplicity of relationships of the network. In an interesting but not often understood sense, such "entanglement" is a type of social insurance against the vagaries of the employer-employee relation, which is often an asymmetrical one at best and an exploitative one at worst. Especially in the informal sector, which is marked by the lack of protection, security, and wages above the minimum, the network penetration also serves as the only means of minimum insurance against sudden firings.

The Tucson household sample shows these networks in remarkable continuity despite constant disruptive pressures, with a variety of households engaged in frequent exchange relations. Most of these clustered households are continuously involved in child-care exchange, house sitting, ritual participation, visitations, and caretaking of persons outside of the household's biological unit. Very few of the clustered households relied in any appreciable degree on nonkin network members for child care, recreation, and other emotive functions.

Our data show that there is significant residential clustering of one portion of all household clusters, which we have termed *primary* household clusters. Primary clusters are those in which exchange relations of kin groups with the interviewed household occur within a residential area of less than a mile. Secondary clusters are those with which exchange relations of kin groups are maintained but are not centered on the household interviewed and are more than a mile away. Half of all household clusters were primary and the rest were secondary. There was little significant size difference between the two types: the median was 4.12 households per cluster, and all other socioeconomic characteristics remained constant. For analytic purposes both types may be collapsed for the rest of this discussion except where noted.

Generally, the most frequent exchange within clustered households was baby sitting for daughters and daughters-in-law. The differences between clustered and unclustered households was statistically significant at the .005 level of probability, with unpaid child care in clustered households being provided by grandparents. There was no statistically significant median age difference between clustered and unclustered households (52 and 48 respectively), and the median yearly income for all households was $25,164 with a per capita income of $4,934.[34]

Yet, such characteristics are only statistical aggregates that do not indicate the qualitative manner in which such clustering is distributed in historical context. By being attentive to the manner in which the life cycle partially determines such distribution, as well as the effect of the penetration of economic and political forces into the household, an understanding of the viability and limits of household clustering is gained.

Clustering in the Life Cycle and the Formation of
Funds of Knowledge: Social Exchange Formation and
Cultural Emergence

Household clustering is usually centered on an ascending generation in which kin live close to children and their families of orientation and in which exchange relations are maintained and mobilized.[35] Once death occurs in the ascending generation, there is a likelihood of lateral partition. In addition, unmarried siblings move out, and although their kin ties seem to wane, this occurs only superficially. There seems to be an initial process of choosing kith over kin, but as children are born and grow, the kin networks are mobilized to meet occupational and experiential demands.

For the unmarried young adult there is peer preference over kin ties. This seems to dominate until marriage, at which time the new household becomes attached to a parental household. These household clusters begin to become trigenerational, and a "core" appears once the birth of grandchildren occurs. Such dynamics form the basic characteristic of the assembly process of clustered households and the "American" version of dispersal seems to be valid only for a limited period within the life cycle of the total household cluster. In fact, the preference for density of relations whether parental, consanguineal, or friendship, becomes more important than occupational stability in some cases. In addition, given the density of relationships, intermarriage with non-Mexicans does little to change either expectations for relationships from the Mexican pattern or their behavioral expression in exchange. I term this phenomenon the *black hole* occurrence, in that Mexican extended clusters seem like celestial black holes that incorporate and consume anything within their relational distance, including non-Mexicans who intermarry.

There is a general trend found in most household clusters that in spite of familial fracturing due to exogenous or endogenous variables, a strong recapitulation process seems to develop and mobilize both extended relations and the cluster effect beyond subsistence or other economically functional reasons. Such recapitulation seems to be indigenous to the implicit lifeways of the population and to be learned early in the life cycle.

Mexican household clusters emerge in historical circumstances that provide a type of "characteristic" that is unique to the household being described. For example, in some households the worlds of work and recreation singularly mark the activities and relations of the household, in part because of the place in the life cycle the household head occupies and also because of the generational context in which such a household emerges. In others, basically made up of upper-middle-class, white-collar professionals, secular and religious rituals seem to be the underlying "cultural" glue for much of the operant exchange relations. Yet, in still others, such as some blue-collar "core" clusters, emergence basically stems from partly fractured settings and is reflective of the hopscotching previously discussed. However, it may also be the case that such clusters are supported by a religious, familial, and nationalistic ideology that provides the underlying rationale for the expansion and development of the household cluster itself. In some households an overcompensating ideology constructed of an extreme work ethic, religious observance, and patriotism seems to be utilized to explain away the effects of occupational risk and injury, current trends in the dissolution of young U.S.-Mexican households,[36] and racial and ethnic discrimination.

In addition, each household cluster has accumulated and discarded funds of knowledge[37] that form the basis of material survival and contain much of the previous generation's repertoire of information and skills used for subsistence. Thus, each case presented here has at its core either historical or contemporary rural experience important to the formation of the funds of knowledge particular to each household and cluster. Such funds also have the borderland region as an important historical and contemporary cultural reference point. What provides such funds with the potential for expression is that they are rooted in daily, useful skills and information of a very broad nature, and include mechanical, historical, creative, computational, and design mastery.

These funds are not only reposited within nuclear settings but are also part of the repertoire of information contained within the clusters of households in which younger generational cohorts learn the substance of the corpus of information and have the opportunity to experiment with it in a variety of settings. They are, in fact, the currency of exchange not only among generations but also among households, and therefore form part of the "cultural glue" that maintains exchange relations between kin. Such funds are dynamic in content and change according to changes in empirical reality and may mitigate the more pernicious effects of household poverty.

Poverty and Clustered-Household Functions: Access to Limited Resources

In 1980, the poverty rate for U.S. Mexicans in the five southwestern states of the border region was slightly less than 22 percent—a drop of 4.5 percent from 1970 (Stoddard and Hedderson 1987, 56), although Moore (1988) cites a higher percentage from more current census data for "Hispanic" poverty.[38] However, poverty was very much concentrated in the southern border counties of the U.S.-border region so that the probability of higher income is greatest in the western coastal counties and decreases consistently as one moves east toward the lower Rio Grande valley of Texas such as Starr County, where the percentage of families in poverty is 45 percent (Stoddard and Hedderson, 56 and 59). Yet for the most part, such poverty areas are rural rather than urban and the pattern of poverty is very much a consequence of the organization of industrial agriculture in those areas in which sectors of the U.S.-Mexican population are relegated to poorly paid, rural farm wages that are intermittent at best and nonexistent for much of the crop year.

However, even in poverty-ridden urban situations underclass characteristics are counterindicated. Heavily U.S. Mexican, South Texas cities like McAllen, Laredo, and Brownsville have among the lowest of household income, highest percentage of public assistance, and highest poverty levels.[39] Yet in these same "poverty" areas, more than 50 percent of households are owner-occupied, which indicates stable populations, with older housing stock, but residents living longer in one home.[40] This also points to the importance of low-cost home ownership in order to improve social stability for Mexican households in poverty circumstances.

However, even poverty figures do not support the presence of a U.S.-Mexican borderlands "underclass" in regard to household structures in which young unmarried women with children under eighteen predominate. The National Center for Health Statistics' Hispanic and Nutrition Examination Survey (HHANES) showed that most U.S.-Mexican single heads of household were middle aged (forty-five to sixty-four years) and that their single status resulted from divorce or separation rather than from widowhood or from never having been married (Trevino et al., 9). This seems to be borne out by the fact that only 12.8 percent of U.S.-Mexican householders were composed of single females with children under eighteen and no spouse present (*Social and Economic Characteristics of the Spanish Origin Population* 1982, 41).[41]

As well, U.S.-Mexican women in poverty circumstances contradict expected marital behaviors of unwed single mothers in underclass situations. It is more likely that single-parent U.S.-Mexican women will marry soon after their first child's birth (Testa 1988, 27 in James 1988, 14).[42] Of single U.S.-Mexican women who did become pregnant, 45 percent did marry the father of the first child.

It is highly likely that for single, female U.S.-Mexican parents, one of the most important factors to prevent the development of underclass characteristics may lie in the ability of women to mobilize male labor and resources in times of need within household clusters. These seem to be an underlying strength in U.S.-Mexican household relations as James (1988, 27) has shown and as has my own work in the samples of households discussed.[43]

Thus even single-headed, U.S.-Mexican households do not conform to the often cited characteristics of female head of households for the underclass. Similarly James (1988)[44] and Moore (1988) question the behavioral, ecological, structural, and processual applicability of the same sort of underclass category to U.S. Mexicans,[45] and I would suggest strongly that it is due to available circumstances for the development of viable clustered households.

The Emergence of the Mexican Child in Social Density

There is one other dynamic aspect that should be considered in understanding the evolution of expectations for such clustering and the acquisition of funds of knowledge.[46] The probability of such clusters to be constructed and their attending funds of knowledge to continue, rests partially not only on an appropriate economic and social context to which they become rooted but also on the early expectations learned by children in such contexts. It is highly likely, based on the findings on social density described in the case studies, the empirical evidence presented from our Tucson studies, and the substance of various works cited in the literature, that U.S.-Mexican children will emerge within social platforms in which they will learn and internalize analogous "thick" social expectations.

The empirical record on Mexican children, however, is scant in regard to early childhood socialization, and the emphasis has been on non-observational attitudinal studies. The recent study by Vélez (1983) of mother-infant interaction, however, has provided insight crucial to understanding the possible genesis of Mexican expectations and potentialities. Her work provides the probable link between early childhood experience and the formation of these expectations in clustered-household settings and establishes the theoretical basis for understanding the phenomenon.

The original postulate in the work asserted that there would be significant variations in the mothering styles of Mexican-American mothers and of Anglo mothers that could be attributed to cultural expectations and that such expectations included the probability of Mexican mothers' providing more proximal stimulation to infants, being more responsive to their infant's signals, and expressing such differences about infant rearing in their beliefs and values (1983, 11).

In her findings the actual interaction between mothers and infants showed little significant differences in frequency and quality. *Greater significance for the emergence of the social personality of the Mexican infant was in the social context in which such interaction actually took place and the role of others in the infant's early social experience* (1983,

80). Vélez found that even though she introduced a variety of social and economic controls to match her sample, the Mexican mother's social density was much greater, contact with infant and mother by other relatives was significantly more frequent, and greater stimulation of the infant by others was also statistically significant. Thus, the Mexican infant had a social context packed with tactile and sound stimulation, was surrounded by a variety of relatives, and at the behavioral level was seldom really alone. This last finding was also supported by the fact that even though Mexican children had their own rooms available, 92 percent of the Mexican children slept in their parents' room while 80 percent of the Anglo children slept in their own room.

Although this was a working-class sample, we have the impression from our present study that the same phenomenon extends to middle-class Mexican-American households. If this is the case, then it appears that the early thick social contextual surrouding may lead to the emergence of social expectations and dimensions different from non-Mexican populations that do not have equivalent social characteristics. Such differences, I would suggest, include the internalization of many other significant object relations with more persons, an expectation of more relations with the same persons, and expectations of being attentive to and investing emotionally in a variety of such relations. Within such psychodynamic and psychosocial processes, the cultural expectation of *confianza* is cradled and it is from these processes that anticipations for exchange relations emerge. Early experiences give such a cultural expectation its substance, verification, and reinforcement throughout the life cycle.

Such thick contexts are the social platforms in which the funds of knowledge of the cluster households are transmitted. Thus some understanding of their models of transmission gives an insight into the possible basis of cultural conflict with formal educational models that seek to shape Mexican children culturally and socially to the appropriate industrial model for the region and nation.

Fund Transmission and the Basis for Cultural Conflict

Further analysis of the manner of informational transmission to children among U.S.-Mexican households suggests additional support for the probability of culturally constituted methods; reveals emotive implications for children and their self-esteem; and identifies possible sources of cultural conflict for U.S.-Mexican children in the schooling process.[47]

Ensconced within thick, multiple relations, Mexican children have the opportunity to visit and become acquainted with other household domains as well as the relationships within those domains. Such clustered households provide the opportunity for children to become exposed to an array of different versions of the funds. However, what is of particular importance is that the child not only is exposed to multiple domains but the child is also afforded the opportunity to experiment in each domain. From our findings in current and past studies,[48] the transmission process is largely an experimental one in which specific portions of the fund may be manifested by an adult but the manner of learning is in the hands of the children themselves. Children will be expected to ask questions during the performance of the household task. Thus the question-answer process is directed by the child rather than the adult. Once the answer is received, the child may emulate the adult by creating play situations of the learned behavior.

Another important aspect of this behavior is the wide latitude allowed for error as well as encouragement to take responsibility for further experimentation. For instance, a child's observing and "assisting" an adult to repair an automobile leads to attempts by the child to experiment on other mechanical devices as well as on junk engines that may be available. The usual adult direction is to "finish it yourself and try your best, no matter how long it takes." Even when the child is stuck at one point, the adult usually does not volunteer either the question or the answer. In such a sequence children are taught to persevere, experiment, manipulate, and delay gratification.

Because of multiple occasions for experimentation there are also multiple opportunities to fail and to overcome that failure in different domains. It is highly probable that there will be a variety of different kinds of domains the child may observe; and the child will become able to perform tasks adequately in one or more domains in which he or she has been successful.

A major and important characteristic in the transmission of funds of knowledge is that multiple-household domains provide an opportunity for a child to be part of a zone of comfort that is familiar yet experimental, where error is not punitively dealt with and where self-esteem is not endangered. Multiple domains increase the probability of non-stressful and generally neutral zones of comfort where little criticism is expressed and a child cannot be faulted. When an adult is impatient and judgmental, the child often has the opportunity to experience other adults in different domains where such behavior is not present. The child thus learns very early to use a comparative approach to evaluate adults and to avoid discouraging or punitive persons because there are others available who are not.

Such zones of comfort also allow self-evaluation and self-judgment because the feedback process is in the hands of the child. The only exception is when the child is in danger or cannot physically perform the task. But the outstanding characteristic that eventually develops for the child is contextual familiarity that is predictable and manipulable. If the probability of error may be costly, then the child is not encouraged to experiment.

The child learns quickly that there are constraints, but these are so obviously in his or her favor that such an understanding becomes the underlying basis for zones of comfort. In emic terms, such zones of comfort, as well as the relationships that support their expression, become the basis of *confianza*[49] (mutual trust) and place the child within the appropriate cultural frame for adulthood.

Zones of comfort and their cultural frame, however, are threatened by the introduction of the traditional pedagogical approach to learning. From our observations, female children's play is very much marked by the emulation of teacher originated and directed "playing school" sequences in which there is little active student-controlled interaction, as well as expectations of rote or uncreative responses to instruction.[50] In addition, the school model of learning and transmission is emphasized by parents during homework periods, with strong punitive measures either threatened or carried out if tasks are not completed. This use of the schooling model created one of the few sources of adult-child conflict in households observed. Such basic cultural conflict becomes further exacerbated when understood within a larger cultural framework of human emergence. For the U.S.-Mexican adult, who has emerged within both culturally constituted zones of comfort and formal educational settings, self-doubt, negation, and cultural resistance will emerge together.

Conclusions

This work has illustrated that U.S.-Mexican households in the borderlands have long been part of the dynamic economic and technological transformations that have emerged in the region. That part has usually involved such households in the mobilization and creation of exchange relations with kin that serve as the basis for resistance, defense, and acceptance of political and economic pressures. While it is accurate to suggest that increasing specialization threatens the funds of knowledge upon which such relations rest, nevertheless, the same basic construction and reconstruction of exchange based on social density seems to emerge. However, such emergence seems to take different forms dependent on the life-cycle stage.

As the work has indicated, the structural and class complexity of the population, as well as proximity to the border, partially influences the shape and character of the household clusters, such as the cross-border and balanced households with their generational hopscotching phenomena. In some ways, U.S.-Mexican households occupy a positive position in relation to sudden changes in economy and policy. They are able to bring to bear more members of larger households to generate income. They are able to mobilize relationships and skills in order to support household members who need technical assistance. They also are able to cross political frontiers to take advantage of available economic opportunities to offset limited income. The negative aspect is that the blue-collar occupations are dangerous and place men, especially, at occupational risk.

Ideologically such households may also become hypnotized by national cultural prisms that accentuate patriotism and reduce regional cultural history to self-destructive ethnic reference. The Americanization educational programs[51] of the past and the monocultural Anglo-dominant schooling of the present create an ethnic situation of cultural conflict, self-doubt, and uncritical acceptance of destructive ethnic stereotypes. In this sense, even the positive survival values of clustered living are offset by national stereotypes and educational values that accentuate individualism and self-serving vertical mobility. These deny the cultural efficacy of the population by framing them within derogatory stereotypes so that U.S. Mexicans are reduced to being "lazy Mexicans" who have to compensate for apparent deficiencies by working harder in more dangerous occupations, or are even willing to give up their health. The paradox and tragedy is that some part of the Hispanic population comes to believe that which has been composed and comes to deny its own cultural validity.

Cultural conflict is certain when educational institutions have constructed very opposite operational and pedagogical principles that may not take advantage of the cultural and practical skills Mexican children carry to a schooling process that is based on an industrial form of instruction. Nevertheless, children in household clusters have the opportunity to emerge surrounded with dense relations and contexts in which zones of comfort for learning and experimentation exist. The zones of comfort provide children with the opportunity to learn by trial and error without much negative reinforcement in broad arenas of social and historical funds of knowledge not probable in nuclear families.

Finally, U.S.-Mexican household clusters are not dependent on residential context for exchange but on consanguineal or affinal ones. Unlike the highly mobile, nuclear-based familial systems of the U.S. middle class in which neighborhood and institutions are the major means of social and economic articulation outside of the immediate nuclear family, the U.S.-Mexican middle-class, and working-class household-clusters exchange is primarily focused on expanding familial consanguineal, and affinal networks. These provide the social platforms that help develop much of the U.S.-Mexican population into creative, nonpassive, resistant human beings. In spite of being a part of every change in industrial technology and form of organization, of being unsettled and resettled by need and deportation, and of being pushed into an assimilationist perspective regarding language and cultural identity, U.S.-Mexican households remain vibrant and creative units because of their ability to mobilize relations in time of need and to reinforce relations through ritual.

For U.S.-Mexican households, "industrial disorder" has been a constant condition of operation inherent in dynamic economic and technological forces that have sought to control their labor and energy in a border region that has supported ethnic and class stratification. The response of households has been to rely on mechanisms that provide some means of security, protection, and value to future generations.

Policy Implications and Research Futures

There are a number of policy implications that might be considered as the aftermath of understanding the full range of possible and probable outcomes of the various household strategies mentioned in this study.

Educational Policy
The educational policy implications seem rather clear: What is needed is a critical reexamination of the cultural basis of evaluation and as-

sessment of U.S.-Mexican children, a close analysis of the cultural basis of instruction and pedagogy, and field testing of the nature of the social relations between U.S.-Mexican children, their parents, and the educational institutions that serve them.

Concerning evaluation and assessment, some attention should be paid to more dynamic assessment (Campione, Brown, and Ferrara 1982) that seeks to measure children's learning potential. The process would involve the use of mediated learning practices within the assessment context, with the assessor actively participating in teaching skills to the child. Such an approach is predicated on the modifiability of the child, not on stable, easily measured characteristics. Using this approach, Feurestein (1979) even demonstrated significant gains for educable mentally retarded students through instruction based on learning potential.

Second, the very basis of instruction should be reexamined. In contrast with the traditional highly individualized competitive instructional systems, "cooperative learning systems" might be more appropriate for children for whom social interaction is both a highly developed skill and an expectation. Such systems are based on the idea that students accomplish their academic tasks in heterogeneous groups, usually assigned by the teacher, and each student's effort contributes to the total group effort. Cooperative learning may be an important innovation in relation to education and culture for three reasons: first, it may be more compatible with the cultural norms and values of U.S.-Mexican children and seems to be highly compatible with their learning experiences; second, it may contribute to better interethnic relations in the classroom; third, and most important, such approaches lead to much higher academic gains for minority students (Kagan 1986).

Last, the social basis of instruction between child and teacher, as well as the social basis of relations between teacher and parents must be carefully considered. If, as I have pointed out, the child's and parents' expectations for relations with others is based on social density, then the school-based model of instruction is in direct contradiction and opposition to those expectations. If anything, the school-based model of instruction is organized around single-stranded, teacher-to-student interaction, in which parental involvement is restricted to occasional contact or is defined within highly formalized contexts such as parent-teacher organizations. There is little in the triad of children, teacher, and parents that crosscuts either generational, class, educational, ethnic, or status differences except the single strand of informational and assessment authority directed by the teacher.

Border Policy
Clearly, present immigration policies do not seem to have been efficacious in "keeping people out," which is a questionable goal at best, and pernicious at worst. It has contributed to the creation of artificial cultural differences between border populations that become exacerbated during periods of economic instability along the border. Within both Mexican and American nationalistic ideologies the effects of this policy are not even questioned.

On the other hand, such a policy has created the basis of ethnic identity as a negative reaction to tighter immigration-control measures and in some cases has created the basis for cultural loss and identity confusion. This chapter has not dealt with the fear, trepidation, and harassment that border enforcement creates for both native-born and foreign-born U.S.-Mexican households, but certainly this is an important consideration in relation to the creation of ethnicity and revitalization politics.

However, a creative border policy that does not eliminate cross-border relations and cultural identity could be generated along the two thousand-mile border and four hundred-mile-wide belt that comprise the borderlands. Such a policy would include the extension of political, legal, occupational, and juridical rights and duties to members in the region rather like some propositions discussed among nations in the European Common Market that share political borders. While Mexican national and U.S. "national security" concerns certainly militate against the establishment of such a policy, nonnationalistic frames of discussion that respect the cultural and social rights of human populations and openly question traditional national boundaries and their policies on both sides of the present Mexican and U.S. border need serious consideration. While there is great concern over the cultural rights of Native American tribal peoples divided by the U.S.-Mexico border, there is little discussion of the cultural rights of U.S. Mexicans.

Theoretical Policy on U.S.-Mexican Minority and
Underclass Populations
Finally, a brief discussion should be provided of what can be described as a critique of theoretical policy on minority and underclass[52] populations in the United States. From the point of view of some students of ethnicity[53] including myself, there is a basic conceptual error made by those concerned with ethnicity and minority statuses who hunt for

"cultural reasons," or in underclass discussions for "structural reasons," for U.S.-Mexican populations' lack of political participation, poverty and low income, lack of educational attainment, high rates of certain types of crimes, and gang involvement. These aspects and reasons become conceptually conflated into one conceptual apparatus—minority underclass status. In an interesting and unintended way, category becomes explanation and status designation serves as explanation for condition.

On the other hand, from the point of view of the "minority" population, except within some bourgeois circles, few members of culturally different populations consider themselves as minorities or the underclass. In the Southwest, for the most part, few U.S. Mexicans consider themselves apart from the physical and social environment of the border region. The proof is in the maintenance of U.S.-Mexican cross-border familial relations through three and four generations. Similarly, regardless of language, most U.S. Mexicans will consider themselves as Mexicans culturally and as citizens of the United States politically.

On social grounds, few U.S. Mexicans appreciate or emulate gang members who constitute a small proportion of the teen-age population, probably no more than 6 percent. (Vigil 1989). They are considered by most U.S. Mexicans as multiply marginal[54] individuals caught up in self-destructive systems of behaviors that are in extreme contrast with the conservative expectations of most U.S. Mexican households.

Politically, U.S. Mexicans will vote, as the Kennedy years illustrated, but will correctly assess the limits of the class interests of most politicians and, with some degree of accuracy, the close relations between most politicians and their campaign contributors. Economically, most U.S. Mexicans work, and will work, two or more jobs to make ends meet. Most members of the family in one way or another will contribute their labor and energy to stabilize thier immediate household and the other households to which they cluster. This "insider's" view is quite at variance with both the academic and the nation-state characterization of the U.S.-Mexican population as a minority.

An implicaton that might be drawn from this description is that to lump and categorize culturally different populations in a pluralistic setting, like that of the border region, within only poverty, underclass, or minority categories is to frame them ideologically as either passive or merely responding to a world constructed by others (C. smith 1984, 194). The burden of Anglo society then becomes to lift them above their condition or to make them lift themselves up by their bootstraps as if either of the two conditions were empirically real. Or, in a different version of the same sort of approach, an overemphasis is placed on the significance of extra-local pressures, thus undervaluing the manner in which local-level populations defend their interests and rights (Ortner 1984, 142–43).

Yet, from a historical point of view, minority status is the creation of a border policy eighty years after war and conquest that overtly seeks to replace cultural continuity and social relations with citizenship that demands a cultural eraser. United States educational institutions try with culturally alienating methods and approaches to guarantee what border policy begins. Simultaneously minority status is guaranteed by an appropriation process under which U.S.-Mexican households constantly have to defend themselves ideologically while trying to retain a modicum of control over their labor and energy. For reasons of conquest a border was created. As a result of state political control over borders, ethnic identity was created. For reasons of Mexico's national expediency, U.S. Mexicans are derided as culturally second rate. For reasons of labor market use, the U.S. attempts to standardize U.S. Mexicans in terms of citizenship and denies culture as a significant and useful category of recognition. The outcome is to "minoritize" such populations, or as Williams (1989, 438) has labeled it, to create an "ethnic" division of labor. Such national frames underlie the theoretical gestalt that guides and defines the cultural rights of human beings in the region. Yet, such a frame includes a type of cultural prism that is not value free or culturally neutral. It becomes apparent only when we analyze the way in which many U.S. Mexicans have to survive the educational and institutional shocks of nonacceptance and worse of nonappreciation as culture makers and defenders. U.S.-Mexican households must defend themselves not only against economic and political appropriation but also against a national cultural frame of reference that defines the cultural content of all national institutions, including education, the expressive arts, communications, politics, and the world of work. "English only" is one example of the refraction of such a cultural prism; the educational classroom is another. From my point of view, it is time to call for a much more dynamic theoretical approach. It should address the history and culture-making processes by which populations placed in structurally plural situations respond to and reduce the effects of economic appropriation and political and social dominance within and through their households. Such a dynamic point of view would equally question the underlying frames of the ideology that create the theoretical rationales for characterizing whole populations as minorities.

Research Futures

The present population faces new challenges by new versions of the old stereotypes and relations. International processes now make overt the characterization of the areas in the IndoMesitzoAmerican region as cheap-labor regions to be exploited under the mantle of the Free Trade Agreement. This will formalize the distorted relation between nations and populations and provide further linguistic and cultural rationalizations for hierarchy and its accompanying behavioral, linguistic, and attitudinal categories of minoritization of the Mexican population.

Even in hallowed university arenas in the Southwest some expected surprises of such relations emerge with Mexicans and other Latinos and Latinas increasingly captured and constrained to "ethnic studies" or as targeted "add ons" of employment opportunities. Not unlike the expected segmented labor structures of the past industrial world of the region, Mexican faculty are shuttled through and to "special" units since we are not expected to participate as intellectual colleagues in the other domains. Instead of being perceived as important intellectual and academic innovators who create and develop the academy beyond its intellectual, class, gender, and cultural constraints, we often are defined and regarded as a tolerated presence.

Even without such constraints, as a few more of us become part of the university context, serious backlashes become manifest with characterizations of more than one Mexican scholar in the same department, administration, or college as comprising a "Mexican mafia."

Within the academy, too many of my colleagues readily repeat the minority stereotypes of the population and hide behind the masks of confidentiality within search committees, hiring operations, and peer and tenure evaluations. For "Mexicans" what is reproduced just as stupidly, just as sexist, and just as racist and ethnocentric, are the premises and attitudes underlying the past and provided with new energy in the present. However they do reveal the distorted relations between us and make their resistance more rational.

Therefore, future research of U.S. Mexicans will have to be much more inclusive geographically and economically. Intensive household analysis on both sides of the political border must be done in order to understand the impact of the Free Trade Agreement and the further restructuring of the region. As has been discussed, the ability of Mexican households in the United States to withstand the effects of technological and economic shifts has been a constant one. However, within U.S.-economic restructuring of which the Free Trade Agreement is one important segment, heightened ethnic cultural processes may be put into motion like those begun after 1929 and U.S.-Mexican household formation impacted upon in important, but not yet known, ways. Last, but not least in relation to cross-class understandings, intensive analysis of U.S.-Mexican professional households needs to be accomplished simultaneously in order to understand the dynamics of the conflict over scarce resources between U.S. Mexicans and their non-Mexican professional cohorts.

NOTES

1. An extensive literature on "pluralism" differentiates between cultural, social, and structural pluralism. In the 1960s and early 1970s a number of British-influenced anthropologists and social scientists developed theoretical models of plural societies—Leo Despres (1967), Kuper (1969), Kuper and Smith (1969), Smith (1960; 1965; 1969a,b,c), and Van Den Berghe (1967; 1970)—all of whom were strongly influenced by the earlier work of Furnivall (1948). Smith (1969a) defines the differences between structural, social, and cultural pluralism by suggesting that structural pluralism exists in societies where there are separate institutions for different parts of the populations, and rights and duties within the society are determined by those differentiated institutions. Social pluralism exists where in a single society there is a diversity of ethnic, religious, political, and other institutions and where participation by an individual in one such institution defines membership in others. These may be parallel and analogous memberships in social clubs, religious sodalities, or political parties, but all members of all groups have equal rights and duties granted by the state. Cultural pluralism refers to a diversity of ethnic, religious, political, and other institutions, but individual participation in such diverse groups does not determine membership in others.

Obviously, in any complex society, aspects of each exist. For instance, in the United States, Native Americans exist within structurally characterized reservations, participate in exclusive ritual and religious associations, and simultaneously belong to differentiated ethnically dominated voluntary associations.

In the U.S.-Mexican case, both social and cultural pluralism have been the outcome of the border experience. Yet there are structural conditions between nations that, in part, strongly influence the maintenance of economic and political disparities between U.S. Mexicans and Anglos. Certainly, the record of the miseducation of Mexicans—relegating children to learning tracks, segregated schooling, and "educationally mentally retarded" classes—is an example of the type of structurally defined condition that has strongly determined the participation of adult U.S. Mexicans in the labor market.

2. Thus Native American households were structurally relegated to existence within political and economic reservations under the domination of U.S. federal governmental bureaucracies. Household strategies of survival are made integral to the fortunes of their tribal authorities' relations with federal bureaucracies, to the limits of the physical environment, and the efficacy of traditional economy and technology to penetrate industrial forms of organized labor and production. The Native American household is thus very much influenced and constrained by, and adjusts its labor and production according to, indigenous tradition, tribal organization, and federal penetration.

Other populations in the United States also have to cope with distinctive structural and substantive economic and social disparity, e.g., African American populations throughout the country and Puerto Ricans on the East Coast. As Kennedy (1980), Stack (1974), and Valentine (1980) have shown, such populations develop a number of creative household approaches to mitigate the effects of such conditions, including the extensive use of social networks and helping systems. Yet the regional context for Puerto Ricans and African Americans differ markedly from that of U.S. Mexicans, so careful analytical distinction should be made of each type of adaptive and coping mechanism in relation to an appropriate economic and political context. While similar networks operate among African Americans and Puerto Ricans, most studies seem to locate the necessity of such relations in the effects of racism, economic disparity, and the accompanying large proportion of female-headed households. For African Americans the percentage of households headed by a female, 40.6 percent is almost the same as for Puerto Rican households, 36.5 percent (Bean and Tienda 1987, 192). In comparison, only 18.9 percent of U.S. Mexican households were headed by females, and among U.S. Cubans, 16.0 percent so that different sets of explanations seem to be required for the emergence of similar cultural and social behaviors.

3. I use the term *Mexican* to describe those born in Mexico as well as those of Mexican parentage born in the United States. Although *Chicano* or *Mexican American* is also used for those born in the U.S. of Mexican heritage, *Mexican* is the generally preferred term used by the U.S.-born population. See C. Arce (1981), Garcia (1982), and C. Vélez-Ibanez (1983).

4. *Social platform* refers to the contention that human beings emerge and end from the social constructions created by inherited historical relations and their cultural understandings, familial relations, and all nonfamilial, social, economic, and political relations and events. Through the life cycle all individuals learn, reject, and/or reconstitute relations and events as their own. The earliest platform for the neonate is the suckling and bonding process between mother and child. A review of the literature by Bateson (1978), Erickson (1963), Goffman (1961), Hallowell (1959; 1968), Horner (1979), Laing (1963), Mannheim (1952), Schwartz (1968), and Wallace (1961) is instructive on the concepts of emergence, social construction, object relations, and life-stage development.

5. The border region witnessed the introduction of large-scale, irrigation-based farming by the Riverine Hohokom peoples between 300 B.C. and A.D. 1450; the penetration of mining, farming, and ranching by Spaniards and their entire cultural and political structures; the attempted consolidation by a centralized mestizo population during the Mexican period; and the Anglo introduction of large-scale, industrially organized mining, construction, commerce, and animal production, as well as the present service, electronic, military, and modified mining and border-related twin-plant production. Most historical periods were also filled with raids, warfare, conquest, and subjection of one population over another. The American period is also marked by large-scale land clearing; land speculation; control of mineral, water, and natural resources by national corporations; and state ownership of more than half of the available land area.

Throughout the borderlands of northwest Mexico and the southwestern United States, the Mexican population has been part of major transformations. It has been a population subjected to constant demographic shifts, ecological pressures, and economic uncertainty. The nineteenth and twentieth centuries are replete with periodic large movements of Mexicanos moving north and east and west, enlisted or attracted by farming, mining, and railroad recruiting agents and contractors, or pushed out by the Mexican revolution, depressions, natural calamities, and great economic changes. New capital and technologies that have penetrated these regoins have always transformed the regional ecology of the borderlands. In the modern period, the location in the borderlands of a labor market necessitating a combination of technical skills and labor manipulability is clear. This has stimulated lineal and cyclical migrations of Mexicanos among border states (Vélez 1980, 218). In the period 1917–21 alone, 72,000 Mexican farm workers were admitted to the United States without the restrictions of the Immigration Act of 1917 (an $8 head tax, literacy test, and prohibition of contract workers). Such restrictions were also waived for nonagricultural workers from Mexico for the railroads, mines, and construction companies. In that period, Mexicans worked in iron and auto works in the Midwest, building trades in Arizona, railroad building in Southern California, and slaughterhouses in Kansas and Chicago (Vélez, 1980).

Periodically, as the economy cools off, Mexican labor has also been voluntarily or forcefully pushed back across the border when no longer needed. During these cooling periods and during periods of high industrial and building development in various states, Mexicanos migrate from New Mexico, Arizona, and Texas to California, and most recently some from California, New Mexico, and even Wyoming are moving into Arizona.

6. The ten states that comprise the U.S.-Mexico border region are, on the Mexican side, Baja California Norte, Baja California Sur, Sonora, Chihuahua, Nuevo Leon and Tamaulipas; on the U.S. side, they are California, Arizona, New Mexico, and Texas.

7. See the works of Diez-Canedo (1981), Fernandez-Kelly (1987), Martinez (1983), Garcia y Griego (1983), Tiano (1985), Gonzalez-Archegia (1987), and Porras (n.d.), all indicate the U.S. orientation of the Mexican border economy. Mex-

ico supplies cheap labor, cheap agricultural products, mostly female-assembled goods, and playgrounds for U.S. sybarites. The U.S. supplies chiefly finished goods and technology. This relationship extends to income in border transactions earned by Mexico. In 1986, $1.2 billion was spent in Mexico by Americans and Mexicans spent $1.5 billion in the United States (Gonzalez-Archegia 1987, 6).

In 1986, Mexico imported $11.4 billion in goods while exporting $16.0 billion, of which almost 40 percent was oil. The resulting advantage to Mexico is largely erased by the enormous debt of $107.4 billion, largely owed to American public and private institutions (U.S.-Mexico Report, July 1989, 11), and the attending annual interest of $14.5 billion (U.S.-Mexico Report, April 1989, 18–19).

However, without U.S. investment, the Mexican maquiladora industry (basically U.S.-owned plants used to assemble U.S. manufactured products in Mexico that are then sent back to the United States for sale), could not provide employment for 400,000 persons, mostly along the border. Such employment is, in large part, responsible for the fact that real income for Mexico's six northern border states is higher than the per capita income of all of Mexico (Stoddard and Hedderson 1987, 59).

8. Part of this chapter and the statistical information have been previously published in Carlos G. Vélez-Ibanez, "Ritual Cycles of Exchange: The Process of Cultural Creation and Management in the U.S. Borderlands," in *Celebrations of Identity: Multiple Voices in American Ritual Performance,* ed. Pamela R. Frese, 120–43 (Westport: Begin and Garvey, 1993). As well, portions have been published in Carlos G. Vélez-Ibanez, "U.S. Mexicans in the Borderlands: Being Poor Without the Underclass," in *In the Barrios: Latinos and the Underclass Debate,* ed. Joan Moore and Raquel Pinderhughes, 195–220 (New York: Russell Sage Foundation, 1993).

9. Wolf (1988, 108). See also Goody (1983), Cohen (1969), Corrigan and Sayer (1985).

10. The socialist state's purported ideological intent, to release social labor from the marketplace, is of questionable utility in practice, since the state organizes social labor through conscription and regulation and sets it to work; wages are set by a privileged centralized management and policy unit. Capitalist systems mobilize social labor by purchasing labor power and sets it to work for wages according to the "market," which is largely asymmetrical, since the buying and selling of labor power is not an even exchange. Under both ideologies the quest for household labor by the state or by market responses is part of a constant struggle against which household members have to balance available labor power, consumption, and exchange in order to meet both culturally constituted "demand" and subsistence needs.

11. The history of Mexicans in the labor movement in the Southwest is replete with organized examples of entire kinship systems and households mobilizing against racial discrimination, low wages, poor housing, and the infamous company stores.

12. Density of relationships refers to many-stranded or multiple relations described as "the extent to which links which could possibly exist among persons do exist" (Mitchell 1969, 18). These relations also have a vertical and horizontal

directionality (Lomnitz n.d.). The vertical relations are largely unequal ones between people of different statuses or power positions, with an exchange of favors and resources tying specific persons to networks of supporting power groups. The horizontal relations are based on generalized reciprocity of basic equals. The relations with which we are concerned here are horizontal ones that emerge as central to political coalescence in central urban Mexico, to economic cooperation in Mexico and the U.S. borderlands, to clustered housing patterns in Tucson, Arizona, and to neonate emergence in socialization processes.

13. On the Mexican side of the borderlands, some of the same structural characteristics apply but with a greater skewing of income distribution and occupational categories. Nationally, 54 percent of the population receive income below the minimum wage while 84 percent live in poverty (*U.S. Mexico Report,* April 1989, 16). See the *X Censo General de Poblacion y Vivienda, 1980.* In 1980, the minimum wage in Mexico was approximately 6,390 pesos monthly, and the exchange rate was 22.50 pesos to $1.00. It should be noted that since 1980 the twin forces of inflation and devaluation have reduced real wages considerably. Thus, for example, in 1980, maquiladora workers in Sonora earned approximately 1400 M.N. a week, or $62. In 1989, while these same workers averaged 60,000 M.N. a week, the real income was only $24. According to one source (*U.S. Mexico Report,* July, 1989), the minimum wage earner's purchasing power has decreased by 70 percent in the past twenty years.

In the six Mexican border states, 72 percent of the population earns the minimum wage of $284 or less monthly. At the upper end of the distribution, only 3 percent of the population earns more than $954. Approximately 25 percent of the population earn income between the minimum wage and the upper reported limit. This income distribution is also reflected in the occupational structure of the Mexican borderlands. Seven percent are upper white-collar occupations; eighteen percent are categorized as self-employed; 69 percent are in blue-collar jobs; and 6 percent in unpaid labor. The category of self-employed captures two different populations. The first is composed of persons who have established their own small businesses and who are largely a part of the lower end of the formal sector. The second is composed of persons who are largely part of the informal sector and who include street vendors, cab drivers, scavengers, street barbers, gardeners, and countless other occupations marked by easy entry, low skills, and the need for few resources. (See Eames and Goode 1973, 1980; Lloyd 1982). Finally, 1 percent are officially categorized as unemployed. This figure does not accord with other national estimates of real unemployment that ranges from 30 percent to 45 percent especially if a consideration is given to "disguised underemployment." According to U.S. Mexico Report (April, 1989), fourteen million persons in Mexico are part of an underground economy distributed among industrial and agricultural sectors.

14. See Bean and Tienda, (1987, 323). I have taken the liberty of recomputing figure 9.3 and combining men and women in single occupational categories.

15. See Bean and Tienda, 199.

16. See Bean and Tienda, 199. Our previous work done in Tucson, Arizona, clearly indicates that mean per-capita income in 1980 for 76 percent of the

Mexican population was $5,202 and for 24 percent of the Mexican population, $8,398. For the Anglo population the percentages were almost exactly reversed, with only 25.5 percent earning $5,202 and 74.5 percent earning $8,398. In comparing mean household income, 76 percent of the Mexican population earned $14,488 while 24 percent earned $21,994. Only 25.5 percent of the Anglo population earned $14,488 while 74.5 percent earned $24,245. See Vélez-Ibanez et al. (1984).

17. See Bean and Tienda, 199.

18. See Bean and Tienda, 199 for data on household income origins and 188 for a discussion of household size. From our own work in Tucson, Arizona, exchange of labor between households releases labor for the marketplace at some time during the work and life cycle of the household.

19. See Eli Ginzberg (1976). For Ginzberg, the essential characteristics of the secondary labor market include lack of occupational stability, security of employment, and above-average earnings.

20. See J. Heyman (n.d.). As well, political and commercial life has been strongly linked. As early as 1890 or so my own grandfather made Conestoga wagons and stagecoaches in Magdalena, Sonora, situated 120 miles south of Tucson and sold them for resale to Don Federico Ronstad in Tucson, who had sold my grandfather some of the materials with which to construct the finished products. My own father lived in Tucson with his mother's sister and attended Tucson elementary and secondary schools in order to learn the accounting and English necessary to maintain my grandfather's business in Magdalena.

21. During the depression between 1929 and 1935, repatriation and deportation measures were instituted in the United States and a half million persons of Mexican origin were "voluntarily" forced to Mexico. Of interest is that one-third were American citizens. See Hoffman (1974).

22. See for example, Dickerson (1919); Meriam (1933); Stanley (1920). Stanley is especially instructive in regard to the rather ethnocentric premises on which such programs were based. The author contends that Mexicans basically are "handicapped by the lack of home training, by shyness, by an emotional nature, all of which interfere with their progress in the conventional course of study" (715). Equally a problem according to the author, is that "they appear dull, stupid, phlegmatic . . . restive in school and truant whenever possible." She concludes that "We need to cultivate the creative ability [drawing, penmanship, handiwork] rather than the critical and analytical for . . . the Mexican illustrates as he does in the large what is true only in a lesser degree of most of us" (715).

23. See especially the self-exposition by Richard Rodriguez (1982).

24. "Operation Wetback" was an INS sponsored program of explusion of undocumented Mexican labor during fiscal 1954 and allegedly resulted in the departure of 1,300,000 "illegals" according to INS authorities. See U.S. Department of Justice, *Annual Report of the Immigration and Naturalization Service* (1954, 31).

25. See especially Cornelius (1988), Chavez (1988), and Chavez et al. (Forthcoming).

26. See Cornelius, 4.

27. The cultural implication for some U.S. Mexicans is to differentiate themselves as "American Mexicans" from the "mojados" (wetbacks). Analogous processes are set in motion for Mexicans in Mexico with differentiations made between themselves as real *Mexicanos* and the despised *"pochos"* from the United States. The latter term is basically derisive of the linguistic and value systems of the U.S.-born Mexican.

28. According to recently unpublished data of our Tucson Project Study (Carlos G. Vélez-Ibanez and James B. Greenberg, Multidimensional Functions of Non-Market Forms of Exchange among Mexicans/Chicanos in Tucson, Arizona, NSF Project BNS-8418906, 1986), 80 percent of the respondents indicated that they mostly or only speak English at school while on the job 37 percent used both English and Spanish and most of the remainder (59 percent) used mostly or only English. Only 8.9 percent used only English at home and 7.1 percent used mostly English at home; 30 percent spoke only Spanish, 36 percent mostly Spanish, and 18 percent spoke both at home (Gerardo Bernache and Ramon Gomez, "Partial Report #1, Tucson Project" [Tucson, Arizona: Bureau of Applied Research in Anthropology, March 27, 1989], 16, manuscript).

29. Portions of the section on cross-border clustered households have been previously published in Vélez-Ibanez (1988a), especially 35–36.

30. A second type of variant is the Mexican economic elites who have taken up semi-permanent and permanent residence in the United States along the U.S.-Mexican border. Although Mexican political elites have long settled in semi-permanent or permanent residency in the United States as the aftermath of revolutionary activities in Mexico in the late nineteenth and early twentieth century, the monetary devaluation crisis that began in 1981 and continued through 1985 pushed out Mexican capital and its owners for the first time. In the period 1981–85, $34.2 billion left Mexico of which three-quarters was invested in the United States. See Murguia (1986).

With the flight of capital, Mexican elites purchased homes in wealthy areas in La Jolla, California, Tucson, Arizona, and in parts of Texas and New Mexico. However, the mobilization pattern of migration as well as place of choice seems to be the same as that of working-class (Murguia 1986, 13). Both elites and working class mobilize kinship, fictive kinship, and friendship, and use these as contact points, institutional access, and a residential platform on which to arrive. This is certainly the case in Tucson, Arizona, in which entire condominium complexes have been purchased by Sonorenses who have had long-standing dense relationships with each other. Business investments, ritual and secular activities, and household exchange are basically kept to the inner network of elites.

Yet most recently, even semi-permanent residence and rather closed elite networks have begun to change due to intermarriage with other Hispanic elites as well as with non-Hispanics. The latter is usually a result of university attendance in either a southwestern university or one of the East or West Coast elite universities.

31. The work by Keefe and Padilla (1987), show that for the most part there is a clear disengagement from Mexican relatives and a greater exchange relation with localized kin networks. While the latter is generally true of Tucson Mexicans,

their rate and volume of disengagement are artifacts of proximity to the border, economic opportunity of exchange, and remaining relatives. It is not unusual along the border for almost complete familial networks born in Mexico to migrate to adjoining U.S. states so that the remnants left in Mexico are largely the elderly and the very young.

The Keefe and Padilla studies were carried out among nonborderlands populations and with a sample of persons largely residing in two California counties (Santa Barbara and Ventura), from the case studies they presented were not part of cross-border networks which could be maintained. There is little indication in the quantitative or qualitative material analyzed in this work and others (Keefe 1978; Keefe et al. 1978; 1979) that attention was directed to this phenomenon. Given the distance from the border and lack of historical connections between the families studied and the border region, it is understandable that Keefe and Padilla should not have found significant cross-border networks.

32. See Oscar Ramirez (1980, 2).

33. See Vélez-Ibanez (1983, 156) in which *confianza* is defined "as the willingness to engage in generalized reciprocity."

34. Gross monthly income for the sample of forty interviewed and observed clustered and unclustered households was $2,097 with a mean of 5.1 persons per household. Approximately 80 percent of income was earned from wages or salary with 20 percent earned in the informal economy with weekend labor, bartering, and used-articles sales. Income was generated by two or more household heads and members in 40 percent of the households, 40 percent by male heads only, and 20 percent by female heads only. The male and female heads percentages do not represent single-parent households but only that either a male or female head was employed. Eighty-four percent of the Tucson sample was married, 5 percent were single, 5 percent divorced, and 5 percent were widowed. The percentage of true single parents with children was only 5 percent.

35. The case studies use pseudonyms to protect the identity of the informants as well as to maintain confidentiality. I have also changed some events as well as relationships in order to protect well-known households from public embarrassment. In some cases it was impossible to change the ethnographic details without distorting the substance of the relationships and behaviors described. I have tried to be most careful in balancing appropriate ethnographic detail with the necessity of keeping confidential the lives of our informants.

Of the possible sample forty households, I have selected three as being fairly typical of the social and cultural heterogeneity of Tucson's Hispanic community and reflective of the household occupational and income characteristics discussed. One case illustrates the early life cycle of a working-class household headed by a single person; a second, a middle-class household in which intermarriage with an Anglo seems to be relatively unimportant in the social and cultural systems in which they participate; and a third, of a working-class, late cycle "core" household of a retired couple.

36. Bean and Tienda (1987, 186) show that there is a trend of increasing marital instability among Mexican females aged fifteen to sixty-four compared with non-Hispanic whites. Comparing 1960–80, 15.8 percent of non-Hispanic

white women experienced marital instability in 1960 while 18.7 percent of Mexican women experienced marital instability. In 1980, 23.3 percent of non-Hispanic white women had experienced marital instability while 21.2 percent of Mexican women had experienced the same. It must be noted, however, that the percentage difference between the two populations is much greater when based on the southwestern states alone with 31.6 percent of non-Hispanic white women and 22.7 percent of Mexican women experiencing marital instability.

37. A significant difference between clustered households and nuclear-based ones, is that clustered households seem to share in what I have termed broad funds of knowledge (Vélez-Ibanez 1988a; 1988b), which include a great array of familial, household, neighborhood, and institutional contexts. The funds of knowledge include information and formulas containing the mathematics, architecture, chemistry, physics, biology, and engineering for the construction and repair of homes, the repair of most mechanical devices, methods for planting and gardening, butchering, cooking, hunting, and "making things" in general. Other parts of such funds included information regarding access to institutional assistance, school programs, legal help, transportation routes, occupational opportunities, and the most economical places to purchase services and goods. Our impression is that clustered households are much more self-sufficient and do not depend as greatly on the market for technical assistance.

The borderlands region has been a particular focus for the complex development of such funds. Border populations constantly emerge as creators of experience by adjusting, coping, learning, manipulating, resisting and experimenting with traditional, syncretic, and novel ways of making a living, using scarce resources and limited skills, and expanding as well as constricting the funds of knowledge necessary for survival.

Such funds are the accumulated and experimented information and practices used and manipulated by Mexican households, and shape the social platforms on which progeny may emerge as human cognitive and emotive personalities. These funds at one time were part of rural or small urban settings such as ranchos in Sonora, mining towns in southeastern Arizona, and developing cities like Albuquerque or Tucson. There funds have been, and for immigrating households in the present still are, useful skills and information associated with making a living in a small-scale productive system.

Yet, because of such rapid technological change in the region there is a process in which such funds become "commoditized" so that only portions of those funds are useful for the market and, depending on the rapidity of economic and social mobility, become increasingly narrowed and constrained.

The funds are never static to the region's dynamism. Most males, for example, will have held an average of 5.3 jobs during their lifetimes. The most important characteristic of such changes is that such individuals are able to shift from low-paying service work in restaurants to high-paying industrial work in the mines in this region, and then back to low-paying work as musical sales clerks in a store once the copper market becomes weakened. What is of importance is that with each job shift there is an accumulation in the knowledge base that is required to work successfully. In the example cited above, the individual accumulated information about food serving, food preparation, spoilage, recipes, and the operation of a restaurant. Second, depending on the specific area of mining, it will not be unusual for the individual to learn geological information, hydraulics and mechanics, chemistry and physics, and computational skills. In the last occupation, an individual will gain access to the entire gamut of musical presentation, composition, and names of artists, groups, and musical styles. Yet such information will not be retained by the single individual alone and because of the clustered network phenomenon each job and contact contributes to the larger fund of knowledge. Because of the limited level of wealth and income for most U.S.-Mexican households, such funds are in constant use, and transmitted to following generations.

38. Moore (1988, 2) states that the percentage of poverty among Hispanics had grown from 22 percent in 1979 to 28.2 percent in 1987. This is an aggregated figure of all Hispanics including Puerto Ricans that would raise the poverty percentage to that level. In disaggregating Mexican from Puerto Rican household income in 1980, the differences in income between groups becomes clear in that for household income below $14,999 or less, Puerto Ricans are likely to have 10 percent more of their families earning between $5-9,999 than U.S. Mexicans and 12.2 percent more Puerto Rican families earning $5,000 or less than U.S. Mexicans (U.S. Bureau of the Census 1982: 41).

39. See pp. 40-41, and 44-45, *The Changing Profile of Mexican America: A Sourcebook for Policy Making,* San Antonio, Tomas Rivera Center, October, 1985.

40. Ibid., 48.

41. U.S. Bureau of the Census 1984.

42. Mark Testa (1988), "Ethnic Variations in the Formation of Independent Households by Adolescent Welfare Mothers." Paper prepared for the Population Association of American Session on Welfare Policies, April, from a study conducted in Chicago.

43. Other populations in the U.S. also have to cope with distinctive structural and substantive economic and social disparity, e.g., African-American populations throughout the country and Puerto Ricans on the East Coast. As Kennedy (1980), Stack (1974), and Valentine (1980) have shown, such populations develop a number of creative household approaches to mitigate the effects of such conditions, including the extensive use of social networks and helping systems. Yet the regional context for Puerto Ricans and African Americans differ markedly from that of U.S. Mexicans, so careful analytical distinction should be made of each type of adaptive and coping mechanism in relation to an appropriate economic and political context. While similar networks operate among African Americans and Puerto Ricans, most studies seem to locate the necessity of such relations in the effects of racism, economic disparity, and the accompanying large proportion of female-headed households. For African Americans the percentage of households headed by a female, 40.6 percent is almost the same as for Puerto Rican households, 36.5 pecent (Bean and Tienda 1987; 192). In comparison,

only 18.9 percent of U.S.-Mexican households were headed by females, and among U.S. Cubans, 16.0 percent, so that different sets of explanations seem to be required for the emergence of similar cultural and social behaviors.

44. Franklin J. James, (1988), "Persistent Urban Poverty and The Underclass: A Perspective Based on the Hispanic Experience," Paper prepared for a conference on persistent poverty convened at Trinity University, San Antonio, April 8, the Tomas Rivera Center, 1–42.

45. James (1988, 1–42) states that his analysis has found greater patterns of separation of Hispanics by class but that such separation does not have the same characteristics as for blacks since U.S. Mexicans have access to mainstream businesses and organizations. In conjunction with such separation, U.S. Mexicans do not have great rates of out migration from their settings and the young males, especially, are strongly motivated to work and to move among other Mexican populations. As well, James states that the U.S.-Mexican family's structure and functions differ from African Americans and presumably Puerto Ricans in New York. He cites J. Moore (1988), and states that among Mexicans, family needs supersede individual ones and families serve as a place of refuge in times of need. Within that context, then, the women's roles are highly valued as mothers with attending support created for those roles to be fulfilled. He concludes from an analysis of case material in Denver, Colorado that compares U.S. Mexicans with African Americans within the same urban poverty contexts that (1) the pace of metropolitan spatial decentralization is slower in the Southwest because cities are generally newer; (2) Hispanics were not victims of economic dislocation to the same extent as African Americans; (3) there is less prevalence of underclass behavior among poor Hispanics than blacks; (4) Hispanics had high educational drop out rates; (5) there was high fertility of husband-wife families not linked to underclass behavior; and (6) that immigrant status was independent of underclass category. Finally, James (34) states that "the profile of persistent poverty in Denver supports the conclusion that the main causes of persistent poverty among Hispanics lie outside standard models of the underclass."

In comparing U.S. Mexicans and African Americans within the same city and neighborhoods, the "underclass" concept fails to develop heuristically or as a necessary or sufficient explanation. James's (1988, 27) analysis of both populations in Denver's most impoverished neighborhoods clearly undermines the concept by showing that U.S. Mexicans in identical urban situations differ significantly in work and employment, support from friends, the church, family, and other community based organizations.

Moore (1988, 5) states that the sunbelt where most U.S. Mexicans live is very different from the rustbelt where Wilson's model might be applicable. She states that unemployment in the Southwest was 8 percent for U.S. Mexicans in 1988 compared with 12 percent for African Americans and 5 percent for Anglos (4). For Moore the borderlands area is an arena in which binational economies operate and where economic process are tied at productive, labor, and consumptive levels.

Critiquing the applicability of Wilson's neighborhood "concentration" processes of successful parts of the population engaged in "flight out" and only the poverty part of the population "staying in," Moore (6–7) states that before the 1980s U.S.-Mexican communities were vertically integrated communities but that even poor barrios studied a generation ago were reasonably stable with effective neighborhood institutions that were not the case in Puerto Rican neighborhoods. As well, she states that there is no evidence of a middle- and working-class exodus from Mexican neighborhoods. To reinforce this assertion, Moore cites Hansen and Cardenas's (1987) data for San Antonio, Texas that shows that most (85 percent) of the businesses in Mexican neighborhoods were U.S.-Mexican owned. Other institutions such as the church with their voluntary associations and neighborhood centers were institutionally strong.

46. Portions of this section were previously published in Vélez-Ibanez (1988a), 40–41.

47. Portions of this section appear in Carlos G. Vélez-Ibanez and James B. Greenberg, "Formation and Transformation of Funds of Knowledge Among U.S.-Mexican Households," *Anthropology and Education Quarterly,* 23, 4:313–35.

48. See Carlos G. Vélez-Ibanez and James B. Greenberg, (1986), "Multidimensional Functions of Non-Market Forms of Exchange Among Mexicans/Chicanos in Tucson, Arizona": NSF Project, BNS-8418906. Also, Luis C. Moll, Carlos Vélez-Ibanez, and James B. Greenberg (1988).

49. *Confianza* is a cultural construct indicating the willingness to engage in generalized reciprocity. For a full discussion, see Vélez-Ibanez (1983, 10–16).

50. See Tapia (1989).

51. See for example, Dickerson (1919); Meriam (1933); Stanley (1920). Stanley is especially instructive regarding the ethnocentric premises on which such programs were based. The author contends that Mexicans are "handicapped by the lack of home training, by shyness, by an emotional nature, all of which interfere with their progress in the conventional course of study" (715). Equally a problem according to the author, is that "they appear dull, stupid, phlegmatic . . . restive in school and truant whenever possible." She concludes that "We need to cultivate the creative ability [drawing, penmanship, handiwork] rather than the critical and analytical for . . . the Mexican illustrates as he does in the large what is true only in a lesser degree of most of us" (715).

52. See W. J. Wilson (1987) for the analysis of the concept of the underclass and for a lucid discussion of the idea as it might pertain to Hispanics, see J. Moore (1988).

53. See the excellent review by B. F. Williams (1989).

54. See Vigil (1988), a fine discussion of his concept of multiple marginality that alludes to class domination, ecological constraints, familial disruption, and racism as the conflation that selects certain personalities to engage in gang behavior.

REFERENCES

Arce, C. 1981. A Reconsideration of Chicano Culture and Identity, *Daedalus* 110:171–91.

————. 1982. Dimensions of Familism. Paper presented to the Pacific Sociological Association, April 22, San Diego, California.

Bateson, G. 1978. *Steps to an Ecology of Mind.* New York: Ballantine.

Bean, F. D., and M. Tienda. 1987. *The Hispanic Population of the United States.* New York: Russell Sage Foundation.

Bernache, G., and R. Gomez. 1989. Partial Report #1, Tucson Project, Bureau of Applied Research in Anthropology, March 27, Tucson, Arizona.

Campione, J., A. Brown, and R. Ferrara. 1982. Mental Retardation and Intelligence. In *Handbook of Human Intelligence.* Ed, R. J. Sternberg, New York: Cambridge University Press.

Chavez, L. R. 1988. Settlers and Soujourners: The Case of Mexicans in the United States, *Human Organization* 47:95–108.

Chavez, L. R., E. T. Flores, and M. Lopez-Garza. N.D. Here Today, Gone Tomorrow?: Undocumented Settlers and Immigration Reform. *Human Organization.* Forthcoming.

Cohen, Y. A. 1969. Ends and Means in Political Control: State Organization and the Punishment of Adultery, Incest and Violation of Celibacy. *American Anthropologist* 71(4): 658–87.

Cornelius, W. A. 1988. The Role of Mexican Labor in the North American Economy of the 1990s. Paper prepared for the Fourth Annual Emerging Issues Program for State Legislative Leaders: The North American Economy in the 1990s, December 7–10, University of California, San Diego.

Corrigan, P., and D. Sayer. 1985. *The Great Arch: English State Formation as Cultural Revolution.* Oxford: Basil Blackwell.

Despres, L. A. 1964. The Implications of Nationalist Policies in British Guiana for the Development of Cultural Theory. *American Anthropologist* 66: 1051–77.

————. 1967. *Cultural Pluralism and Nationalist Politics in British Guiana.* Chicago: Rand McNally.

————. 1969. Differential Adaptations and Micro-Cultural Evolution in Guyana, *Southwestern Journal of Anthropology* 25:14–44.

Dickerson, R. F. 1919. Some Suggestive Problems in the Americanization of Mexicans. *Pedagogical Seminary,* Sept. 288–93.

Diez-Canedo, J. 1981. *Undocumented Migration to the United States: A New Perspective.* Translated from the Spanish by Dolores E. Mills. Albuquerque: Center for Latin American Studies, University of New Mexico.

Erickson, E. H. 1963. *Childhood and Society.* 2d ed. New York: Norton.

Fernandez-Kelly, P. 1987. Technology and Employment along the U.S.-Mexican Border. In *The United States and Mexico: Face to Face with New Technology,* ed. Cathryn L. Thorup. New Brunswick, N.J.: Transaction Books.

Feuerstein, R. 1979. *The Dynamic Assessment of Retarded Performers: The Learning Potential Assessment Device, Theory, Instruments, and Techniques.* Baltimore, Md.: University Park Press.

Furnivall, J. S. 1948. *Colonial Policy and Practice: A Comparative Study of Burma and Netherlands India.* London: Cambridge University Press.

Garcia, J.A. 1982. Ethnicity and Chicanos: Measurement of Ethnic Identification, Identity, and Consciousness. *Hispanic Journal of Behavioral Sciences* 43(4): 295–314.

Garcia y Griego, M. 1983. *Mexico and the United States: Migration, History, and the Idea of Sovereignty.* No. 7. El Paso: Center for Interamerican and Border Studies, University of Texas.

Ginzberg, E. 1976. *Labor Market: Segments and Shelters.* Washington, D.C.: U.S. Government Printing Office.

Goffman, E. 1961. *Asylums: Essays on the Social Situations and Other Inmates.* Garden City, N.Y.: Doubleday.

Gonzalez-Archegia, B. 1987. California-Mexico Linkages. Paper presented at First Annual California-Mexico Business Conference, October 28–29, Los Angeles, California.

Goody, J. 1983. *The Development of the Family and Marriage in Europe.* London: Cambridge University Press.

Griswold del Castillo, R. 1984. *La Familia: Chicano Families in the Urban Southwest, 1848 to the Present.* Notre Dame: University of Notre Dame Press.

Hallowell, A. I. 1968. Behavioral Evolution and the Emergence of the Self. In *Evolution and Anthropology: A Centennial Appraisal,* ed. B. Meggers. Washington, D.C.: Anthropological Society of Washington.

Henry, J. 1963. *Culture Against Man.* New York: Random House.

Heyman, J. N.D. The Power of the United States Border Over Mexican Lives: The Case of Cross-Border Kinship. In *The U.S.-Mexico Border in Anthropological Context,* ed. C. Vélez-Ibanez, J. Greenberg, and R. Trotter. Forthcoming.

Hoffman, A. 1974. *Unwanted Mexicans in the Great Depression.* Tucson: University of Arizona Press.

Horner, A. J. 1979. *Object Relations and the Developing Ego in Therapy.* New York: Jason Aronson.

James, F. J. 1988. *Persistent Urban Poverty and The Underclass: A Perspective Based on the Hispanic Experience.* Paper presented to the Conference on Persistent Poverty, April 8, at Trinity University, San Antonio.

Kagan, S. 1986. Cooperative Learning and Socio-Cultural Factors in Schooling. In *Young Language: Social and Cultural Factors in Schooling Language Minority Students.* Los Angeles: California State University.

Keefe, S. E. 1979. Urbanization, Acculturation, and Extended Family Ties: Mexican-Americans in Cities. *American Ethnologist.* 6(2): 349–65.

Keefe, S. E., and A. M. Padilla. 1987. *Chicano Ethnicity.* Albuquerque: University of New Mexico Press.

Keefe. S. E., A. Padilla, and M. L. Carlos. 1978. *Emotional Support Systems in Two Cultures: A Comparison of Mexican-Americans and Anglo-Americans.* Occasional Paper No. 7. Los Angeles: Spanish Speaking Mental Health, UCLA.

———. 1979. The Mexican-American Extended Family as an Emotional Support System. *Human Organization.* 38(2): 144–52 (summer).

Kennedy, T. R. 1980. *You Gotta Deal with It: Black Family Relations in a Southern Community.* New York: Oxford University Press.

Kuper, L. 1969. Plural Societies: Perspectives and Problems. In *Pluralism in Africa,* ed. Leo Kuper and M. G. Smith, Berkeley: University of California Press.

Kuper, L., and M. G. Smith, eds. 1969. *Pluralism in Africa.* Berkeley: University of California Press.

Laing, R. D. 1963. *The Politics of the Family and Other Essays.* New York: Vintage Books.

Litwak, E. 1960. Geographic Mobility and Extended Family Cohesion. *American Sociological Review* 25: 9–21.

Lomnitz, L. N.D. Horizontal and Vertical Relations and the Social Structure of Urban Mexico. Unpublished ms.

Martinez, O. 1983. *The Foreign Orientation of the Mexican Border Economy,* Border Perspectives, No. 2. El Paso: Center for Interamerican and Border Studies, The University of Texas.

————. 1988. *Troublesome Border.* Tucson: University of Arizona Press.

Mannheim, K. 1952. The Problems of Generations. In *Essays on the Sociology of Knowledge,* 2d ed., ed. Paul Kescskemeti. London: Routledge and Kegan Paul.

Meriam, J. C. 1933. Activity Curriculum in a School of Mexican Children. *Journal of Experimental Education,* June, 304–8.

Mitchell, J. C. 1969. *Social Networks in Urban Situations.* Zambia: Manchester University Press for the Institute for Social Research, University of Zambia.

Moll, L. C., C. G. Vélez-Ibanez, and J. B. Greenberg. 1988. Community Knowledge and Classroom Practice: Combining Resources for Literary Instruction. Innovative Approaches Research Project Grant, Development Associates. Manuscript.

Moore, J. 1988. *An Assessment of Hispanic Poverty: Is There an Hispanic Underclass?* San Antonio: The Thomas Rivera Center.

Murguia. V. de. 1986. *Capital Flight and Economic Crisis: Mexican Post-Devaluation Exiles in a California Community.* San Diego: Center for U.S.-Mexican Studies, University of California.

Ortner, S. 1984. Theory in Anthropology Since the Sixties. *Comparative Studies in Society and History* 26:126–66.

Porras, A. Salas. N.D. Crisis, Maquiladoras y Estructura Sociopolitica en Chihuahua, Sonora y Baja California. Manuscript.

Ramirez, O. 1980. Extended Family Support and Mental Health Status Among Mexicans in Detroit. *La Red* 28:2 (May).

Riding, A. 1989. *Distant Neighbors: A Portrait of the Mexicans.* New York: Random House.

Rodriguez, R. 1982. *Hunger of Memory, the Education of Richard Rodriguez: An Autobiography.* New York: D. R. Godine.

Schwartz, T. 1968. Beyond Cybernetics: Constructs Expectations, and Goals in Human Adaptation. Paper presented at symposium 40, The Effects of Conscious Purpose on Human Adaptation. Wenner-Gen Foundation for Anthropological Research, Burg Wartenstein, Austria.

Sena-Rivera, J. 1980. La Familia Hispana as a Natural Support System: Strategies for Prevention. In *Hispanic Natural Support Systems,* ed. R. Valle and W. Vega, 75–81. Sacramento: State of California, Department of Mental Health, Office of Prevention.

Smith, C. 1984. Local History in Global Context: Social and Economic Transitions in Western Guatemala, *Comparative Studies in Society and History* 26:193–228.

Smith, M.G. 1969a. Institutional and Political Conditions of Pluralism. In Kuper and Smith, 1969.

———. 1969b. Pluralism in Precolonial African Societies. In Kuper and Smith, 1969.

———. 1969c. Some Developments in the Analytic Framework of Pluralism. In Kuper and Smith, 1969.

Stack, C. 1974. *All Our Kin: Strategies for Survival in a Black Community.* New York: Harper & Row.

Stanley, G. C. 1920. Special Schools for Mexicans. *Survey* 44: 714–15 (September 15).

Stoddard, E. R. and J. Hedderson. 1987. *Trends and Patterns of Poverty Along the U.S.-Mexico Border.* Borderlands Research Monograph Series. Las Cruces: New Mexico State University.

Tapia, J. 1989. The Recreation of School at Home Through Play. Bureau of Applied Research Report, January 25, Tucson, Arizona.

Tiano, S. B. 1985. *Export Processing, Women's Work, and the Employment Problem in Developing Countries: The Case of the Maquiladora Program in Northern Mexico.* El Paso: Center for Interamerican and Border Studies, University of Texas.

Trevino, F., D. B. Trevino, C. A. Stroup, and L. Ray. 1989. *The Feminization of Poverty among Hispanic Households.* San Antonio: Tomas Rivera Center.

U.S. Bureau of the Census. 1982. Spanish Origin Population, United States Summary. *Statistical Abstract of the U.S.* 10th ed. no. 46. Washington, D.C.

U.S. Department of Justice. 1954. *Annual Report of the Immigration and Naturalization Service.* Washington, D.C., 31.

U.S.-Mexico Report. 1989. Las Cruces: Joint Border Research Institute, New Mexico State University, 18–19 (April).

U.S.-Mexico Report. 1989. Las Cruces: Joint Border Research Institute, New Mexico State University, 11 (July).

Valentine, B. 1980. *Hustling and Other Hard Work: Life Styles in the Ghetto.* New York: Free Press.

Van Den Berghe, P. 1967. *Race and Racism: A Comparative Perspective.* New York: John Wiley & Sons.

———. 1970. *Race and Ethnicity.* New York: Basic Books.

Velez, M. T. 1983. The Social Context of Mothering: A Comparison of Mexican-American and Anglo Mother Infant Interaction Patterns. Ph.D. Diss., Wright Institute of Psychology, Los Angeles.

Vélez-Ibanez, C. G. 1980. Los Movimientos Chicanos: Problemas y Perspectivas. In *Las Relaciones Mexico/Estados Unidos,* ed. David Barkin. Mexico D.F.: Editorial Nueva Imagen.

―――. 1983. *Bonds of Mutual Trust: The Cultural Systems of Rotating Credit Associations among Urban Mexicans and Chicanos.* New Brunswick, N.J.: Rutgers University Press.

―――. 1988a. Networks of Exchange Among Mexicans in the U.S. and Mexico: Local Level Mediating Responses to National and International Transformation. *Urban Anthropology and Studies of Cultural Systems and World Economic Development* 17(1): 27–51.

―――. 1988b. Forms and Functions Among Mexicans in the Southwest: Implications for Classroom Use. Paper presented to invited session Forms and Functions of Funds of Knowledge within Mexican Households in the Southwest, November 20, American Anthropological Association.

―――. 1989. Transmission and Patterning of Funds of Knowledge: Shaping and Emergence of Confianza in U.S.-Mexican Children. Paper presented to Society for Applied Anthropology, Annual Meeting, April 5–9, Santa Fe, New Mexico.

―――. 1993a. Ritual Cycles of Exchange: The Process of Cultural Creation and Management. In *Celebrations of Identity: Multiple Voices in American Ritual Performance.* ed. Pamela R. Frese, 120–43. Westport: Begir and Garvey.

―――. 1993b. U.S. Mexicans in the Borderlands: Being Poor Without the Underclass. In *In the Barrios: Latinos and the Underclass Debate,* ed. Joan Moore and Raquel Pinderhughes, 195–220. New York: Russell Sage Foundation.

Vélez-Ibanez, C. G., J. B. Greenberg, and B. Johnstone. 1984. The Ethnic, Economic and Educational Structure of Tucson, Arizona: The Limits of Possibility for Mexican-Americans in 1982. In *Proceedings of the 1984 Meeting of the Rocky Mountain Council on Latin American Studies,* 154–64. Las Cruces: Center for Latin American Studies, New Mexico State University.

Vigil, D. 1988. *Barrio Gangs: Street Life and Identity in Southern California.* Austin: University of Texas Press.

―――. 1989. Personal communication.

Wallace, A. F. C. 1961. *Culture and Personality.* New York: Random House.

Wilson, W. J. 1987. *The Truly Disadvantaged: The Inner City, the Underclass and Public Policy.* Chicago: University of Chicago Press.

Williams, B. 1989. A Class Act: Anthropology and the Race to Nation Across Ethnic Terrain. In *Annual Review of Anthropology,* ed. B. Seigel, A. R. Beals, and S. A. Tyler, 401–44. Palo Alto, Calif. Annual Reviews.

Wolf, E. R., 1988. Afterword. *Urban Anthropology and Studies of Cultural Systems and World Economic Development* 17(1).

Chapter 7

Disorders of Our Own: A Conclusion

Roy A. Rappaport

I. On Coming Home

The essays making up this volume have all been concerned with disorders affecting our own country. Anthropology, it seems, is coming home to America, one of the societies from which it first sprang and from which it then departed on its voyages to strange places. A majority of us have, of course, worked, and may continue to work, abroad in societies we chose because they were very different from our own and because they were separated from our own by great distances. For better or worse, no place is very far from anyplace anymore, but many, perhaps most, of us will, and probably should, remain in our exotic diaspora to provide continuing accounts of how the erstwhile separate worlds ethnographers describe articulate to, resist, and become absorbed into an increasingly integrated world system. At the same time, more and more of us should, and probably will, take up research in our own society, and more and more of this domestic research is likely to focus on domestic troubles.

The essays appearing together here came out of two years of conversation in which the authors not only spoke to but actually listened to each other carefully. They are in essential agreement on the need for anthropology to engage problems facing its own society and for it to become appropriately active in their amelioration, but are nevertheless, so diverse in so many respects that no attempt (on my part at least) could summarize or synthesize them. The best I can do in this conclusion is, first, to reflect on some of the difficulties inherent to the engagement of anthropology with the ills of its own society, particularly when it focuses on social values that it itself in some degree shares—like the pluralism, participation, community, and equality that in one way or another concern all our authors. I will move on to the problem of defining social problems, then to the matter of correction and, finally, to the place of anthropology in what Stephen Toulmin calls "Post-Modern Science."

Domestic Anthropology and Its Difficulties

The repatriation of anthropology, which has been going on for some time (see, for instance, D. Messerschmidt 1981, and a decade earlier, Dell Hymes 1972) has recently been gaining momentum, but is not quite one and the same as a concern to engage contemporary social problems. In conducting research in America it may, however, be difficult to avoid conducting research on the problems *of* America. For anthropology to come home is for it to come face-to-face with paradox, dis-ease, and so multitudinous an array of quandaries, dilemmas, crises, inequities, dangers, stresses, burdens, tribulations, and disorders—cultural, social, organic, and ecological—that they cannot all be named, much less studied as such.

Anthropological research on American society and culture is not new, of course. MacLennan reminds us of the work of Warner and others in the 1920s and 1930s and Peacock recalls the importance of Weber's American experience in the development of his concept of cultural systems. Nor, obviously, is the application of anthropology to contemporary problems at all novel (see Baba 1986 and Eddy and Partridge 1984). One of the points this volume seeks to make (that anthropology, although it does not have *solutions* to the problems of the world in general, or of our society in particular, does have some more or less unique contributions to make to their understanding and therefore to their amelioration) has not only been argued before (see especially Wulff and Fiske 1987) but, all but the most disillusioned of our colleagues would agree, has been demonstrated before. The converse, namely that the benefits of engagement are reciprocal—that grappling with contemporary social and cultural problems may not only enlarge understanding of those problems and increase anthropology's influence in society at large, but also expand anthropological theory and method *generally*—is another, and less familiar, implication of this volume (see also Messerschmidt 1981).

The ultimate aims of all the authors, as I see them, are derived from, but are not a simple sum of, the two previous points. They are first, to relocate both engaged and domestic research within anthropology—in short, to move them away from the discipline's periphery *toward* its center (there is no claim that engaged domestic research should take control of anthropology's center)—and second, to move anthropology as a whole toward a more central position in our society's attempts to reflect on its difficulties and to deal with them—to "anthropologize," so to speak, public discourse about contemporary problems.

There are impedances, however; some of them, as Forman has pointed out, internal to our discipline itself. Neither the repatriation of anthropology nor its increased engagement have been unambiguously encouraged by our own ideology or institutions. Anthropology, on the whole, has always valued its theoretical concerns more highly than its practical ones, perhaps properly so, although it can at least be argued that the theoretical and practical should be mutually formative. Nevertheless, the attitudes of many academically oriented anthropologists toward the application of their discipline to the problems besetting our own and other societies are even more doubting than commendable modesty would justify, running from skeptical through suspicious to cynical. It may not be surprising, therefore, that despite the fact that a large number of our colleagues (inside as well as outside the academy) do applied work, or at least devote critical thought to contemporary problems, such concerns are underrepresented, to put it mildly, in our graduate curricula. It is in academia that anthropology defines and reproduces itself and, as things now stand, in the course of doing so anthropology continues to relegate engagement, whether fully "applied" or simply "critical," to its margins.

As for anthropology's homecoming, it may be suggested that repatriation does not conform very well to the ideal of the lone fieldworker's questing after eternal verities in otherworldly places where malaria is endemic or frostbite a recurrent danger, nor to such thisworldly considerations as academic hiring practices. Geography remains more important in the configuration of departments than it does in the intellectual life of the discipline and contemporary America has not yet been admitted as a bonafide member to the class of anthropological culture areas. Its students, therefore, remain institutionally anomalous, and there may well be more university positions open to Melanesianists than to anthropologists of the United States.

Valorization of the foreign and strange may also have been encouraged by certain pseudomethodological or epistemological dicta, the validity of which we may have convinced ourselves as we retailed them to freshmen. This takes some discussion.

Until recently it was truistical to cite the difficulty or even impossibility of doing penetrating research on a society into which one had been enculturated and socialized. This dubious principle has been proclaimed in some classic places. Ruth Benedict put it as follows in the first chapter of *The Chrysanthemum and the Sword*: "A Japanese who writes about Japan passes over really crucial things which are as familiar to him and as invisible as the air he breathes. So do Americans when they write about America" (7). A little later she changes her metaphor and elaborates:

> The lenses through which any nation looks at life are not the ones another nation uses. It is hard to be conscious of the eyes through which one looks. Any country takes them for granted, and the tricks of focusing and of perspective which give any people its national view of life seem to that people the God-given arrangement of the landscape. In any matter of spectacles, we do not expect the man who wears them to know the formula for the lenses, and neither can we expect nations to analyze their own outlook on the world. When we want to know about spectacles, we train an oculist . . . (14)

There is, of course, something to Benedict's discussion and others like it, but I don't think very much. We are, to be sure, well warned in the first passage against the invisibility of the absolutely familiar but the difficulties such invisibility may generate may be more than offset by the high sensitivity to subtle differences that also accompanies familiarity. It may in fact be, as Mary Catherine Bateson has suggested (personal communication), sensitivity to such differences that make it difficult for domestic anthropology to ignore domestic difficulties. As insiders anthropologists of the familiar are likely to be struck by phenomena and changes in them that seem out of the usual order, and thus trouble for the society as constituted.

The second passage is blatantly fallacious. Individuals, *not* nations, analyze the "outlooks" of nations and we understand, much better than did our forebears in Benedict's day, that *no* individual reflects or represents "in small" the culture of his or her nation, that *no* nation is culturally monolithic, that *all* nations are crisscrossed by class, gender, ethnic, racial, regional, and other distinctions. It follows that familiar cultural terrains are not all separated from strange cultural regions by national borders, and while it may not be possible to find within the United States any group as culturally strange to us as, say, New Guinea

Highlanders it is not hard for anthropologists to find, should they want to, people from whom they are separated by considerable cultural distance. It may, indeed, be hard to find any from whom they are not. The cultural differences separating most American ethnologists from their fellow citizens are too great, too obvious and occasionally too painful to sink easily into invisibility. It is an irony that whereas the study of anthropology itself may help us bridge the cultural chasms lying between us and those who came to maturity in other societies or ethnic groups it may alienate us from those among whom we ourselves grew up. This alienation also has its compensations. At the same time that familiarity increases sensitivity to that which is out of order in the operation of society as constituted, a degree of alienation frees us from the society's own acccounts of itself.

It is also ironic to observe that some recent writers have, in effect, stood Benedict's injunction on its head. Their claim is that ethnographies done among peoples foreign and strange to us are bound to misrepresent their subjects because cultural "others" are so different from ourselves that we cannot comprehend them clearly enough to represent them adequately. It is further claimed that inadequate representation of the "other" is likely to, or even perforce must, contribute to the "other's" subordination. The likelihood that our representations will be inadequate has also been emphasized by some third world anthropologists who have stressed insufficient time in the field and less than nuanced control over local languages (see Owusu 1978).

If we took fully to heart the strictures from both sides, all ethnography would cease forthwith, but a large corpus of successful ethnographies, both domestic and foreign, demonstrate that it is realistic to construe this dilemma in less desperate terms. John L. Aguilar (1981) in the volume edited by Messerschmidt already cited, has discussed the comparative benefits and difficulties of "insider" versus "outsider" ethnography, and his discussion is exemplified or elaborated by every other essay in that volume. We might note, recognizing that the essence of the ethnographic method combines participation with observation, that the central problem of doing the ethnography of the strange is to gain more than an outside objective observer's knowledge of a society and culture in which the ethnographer has not participated. The problem of doing the ethnography of the familiar is, conversely, to gain more than a participant's inside knowledge of a society and culture in which the ethnographer has been more or less immersed. If either or both are, as critics have proclaimed, impossible, we can only note that many people have, nevertheless, done one or the other, and a few have done both, very well.

The ethnographic study of American subcultures—our own or others—is, of course, different from the study of U.S. culture and society "in general"—the general symbolic and social structure or system within which subcultures have their places. Problems like those with which this book is concerned, those surrounding democratic participation and cultural pluralism, and many others as well, may be manifested and experienced differently by members of different subcultures but must be understood to afflict the society as a whole. Whereas ethnography has an important, even central, role to play, we cannot rely entirely on ethnographic methods in approaching national difficulties but must employ national and global systemic concepts as well. The problems attending such studies are different from those attending "simple" ethnography. Distortion and error is less likely to arise from the invisibility of the familiar or the incomprehensibility of the strange than from the fact that, familiar or strange, alienated or not, our lives are directly and obviously affected by events in our own societies. We are not merely interested in events in our own society but are ourselves parties to them with interests in them. We are often inescapably invested in the matters we seek to investigate. Our studies, therefore, are vulnerable to biases arising from the conjunction of our own values and interests with the phenomena we attempt to explore. Our position in this respect, however, may not be significantly different from those of sociology, political science, and economics; social sciences that have traditionally worked mainly at home, with this qualification: they have always claimed more objectivity for their methods than we have for ours. But this difference can be reduced without costing us our anthropological souls, and we should be no more crippled by the possibilities of bias than are they. We will return to these matters in later sections. Here I would note that the arguments some anthropologists, like Benedict, have raised against domestic anthropology seem no more compelling than those that other anthropologists have raised against doing anthropology abroad.

Anthropology has hardly come home to an open-armed welcome from the discipline itself. There have been, and remain, traditional impedances, both ideological and institutional, to the continuing development of domestic anthropology. It would be an exaggeration to claim

that anthropology's future lies *entirely* at home but the claim that anthropology at home is crucial to anthropology's future is actually quite
modest, and anthropological barriers to domestic anthropology should
be removed or dissolved. This calls for nothing radical. All that need
be done is to increase the numbers of anthropologists of America hired
by academic departments, make room for their interests in our curricula,
refrain from discouraging students from doing doctoral research in the
United States, increase our engagement with matters of concern to publics
outside of anthropology and encourage the development of nonacademic
anthropology. The statement to the profession appended to this volume
includes more specific suggestions.

The Changing Significance of Domestic Anthropology

But why should anthropology focus on the United States more than it
has in the past? It has been coming home for a number of reasons,
some of which are simple, straightforward, and very practical, like increasing difficulties in obtaining the funding and the research visas requisite to foreign field study, a growing inclination of Third World elites to
associate anthropology with colonial pasts, and development economics
with national futures (as Peacock notes, to be an object of anthropological inquiry has been, ipso facto, to be marginalized), and finally, the
discomfort of many contemporary anthropologists with the discipline's
erstwhile ambiguous relationship to colonizing powers (I, for one, think
that we tend to exaggerate our ancestors' complicity in colonialism and
are inappropriately judgmental with respect to them, but this is not the
place to argue the matter).

There are more theoretical reasons for anthropology's repatriation.
No anthropologist could possibly believe the often-heard comment that
anthropology would soon have to go out of business anyhow because
its traditional subject matter is disappearing. By the same token, no
anthropologist could possibly deny that the circumstances of the communities traditionally constituting enthnography's subject matter are
changing more or less rapidly and radically. The implications are important. It is obvious, for one thing, that the fiction of the "ethnographic
present" which may at one time have had its heuristic uses no longer
does. All ethnography must now be located in history as well as geography. This requirement in itself does not constitute a brief for anthropology to turn more of its attention to its own society but it does
point in the direction of more profound considerations that do.

As Marcus and Fischer (1986, Introduction, Passim) have discussed at length, anthropology, since its own prehistory in the accounts of native customs brought back to Europe by explorers during the sixteenth, seventeenth, and eighteenth centuries, has constituted a critique, sometimes explicit but always at least tacit, of the societies and cultures from which its practitioners have come. Its descriptions of customs, institutions and systems of reasoning differing radically from those of Europe have served in their mere expression to call into question whatever claims might be advanced for the natural validity of Western practices and understandings. Ethnography and, before it, proto-ethnography revealed as conventional and relative that which had been taken to be natural and absolute.

The use of ethnography as a set of "countermirrors," revealing not reflections but inversions of our own culture ("In Samoa adolescence is *not* a time of *sturm und drang*"), has depended on difference, the radical otherness of the subject matter. It is this radical otherness that is being broken down or dissolved by processes of multinational or even global magnitude. Whether these processes and forces are to be accounted for fully by the special character of late capitalism, as Jamieson (1984) seems to propose, on whether (as I believe) developments in electronic technology and high-speed transportation are also elemental contributors, need not detain us. The point is that "we" and "the other," although profound differences continue to separate us, have come to stand on the same political-economic ground, that this makes for complications, to say the least, in the relationship of their institutions to ours and, correspondingly, changes the nature of the critique of our institutions and understandings that accounts of theirs have constitued for several hundred years. Furthermore, if the grounds on which others now stand are no longer discrete cultural islands but, increasingly, of culturally particular but nevertheless functionally specialized components of an increasingly coherent global system, that global system has its origins in, and continues to be energized by, industrial, technological, informational and financial processes now centered in and emanating largely from the United States, Western Europe, and Japan.

We have been led from theoretical and methodological considerations to matters of substance, cause, engagement, and praxis. The societies in which anthropologists have traditionally worked are at least as troubled by social, political, medical, and ecological problems as is America and some of their problems are more immediately life threatening. The domestic difficulties with which this book is concerned can, nevertheless, stake strong claims on our attention. Although it would be a serious mistake to claim that all of the troubles afflicting the societies that we have traditionally studied are to be accounted for by what goes on in the United States and other core or metropolis societies, it is reasonable to suggest that in an increasingly coherent world the disorders, or even simply the demands, of core societies may generate disorder in societies of the periphery ever more powerfully, more pervasively, and more profoundly. Inasmuch as the disorders of our own society are not simply our own problems but, with accelerating globalization increasingly generative of disorders in others, it follows that their understanding and amelioration are more fundamental, if not always more pressing, than are solutions to problems confined to more or less localized areas in the periphery.

Research in the United States is not a substitute for or alternative to research in Papua New Guinea, Indonesia, or Brazil. Ethnographies now done in those societies not only continue to be of value in their own right but also continue to be valuable as critiques of our own society, no longer by simple virtue of the cultural distinctiveness that they bring to our attention but by virtue of exposing what forces loosed from our own society have done, or are likely to do, to that distinctiveness, and how and at what price those forces are resisted. Domestic research, on the other hand, not only may analyze the effects of those same forces as they operate at home but also, we may hope, elucidate the nature and wellspring of those forces themselves. All of this is to say that engaged anthropology should not be confined to home but, like charity, would do well to begin there.

Knowledge and Values

The Introduction and all of the chapters in this volume make it clear that the authors take engaged anthropology to be value driven. Some discussion is warranted in light of the prevalence of value-neutral concepts of science, and even of social science.

First, that it is logically impossible to evade value consideration seems obvious. Even the most abstruse of disciplines, those whose subject matters are most remote from human affairs, for example pure mathematics and extragalactic astronomy, are driven by values of high generality among which the value of knowledge per se must be prominent. Such a value, virtually by tautology, must have a place not only in all learned fields but in all learning. As such it would seem to be of such high generality as to be unexceptionable, but exception has, in fact, been taken to it by respectable authorities. Folk wisdom—not to be sneered at—warns us of the dangers of small amounts of knowledge, and Ecclesiastics (1:18 KJV) tells us "in much wisdom there *is* much grief: and he that increaseth knowledge increaseth sorrow." In Genesis the Fall follows from eating of the Tree of the Knowledge of Good and *Bad* (*not* Evil), and is, thus associated with the mere acquisiton of knowledge in general and of distinction, moral and otherwise, in particular. "Eden" glosses as "bliss," or "place of bliss," and thus there is sacred support for the folk dictum "ignorance is bliss." The scriptures are, of course, open to charges of obscurantism but, at considerable distance from Genesis, the Pragmatisms of Charles Sanders Peirce (1878), and especially of William James (1907; 1909), at least raise questions about the value of some knowledge.

I have no interest here in impugning the value of knowledge for its own or any other sake. I am only underlining the point, not at all original but implicit throughout this book, that scientific claims to value neutrality are self-deluding. As Bertram Russell is supposed to have somewhere said "He who claims to have no metaphysic has a bad one," so those who claim to operate free of values obviously have not examined the values in terms of which they are in fact operating. To the extent that their values remain hidden from them or, if not hidden, simply taken for granted (the invisibility of the familiar) their values are not in their possession. They are, rather, pessessed by and thus the creatures of their values, and as such they may endanger knowledge by attributing absolute and natural status to accounts the biases of which, being unrecognized, go uncorrected.

It is one thing for anthropology to be *motivated* by *general* values, another for it to *promulgate particular* values, and yet another for it to analyze the *value structures* of the societies it studies.

Marcus and Fischer take a position on this matter at the end of *Anthropology as Cultural Critique:*

> We end with a word about the moral or ethical dimension that one might expect any project of cultural critique prominently to express. For some, advocacy or assertion of values against a particular social reality *is* the primary purpose of cultural critique. However, as ethnographers for whom human variety is a principle interest and any subjects are fair game, we are acutely sensitive to the ambivalence,

irony, and contradictions in which values, and the opportunities for their realization, find expression in the everyday life of diverse social contexts. Thus, the statement and assertion of values are not the aim of ethnographic cultural critique; rather the empirical exploration of the historical and cultural conditions for the articulation and implementation of different values is. In this essay, then, we have paid attention to the media of expression and the embedded problematics of value, conceived as questions of aesthetics, epistemology, and interests which ethnographers confront both in their engaged field research and in their experimenting with innovative ways to write about it. (167; emphasis in original)

This passage, with which I am in considerable sympathy, demonstrates (although it was not the author's intention) that although motivation, analysis, and promulgation may be easy enough to distinguish *logically* they may be difficult or impossible to keep apart in practice, or so I will argue in the next section.

Pluralism in America and Anthropology
We are now in a position to consider two of the values constituting the central concern of this book, the complex and, in some degree, paradoxical relation between them, and the further complex and involved relationship between them and anthropology. As Shepard Forman put it in the Introduction, *"Diagnosing America* is an outspoken call for a *committed* and *engaged* anthropology, one that expresses a vision of American culture and society rooted in values of cultural pluralism and democratic participation that we believe to be strongly held." Pluralism and participation are, by this statement and in full agreement with Marcus and Fischer, proper objects of anthropological study because they are asserted to be values "strongly held" by Americans. The cultural heterogeneity of America is brought immediately to mind by Forman's assertion, however, because it is *not* the case that cultural pluralism, which is indubitably an element of American ideology and is strongly supported by the American constitution, is a value strongly held by *all* Americans. It certainly is not as far as race is concerned. An important general-circulation periodical, the *New Yorker* recently (July 1, 1991, 21) put the matter as follows:

Somewhere in the enormous space between the ideals of American democracy and the history of American race relations, the darkest part of the American character long ago formed. That space has narrowed greatly since the days of slavery and the campaigns of extermination against Native Americans but it remains a zone of fierce hypocrisy and denial.

Forman, and the others following him, are thus proposing that anthropology take or advocate a particular position with respect to a contested value. This value, cultural pluralism, is, moreover, closely related to one that animates anthropology. As Marcus and Fischer put it, "human variety" (which is at least related to cultural pluralism), is a "principle interest" of ethnographers. In the absence of human variety, anthropology could not exist. This does not mean, we should note in passing, that anthropology is interested only in variety and particularity; it is also interested in human universals and in the relationship between the *varieties* of which "human diversity" is constituted and the human universals that those varieties, each in its own way, realize. The concepts of human universals and human varieties entail each other. All of this is to say that human variety is not simply one of anthropology's principle interests, unless interest is to be understood here in the sense that a stockholder is said to have an interest in a company. It, along with human universals—universal physical, psychic, social and cultural needs, weaknesses, problems and capacities—stands among anthropology's ultimate concerns. Thus, a high-order value-motivating anthropology generally, and somewhat more specifically, constituting its raison d'être and demarcating its field of study, comes close to coinciding with what is taken to be a high but contested value of American society and as such is the subject matter of this book.

They come close but don't quite coincide. The concern to understand human variety and its relation to *humanity* (i.e., that which is common to all human varieties) does not logically entail cultural pluralism as the term is used by all authors in this volume (except Vélez-Ibanez, who uses it to designate an objective condition as well as a value). Cultural pluralism, as it is understood here, does more than take diversity to be an interesting phenomenon. It, at the least, tolerates diversity but may even celebrate it and attempt to preserve it. American anthropology's history has not been entirely free of racism or other antipluralistic manifestations, but it is noteworthy that modern anthropology has overwhelmingly supported cultural pluralism, first by helping to give voice to minorities otherwise silent or whose understandings and concerns can find no place in the society's dominant discourse; second, by arguing, tacitly or explicitly, for the value of the cultural varieties they attempt to make comprehensible to the world at large; third, by publicizing the fact that an overwhelming majority of anthropologists agree that so-called races do not differ in innate intelligence (whatever that may be) or other genetically based abilities; and fourth, by elucidating the factors, by and large value choices on the one hand and discrimination on the other, that account for a group's "failure" to "succeed" in the dominant culture's terms. Whether anthropologists represent others well, or whether they have any right to represent others at all is beside the point. The point here is that it is in the nature of modern U.S. anthropology to act in ways conforming to the U.S. value of cultural pluralism. It can hardly do otherwise without becoming something other than anthropology.

Anthropology's pluralistic convictions prevail in its foreign as well as in its domestic research (although operating at the level of cultural varieties of human culture generally, rather than at the level of *subcultural* variance of particular cultures) but additional complications enter, in the domestic arena.

If, in its mere practice, anthropology is compatible with a value of the society under study, in this instance cultural pluralism, and if the audience for a study's results are members of the society under study, then anthropology can hardly avoid promulgating that value unless it remains silent or addresses itself only to itself. And if the communication of information about the nature or condition of a social system into that system (whether or not the message explicitly promulgates a value) ipso facto constitutes a significant action within that system, then the separation of the study of a system from participation in it breaks down. (Anthropology is not alone in having to face this problem. Consider the effects of opinion surveys on the opinions surveyed.)

We may pause here to recognize that the uses and consequences of anthropological participation at home and abroad are very different. Participation in the life of a strange community, being unorganized by our own preconceptions and misconceptions, but rather by the flow of events in that community's life, can provide us with understandings that we otherwise might never have imagined. It can provide us with inside knowledge, in some instances experiential, the depth and scope of which is beyond the reach of unaided objective observation. The anthropologist's participation in the life of a community of which he or she is not a member—the participatory component of participant-observation—is part of the study. When the anthropologist works in his or her own society the situation is inverted. As insiders, anthropologists of the familiar already possess inside knowledge of the society's life, and know, perhaps all too well, what it feels like to live that life. What is most needed to enlarge anthropological understanding in such circumstances is an increase, so to speak, in the proportion of objective observation to subjective participation in whatever programs of participant-observation are employed. The main point here, however, is that whereas participation in the life of a society of which the anthropologist *is not* a member is part of his or her study, observation in a society of which the anthropologist *is* a member is *an act of participation* in the life of that society.

In sum, we may be able to *distinguish* logically anthropology's motivating values from the values constituting elements of its subject matter, and both from the promulgation of the latter, and we may further *distinguish* between the study of a society from participation in it, but we delude ourselves if we think that we can *separate* them in practice. I nod assent to Marcus and Fischer when they tell us that "the statement and assertion of values are not the aim of ethnographic cultural critique; rather the empirical exploration of the historical and cultural conditions for the articulation and implementation of different values is." It is not to contradict them to propose, however, that in domestic research the empirical exploration of values in their contexts can hardly avoid asserting, tacitly if not explicitly, those (or contradictory) values as well.

To recognize that virtually any study in our own society, certainly any study of our own society's disorders, constitutes a form of active participation in this society and, further, that this participation, whether or not we guard against it, is likely to be in some degree partisan, is not to plead guilty to offenses that necessarily impeach our results. What *will* impeach our results, now that we have lost whatever innocence concerning the value-free nature of our work we once may have had, is to plead innocent. We can no longer get away with that. It follows then, that if we are to protect the integrity and credibility of our work, we must specify our relationship to it. That is, we must make our own values, intentions, interests, and biases clear, to the degree that we understand them, as have every one of this book's authors. Recent developments in reflexive anthropology, although sometimes excessively self-concerned, point in the right direction for, on the one hand, they force to the analyst's consciousness values, biases, and intentions of which he or she may not have been fully aware and, on the other, they indicate to readers what those biases and blind spots may be and thus suggest to them how to assess the accounts offered them. The explicit location of anthropologists in such accounts has the further virtue of demonstrating the partial nature of any anthropological account. Because any account is constructed from a particular point of view, no account can see everything.

Other considerations point in directions that seem to lie at angles widely deflected, or even opposite from, the reflexive position. The reflexive movement, as I understand it, is, in part, a reflection of skepticism concerning the possibility of objectivity. With increasing distance from value-neutrality in the study of a society in which the anthropologist has participated as a member there is, however, increasing need for precise, accurate and well-grounded empirical data, data that can stand up against cross-examination by those who will seek to refute it. If credibility is to be achieved we must combine the self-specification characteristic of the reflexive movement not only with the interpretive frameworks on which it stands but also and, I think, more crucially, with more rigorous empirical (including quantitative) methodologies than much recent anthropology has favored.

Pluralism, Participation, and Individualism

We have moved from the consideration of an American value, cultural pluralism, and its relationships to its anthropological analog, human diversity, to the inevitable participation of domestic anthropology in the society that generated it. We are thus led to the second of the American core values with which this book is concerned, namely democratic participation.

The relationship between cultural pluralism and democratic participation is more problematic than this volume has so far indicated. Like other matters already discussed, they are easier to distinguish than they are to separate. They are not, however, inseparable and their relationship is asymmetrical.

Cultural pluralism as the term is understood in this book (except in Vélez-Ibanez' usage) is not a synonym for *multiethnicity. Multiethnicity,* and *cultural heterogeneity* are descriptive terms and as such merely designate the condition of a society made up of more than one ethnic or cultural group (e.g., Serbs, Muslims, and Croats), whatever relations among these groups might be. Cultural pluralism designates a value. It not only denotes a positive evaluation of diversity—a caste system can ideologize such an evaluation—but further denotes equal valorization of each of the cultural varieties constituting that diversity. Equal valorization entails both protection of the distinctiveness of all the cultural varieties constituting the society's diversity and freedom for all members of all of them to participate, to the limits of their capacities, in the full spectrum of the general society's life. The recognition of cultural, ethnic, or racial differences combined with the overt or covert denial, on the basis of these distinctions, of full rights of participation, is what is meant by *discrimination,* which is, of course, a form of oppression. To the extent that discrimination prevails, cultural pluralism does not. Democratic participation is, thus, logically requisite to cultural pluralism.

The reverse is *not* the case. Cultural pluralism is, as we have already noted, a contested value in the contemporary United States, but all those who contest it cannot be easily dismissed as bigots and racists. The position of at least some critics is that unless the concept of democratic participation is reduced to participation in political institutions and political participation to the right to vote and, perhaps, to unimpeded access to public services, democratic participation and cultural pluralism are, in some degree, mutually exclusive, simply because cultural pluralism entails distinction, distinction when applied to social groups involves some degree of separation and although separation does not *logically* entail inequality, history does strongly suggest that the concept of separate but equal has in fact served as an ideological cover for discrimination of the most malignant sort.

A position that takes the social doctrine of separate but equal to be socially if not logically self-contradictory (at least for complex societies) must, consciously or unconsciously, place high value on cultural homogeneity and, implicitly or explicitly, take the diversity constituting the stuff of cultural pluralism to constitute barriers to democratic participation. Such a position does not stand directly opposed to cultural pluralism. It tolerates diversity, but takes it to be as much a problem to be ameliorated as a value to be celebrated. It has generally taken diversity to be a continuing condition, but the characteristics distinguishing the particular varieties of which that diversity is at any time comprised to be more or less transitory, "melting" particular ethnic categories into the "mainstream" in a few generations. It further assumes that with the disappearance or attenuation of whatever cultural characteristics distinguish members of any particular ethnic category from the unmarked mainstream, impedances to their full democratic participation will also become weaker or even disappear.

We may also recall here, if only in passing, Peacock's discussion of another strongly held American value, namely individualism, noting that the Bill of Rights, the Declaration of Independence, and American ideology generally all focus on *individual* rights to life, liberty and the pursuit of happiness. To the extent that cultural diversity is tolerated or positively valued by Americans, I would suggest, it is derived from the individualistic principle that people have a prima facie right to practice what pleases them as long as no one else is damaged. I would also suggest, however, that individualism and cultural pluralism do not live as compatibly in American ideology as this last observation may seem to imply. Many Americans, perhaps most Americans other than those of African ancestry, understand the immigration of their ancestors to this country as escape from oppressive regimes or from stifling and deprived peasant or proletarian cultures. (This, in fact, is one of our central myths, a version of which is inscribed on the pedestal of the Statue of Liberty). They are therefore inclined to understand assimilation as a form of liberation.

I have suggested that the relationship between pluralism and participation constitutes *something* of a contradiction. It is hardly absolute. Whereas their opposition may not be amenable to logical mediation, it is not unamenable to all resolution nor is the possible incompatibility of individualism and cultural pluralism. Social systems are not as rigid as logical systems, and resolutions between the preservation of cultural particularities and democratic participation in the more encompassing society arc continually negotiated, as Vélez-Ibanez's chapter makes clear, in the decisions that individuals and groups continuously make in their everyday lives. Anthropology, be it noted, is better equipped to observe and elucidate such negotiations than are other social sciences for methodological reasons too obvious to require discussion.

Racism, Theory, and Anthropological Engagement

A position that places high value on cultural homogeneity combined with democratic participation may judge cultural diversity as no more than tolerable but, because it is based on the assumption of a radical separation between genetic and cultural modes of transmission is not in any sense racist. It follows from such an assumption that full assimilation to American (or any other) culture is regarded as possible for anyone, whatever his or her genetic heritage.

To say that this fundamentally liberal public position coincides with fundamental anthropological doctrine does not adequately represent the intimacy of their relationship, especially during the early decades of this century when eugenics was striving for political as well as theoretical ascendancy. Immigration from southern and Eastern Europe was still at its height at that time, with the eugenicists denying that people of Slavic, Baltic, Balkan, Italian, or Syrian ancestry (to say nothing of Jews, Asians, or Africans) could successfully be integrated into a culture of Anglo-Saxon origin because culture and cultural differences, in their view, were to be accounted for by genetic differences. They also asserted that there are superior and inferior cultures because there are superior and inferior genetic types, or races (corresponding, more or less, to nationalities or ethnic groups). They further claimed that the distinctive personal and moral characteristics of members of the groups they distinguished are also genetically determined, and that the quality of culture, character, and genetic material deteriorates with increasing distance from germanic northwestern Europe, the home of the "master race" (Madison Grant actually used the term [(1916) 1920, 87]. The eugenicists were very influential, succeeding in getting the Immigration Act of 1924, the most restrictive in the history of the republic, passed into law by Congress, and many states adopted codes based on model laws against "miscegenation" that the eugenicists had written.

In what may have been its finest hour, anthropology led intellectual resistance to the eugenics movement. In the course of this confrontation anthropology clarified its own concept of culture as independent from genetic processes (see especially Kroeber 1917), a concept seminal in anthropology at the same time that it served as social-philosophical reinforcement for what has probably become the predominant public understanding of the matter, an understanding also based to a considerable degree on the successful assimilation into U.S. society of categories of persons whom the eugenicists claimed were unassimilable. We may be reminded here of an earlier assertion, namely, that in engagement with the world's problems anthropology expands its own theory and method.

Just how much credit anthropology is to be given for the ultimate disgrace of eugenics, an explicitly racist ideology masquerading as a scientific theory, cannot really be assessed. As World War II approached, leading eugenicists did a fair job of disgracing themselves and their movement through their open admiration of Nazi Germany (which enacted sterilization laws based on model codes American eugenicists had written). Whatever the case, anthropologists *as* anthropologists were engaged as important actors in the affairs of their own society during this episode (see Chase 1977), in the course of which they elaborated their own understanding of culture and the relationship of cultural diversity to human universals while, at the same time, communicating their clarified understandings to a general public. Their understandings, based on both empirical research and theoretical constructs, developed in public debate and carefully argued in general circulation periodicals, bore directly on questions concerning capabilities and possibilities for full participation by persons of all ancestries in the entire spectrum of American social, economic, and political life. This is to say that a *particular* position with respect to a highly contested public value, that of democratic participation, was *intrinsic* to understandings grounded in generally accepted anthropological observation and theory. Thus, to expound that anthropological understanding publicly was ipso facto to promulgate that value. The choice was not whether to make presentations to general publics value-neutral or partisan but, simply, whether to bring anthropology into a public debate on which its competence had bearing. Anthropologists could, after all, have stayed out of it.

Our discussion of democratic participation in general thus brings us back to questions concerning the democratic participation of anthropology in American society. Does it have a right to participate? Even if it does, does it compromise itself by doing so? Can it avoid participation even if it aims to? Does it have a *duty* to participate?

This is the moment for some recapitulation. We have already noted, following innumerable others, that anthropology is in its nature critical. Even when we conduct studies elsewhere we mount tacit if not explicit critiques of our own society, and these critiques can be highly influential. *Coming of Age in Samoa* was, after all, a best seller. When we conduct studies at home we go even further. We may not only be ipso facto mounting a critique of our society but participating in it, and the promulgation of values, some of which may be contested, is, in some instances at least, likely to be unavoidable. It may be that some domestic research on contemporary problems can confine itself, more or less effectively, to "the empirical exploration of the historical and cultural conditions for the articulation and implementation of particular values."

I would certainly agree with Marcus and Fischer that such exploration is among an engaged anthropology's primary aims, but it may not always be possible to maintain such purity. I would propose, however, that we are not undertaking anything in its nature illicit if we proceed beyond the unexceptionable attempt at value neutrality advocated by Marcus and Fischer. We can, if we feel that we must, justify ourselves by noting that rights of democratic participation in the affairs of our own society should extend to us no less than to everyone else, that we did not take oaths of political or social celibacy when we received our doctorates, and that there is no more reason for us than for anyone else to check our experience, method, theory, and knowledge at the door before entering public arenas. If we need further justification we can remind ourselves that other disciplines, for instance, economics and political science, no more qualified than ours to address public issues publicly, do not shrink from doing so. Needless to say, we cannot contribute to the formation of a pluralistic—and therefore more comprehensive or even holistic—public discourse by talking only to ourselves about issues that also matter to others. We should, in this regard, never forget that anthropology's debate with eugenics was no academic argument, nor that anthropology could not have provided a continuing rebuttal to the eugenicists if it had remined publicly silent. It can even be argued, and all of our authors tacitly do so argue, that its duty was not to remain silent.

At this point it is well to remind ourselves of cautionary notices already posted and to post additional ones. The further we move from value neutrality the heavier our responsibilities become. The need for the anthropologist to specify his or her relationship to the subject matter increases with that distance, and the more publicly contested the terrain onto which anthropologists venture the more solid and rigorous their work must be. Engaged research must be of the highest quality because there is more at stake than winning debates in journals. We should also keep in mind that no salvific truths have been vouchsafed to us alone, and that modesty becomes us because we have a good deal to be modest about.

On Anthropological Values

A warning against another danger, much more fundamental, much less obvious, much more difficult to grasp, and much harder to heed, must finally be posted. Some preliminary ground work is required.

To say that an engaged anthropology is value informed is not to say that it is equally well guided by any or all values that any anthropologist cherishes, that whatever value is chosen by the researcher will do, so long as he or she makes it explicit. Some values can guide us well. Others could lead us into disgrace.

It would, perhaps, seem obvious that anthropology and, for that matter, all disciplines, select their guiding values on substantive grounds. More specifically, it would further seem proper that for a discipline that styles itself "the science of humankind," humanistic values, an ultimate valorization of the quality and meaningfulness of human life, should be regnant. Most of us would, I think, be quite sympathetic to such a position that, it can be fairly said, pervades this volume, and becomes particularly poignant in Blakey's contribution. Nevertheless, questions could be raised, and they would not be academic, with respect to possible contradictions between humanistic and ecological values. I am not suggesting that humanistic values be either dismissed or subordinated to ecological values, nor am I proposing that apparent contradictions between humanistic and ecological values are irreconcilable (I don't think they are, but their reconciliation is one of the most profound and difficult problems now facing humanity. The matter is broached later in this chapter). What I *am* questioning is whether any *particular* set of *substantive* considerations can be sufficient in and of itself to serve directly as, or even as a criterion to select, the values informing engaged anthropology.

The problem to which such questioning points goes deeper than the simple matter of substance. The objection just raised to substantive particularity points to another consideration, formal or logical rather than substantial in nature, that must also be given weight: the level of generality of the values informing engaged anthropology. I suggest that they must be of very high generality or, to put it conversely, their specificity must be very low if anthropology is to maintain its integrity.

This may not be immediately apparent. Illustration will be useful. Democratic participation, a value with which this volume has been continuously concerned, can continue to serve us here. Its salient characteristic in the present context is its high generality. It seems to be only a short logical step lower in generality than the fundamental principles of "life, liberty and the pursuit of happiness," for the realization of which the society under consideration represents itself to itself to have been founded. As already implied, a tautological entailment of this value's high generality is its low specificity. It is of the essence in this context that high valuation of democratic participation does not specify the social conditions that do or do not qualify as instances or realizations of it. As such "democratic participation" may seem vacuous. But general principles or values, like democratic participation or, even more fundamentally, liberty, are not mere pieties because they are devoid of particulars or even downright vague. High order, or general values, like democratic participation, or the "inalienable rights" proclaimed in the Declaration of Independence, or those stipulated in and protected by the Constitution, can and do serve as criteria against which historically particular and highly specific organizations of social, economic, and political relations can be assessed. Conversely, to elevate any *particular* historical or hypothetical social or political arrangement that can make a claim to fulfill the requirements of democratic participation (say open elections for congressional representatives) to the level of general principle or value is a form of fallacy, an error in logical typing (roughly, mistaking the properties of a particular member of a class for those definitive of the class as a whole). This fallacy, which commonly mistakes instruments for goals (e.g., busing for school integration, school integration for equal educational opportunity, equal educational opportunity for full democratic participation, democratic participation for liberty) may have unfortunate practical consequences, particularly those associated with rigid orthodoxy: inflexible, doctrinaire commitment to particular programs for realizing values that may be as well or better realized by other means, or even the sacrifice of the goal to institutionalizing particular means for achieving it. The danger to an engaged, value-guided anthropology of falling into such a fallacy is patent: to the extent that it does it subordinates itself to, and thus becomes an instrument of (old left jargon would have said "a tool of") particular political, social, or economic agendas, interests, or parties. This would constitute a degradation of anthropology and, needless to say, not what the contributors to this volume have in mind. To put what we do have in mind into crude but clear (if oversimplified) terms, it is not to politicize anthropology but to try to "anthropologize" public political and social discourse. I would suggest that our political positions, whatever they may be, should be outcomes of our anthropology, not vice versa.

The generality of the principles or values guiding what we mean by *engaged anthropology* may help to distinguish it from what may ordinarily be meant by *applied anthropology*. The two should not be sharply separated, however, and even the distinction is not clear. *Applied anthro-*

pology, as the term is ordinarily understood, designates analyses of particular situations or processes for the purpose of comprehending their human consequences, social, cultural, biological, and ecological, and, in some instances, for the further purpose of informing actions that will affect those situations and processes or their consequences. The account of engaged anthropology developed throughout this volume but made more explicit in this conclusion suggests that application and engagement should relate to each other as the specific and general aspects of a more-or-less integrated enterprise. Applications, this is to say, should be informed by the general values or principles inherent in engagement as here conceived. The normative "should" needs to be emphasized because it is not only possible but common for applications to be devoid of praxis, that is to be developed without the guidance of the general principles or values we have associated with engagement. Applied anthropologists, this is to say, sometimes design studies based on problem definitions and program goals derived from the concepts of clients with whom they may disagree on fundamental grounds.

II. On the Nature of Trouble

In the first part of this chapter, we discussed some of the difficulties American anthropology may have in engaging the troubles of its own society, but we have not yet considered just what it is that constitutes "troubles," to use as noncommittal a term as possible, or how they are to be recognized.

Symptoms and Solutions

It is probably fair to say that the definition or concept of troubles has never struck anthropologists as particularly problematic. They often take such matters as givens, sometimes given by others. Thus, applied anthropologists have often (certainly not always) accepted a priori definitions of problems written into requests for proposals (RFPs) by their clients (usually government agencies), their mission then being, first, to collect and analyze data bearing on the matters so defined and then to make recommendations that help their clients meet whatever their goals may be (which, of course may not be altogether clear, unexceptionable, or even fully known to the anthropologist). There are, in the nature of such things, what economists call *disincentives* that discourage the anthropologist from taking issue too strongly with clients' definitions: proposals responding to RFPs are generally in competition with others.

Even when anthropologists are free from such constraints they may take troubles to be given not by others but by the nature and force of the phenomena themselves. Some trends and conditions, for example, growing homelessness, prevalence of drugs, global warming, increased disparity between the rich and poor, increasing illiteracy, ecological degradation—are so evident and so painful that it would be ludicrous to establish criteria against which they would have to be adjudged "ills" or "disorders" or "problems." If we are bleeding, we don't need anatomy lessons to know that we are hurt, and substantial numbers of anthropologists have devoted themselves to the study and amelioration of, for example, drugs and homelessness and ecological degradation without, I presume, worrying very much about whether or not the objects of their studies are properly regarded as problems or troubles.

It is impossible to argue against anthropologists' focusing on drug use or illiteracy or declining democratic participation, but, as we noted at the beginning, there is such a multiplicity of quandaries, dilemmas, crises, inequities, dangers, and stresses facing society that they cannot all be named, much less studied. Furthermore, actions taken to ameliorate one may exacerbate others.

The possibility of amelioration points to a further complication: what are taken to be solutions may, in fact, be parts of the problems they are meant to address, or may even constitute problems in their own rights, sociocultural equivalents of what are called in medicine *iatrogenic disorders,* disorders induced by treatment. Furthermore, the solutions of one age are likely to become the problems of the next. It could plausibly be argued, for example, that the Taylorism that is the primary object of Dubinskas's critique constituted a great leap forward early in the century. As such it would provide an instance of an evolutionary rule that deserves more recognition than it has generally received: every evolutionary advance sets new problems (often latent) as it responds to and ameliorates old ones. If this observation is apt, it follows that Dubinskas's comparison of Japanese and American industrial management policy illustrates what was characterized by David Kaplan (1960) as, "the advantage of evolutionary backwardness." It should also be noted here that although Taylorism is a form of industrial management it obviously has social and political analogies, as even a cursory comparison with MacLennan's discussion of impedances to democratic participation makes clear.

A particularly U.S. approach to solution that is itself highly problematic is that which is called in common parlance *trouble shooting* or *problem solving*. Its salient characteristic is that it attempts to identify particular features of complex states of affairs (say high rates of teenage pregnancy) that "need fixing." It tends to isolate discrete "problems" for which "solutions" conceived as repairs or cures can be sought. Free condoms and sex education are thus taken to be cures for what someone (not necessarily the adolescents themselves) thinks ails inner-city teenagers. Sometimes such repairs do have positive effects, but the decontextualization they entail is at best likely to limit success and may even make matters worse. It is what might be called a *generative mistake* (a mistake that will engender further mistakes) to attempt to isolate, and thus take to be simple and discrete, what may in fact be an inseparable aspect of a complex situation. Even to label a problem (e.g., the drug problem, the problem of illiteracy) may reify it, which may ramify the primary error and thus exacerbate the condition that it has misconstrued.

If all of this is obvious, it points clearly to the fact that whatever it is that constitutes social ills or disorders or problems may not be at all obvious. What are usually taken to be problems, ills, pathologies, or disorders are often better thought of as symptoms than as diseases. The real problems, as Katherine Newman makes abundantly clear in her chapter, are the conditions or processes generating such symptoms, not the symptoms themselves. She further argues that the problem immediately underlying many or even most of the symptoms from which inner-city populations suffer is poverty. If she is correct, it follows that the alleviation of poverty is likely to do more to decrease the incidence of teenage pregnancy than carloads of condoms distributed free along with operating instructions in inner-city high schools, by changing conditions that lead some young people to act in ways that increase the likelihood of pregnancy.

It is worth making explicit that mistaken solutions, such as condom distribution without changes in the social conditions that encourage pregnancy, are not only likely to be ineffective but downright harmful, for they make the easy assumption that MacLennan, quoting the Lynds on Middletown, implies may be typically American: "The system is fundamentally right and only the persons wrong, the cure must be changes in personal attitudes, not in institutions themselves." Such assumptions underwrite diagnoses that blame victims for the consequences of social conditions over which, it seems obvious to anthropologists, they have no control. Thus, if boys and girls continue to behave in ways that may result in pregnancy after they have been offered the gift of free condoms, they are likely to be blamed for their own degraded states. Or, if those judging their behavior are more enlightened, they may take what seems to them the young peoples' lack of forethought and responsibility to be a consequence of deficiencies in socialization for which education in mainstream values is the cure, also probably misguided in the absence of what may be called *mainstream conditions*. As Newman has put it, problems to reduce teenage pregnancy and delinquency "will have little effect absent a Marshall Plan for full employment."

It is not at all clear that high rates of teenage pregnancy are more troubling to the populations in which they occur than they are to others worrying about the increasing demands they fear a burgeoning underclass will make on public services, and the increasing dangers such an underclass is thought to pose to others. Be this as it may, although the direct alleviation of what we are now calling *symptoms* may sometimes be necessary, solutions aimed at assuaging pain without correcting the conditions generating that pain are not true solutions. The so-called solutions are particularly troubling parts of the problems they purport to address, social analogues, possibly, of neurotic behavior, behavior that tends to *maintain* emotional disorders by *temporarily* alleviating, often at great cost to the neurotic, the anxiety generated by those disorders. For example, a county bureau of substance abuse to which I was once a consultant dispensed large amounts of money to a range of agencies running a variety of programs to keep addicts relatively comfortable on methadone, away from such mischief as armed robbery, and generally out of the public's sight. The combined effect of these programs was not to reduce drug use but to make it less threatening to the public at the same time that it not only kept a surprisingly large substance abuse bureaucracy employed but made the county safer for drug traffickers. Such programs are, to reach for another medical metaphor, social equivalents of topical anaesthetics. They don't cure anything, but they do stop it from hurting for a while.

Even if we agree that we should not take symptoms to be diseases, the disparate nature of the sorts of difficulties raised in the last pages—the material matter of poverty on the one hand, the structural (more specifically cybernetic) disorder of turning off "pain" signals while leaving the source of those signals intact—leaves questions concerning the nature, recognition, and definition of disorders unresolved. Should we construe poverty to be the real problem underlying teenage pregnancy, drugs, and other troubles besetting society, or should we take the real problem to be whatever it is that generates that poverty, for instance, the deindustrialization of American cities? Or is it the globalization of the economy that, at one and the same time both deindustrializes some American cities and, as Vélez-Ibanez points out, overindustrializes the U.S.-Mexican border region? Such regresses can go on indefinitely but it is heartening to know that they are not, like logical regresses, infinite, nor are they likely to be very many layers deep, although casual structure may be reticulate and synergistic. Problems, ills, disorders, or "dis-eases" can surely be identified at many levels and it may be a mistake to take any particular level to be key. Disorders of varying depth and nature (material, structural, conceptual, ideological) will have to be considered, after which their relationship to each other, their generality and the usefulness of their identification can be approached.

Undertheorizing, Overtheorizing, and False Solutions
It is probably safe to say that the recognition and definition of social disorders is undertheorized in anthropology. It is possible that one of anthropology's core values, cultural relativism (virtually a corollary of cultural pluralism) tends to make us wary about formulating general concepts of problems or disorders, or even recognizing disorders as such when we see them. Be this as it may, the matter is not undertheorized in all of the other social and behavioral sciences, and it will be helpful to glance at one of them. Economics, it is fair to say, constitutes the dominant discourse of public affairs in our society. This discourse is itself hegemonic in the society's most powerful sectors—government, finance, and production—and is more influential by magnitudes than any other social science or any other social discourse.

Because economics is strongly empowered, aspects of its theory and method may, when inappropriately applied, contribute to serious social political and ecological disruption. It is, for example, usual for economists to use cost-benefit analyses and projections of comparative cost effectiveness in their evaluations of symptoms, problems, and solutions. Such methods require the use of common metrics, usually monetary, and such metrics are therefore applied to wide ranges of disparate things. Thus, for purposes of assessing compensation for maritime oil spills, monetary values have been assigned to the various constituents of marine ecosystems (including noncommercial species on the grounds that commercial species feed on them). This seems a reasonable part of a procedure for fixing amounts that polluters should compensate individuals or publics whom their activities have damaged, but two related issues are raised here.

First, not all social and ecological problems can be adequately characterized or described in quantitative, let alone monetary, terms. Indeed, in a logical sense *none* of them can. Any operation of quantification requires that *something* be counted, measured, or weighed, but such somethings cannot, *as such,* themselves be simple quantities. They are structures (e.g., social, political, "Levi-Straussian") or entities (e.g., organisms, species populations) or world concepts (e.g., Heraclitian *Logos,* Navajo *Hozho,* Egyptian *Ma'at,* Walbri *Djugaruru,* anthropology's "cultures"), virtues (e.g., honor, justice, truth, faith), or qualities (e.g., ecological or ritual purity or pollution). Whereas some *aspects* of *some* of these somethings can be meaningfully quantified and even given plausible monetary values, others cannot. For example, during a visit to Bristol Bay, Alaska shortly after the *Exxon Valdiz* catastrophe in 1989, a National Academy of Science panel on which I was serving was continually told by Yupik speaking Native Americans that an oil spill of similar magnitude in their vicinity would be even more devastating because their coast, in contrast to Prince William Sound, was in wetlands harboring hatcheries for most of the fish species on which they depended. Pollution of their hatcheries by oil, they plausibly claimed, would destroy them. Whereas they could be compensated for the loss of their commercial fishery, the loss of their subsistence fishery could not be mitigated because, ever since they had converted to Christianity, Yupik culture (even old monolingual Yupik speakers used the term) had been reproduced through teaching subsistence activities to the young in summer fishing camps. The destruction of the fishery would therefore, in their view, be tantamount to the destruction of Yupik culture for which no compensation could possibly be adequate or even reckoned. Most anthropologists would agree that there is no way to assign monetary values to cultures. They are, as we say, priceless. More generally, we would also agree that many of the things humans take to be most important are, in their nature, beyond the reach of quantification. There is no way to incorporate such nonmetrical values into economic discourse.

The second issue is less anthropocentric, more general and perhaps even the heart of the matter: the world on which the monetary metric is imposed is not as simple as the metric itself. Living systems—plants, animals, societies—are complex beyond full human comprehension. Each, moreover, requires a great variety of *particular* materials, generally derived from a variety of sources, to remain healthy. As the experiences of mariners voyaging before the mid-nineteenth century attested, humans can stuff themselves with protein-rich foods, but if they don't get enough vitamin C their teeth will fall out. Vitamin C and protein are nutritionally incommensurable, and thus not interchangeable. An analogous point can be made concerning the constituents of ecosystems. Each species occupies a more or less distinct niche, which is to say that it makes a more or less distinctive contribution to the operation of the whole system. Distinct species are, as it were, ecologically incommensurable, but because these constituents can be assigned prices (monetary values) they become fully commensurable *as commodities. The point is that the logic of commodity on the one hand and biology, both organic and ecosystemic, on the other, are not only at variance but at odds.* To the extent that monetary standards are dominant their application forces the great range of qualitatively distinct organisms, materials, and processes that together are necessary to sustain or even constitute life into arbitrary and specious equivalence. It follows that decisions guided by the terms of such artificial equivalence are likely to simplify, which is to say degrade and thus to disrupt, the ecological systems in which they are operative. It hardly need be said that the application to ecosystems of large amounts of energy, in its very nature mindless, under the guidance of the simplifying or even simpleminded and often selfish considerations that money makes virtually omnipotent (and when united with a capitalist ideology even sacred) is in its nature stupid, brutal, and almost bound to be destructive. It is in full accordance with such monetized logic to rip the top off a complex ecosystem like West Virginia to get at a simple substance, coal, particularly if environmental damage can be ignored as an "externality." This critique raises a number of issues.

First, the characterization of monetary metrics as stupid is not meant to be insulting. It is to be taken in a formal or analogic sense. Informational systems, among which evaluative conventions are to be included, are stupid if their capacities are inappropriate for or insufficient to the task at hand, namely to assess significant consequences of alternative courses of action. Monetary standards when applied to ecological systems are stupid in that they are *in their nature* incapable of recognizing *qualitative* distinctions between and interdependences among the constituents of those systems, and thus cannot take them into consideration in developing courses of action. Such actions are, therefore, likely to be destructive. When subordinated to a logic of commodity and to a monetary metric, ecosystems are conceptually fragmented into local agglomerations of more or less discrete "natural resources." Actions informed by such concepts cannot help but fragment the physical world.

Second, this criticism of monetary criteria is not meant to be a critique of capitalism or of human greed or anything of the sort. It is, rather, an attempt to point to a deep epistemological error. To be more explicit, the application of a common monetary metric to dissimilar things *reduces their qualitative distinctiveness to the status of mere quantitative differences.* Either-or distinctions are dissolved into more-less differences. The most appropriate answer to questions like What is the difference between a forest and a shopping mall? becomes something like $100,000 per acre. Evaluation becomes nothing more than what is called the bottom line, the result of operations of addition and subtraction of dollars and cents. Such results are *in their nature incapable* of representing such matters as changes in species diversity, biomass production per unit area, transpiration and run-off rates or CO_2 production.

In sum, an ecological logic, which is based on relations of mutual dependency among qualitatively distinct things and is fully compatible with the values of cultural and aesthetic preservation, is displaced by a monetary logic *incapable in its very nature* of recognizing qualitative distinctiveness per se, but which subordinates all distinctions to simple-minded calculi of more or less. The representational shortcomings of such calculi are not confined to their imposition on ecological systems. They are no better at representing the value of Yupik culture to Yupik speakers or to the world at large, or the beauty of landscapes and the pleasures of walking through them, or of problems of health (the price of a cancer operation can easily be determined, but it bears no relation to the benefit of a successful outcome, nor can the cost to the nation of inordinate frequencies of stress disease in minority populations be adequately represented in monetary terms).

This discussion is not meant to be a *summa contra oeconomia.* That certain forms of analysis popular in economics are not properly applicable to biological systems, and that they are devoid of cultural sensitivity, does not invalidate them, nor even distinguish them in particular, or economic analyses in general, from modes of analysis favored by other disciplines, including our own. It is probably safe to say that no mode of analysis can properly claim universal adequacy or even applicability. The criticism here is not primarily of monetary metrics in particular or economic analyses in general so much as it is of their privileged status, a status derived from economics' favored position as this society's regnant social science. As such its modes of analysis, such as cost-benefit analyses based on monetary metrics, are likely to be granted universal and ultimate bottom-line authority. Its undoubted analytic capacities would be more useful and its analytic shortcoming less destructive if it were not so powerful and influential that its limitations go unrecognized. Consequently, it leaves little room in the minds of the public for other approaches that may be able to take into consideration what economics cannot and little ground for the public to believe that other discourses, even if persuasive, could possibly be taken seriously in a world in which money not only talks but constitutes the lingua franca. Under these circumstances essential public concerns that cannot be put into economic terms are not only likely to remain inaudible but unarticulated.

If anthropological approaches to social ills or disorders have been undertheorized it may be proper to characterize some economic approaches as overtheorizing. That is, their application to aspects of the world with which they are incompatible does not remain empirically wrong because with their empowerment they are able to coerce the world into conformity with the commoditized images they provide. Under their domination ecosystems and landscapes, reduced to concatenations of commodities, tend to become simplified, degraded, decreasingly distinctive, and decreasingly capable of maintaining themselves. To put this a little differently and more generally, a mode of description, analysis, or explanation when sufficiently empowered can become "performative" in J. L. Austin's (1962) sense, not only providing a model for the world but reshaping the world to comply with itself. The problem, then, is not that the account is empirically wrong but that it isn't, that it can make itself true. But the "truth" that it imposes on the world is of degradation, ecological and otherwise. This is iatrogenic disorder with a vengeance.

Values, Power, and Disorder
We have been considering what we may be tempted to take to be a problem or disorder in the deeper sense, one underlying or generating the multiple symptoms of ecosystemic disruption, namely incompatibility between discourses or logics. In the instance at hand one is economic, the other broadly biological. But such inconsistencies by themselves can-

not be considered disorders, for the world is full of distinct kinds of things and processes, each with, to some degree, a logic of its own, and each of these logics is valid in no more than a limited domain. This may be obvious during a time when only diehard ideologues are able to maintain even semblances of belief in any single "totalizing" conceptual system, but even if we don't take either economic or biological discourses to be capable by themselves of rendering adequate accounts of contemporary humans operating in ecological systems, how is the *relationship between* the monetary logic of the economic account and the ecosystemic logic of the biological account to be conceived? Are they simply and straightforwardly competitive, are we to take elements from each and formulate some sort of eclectic construction, or are there principles in accordance with which we can "put them in order," that is, decide that one is superordinate or prerequisite to the other? Bearing in mind that the discourses we devise, although they may be meant to be descriptive or explanatory, serve as guides to action we may ask by what logic or combination of logics should we proceed?

I believe that there are general principles in accordance with which one discourse can be given precedence over another, at least in some cases, including the general one discussed in the last section. In that case a simple principle, at once logical and substantive, pertains: that of *contingency.* The existence of any and all economic systems is contingent on the existence of biological-ecological systems, but the converse is not the case. Organisms appeared on the planet some billions of years before economic systems (that is, symbolically constructed systems for organizing production, exchange, and consumption), which appeared only recently in one primate line, plausibly, at least initially, as part of that line's species-specific means for fulfilling what are essentially biological functions. This is to say that the relationship of the economic to the biological-ecological is a relationship of the special, instrumental, and contingent to the general, fundamental and ultimate. (By *ultimate* I mean valued as end in itself, rather than valued as instrumental with respect to higher goals.) *Implicit in this account of the relationship of the economic to the biological-ecological is that, generally speaking, ecological and biological considerations, being more fundamental, should take precedence over economic considerations and that, in general, economic systems should be adjusted to the requisites of the biological-ecological systems on which they are contingent.* This obviously accords with both common sense and possibility: the requisites of organisms and ecosystems, being aspects of nature are not easily modified by humans and then only slightly. Economic systems being conventional can be modified quickly and profoundly although it is sometimes painful to do so, and resistance may be great, as Dubinskas's contribution makes clear.

We have identified here a common form of disorder: *the subordination of the fundamental and ultimate to the contingent and instrumental.* Blakey's contribution to this volume bears witness to the awful and disgraceful consequences of violating proper relations of contingency. It is no criticism of him to observe that he could have gone much, much further, counting such pathologies as gunshot wounds, drug addiction in adults, adolescents and infants, low-birth-weight babies, malnutrition, and so on along with the conditions he did discuss. As we have already observed, the subordination of the fundamental to the contingent is also likely to generate such ecological and biological symptoms as the degradation of West Virginia's ecosystems and the destruction of the atmosphere's ozone layer. In the one case a commodity, coal, and the short-run interests of its producers and some of its users take precedence over long-run ecosystem integrity. In the other, aerosol's uses are valued more highly than the need to screen life from overexposure to ultraviolet radiation. This form of disorder is ubiquitous, producing political and social as well as biological and ecosystemic symptoms. We will return to its products shortly, but two observations concerning its nature are in order.

First, when we speak of the subordination of the fundamental to the contingent and instrumental, and of the higher valuation of aerosols than of conditions requisite to health and even to life we are speaking of *values* and their disordering. We are, thus, raising an issue similar to that raised earlier when the nature of the values proper to the task of guiding engaged anthropology was discussed. There we were concerned with the relationship of the general to specific. Here we have been concerned with the relation of the fundamental to the contingent and instrumental. Both discussions imply that similar relations of generality/ specificity and fundamental/contingent should prevail in relations between incompatible discourses, both in engaged anthropology and in the societies it studies. The present discussion, which uses the term *disordering,* further implies that there are proper orders for value structures, that these proper orders entail certain relations among the general and fundamental on the one hand and the specific, instrumental, and contingent on the other, that these proper orders can become disordered, and when they are out of order, the substantive difficulties we are calling *symptoms* are likely to manifest themselves.

Second, these values are, obviously, not free-floating in society. They are held and promulgated by different institutions, different interest groups and different individuals. Such institutions, interest groups, and individuals are differentially powerful and probably become even more so as a concomitant of sociocultural evolution in general and technological evolution in particular. As a consequence, the ever-more powerful become ever more able to elevate their *particular* values, which are likely to express or ratify their ever-more-narrowly defined special interests to positions of predominance in the larger society, with social and political results that may be formally similar to the degradation of ecosystems already discussed. We may recall in this context Charles Wilson's famous response, during senate confirmation hearings on his appointment to the position of Secretary of Defense, to questions concerning possible conflicts of interest in moving to that post from the presidency of General Motors. "What's good for General Motors," he said, "is good for America." We may be pardoned for doubting the absolute benevolence of General Motors toward the country as a whole but no matter how public-spirited or benign General Motors might be, what is good for it *cannot* in the long run be good for the United States. Quite aside from Dubinskas's powerful critique of mechanistic management systems of the sort that General Motors spectacularly represents, and at a yet more fundamental level, for a society, such as the United States (the persistence and prosperity of which is an end in itself), to commit itself as a highest value to what may be good for one of its instrumental special-purpose subsystems, such as General Motors (or even the entire automotive industry), is for it to over-specify or narrow the range of conditions under which it can persist. *It reduces its evolutionary flexibility or adaptiveness, at the same time that it is likely to increase its social, economic, and political inequalities, and to degrade its environment.*

Adaptation has just entered the discussion. The concept is complex and the term is used in a range of ways, some of which seem virtually to contradict others, largely as a consequence of its subsumption of processes of both transformation on the one hand and continuity on the other (For a fuller discussion of the matter, see Rappaport 1984, 411–31.) Here I will only make clear that in my usage the term designates the processes through which relatively autonomous living systems of all

classes (organisms, social groups, societies, ecosystems) maintain themselves in the face of continual and potentially perturbing changes in both
internal and environing conditions. Persistence in the presence of such
conditions requires both continuous reversible responses to more-or-less
continuous fluctuations in environing and internal conditions (e.g.,
weather changes) and occasional discontinuous less-reversible or even
irreversible structural transformations in response to long-run directional
changes in those conditions (e.g., climate changes). It is obvious, in
terms of such a characterization, that flexibility, the ability to respond
in timely, appropriate, and roughly calibrated fashion to perturbations,
often unpredictable in occurrence and sometimes even unforeseeable in
nature, is central to adaptive capacity, and we have just noted that *getting
values out of order has negative implications for adaptive capacity generally as well as for democratic participation and ecosystemic integrity
specifically.* We have also observed that sociocultural evolution, perhaps
most directly in its technological aspects, may exacerbate these disorders,
for at one and the same time technological advances both elaborate the
division of labor and empower its burgeoning sectors differentially. Furthermore, with such advances, communication media become increasingly concentrated, powerful, and expensive to control and operate. It
is, therefore, increasingly possible for particular discourses postulating
particular values to gain predominance while others are, de facto, suppressed, repressed, or ignored. The suppression or repression of political
and social discourses is, of course, closely related to oppression if not,
indeed, definitive of it. With media concentration, furthermore, it is
increasingly possible for hegemony to replace brute domination as the
general means for maintaining the privileged status of particular discourses, thus hiding oppression behind what has long been called *false
consciousness*. Again we may be reminded that every evolutionary advance sets new problems as it solves or ameliorates old ones. We may
think here also of all-purpose money, the appearance of the state, the
development of high-energy technology and, later, electronic-information
technology. We may even recall more ancient advances: the division of
labor above the household level and, long before that, the appearance
of language that, for all its virtues, facilitated enormously the transmission of various forms of lie (Rappaport 1979a).

Our discussions of monetization and of the elevation of special
interests to the status of general principles may have suggested that this

form of disorder is specific to capitalism. Capitalism may encourage the domination of special interests, but the form is much more widespread and general. The difficulties encountered by the Roman Catholic church as a consequence of its continuing opposition to mechanical and chemical means of birth control provide a case in point. Not only has it suffered widespread defection by communicants and challenges to its general authority by such prominent theologians as Hans Kung (1971) but its stand seems also to have resulted in changes in the attitudes of many of those remaining in the church toward its teachings: they now take them to be much less absolute and binding. It seems, not only to this outsider but to many Catholics as well, that artificial means of birth control could be made acceptable through reinterpretation of what is called *natural law,* on which the prevailing position now stands, without challenge to the articles of faith enunciated in creeds and accepted in the devotional act of communion. In contrast, I would suggest that the attribution of a degree of sanctity equivalent to that surrounding such articles of faith as the Immaculate Conception to specific rules concerning nonimmaculate nonconception bears formal resemblance to, if it is not, indeed, an instance of, what the Protestant theologian Paul Tillich (1957, 11) called *idolatry,* which he characterized as "absolutizing the relative." Similarly, attributions of ultimacy to that which is socially specific, historically situated, and instrumental, for instance particular economic interest or even particular modes of economic organization, like capitalism or socialism, also, obviously, "relativize the absolute." This disordering of relations between the ultimately sacred, consisting of postulates that must, in their nature, be represented as eternal verities and therefore fundamental and immutable, and the merely sanctified, consisting of rules and understandings that being embedded in life and history must be represented as contingent, instrumental, and flexible, cannot avoid undermining the very principle of sanctity, a principle that has been—quite possibly since the emergence of language—a primary foundation of human social life (see Rappaport 1979a, 1979b). It is not surprising, in this light, that Tillich took idolatry to be an evil. We may note that idolatry is similar in form to the promotion of the interests of General Motors (or any other sector of the U.S. economy, or even the economy as a whole) to a position of predominance in U.S. society generally. Whatever its moral status may be, idolatry and structurally similar disorders are maladaptive, a matter to which we shall return.

Disorders and Levels of Generality

Problems, as we have noted, can be identified at various levels of generality, from the highly specific and substantive, like teenage pregnancy in the Bronx or ecological degradation in West Virginia, to the very general and formal, like inversions in relations between the fundamental and contingent. These, in turn, subsume inversions in relations between such substantive discourses as the economic and ecological and such classes of institutions as the economic and political. Between the extremes of specificity and generality lie such epistemological errors as the reification (possibly following an innate tendency of language itself to create "things" by naming them) that results in mistaking aspects of complex circumstances or systems for discrete (and therefore "fixable") entities, and the application of single metrics to incommensurable and even nonmetrical aspects of the world.

Whereas specific substantive difficulties may best be thought of as symptoms, the causes of which need to be discovered, the formal disorders just noted are better conceived as disorders (*sensu strictu,* i.e., deformation of structures) or dis-eases that underly symptoms.

Although it is clear that troubles or problems can be identified at many levels, questions remain concerning the levels at which it may be *useful* to identify them. Discussions so far suggest: at any and all of them. Symptoms *should not* be ignored because they are indices (in Peirce's 1897, 1955 sense of "index") of underlying disorders. They *cannot* be ignored because they are the immediate loci of pain, and pain itself may require immediate relief. But relief is one thing and correction is another, and it is at deeper levels, at the levels of underlying disorder that correction probably must take place. Direct treatment of symptoms for instance, free condoms and sex education for teenagers, and increased welfare payments to alleviate poverty may be necessary, but such actions by themselves are more likely to secure than to cure the symptoms: they make their perpetuation tolerable. Moreover, even if they could, symptoms are innumerable and therefore direct treatment of them all would be so expensive, so demanding, and so full of contradictions as to be impossible.

Whereas symptoms are beyond number, underlying disorders are not. Their forms are probably few and it may be possible to conceive them to be distributed among a limited number of classes each of whose members not only bear family resemblance to each other but may together constitute more complex and comprehensive disorders. Before identifying some of them it will be useful to recapitulate and make explicit what has so far been said about some of those clustering around questions of discourse, or logic.

1. *No* discourse or logic *by itself* is capable of comprehending all crucial aspects of the world. Any adequate grasp of the world relies, therefore, on the use of multiple discourses or logics.

2. There are, however, disagreements, incompatibilities, or even contradictions between and among these discourses or logics.

3. These discourses are not only incompatible but incommensurable. Therefore, evaluations of their disagreements cannot be reached through simple bottom-lining operations.

4. These discourses are differentially empowered. The sovereignty of any one over others is an outcome of such differentials.

5. The relations of dominance and subordination maintained by power differentials between and among discourses is likely to be at odds with those that would follow from the logic of contingency. It was proposed, however, that contingency's logic provides a criterion in terms of which discourses as "wholes" *should* be ordered.

6. Contemporary violations of contingency relations subordinate long-run ecological, biological, social, and cultural considerations of the many to short-run economic interests of the few.

7. A multiplicity of the symptoms by which we are pained—the ecological degradation of West Virginia, the prevalence of stress-related diseases among African-Americans, declining democratic participation, downward mobility, and on and on ad nauseam if not ad infinitum—is either exacerbated by or, in some degree, even accounted for by violation of the ordering of contingency.

8. Although the drive to violate the order of contingency relations may be intrinsic to capitalism it is not exclusive to it. Widespread ecological degradation in the Soviet Union and Eastern Europe suggests that this form of disorder (or disordering form) can materialize under a range of conditions. We have also noted the elevation of the specific, instrumental, and contingent to the status of virtual ultimacy in the Catholic church's stand on rules concerning licit methods of birth control, proposing that the consequences of this mistake in logical typing have been severe for

the church, for the control of such diseases as AIDS, and possibly, for the containment of the world's population.

Maladaptation and Disorder

At least some of the forms of disorder with which we have been concerned can, in terms of our characterization of adaptation, be understood to be maladaptations. *Maladaptations* it must be emphasized, are *not* stressors but *impediments to, inhibitions of, or subversions of adaptive processes.*

The matter of maladaptation is much too complex to discuss in any detail here. Fuller accounts can be found in earlier essays (see Rappaport 1977, 1979b, 1984). Suffice it here to note that there seem to be structural properties that a system must possess if it is to respond adaptively to more-or-less unpredictable and even unforeseeable stresses. These structural properties include hierarchical relations, first, between adaptive systems as wholes and their more-or-less specialized subsystems and, second, between the ultimate values associated with systems as wholes and the instrumental values associated with specialized subsystems. The structural properties of adaptive systems also include the closed informational and causal circuits ("feedback loops") requisite to self-regulation and self transformation.

We are now in a position to become somewhat more specific in characterizing maladaptation: it can be regarded as the disordering of adaptive structures, for such disordering will impede, inhibit, or subvert adaptive-response sequences. Such impedances, subversions, misdirections, and inhibitions, I am arguing, will, in turn, generate the sorts of substantive difficulties we have been calling *symptoms.* Their discussion will range beyond those that are illustrated by our contributors.

"Elevation" or "Usurpation" This disorder has already been discussed at length, but is reiterated here to emphasize its relationship to other maladaptive forms. It is constituted by the promotion or elevation of the specific goals or interests of specialized subsystems (e.g., General Motors or the automotive industry or health insurers) or specific sectors (e.g., business, or the economic sector) to positions of predominance in the society as a whole, in the course of which those special goals or interests may lay claim to, or even usurp, the status of society's ultimate or even sacred values. This form, which is capable of generating a large but indefinite number of material symptoms, including ecological degradation,

damage to health, and poverty, as well as general debasement of values is nicely exemplified by President Coolidge's dictum, "the business of America is business," an assertion on the face of it elevating the value of business to a level equivalent to the Declaration of Independence's inalienable rights to "life, liberty, and the pursuit of happiness." In subordinating all other considerations to the interests of business it constitutes an expression of idolatry and as such may, in addition to its material consequences, have severe consequences for the society's morale and morality. Deteriorating morality and morale may, in turn, have material consequences of their own.

Disorders of Information Collection, Transmission, Reception, and Interpretation Disordering of relations among values is hardly the only form of structural disorder constituting maladaptation. Impediments to self-regulation include such matters as:

  a. Failures to *detect* the changes of states in key conditions, for instance, the failure to detect changes in levels of harmful substances in the environment, poverty among urban populations, alienation among citizens.
  b. The delay, loss, or distortion of information transmitted from detecting agencies to system regulators.
  c. What might be called *institutional deafness,* the inability or refusal to receive, interpret, and thus to act on information concerning changes that *have* been detected (for instance, White House reluctance to act in response to information concerning decreases in atmospheric ozone and increases in CO_2).

Such cybernetic failures may be a consequence of inappropriate reference criteria (e.g., the use of economic standards for the regulation of ecological systems), but be this as it may, such failures in information collection, transmission and processing may produce inappropriate responses, inappropriate timing of responses, like too late, and errors in scale of response, like too little as well as too late.

Dubinskas's essay argues that mechanistic management structures do poorly in detecting aberrant conditions, in transmitting accurate information about them in timely fashion, and in hearing and interpreting such information as is transmitted. His argument is as relevant to governments as it is to industrial firms.

Feedback Aberrations In democracies, citizen participation, particularly but not exclusively in the form of the vote, is important in the society's self-regulatory processes. In response to their assessment of conditions and of their evaluations of the performances of elected regulators, citizens either return them to office or replace them. MacLennan in particular is concerned with the increasing failure of American citizens to exercise their franchise as well as with problems flowing from that failure.

Such failure may permit symptoms of all sorts to develop unchecked, especially those following from the domination of elected officials by the special interests that finance their reelection campaigns. Awareness of such domination may contribute to an increasingly pervasive cynicism that further reduces participation. Positive feedback in the form of the vicious circle thus displaces the self-correction of negative feedback.

If diminishing participation in elections constitutes one form of feedback inadequacy, the growing influence of polls may constitute another. American democracy was predicated on feedback from the governed in the form of elections with frequencies of two, four, and six years. The frequency of polls on matters of public interest are, in the contemporary United States, greater by magnitudes—weekly polls on subjects of strong public interest are not unusual. It can be argued that such rapid and frequent feedback is as much a problem for as it is an aid to governance. Following what is *taken* to be the will of their constituents (as read from the evanescent results of putting particularly phrased questions to limited samples of respondents who may or may not answer honestly or seriously and, in any event, may feel differently tomorrow) rather than following their own judgments may paralyze officials to such a degree that they are unable to enact necessary but unpopular programs.

Increases in the concentration, pervasiveness and penetration of mass media may also decrease the effectiveness of public participation in the general cybernetics of the polity, for such concentration increases the capacity of whoever can master and control such media to broadcast particular discourses so powerfully and pervasively that they become hegemonic, silencing other discourses. In lay terms media concentration facilitates the manipulation of the opinions of publics to such a degree that those publics are distracted from, fail to recognize, or misconstrue the disorders afflicting them.

Disorderings of Information Processing by Increased Scale Problems of information processing are likely to be exacerbated by scale and by increases in the numbers of hierarchical levels of government or management (see Dubinskas's chapter).

In particular, the more nodes through which information must pass the more subject it is to editing, delay, distortion, and loss. Thus, the higher the administrator the less accurate, current, or complete the information on which he or she must act is likely to be, and therefore the more likely is an erroneous, inappropriate, or insensitive response on his or her part.

The likelihood of time aberrations also increases. Whereas excessive lag may be a problem, so may be *premature responses* of higher authorities, for if they constantly override subordinate regulators they will destroy them, throwing additional burdens on themselves, perhaps to the point of overload and breakdown. Moreover, premature responses of higher authorities may well be *overresponses*—"too much too soon," resulting in more-or-less irreversible changes when less drastic adjustments would not only have been sufficient but conservative of long-term flexibility. The contribution of high-energy technology to premature override and overresponse is patent. Premature response is facilitated by high-speed communication, a product of high-energy technology, and magnitude of response is freed by high-energy technology from the limitations set by the energy available from local and contemporary biological processes.

The Increased Scope of Economic Systems Several other related trends have flowed from the increased scale of social and economic organization, first in the emergence of states, then in colonial empires and now, in the post-colonial era, in the increased world-wide economic integration coming to be called *globalization*.

First, there is what may be called *oversegregation*. Whole regions or even countries come to specialize in one crop or product. But increasing regional specialization is usually, if not always, accompanied by decreased ecological stability. High-yield varieties of staples planted in monocrop fields are in themselves delicate; moreover, their successful growth usually depends on fuel, machinery, and chemicals delivered from great distances through extensive and complicated networks. Remote as well as nearby difficulties can thus disrupt agriculture anywhere. With the loss of local self-sufficiency that follows from geographical specialization, there is also loss of local regulatory autonomy. The regulatory capacity lost from local systems is not adequately replaced by increasingly remote centralized regulators responding to increasingly aggregated and simplified variables, like monetary values, through operations increasingly subject to such cybernetic impedances and time aberrations as those already mentioned.

We recognize here yet another maladaptive form that has elsewhere been called *hypercoherence* (Flannery 1972; Rappaport 1969, 1971, 1977). The coherence (i.e., the extent to which changes in the state of one component of a system effects changes in other components of that system) of the world as a whole increases to dangerous levels as the self-sufficiency of local systems is reduced. Disruptions originating anywhere immediately spread everywhere.

With loss of self-sufficiency there may be loss of autonomy. Ecological degradation, therefore, has political consequences among which may be increased political centralization and, given the possible inadequacies of centralized agencies to regulate the complex systems over which they preside, this sometimes becomes *overcentralization*. Dubinskas's discussion, although it focuses on private firms, applies to social systems as well. Overcentralization, hypercoherence, and oversegregation can constitute socially, politically, economically, and ecologically destructive vicious circles.

Paradoxically although overcentralization, which may have reached its apogee during the heyday of colonization, remains a problem in the postcolonial period, *undercentralization* of authority may bid fair to become the fundamental problem of the twenty-first century. The power of global capitalism, which operates through the simplified and dissolvant terms of monetary metrics and is able to move billions of dollars from one part of the world to another in an electronic instant, overwhelms the capacities of national governments to contain it, and its strength remains unmatched by that of any global institution yet evolved. The deindustrialization of the North and the impoverishment of the inner cities of which Newman speaks, and the pathologies flowing from such impoverishment that concern Blakey are, in some degree, consequences of a globalization that threatens to reduce the condition of the First World to that of the Third without doing either the Third World or the biosphere any compensating good.

Oversegregation, overcentralization, undercentralization, and hypercoherence taken together may be regarded as constituent elements of a more general structural anomaly we can call the *hierarchical maldistri-*

bution of organization. An increasingly complex and tightly integrated world system is based on decreasingly organized local, regional, and even national social and ecological systems. It seems doubtful that worldwide human organization can elaborate itself indefinitely at the expense of its local infrastructures, and it may be suggested that the ability of the world system to withstand perturbation would be increased by returning to its local subsystems *some* of the autonomy and diversity they have lost. This is not to advocate fracturing the world into smaller, autonomous self-sufficient systems, as undesirable as impossible, but to suggest that redistribution of organization among the levels of the world system would serve the world system as a whole well.

Disconsonance Between Self-Sufficiency and Autonomy Another form of disorder that was approached but not made explicit is mismatch between the degree of self-sufficiency and the relative autonomy of systems and subsystems. *Relative autonomy* refers to the extent to which the regulatory mechanisms on which a system's persistence depends are intrinsic to that system or, to put it a little differently, the extent to which systems (or subsystems) are more or less distinct adaptive units. It is obvious that there should (from the point of view of adaptive success) be consonance between the relative autonomy of a system or subsystem and the extent to which it is capable of persisting on its own, that is, its *degree* of self-sufficiency, the extent to which it can meet its own material needs. This consonance is built into the anatomy and physiology of organisms. Their subsystems—organs—have very little autonomy, as is consonant with their inability to function in the absence of the organisms of which they are parts. Organisms, as distinctive adaptive units, should and obviously do have higher degrees of relative autonomy than the organs composing their parts, but such adaptive wisdom is not intrinsic to the structure of human social systems, and anomalies can develop between autonomy and self-sufficiency. The likelihood that they will is increased by the elaboration of the division of labor, that is, the multiplication of subsystems, the increase in their degrees of specialization, and the increasing identification of particular individuals and groups with particular specialized subsystems. The degree of self-sufficiency of these ramifying subsystems is roughly inversely proportional to their degrees of specialization (to come close to oversimplifying the matter), but their relative autonomy may be inappropriate to such degrees of self-sufficiency.

Sometimes, as Dubinskas's contribution makes clear, subsystems enjoy less autonomy than they need in order to function well in their specialized tasks. In colonial domination, what had been more-or-less-autonomous adaptive systems are reduced to the status of subsystems of more inclusive economic and political systems and are thus deprived of effective self-regulatory functions.

Often, however, the inverse is the case. Subsystems particularly in the form of industrial or financial firms, come to enjoy more autonomy than their self-sufficiency warrants and more than the general interests of the larger social system of which they are parts can tolerate. Their excessive autonomy may stand largely on their ability to influence or even control agencies established to regulate them. Thus, the pharmaceutical industry comes to control the Food and Drug Administration, the Senate Banking Committee does the bidding of the savings and loan industry, and industry generally through the Council on Competitiveness, overruled the position of the Environmental Protection Agency on atmospheric gas emissions during the Bush administration. The consequences of this maladaptive form have included thalidomide babies in Europe, ozone destruction throughout the world, and the collapse of the savings-and-loan industry in the United States.

The general problem being considered here is exacerbated by disparities in magnitudes, particularly monetary magnitudes, between the processes to be regulated and those requisite to the regulators. Whereas the savings-and-loan industry does business in volumes of hundreds of billions of dollars annually, the campaign requirements of the members of the Senate Banking Committee stand in the hundreds of thousands or the very low millions and need to be disbursed only once in six years. It is clear that the industry is in a position to influence one of the authorities to which it is supposedly subject for what is, in its own terms, "small change."

Although it is usually not framed in these terms, a continuing need to adjust relative autonomy to prevailing degrees of self-sufficiency, may have to be met by all complex social systems, and the difficulty of such adjustment may increase as a concomitant of social evolution. To recognize inappropriate degrees of autonomy as a maladaptive form does not resolve the matter but does offer, at least tacitly, a rational criterion for correction in a domain in which action has mainly been guided by ideology.

With *inappropriate degrees of autonomy* this brief and incomplete survey of maladaptive forms has come almost full circle, for this last disorder is related to or even an aspect of the disordering of relations of contingency and of fundamental to instrumental values with which we commenced.

The Transformation of Adaptations into Maladaptations We are brought here to what may seem a paradox but what may be intrinsic to the (possibly tragic) nature of things. The account of maladaptation so far developed here has had nothing to say about ethnic hatreds. In this regard it may be suggested that until relatively recently, the most inclusive autonomous adaptive systems have probably been more-or-less ethnically homogenous. Over the last five thousand or so years distinct ethnic or cultural units have often been combined (usually by force) into more inclusive formations, i.e., states, but these, as the late twentieth century has made clear, have often remained unreconciled and unstable conglomerates. Members of cultural and ethnic entities share traditions the positive values of which have been reinforced by, if not indeed constituted by, negative evaluation of others. This is to say that ethnic hostility may have been, through most of humanity's experience, a concomitant of adaptation itself. To the extent that ethnicity no longer bounds autonomously adapting entities this erstwhile aspect of adaptation has become maladaptive. There is nothing extraordinary about the transformation of adaptive into maladaptive features. Species and societies become extinct as a consequence of features that had been the very grounds of their earlier success.

To recognize that ethnic antagonism may have been intrinsic to adaptive processes for millennia is neither to justify its perpetuation nor to accept its inevitability or incorrigibility. On the other hand to assert that such antagonism no longer has adaptive value (if it ever did) makes it no easier to dissolve. It may, however, help us to understand the depth of the problem and to understand that homilies about brotherhood and all God's children are not sufficient to alleviate it.

Racial antagonism may simply be an extreme form of ethnic antagonism. Indeed, in much folk thought and in some bad science, ethnic differences are accounted for by differences "in blood." But whereas ethnic antagonisms may be diluted by diminishment of ethnic distinctiveness, the physical characteristics, labeled "racial" are more resistant to erasure than are foreign last names and stigmatized accents, thus making assimilation difficult.

Several general points should be made in concluding this discussion of structural disorders and the processual malfunctions they produce.

First, it is obvious that some of the maladaptive forms included in our brief catalogue overlap with others and that, more importantly, they are closely related causally, as well as by formal resemblance. It should also be obvious that comprehensiveness has not been claimed for this list. Further structural disorders could surely be identified.

Second, it would be well to reiterate that many of the disorders broached in this discussion are exacerbated by what are appropriately taken to be advances in sociocultural evolution but, as Flannery (1972) may have been first to point out, the pain of these disorders, both they themselves and the symptoms they generate, may lead to their own amelioration by stimulating further structural transformations.

Third, our discipline is properly skeptical these days about the ability of any "totalizing" theory (or, to use a buzzword, "metanarrative") to provide, by itself, an adequate account of anything human. This cannot mean that we are to reject all explicit theories, but that the limitations of each and every one of them must be recognized, that we acknowledge that we need more rather than fewer such theories and that we must consider relations between and among them. The concept of maladaptation may be helpful in conceptualizing the disorders of our society, and in exploring relations among them but it is not sufficient to constitute, by itself, an adequate theory of contemporary distress, pain, or crisis. For one thing the maladaptive *forms* considered here, it is well to reiterate and to emphasize, stand in a mutual causal, or dialectical relationship with the material *forces* that give them *substance*. We need all the tools we can lay our hands on to deal with the ills of the world. The concept of maladaptation is one of them.

III. On Correction

Anthropology has, as yet, even less to say about the correction of troubles than it has about the nature of those troubles. One does not need to be, as the cliché would have it, a rocket scientist, or political scientist, or for that matter, an anthropologist, to know that some current conditions are bad and a good many of them are getting worse. What should be done to ameliorate or correct them is another matter. The destructive potential of inappropriate and oversimplifying theories of correction needs no further discussion.

The systems in which humans participate are so complex that we cannot now, and probably never will be able to analyze them in sufficient detail to predict with much precision the outcome of many of our actions within them. We must, therefore, develop theories of both correction and continuing action that, although based on incomplete knowledge, permit human life, liberty, and community to persist in a world that becomes evermore delicate, in which error is evermore probable, and in which the consequences of error are likely to be evermore severe. Such a condition is not hopeless. It is one thing to say that the complexity of systems is so great as to confound accurate prediction, another to say that we cannot apprehend their salient structural and behavioral characteristics.

The briefly outlined account of adaptation and maladaptation is schematic, tentative, and in some respects no doubt erroneous but it is probably not totally off the mark. No social system is, or ever has been, totally free of what I have called *maladaptive forms,* but the formulation is meant to be normative rather than descriptive. As such it represents an attempt to provide a standard model of relations against which actual states of affairs can be assessed. It is, to use a medical analogy, a general diagnostic tool serving, first, as a means for recognizing maladaptations, that is, structural disorders underlying symptoms; second, for providing rational criteria for critiques of policies, programs, and actions; and third, for establishing grounds for developing plans and taking actions. It tacitly proposes that the goal of policies, programs, and actions developed and undertaken in light of its general and unifying concept is, in broadest terms, to preserve adaptive relations in human socioecological systems, to restore adaptiveness to systems deformed by maladaptations, and to impede the generation of further maladaptations. The goal in specific circumstances is to correct particular maladaptations.

This general concept of adaptation and maladaptation may seem alien to a good many cultural anthropologists who have come of age in disciplinary traditions in which the interpretation of cultural particularities has been elevated to the status of ultimate value. The macroanthropological formulation presented in this conclusion does seem to bear a closer resemblance to the world systems and political-economy movements in contemporary cultural anthropology as well as to some forms of ecological anthropology and is, perhaps, even more closely related to a good deal of theorizing in archaeology (Flannery 1973, Wright 1977). It is also formally similar to some theorizing in biological anthropology and biology (Bateson 1963, Slobodkin and Rapoport 1974). It is not, however, in any way antagonistic to interpretive anthropology; indeed, interpretation is crucial to it, given the central place it proposes for meaning, information, and value.

The concepts of adaptation and maladaptation are not exclusive to anthropology, but the emphasis placed on information, value, and meaning distinguishes the approach outlined here from other systemic models and identifies it as essentially anthropological. It not only has room for the microanthropology of interpretive ethnology, but requires it.

First, we have noted that the domination or hegemony of privileged discourses, particularly when amplified by control of increasingly concentrated mass media, may make other discourses inaudible or unintelligible. It follows that an important first step in rectifying disorders in relations between and among discourses is to make all of them intelligible and audible. Anthropology, perhaps alone among the social sciences has had, since its inception, as one of its central goals, making the understandings of others comprehensible, and anthropology because of its emphasis on participation as well as observation remains the social science best equipped to be useful in this respect. To put this in today's jargon, anthropology is best able of the social sciences to give voice to others, or to help others translate their understandings into terms that people other than they themselves can understand.

An important point must be made here. It is one thing to make a discourse intelligible and quite another to make it *audible*. To publish a monograph on the plight of some other is to inform, at best, a few thousand anthropologists. This degree of audibility is not often sufficient by itself to ameliorate the condition from which the subjects are suffering. If anthropologists are serious about giving voice to others they must give thought to a deep and difficult problem: how is information relevant to the adaptive processes of a social system, (information, that is, concerning both obscure aspects of its states, its disorders and signs of its disorders), to be introduced into that system in ways that will avoid, ameliorate, or correct maladaptations rather than exacerbate them? This problem is as fascinating theoretically as it is crucial practically and as such cries out for anthropological analysis. Such research would constitute a central component of any anthropology of empowerment and disempowerment, and therefore, of any anthropological "theory of correction."

There is a second and related ethnographic component of any

anthropological theory of correction. We observed that the more nodes through which messages pass the more likely is information loss and distortion and, implicitly the more likely are inappropriate, untimely, insensitive, and brutal responses to perturbations. This suggests that *when it is possible,* corrective action at less-inclusive levels is preferable to intrusive programs imposed by even well-meaning central regulators, and that even national and international programs should, when possible, be reformulated in more local and culturally specific terms. These admonitions are especially cogent when the less-inclusive systems are ethnic groups or are geographically defined. Corrective programs undertaken by, planned and organized by, and governed by local people guided by local or ethnic knowledge and understanding are likely to be more knowledgeable, nuanced, culturally sensitive, and less costly and disruptive than centralized programs operating in terms of highly aggregated and simplified information, and thus more likely to be successful in meeting their explicit goals. They also strengthen rather than undermine local or ethnic institutions and thus tend to reinforce or restore their autonomy. In the case of ethnic groups, as local opportunities for meaningful democratic participation are increased, cultural pluralism is maintained and strengthened. Locally devised and governed responses to local manifestations are, when difficulties are not so massive as to overwhelm them, not only more likely to be more effective in meeting explicit goals but are "empowering."

In this regard we should keep in mind that the general disorders considered in the last section affect different populations differently. This point is powerfully made by Newman in comparing differences in the impacts of deindustrialization on inner-city residents, on pink-slipped blue-collar workers, and on discharged executives. Such differences include, as importantly as possible differences in material consequences, differences in the meanings different categories of those affected ascribe to their circumstances. In this respect executives, who have generally accepted individualistic, meritocratic, concepts of social relations are hardest hit psychologically. Anthropologists are the best equipped of social scientists to investigate and illuminate both the understandings that various categories of persons develop in such circumstances, and differences among them.

In sum, an anthropological "theory of correction" would have several features.

First, it would be built on one more general conceptions of disorder or dis-ease. The formulation offered here features the related notions of adaptive structure and maladaptive deformity. Although I have made no claim for the preeminence of these concepts, I do assert that *any* concept of disorder in a world in which processes of global magnitude are ever more powerful and pervasive *must* include a macroanthropological component. Without plausible macroanthropological grounding there is little or no possibility, as Ruth Fredman Cernea (personal communication) has pointed out, of contending with the macroeconomic formulations that currently dominate discussions of social policies. Pleas by anthropologists for the preservation of local cultures, while proper and necessary, are not by themselves sufficient to confront economics and are, in their nature, forensically weak: they not only recognize the subordination of the local cultures they defend but also tacitly acquiesce to anthropology's subordination. If anthropology is to be heard in the councils that matter it must offer concepts of disorder comparable in scope to those of economics and political science.

Second, the "macroanthropological" concept proposed earlier relies on microanthropological research, which is as much interpretive as it is material in its orientation. It aims, among other things, to grasp peoples' understandings of the difficulties they are facing and to help those people make their understandings explicit to themselves and intelligible and audible to others.

Third, at the same time that local understandings are honored in the general formulation proposed here, so is the organic ground on which all living (including cultural) processes are contingent. The approach outlined here is holistic in a traditional sense: it sets the disorders that constitute its subject matter, and the correction of those disorders as well, in an ecological and organic as well as social context. As such it is more encompassing, and thus more general, than the formulations of other social sciences.

Early in this conclusion I suggested that anthropology has at least as much to gain as to give in its engagement with the world's contemporary problems. The rejuvenation of our traditional holism seems to be one of its gifts. Blakey's contribution proposes and justifies strengthened bonds between cultural and physical anthropology, the outline of maladaptive forms is closely related to theorizing in archaeology, a field concerned with decline and fall as well as with emergence, and attention to meaning and discourse obviously connects to such areas as sociolinguistics and language and culture.

Fourth, although the concept of disorders presented here is structural and universalistic the approach to their amelioration advocated here does not favor the imposition of programs devised by outsiders in terms of their own understandings on local systems but *prefers* to strengthen whatever capacities local systems have for correcting themselves of disorders as they themselves experience them. This implies that one of the aims of ethnographic research or disorder is to identify indigenous institutions or processes the strengthening or support of which can lead to culturally appropriate as well as substantively effective corrective programs.

It must be noted that favoring locally shaped responses to disorders is only a preference and as such subject to the classic qualification "other things being equal." At the same time that an engaged anthropology would point in the direction of local actions strengthening local institutions in response to disorders, it would recognize that the amelioration of many problems, political, economic, ecological, and medical, are of such magnitude that they can only be corrected at the global level through institutions that are, at present, too weak or even nonexistent. An engaged macroanthropology would consider, among other things, the levels of organization at which it is appropriate to respond to perturbations of various type and magnitude, what the nature of such responses might be and how they might be organized. It is well at this point to recall earlier admonitions to modesty, for at this point we depart from whatever competence our discipline provides us and are required to enter into conceptual and practical cooperation with other biological, physical, and social sciences.

Fifth, it follows that the structural concept of maladaptation developed earlier, informed by detailed ethnography later advocated, will be likely to favor particular positions on many of the substantive and policy issues continually exercising our political system. An engaged anthropology need not confine itself to research on public affairs but may, and even should engage in information dissemination, planning, and advocacy. To reiterate a point made earlier, this is not to subordinate anthropology to political positions but to allow anthropology to shape or determine political positions. When anthropological analyses appear in public media they represent attempts to "anthropologize" public understanding.

Sixth, the relationship of the anthropologist to public agencies, political movements, nongovernment organizations, or advocacy groups must remain unspecified here. In my view no general principle of association should or even can be specified. What should be governing for the anthropologist is her or his analysis of the disorder. In some instances, analysis may encourage cooperation with public agencies, in other cases opposition.

IV. The Conclusion's Conclusion: Engaged Anthropology and Postmodern Science

Let us now put all of this in the broadest possible context, and take up the place of our discipline in that context.

Our species is one that lives, and can only live, in terms of meanings it itself must construct in a world devoid of intrinsic meaning but subject to natural law. Its situation is perilous because the laws governing the physical aspects of the universe may never be fully known and even if they were their operations are of such complexity that their outcomes will forever remain in high degree unpredictable. At the same time there is nothing in the nature of human thought to prevent it from constructing self-destructive follies that, empowered by ever more powerful technologies, have already developed world-destroying capacities. Humanity is not simply "suspended in webs of meaning" as Geertz (1973) would have it, but is trapped between meanings that may be misunderstandings and laws that may be mysteries.

We have been brought face-to-face with a fundamental problem of what is portentously called *the human condition.* The worlds in which humans live are in part constituted by galactic, tectonic, ecosystemic, and genetic processes, in part constructed socially and symbolically. Humanity's worlds, consequently, are as full of such things as gods, heaven, hell, honor, shame, democracy, and socialism as they are of trees and rocks. But the procedures of discovery, liberated during the scientific revolution from the tyranny of religion, procedures through which humans come to understand the operations of the physical world, are not only inimical to superstition and ignorance but are, in their very nature, inimical to the processes by which the peculiarly human constituents of the world are constructed and ordered. The epistemology of modern science, this is to say, may undermine the sacred and sanctified ontic foundations on which the world's conventional structures stand simply by showing their truths to have been socially and symbolically fabricated. On the other hand, the meanings that humankind constructs may be so at odds with the world's physical constitution as to be reciprocally inimical to it. The lawful emergence, in the course of evolution, of the ability to construct meaning has provided humans with no exemption from physical law, but has increased by magnitudes their capacity not only to conceive the world, but to misconstrue it as well. (We have, for example, considered the disastrous consequences of using the epistemology of money to understand, assess, and make decisions concerning physical environments.) Contradiction between law and meaning may be the root of the deepest problems not only of humanity but, generative of the likes of ozone depletion and global warming on the one hand and the dissolution of the sanctified grounds of society on the other, of the world as a whole.

It may be that anthropology has a special part to play in resolving the contradiction between law and meaning. Two traditions have continued within anthropology since its earliest days. One, inspired by the sciences, seeks explanation and is concerned to discover laws and causes. The other, influenced by the humanities, attempts interpretation and seeks to illuminate meanings. The two traditions have not always lived happily together but the relationship between them, in all its ambiguity, complexity, flux, and tension, reflects the condition of a species that can only live in terms of its own understandings and values but is subject to all the laws, known or unknown, to which the rest of nature is subject. Anthropology's epistemology, in sum, attempts to do justice to both the conditions under which its subjects live in the world and to the complexity of the ways in whch its living subjects know and value their worlds. Virtually alone among the sciences, anthropology values and takes to be true not only objective knowledge induced from observation but inside knowledge gained through participation. Only anthropology has, since its inception, attempted to grasp human situations in ways that represent not only their complexity, texture, generality, and distinctiveness but also their living subjects' direct experience of them. That such a comprehensive grasp is ultimately unattainable does not make it less worthwhile as an aspiration. Be this as it may, that participation is a crucial element of anthropological knowing recognizes participation's role in cultural knowledge generally.

Pluralism, like participation, is a value intrinsic to anthropology, for anthropology seeks to understand the ways in which the multitude of cultures through which a single humanity expresses itself generate, represent, and maintain their truths. It is neither to embrace an extreme relativism nor to deny the reality of natural regularities now lying beyond human grasp but open to objective discovery, to recognize such truths and to try to preserve them. It is in its attempts to preserve the plurality of culturally constructed truths while recognizing the domains of truths that can only be discovered through objective means, that anthropology is able to assist in their continual reconciliation.

The forms of engagement we have advocated in this volume are not unprecedented in anthropology. We only propose to elevate their status. Engagement, particularly with the disorders that disrupt the lives of those among whom we study and learn, decreases our distance from them, makes participation fuller, and makes knowledge gained from participation truer. And when participation is no longer limited to our taking part in the lives of others but allows others to enter on meaningful terms into our enterprises, we soften the distinction between subject and object, and, in some degree, offset the corrosive effects of discovery on construction by strengthening the processes of construction themselves.

At this point research stops being research alone and becomes something more comprehensive for which there is yet no definite name, but which lies in the direction outlined by Stephen Toulmin in his 1982 book, *The Return to Cosmology.* He calls it *postmodern science.* It may hardly be necessary to say that what he means by postmodern science is very different from the cluster of ideas and attitudes coming to anthropology from architecture by way of literary criticism, inasmuch as in literary critical thought postmodern science probably constitutes an oxymoron. In certain respects, in fact, Toulmin's postmodern science is diametrically opposed to literary critical thought. It also will differ from modern science in several ways that suggest that anthropology has already begun to qualify as such.

First, it will return scientists to the systems from which the Cartesian program banished them, relegating them to the status of detached observers. In Toulmin's view, such detachment is no longer tenable on any grounds. He argues that, for instance, the effects of the study of ecological systems on those systems and of opinion polls on the opinions of those polled, and the growing awareness that living systems under study have subjective as well as objective characteristics all demonstrate that scientific detachment cannot be achieved. We should hasten to note, however, that it is one thing to say that detachment cannot be realized and another to say that objectivity is not possible. Passionate commitment to the amelioration of problems bearing directly on us does not preclude their dispassionate analysis. Objectivity in this sense does require some distance but some degree of distance if not naturally there, can almost always be negotiated and it should be kept in mind that even great physical distance never constitutes radical or absolute separation.

This leads to a second difference. Whereas modern science has attempted to develop theory, that is, detached intellectual understanding derived from objective or outside knowledge of particular constituents of the world, leaving praxis to engineers or politicians, an engaged postmodern science, recognizing that participation in the world is inescapable, will incorporate into itself considerations of practice, and must, consequently, develop theories of practice. If participation entails engagement with problems troubling the world—poverty, hunger, ecological degradation, inequality, racism, oppression—and their underlying causes, these theories will, at least in part, be theories of correction, as we have already noted, and that supposes a moral dimension. Here, then, is the third difference: whereas modern science claims to be value-free, postmodern science will be candid about its value dimension.

A fourth difference is implicit. If postmodern science is to be a science of thinking and acting subjects and not merely of inanimate objects, or of subjects treated as inanimate or passive objects, then it will take as valid inside, subjective knowledge as well as outside objective knowledge: Vico's *verum* as well as Descartes's *certum*. Anthropology is further along in this respect than are other social sciences. The very qualities that sometimes lead anthropologists and others to regard anthropology as the least scientific of the modern social sciences—its qualitative concerns, its commitment to context and to holism, its respect for subjective as well as objective knowledge, its consequent emphasis upon *participant*-observation rather than observation pure and simple, its worries about ethnographic representation, its willingness to quantify tempered by awareness of the epistemic limitations of quantification, its humanistic concern with what it is to be human—are the very factors that make it precocious as a postmodern science.

There is a fifth difference. The detailed and specialized observations specified by the methods of modern science have required an even finer division of scientific labor. As a consequence, knowledge has become increasingly fragmented and the organization of the world as a whole has become no serious scholar's business. Postmodern science, Toulmin asserts, must revive concern with Cosmos—the universe as a whole, or perhaps the wholeness of the universe—banished from the considerations of serious scientists since the seventeenth century when the new astronomy and the subsequent Cartesian revolution made forever untenable the simplistic astronomical cosmology that had dominated thought since antiquity. That astronomy ultimately proved to be an inadequate ground for a cosmological model does not mean, however, that no good cosmological models are possible, and in Toulmin's view postmodern science will ultimately be concerned with the world's unity, *both* with understanding the principles of that unity *and* with maintaining it. In sum postmodern science is an order of knowledge *and* action in which both those who seek to discover natural law and those who seek to understand the nature of the world's constructed meanings are reunited with a world that they do not merely observe but in which they participate for better or for worse. It is in respect to this emphasis on the nature of both unity and unification that the engaged anthropology being discussed here differs most radically from the forms of postmodernism that proclaim or even celebrate the world's fragmentation.

Whereas premodern cosmology was based upon astronomy, postmodern cosmology, could be founded, Toulmin suggests, as have others, on ecology. There are many differences between cosmologies built on astronomy on the one hand and ecology on the other. Most obviously, whereas humans could relate to heavenly bodies only through observation, they relate to ecosystems of which they are elements through participation.

To adopt an ecological cosmology is not to reduce all human problems to ecological problems, but to place humanity in the world as a whole. As anthropologists, we must also emphasize that, since humanity's emergence, *Logoi*—conceptual orders grounded in symbols—have been consequential components of cosmos. The concept of *Logos* entails a realization that the world's unity is not only constituted by nature's impersonal forces but, since humanity's emergence, by symbolic and social processes as well. Further, the cultural component has become ever more determining, and not, especially since the emergence of plant cultivation, entirely to the benefit of either humanity or the world as a whole. Inequality and oppression were made possible by plant and animal cultivation and they have become increasingly predominant in human affairs since its emergence. With cultivation, moreover, humans come to construct and dominate anthropocentric systems that, with increasingly powerful technology, have demanded ever more comprehensive management at the same time that they have become increasingly vulnerable to disruption. It is now at least possible that humans could so disrupt the planet's chemical cycles that natural self-regulatory processes could no longer correct them.

Given humanity's powers to disrupt as well as construct, and its domination of ecosystems it itself destabilizes, its responsibility can no longer be to itself alone but must be to the world as a whole. If evolution, human and otherwise, is to continue, humanity must think not merely *about* the world but on *behalf* of the world of which it is a very special part, and to which, therefore, it has enormous responsibilities. If this is true in some general sense for humanity as a whole it is particularly compelling for those, like anthropologists, whose profession it is to think about such matters. We may cite a modern commentator on Heraclitus' concept of Logos: "The particular Logos of Man . . . is part of the general Logos . . . which achieves awareness in man" (Kleinknecht 1967).

The Logos, this is to say, can reach consciousness in the human mind and, so far as we know, *only* in the human mind. This view of human nature is very different from *Homo economicus,* that golem of the economists into which life has been breathed not by the persuasiveness of their theory but by its coerciveness. It is also very different from that of literary postmodernists who speak of fragmented creatures who, living in a world they take to be without depth and dazzled by its shiny but broken surfaces, cannot contribute to analyses of the world's disorders because they have abandoned any notion of either analysis or order. Humanity in the view of the engaged anthropology of which this volume speaks is, in contrast, not only a species among species. It is the only means the world has to think about itself.

REFERENCES

Aguilar, John L. 1981. Insider Research: An Ethnography of a Debate. In *Anthropologists at Home in North America: Methods and Issues in the Study of One's Own Society,* ed. Donald A. Messerschmidt, 15–26. Cambridge: Cambridge University Press.

Austin, J. L. 1962. *How to Do Things with Words.* New York: Oxford University Press.

Baba, Marietta. 1986. *Business and Industrial Anthropology: An Overview.* NAPA Bulletin No. 2. Washington, D.C.: American Anthropological Association.

Bateson, Gregory. [1963] 1972. The Role of Somatic Change in Evolution. *Evolution,* 17. Reprinted in *Steps to an Ecology of Mind,* 346–63. New York: Ballantine Books.

Benedict, Ruth. 1946. *The Chrysanthemum and the Sword*. New York: Houghton Mifflin.

Chase, Alan. 1977. *The Legacy of Malthus*. New York: Random House.

Eddy, Elizabeth and William Partridge, eds. 1987. *Applied Anthropology in America*. 2d ed. New York: Columbia University Press.

Flannery, Kent V. 1972. The Cultural Evolution of Civilizations. *Annual Review of Ecology and Systematics* 3:399–426.

Geertz, Clifford. 1973. *The Interpretation of Cultures*. New York: Basic Books.

Grant, Madison. [1916] 1920. *The Passing of the Great Race or the Racial Basis of European History*. New ed. New York: Scribners.

Hymes, Dell, ed. 1972. *Reinventing Anthropology*. New York: Random House.

James, William. 1907. *Pragmatism: A New Name for Some Old Ways of Thinking*. New York: Longman.

———. 1909. *The Meaning of Truth*. New York: Longman.

Jamieson, Frederick. 1984. Postmodernism or the Cultural Logic of Late Capitalism. *New Left Review*. July-August, 53–92.

Kaplan, David. 1960. The Law of Evolutionary Potential. In *Evolution and Culture*, ed. Marshall Sahlins and Elman Service, ch. 5. Ann Arbor: University of Michigan Press.

Kleinknecht, H. 1967. The Logos in the Greek and Hellenistic World. In *The Theological Dictionary of the New Testament*, vol. 4, ed. G. Kittel, 77–91. Grand Rapids: Eerdmans.

Kroeber, Alfred L. 1917. The Superoganic. *American Anthropologist* 19:163–213.

Kung, Hans. 1971. *Infallible? An Inquiry*. Garden City, N.Y.: Doubleday.

Marcus, George, and Michael M. J. Fischer. 1986. *Anthropology as Cultural Critique. An Experimental Moment in the Human Sciences*. Chicago: University of Chicago Press.

Messerschmidt, Donald A., ed. 1981. *Anthropologist at Home in North America: Methods and Issues in the Study of One's Own Society*. Cambridge: Cambridge University Press.

Owusu, Maxwell. 1978. Ethnography of Africa: The Usefulness of the Useless. *American Anthropologist* 80:310–34.

Peirce, Charles Sanders. [1878] 1955. How to Make Our Ideas Clear. Popular Science Monthly. Reprinted in *Philosophical Writings of Peirce,* ed. Justus Buchler, 23–41. New York: Dover Books.

———. [1897] 1955. Logic as Semiotic: The Theory of Signs. Reprinted in *Philosophical Writings of Peirce,* ed. Justus Buchler, 98–119. New York: Dover Books.

Rappaport, Roy A. [1969] 1978. Sanctity and Adaptation. Reprinted in *Ecology and Consciousness,* ed. Richard Grossinger, 114–43. Richmond, Calif.: North Atlantic Books.

———. 1971. Ritual, Sanctity and Cybernetics. *American Anthropologist* 73: 59–76.

———. 1977. Maladaptation in Social Systems. In *The Evolution of Social Systems,* ed. J. Friedman and M. J. Rowlands, 49–72. London: Duckworth.

———. 1979a. The Obvious Aspects of Ritual. In *Ecology, Meaning and Religion,* R. A. Rappaport, 173–222. Richmond, Calif.: North Atlantic Books.

———. 1979b. Adaptive Structures and Its Disorders. In *Ecology, Meaning and Religion,* R. A. Rappaport, 145–72. Richmond, Calif.: North Atlantic Books.

———. 1984. *Pig for the Ancestors.* 2d ed., 301–445. New Haven: Yale University Press.

———. 1993. Humanity's Evolution and Anthropology's Future. In *Assessing Anthropology,* ed. R. Borofsky, 153–67. New York: McGraw-Hill.

Slobodkin, L. and A. Rapoport. 1974. An Optimal Strategy of Evolution. *Quarterly Review of Biology* 49:181–200.

Tillich, Paul. 1957. *The Dynamics of Faith.* New York: Harper Brothers.

Toulmin, Stephen. 1982. *The Return to Cosmology: Postmodern Science and the Theology of Nature.* Berkeley: University of California Press.

Wright, Henry R. 1977. Recent Research on the Origin of the State. *Annual Review of Anthropology* 6:379–97.

Wulff, Robert M. and Shirley J. Fiske, eds. 1987. *Anthropological Praxis: Translating Knowledge into Action.* Boulder: Westview Press.

A Statement to the Profession: The American Anthropological Association, Panel on Disorders of Industrial Societies

Michael L. Blakey,
Frank Dubinskas,
Shepard Forman, Chair,
Carol MacLennan,
Katherine S. Newman,
James L. Peacock,
Roy A. Rappaport,
Carlos G. Vélez-Ibanez, and
Alvin W. Wolfe

American anthropology stands at a crossroads. We have the opportunity to engage on the major social issues that are confronting our society, or we can remain peripheral to them.

In participating in the lives of the communities we study and seeking to give them voice, anthropologists have, at least tacitly, long stood for a value-driven rather than value-neutral intellectual inquiry. Such participation has not, however, enabled American anthropology to escape entirely from the pervasive Eurocentrism and racism that is deeply ingrained in U.S. society. In fact, anthropology bears responsibility for some of the more ethnocentric theoretical formulations on both race and cultural assimilation. Yet, thousands of anthropologists have invested years, striving to transcend such biases through intense multiracial, multicultural fieldwork. Their efforts express a commitment to cultural pluralism and the integrity and worth of diverse human cultures. They underlie the humanist and normative assumptions that are basic to our academic traditions and frame the way we record and describe human diversity. As part of that tradition, anthropologists have also insisted on, and now need to remind our own society of, the need for pluralism—for a variety of ideas, opinions, and actors—to be fully represented in public life and its major decisions. Self-determination, the right of cultural groups to have a major voice in their own futures, is the political side of our intellectual commitment to pluralism. In the United States, as elsewhere, the emphasis on self-determination achieves concrete form in our support of democratic participation.

The United States today is suffering from a range of disorders—racism and poverty among the most visible of them—that we believe are susceptible to anthropological analysis and anthropologically informed interventions. Indeed, the decade of the 1980s saw an intensification of racial violence, drug abuse, poverty and homelessness, and environmental degradation, coupled with a resurgence of marketplace ideologies of untempered individualism and meritocracy. While these ideologies have long competed with countervailing values of pluralism and participation in U.S. life, their current dominance has marginalized and now risks disenfranchising large segments of the population. Indeed, ideologies of meritocracy thrive on the denial of pervasive discrimination and other barriers to civil rights and economic well-being, not only by society at large, but by social scientists as well. Hence, the 1990s finds the nation at a critical juncture. As the United States becomes more diverse and opportunity less accessible, our commitment to diversity, equal opportunity and political empowerment are being eroded, and particularistic images of success and entitlement are coming to dominate and even replace notions of community and social responsibility.

As anthropologists, we not only developed capacities for local analyses, but also for culturally sensitive understandings of the macrosocial, economic, and political processes that set the framework for and condition the struggle of ideas and values in American life. We are, therefore, in a position to reassert values of cultural pluralism and democratic participation as basic tenets of our society. To do so, however, requires us to address both the positive and negative aspects of our own past, to reassess our strengths, to face our weaknesses, and to rededicate ourselves to the goals and objectives of a social science in the service of the peoples it studies.

Although many anthropologists embrace the ideals of cultural diversity and democratic participation, there is reason to question the extent to which contemporary anthropology as a discipline actually embodies these commitments. First, anthropologists—no less than anyone else— are products of their cultures, societies, and political environments. The ethnic, gender, class, and generational relationships that mark their social experiences also condition their professional lives, including what they teach and the topics and manner of their research. Second, the demographics of the profession continue to belie its intellectual commitment to diversity. African Americans, Asian Americans, Hispanics and Native Americans, among others, are not adequately represented in the field, which would be enriched by their perspectives. Third, problems of racism and inequality have not been prominent among our research topics, and anthropologists who do research in these areas have been viewed as outside the academic mainstream. Fourth, anthropologists have become increasingly submerged in a professional ethic that rewards the development of abstract theory over practice, encourages individual attainment over collaboration, and places a premium on arcane debate over engagement with broader publics and pressing social issues. The most consequential audience for university-employed anthropologists lies within the academic community, and the predominant criteria for tenuring and peer review—in grant competition, publications, and promotion—reinforces our ivory-tower orientation.

Among our actual and potential audiences, anthropology has been and continues to be perceived as a field peripheral to contemporary social issues. It is thought to be a discipline more concerned with exotic, faraway cultures than with communities close to home. When anthropology does evoke a public image it is usually of the far away in time and space—not negative, but romantic—as exemplified by the popularity of Indiana Jones. However, to the degree that a romantic aura surrounds anthropology, it becomes difficult to see its relevance to hard-core practical concerns important to everyday life. Its positive association with the distant and exotic obscures understanding of anthropology's capacity to throw a particular light on national and local social problems such as racism, hunger, poverty, AIDS, and pollution, to name but a few.

Anthropology grows narrower, more constricted in theme and purpose as we compete to serve our professional goals rather than direct the discipline toward the generation of knowledge that has some more useful social purpose. Even when examing cultural groups within the United States, the tendency is to treat them as ethnographic isolates, as subcultures, rather than as integral parts of a national whole. The nature and form of that integration is an expression of stratification and inequality within the larger social, political, economic, and value system and needs to be so understood. Anthropology can contribute to that understanding, but only after it engages in an open internal dialogue as a preface to major reform. We must take stock, examine ourselves, and discuss alternative ways of acting on the world.

In the remarks presented below, we first outline the basic elements of an engaged anthropology. We then reflect on the barriers that now make it difficult to realize these goals. Finally, we offer a set of recommendations that we believe will help to revitalize the profession and give it new standing in the academy and in public forums.

Anthropological Engagement

It is important at the outset to clarify the vision we have for an engaged anthropology. We are arguing for an anthropology that includes prominently among its missions empirically grounded social criticism on the one hand and theoretically guided participation in public policy processes on the other. Our hope is to engage anthropology in the issues of our times in ways that do not subordinate our understandings to the terms of debate set by other disciplines (e.g., economics and political science). Rather, we want to make room, both in anthropology and in public arenas for anthropologists to help reformulate how questions are asked, analyses undertaken, and recommendations made. Below we consider five aspects of engagement that we believe the profession should define as goals for the discipline.

Anthropology as a Source of Social Criticism
An earlier generation of anthropologists—Frank Boas and Margaret Mead prominent among them— were recognized by the public at large as sources of insight on the social issues of their day. Their careers provide models of engagement; at the same time that they helped to frame basic concepts and methods in anthropology, they demonstrated an enviable capacity to rise above the particulars of their own research to express the larger meaning of anthropological understandings for the society in which they lived. Both Boas and Mead saw their audience as extending far beyond the academy; they wrote for, and spoke to, the public at large. They utilized their research to speak to the most critical issues of the moment and claimed the authority to draw from their work

visions of a better society as well as serious criticisms of the world as it actually was. They also self-consciously brought their social concerns back into the discipline.

The heirs to this tradition find little support in contemporary anthropology, although they flourish in other disciplines. Political scientists, sociologists, historians, and economists readily claim a similar kind of authority to speak out on public issues. As one example, Robert Bellah and his colleagues, in *Habits of the Heart,* discuss what they perceive as a lack of commitment to community in modern America. Whatever one may make of their particular approach, they share a vision of social science as "public philosophy," as a source of essential wisdom and serious reflection on the problems that beset the United States. The success of their work demonstrates that there is a tremendous public receptivity to a research-based social criticism.

Is there a public intellectual among us? Despite our special talents for social and cultural diagnosis, we rarely reach for the deeper, more publicly relevant, meaning of our work. Although we do a great deal of research that reflects critically on the nature of social problems in modern America, we fail to speak out on the major issues of the day and our work therefore often goes unnoticed.

To ask for social criticism is not a call for social punditry. Simple commentary comes cheap, and does not offer the kind of careful analysis of the systemic problems that anthropologists are capable of providing. Rather, we believe anthropologists have an obligation to apply their ethnographic, analytic, and interpretive skills to a diagnosis of current problems in the United States. In doing so, we have a primary responsibility to assess carefully the interests served by our work. As a rule, anthropologists have studied certain selected groups (usually non-Western) and written for other select (usually Western) groups. Yet, the subject and audience need not be different. What is unavoidable, however, is that we engage for selective purposes. The anthropologist as social critic needs to be explicit about the choices being made and self-conscious about the interests being served.

Community Engagement

Anthropology has a long history of direct involvement in matters of public concern. Often, it takes the form of strengthening the capacities of communities to act in their own behalf through local programs in education or economic development. Anthropologists bring a special perspective to such research and action because they are not bound by narrow preconceptions or methods, but take a holistic and participant-observer approach. Anthropologists are trained to understand how daily practices are informed by culture, and how organized interventions may fit into or disrupt a cultural universe.

Too often, however, we congratulate ourselves for our proximity to the communities we study without asking the further question of whose interests we serve. We rarely take note of competing interests and claims within communities, too often viewing them as homogenous, and asymmetrically tied to a larger, hegemonic, and external system.

An engaged anthropology assumes a special responsibility to the communities of persons it studies. Rather than extracting knowledge from its social environment in pursuit of purely academic goals, knowledge developed within a community should be democratically produced, analyzed, and reported. This assumes our engaging the community in determining the goals of research and the methods by which it will be carried out. It also includes the community in the dissemination of research results that may involve nontraditional formats such as newsletters, forums, block meetings, or creative performances. Such democratization of knowledge does not preclude more traditional forms of academic discussion and reporting; nor does it diminish the anthropologist's potential role as interlocutor, speaking to powerful institutions outside the community. It does require the anthropologist to consider carefully the various audiences for anthropological research and appropriate strategies for communicating with them.

The democratization of knowledge recognizes its joint elaboration by the community and the researcher, and it basically accords rights in that knowledge to both parties. It also requires further thought regarding appropriate modes of research. It raises questions about the role of the lone researcher in the field and the privatization of data. It suggests that alternative modes of field research, such as a team approach, could reduce the tendency toward overdetermining ownership and control of both data and interpretation in the academy, and open the way to innovative means of validating anthropological findings; for, in meeting the goals of democratization, anthropologists would be called upon to validate their research results in other than academic terms. Indeed, the requirements of such validation may be more stringent than those of academia, for the arenas in which findings are tested may include not only the review pages of journals but also the communities from which they are derived and courtrooms or committee rooms of Congress where they might be presented.

Policy Voices

We often conflate applied anthropology with anthropological approaches to or involvement in public policy, and therefore tend to equate policy-making with problem solving. Yet, with rare exceptions, applied anthropology is in the business of problem solving without the latitude to determine what the problems are to begin with. Practicing anthropologists who apply their skills as ethnographers in the service of government or service organizations often face serious constraints. When organizations put anthropologists on the payroll, they have certain defined objectives in mind. While some anthropologists are able to develop their own research agendas in nonacademic settings, most lack the time and support needed to examine their activities in their larger social contexts or to be reflective and critical about the work that they do.

Anthropology is in the policy process a voice in the minor key, at best. We are readily consulted on some aspects of development issues abroad, but we are not, by and large, sought out for advice on matters of social concern in the United States. Nor have we been energetic in seeking to make our views influential. Most especially, we are not consequential when it comes to setting the intellectual agenda for policy research. Economists, sociologists, demographers, and occasionally psychologists have claimed the high ground in conceptualizing problems of poverty and the underclass, environmental degradation, deindustrialization, and the like, often misappropriating and misusing concepts developed by anthropologists in the course of ethnographic research. Long before policy decisions are finally made, representatives of these fields routinely contribute to the process of decision making by writing accessible books and articles, holding conferences to debate these issues, and presenting analyses and policy recommendations in the national forums where decisions are made. Anthropologists, on the other hand, are effectively absent from the policy institutes and think tanks where theoretical ideas and policy debates are formulated and position papers written that are subsequently funneled to congressional committees and other policy-making bodies.

We should seek access to these critical arenas of policy debate not simply to claim our "piece of the pie," but because the kinds of questions anthropologists ask about the communities we study (and the kinds of answers we formulate) are distinctly different from those of our sister social sciences. Our emphasis on pluralism, our understanding of culture, our appreciation for the informant's perspective, and our longstanding recognition that policies incongruent with local understandings are doomed to failure, add up to a distinctive perspective that policy makers are ready and willing to hear. We are in a position to show how policies can be shaped and to respond to a community's needs and ideas and even to look inside a culture and capture "homeopathic" methods of "correction," modes of correction that are formulated and implemented by communities themselves. Moreover, we can contribute to public debates on critical policy issues (e.g., bilingual education and English only) in ways that celebrate diversity and help to undercut prejudice and discrimination.

Classroom Engagement

Many of us were initially attracted to anthropology as a forum for teaching, as a means of imparting a particular view of human life to students. This humanistic motivation is especially important when we consider that most people we see in the classroom are not going to become professional anthropologists. They may have, at most, one course in the field and then move on. What do we want young people, who may take only one course in anthropology, to take away with them as a perspective that will encourage their own engagement and dedication to cultural pluralism and democratic participation?

First, we must make it explicit and demonstrate through our actions that cultural pluralism and democratic participation are among anthropology's central, guiding principles. We want our students to leave the classroom understanding the essential integrity of human beings of all so-called races and creeds, and with some grasp of the injustices that have prevented them from equal participation. We have traditionally sought to do this by pointing to the great diversity of human cultures and by trying to inculcate an appreciation for it. But we must do more: we must make the denial of equality a central question in our pedagogy. Problems of inequality, the history of racism and race relations, the generation and reproduction of poverty, questions of gender relations, and the burdens of dislocation should be made central to what we teach. A fuller appreciation of diverse cultural traditions is essential to this. We see no contradiction here between the traditional multiculturalism of anthropology and a newer focus on forms of inequality. They are entailments of each other that provide students with deeper understandings of the conditions of their own lives and others around them, that illuminate what they read in the newspaper, and that ought to inform their thinking as citizens of the world in the years to come.

Reengaging Anthropology
An engaged anthropology is fundamentally driven by the values of pluralism, equality, and self-determination. Yet, a critical examination of the discipline's past suggests that they have not always and unambiguously guided the field. Indeed, it is perhaps more accurate to characterize the history of anthropology as contested terrain. As often as we raised a critical voice against racism, ethnocentrism, and sexism, these destructive forces have resurfaced both in our society and in anthropology itself. Anthropologists can make an important contribution to the history of science and to an understanding of society by asking why this has been the case. Such continuous self-criticism constitutes another primary form of engagement.

Any serious review of the history of American anthropology reminds us that anthropologists, even while espousing positive values, have wittingly or unwittingly contributed intellectually to racism, ethnocentrism, and inequality. For example, some physical anthropologists advocated eugenic science for the so-called betterment of humankind, while ignoring its racist implications. More recently, a number of anthropologists accepted modernization theory as the appropriate road to progressive development for new nations while overlooking its ethnocentrism. Similarly, those who saw assimilation as a way of reducing cultural or ethnic conflict in the United States sometimes failed to recognize the positive potential, as well as the structural inequities of cultural pluralism in our society. Sociobiologists, too, can be said to expound a dubious naturalism of conflict between biologically defined groups that tends to justify the successes of some few over the difficulties suffered by many. While postmodernism has been understood by some that we critically examine our ideologies, others see it as an attempt to escape into self-absorption rather than grapple with anthropology's relationship to the pressing issues in the world.

Our discipline, no less than the society it springs from, is implicated in two visions: progressive, critical, and pluralistic; and reactionary, racist, and exclusionary. While we can justifiably claim to have been at the center of these debates, speaking forcefully against bigotry and organized discrimination of all kinds, we must also ask ourselves why these conflicts continue to surface and we must continually scrutinize the biases that exist in contemporary anthropology.

It seems unlikely that any intellectual discipline could persist in isolation from the other societal institutions and public concerns with which it articulates. Anthropological interpretations are influenced by many institutional and cultural aspects: the structure of academic rewards, agendas of funding agencies, concerns of private industry or government, and broader social and cultural forces working to bolster the status quo. If anthropology is to function in an autonomous and critical way, these institutions and political factors need to be understood. We must also seek to better understand the often implicit uses to which anthropological interpretations are put. Anthropology is an important part of the institution of science because it seeks comprehensive explanations of human problems, prospects, and limitations. In so doing, however, today as in the past, anthropology reveals, distorts, and ignores important social dilemmas. Understanding anthropology's place in and interaction with the larger society should be an essential part of our academic inquiry and discourse.

Recommendations

Several impediments intrinsic to our profession stand in the way of an engaged anthropology. These include: the structure and demography of the discipline, romantic images of anthropology, the ivory-tower syndrome, localism deriving from an emphasis on individual fieldwork, intellectual provincialism, and the structure of the academic market. Collectively, these impede anthropologists from social criticism, leadership in policy initiatives, and other forms of engagement. The recommendations that follow assume that anthropology must be self-reflective and self-transformative in order to be engaged, i.e., reflective on and transformative of our way of life. Accordingly, they are arranged to begin with the discipline, move out into the world, then reflect back on the discipline.

We realize that many of these proposals are not new. Many have been discussed, some are being implemented, and others may have been debated and rejected. Taken together, however, we believe they offer a distinct view of disciplinary reform, and we hope they will stimulate debate and action.

The Profession

If anthropology is to act on its commitments, its demographics must truly reflect its ideology. Therefore,

1. The Association should establish a high level Commission on Diversity to monitor progress in the field and by individual departments, and make recommendations for improvement; establish guidelines to be used by departments in their charges to outside reviewers on occasions of program or periodic department reviews; and provide advice on matters pertaining to the work culture of departments.

2. Where African-, Asian-, Hispanic-, and Native-American faculty manifest consistently disproportionate temporary appointments, high turnover rate, and lack of promotion and tenure, internal and external review is called for to examine aspects of the professional environment antagonistic to fairness and respect for ethnic pluralism. Reforms should be instituted and monitored.

3. A similar commitment should be made to ensure the presence of women in all departments and at higher ranks.

4. The Association should vigorously pursue efforts to introduce anthropology more strongly into colleges and schools where large numbers of interested Asian-, Afro-American, Hispanic-, and Native-American students are found. The activities of the Association's Committee on Anthropology in Minority Institutions (CAP-MI) should be supported and expanded.

5. Fully reciprocal institutional bridges should be established between Ph.D. granting departments and undergraduate programs in predominantly African-, Hispanic-, and Native-American colleges.

6. Departments and institutions should reexamine their tenure and promotion criteria and recognize nontraditional forms of engaged work as legitimate and important forms of productivity for tenure and promotion.

Research

Although there are occasions when ethnologists have collaborated on common problems, anthropology idealizes the lone researcher and the individual interpretation of social facts and cultural events. This is reinforced by academic tenure requirements within the U.S. university system. The result is that the anthropologist, working alone, is publicly perceived as possessing detailed, in-depth information that is interesting but not necessarily compelling in the policy arena. National policy initiatives need to be based on generalizations that hold across communities and are unattainable from single-data studies. We must encourage collaboration and teamwork in comparative research (across sites) on large societal issues. For example, how much more compelling would an anthropology of homelessness be if it were based on in-depth fieldwork in New York, Chicago, Los Angeles, San Antonio, Atlanta, and Calcutta!

1. Faculty and students should be encouraged to engage in research and action related to issues in our own society and communities, including the fundamental questions of ethnocentrism, environmental degradation, racism, sexism, poverty, and inequality.
2. The Association and funding agencies should collaborate in establishing an RFP and review procedure to coordinate and encourage the creation of cross-site teams of researchers whose work would seek to incorporate the goals and ideas of the communities with whom they are engaged.
3. Researchers should actively seeks ways to interweave localized field research with cross-site comparisons, perhaps in units such as the task forces organized within the American Anthropological Association, to permit the generalization demanded by policy makers while building on ethnographic strengths.
4. Efforts should be made to balance a comparative (e.g., research on other industrial societies) focus with a domestic focus, perhaps by creating a unit for the Anthropology of the United States within the American Anthropological Association.
5. Anthropologists should make every effort to create institutes within or linked to their departments dedicated to engaged research in the United States.

Teaching
The public nature of most universities demands a constant reassessment of their role in educating students, and their obligations to the communities they serve and in which they are located. These concerns can be joined in ways that ensure the highest of scholarly standards and academic functions while integrating social needs and goals. Anthropology has a role to play that goes well beyond the diversification of curricula to include other, non-Western cultures. This is a particularly

urgent matter. In recent years, we have witnessed a shocking escalation of racial violence and inter-ethnic tension on university campuses across the nation. Anthropology must respond vigorously to this crisis with a series of curricular initiatives and vigorous efforts toward institutional reform.

1. Anthropology departments should consciously seek to reflect a pluralistic set of approaches to theory, method, and choice of subject, including a focus on the United States.

2. Departments should teach "engaged" anthropology, including racism, sexism, inequality, poverty, hegemony, and ethnocentrism, and possible approaches to their correction, as part of introductory or other courses reaching broad audiences.

3. These courses should balance pluralistic affirmation of the worth and significance of world cultures with the history and identity of particular traditions (African, Asian, European, Hispanic, Native American) of the students, and should honor subject matters that people of color and women bring to the study of anthropology.

4. Pre- and postdoctoral training fellowships should be established for engaged research in U.S. communities on major societal problems.

5. Departments should be urged to introduce seminars or other forums for conscious reflection about engaged anthropology, which encourages (a) knowledge of the place of anthropology in social and policy sciences and intellectual history, (b) humanistic awareness from philosophy and other fields that frame issues facing anthropologists, and (c) examination of the sociopolitical influences from which particular theoretical and methodological approaches developed.

6. Departments should encourage students to obtain skills in quantitative methods and policy analysis necessary for an academically sound and institutionally effective engaged anthropology.

7. Anthropology departments should encourage their faculty and students to take leadership roles in interdisciplinary programs, including American Studies, which can help to describe and explain the United States as a multicultural entity.

8. Anthropologists should be engaged in and, if necessary, initiate, university-wide efforts to understand and address rising incidents of bias and harassment on U.S. campuses.

9. Anthropologists should involve themselves in and help lead overall reform of core curricula in their universities to ensure the multicultural learning that will result in healthy multicultural university environments.

Outreach

A truly engaged anthropology needs to communicate with audiences larger and broader than itself. In addition to incorporating the subjects of its study as active participants, anthropologists must share the results of their work with the communities they study and with broader audiences. We applaud Association efforts in this regard and encourage expansion of the resources necessary to meet broad outreach goals. To help accomplish this, we recommend:

1. Anthropologists seek ways to help expand the financial resources of the American Anthropological Association to publicize anthropology, through such efforts as "Friends of Anthropology" endowments.
2. The Association create a journal for writing identified as anthropological on serious social problems and addressing an audience wider than the discipline; this could be the initiative of a newly formed society on the anthropology of the United States.
3. The Association make special efforts to develop ties with policy institutes and public agencies, which can be used to expand available internships and job placements.
4. The public-relations capacities of the Association need to be supported at a much higher level to engage the mass media in the presentation of anthropologists' findings in the United States, especially those bearing on pressing societal problems.
5. The American Anthropological Association continue to organize panels on particular topics of social concern (poverty, underclass), and invite foundation and other policy-determining people to attend, as exemplified by the Plenary on Racism in America: The Divided Society, held at the American Anthropological Association meetings in Washington, D.C., in November, 1989. The proceedings of such meetings should be disseminated to individuals and agencies dealing with these issues.
6. Anthropologists involve themselves in local media coverage of

community issues on which the profession can make a contribution.

Feedback into Discipline

Genuine engagement of anthropology with disorders of the contemporary world entails more than bringing the wisdom of the former to bear on the latter, all to the general benefit of humankind. Both modesty and realism propose that in transactions between anthropology and the world's problems, anthropological theory and method are at least as likely to be enriched as the disorders are to be ameliorated. If it is to deal adequately with the ills of humanity in all their living complexity, anthropology will not be able to avoid expanding itself in various ways.

Not all the dimensions of such expansion can be foreseen, of course, but we have already mentioned the participation of members of distressed communities in problem definition and analysis as well as in data collection and control. Such inclusion not only broadens anthropological perspectives and enhances interpretation, but it democratizes and pluralizes a profession whose members are characterized by a high degree of sociocultural homogeneity, and who operate in an environment in which individualism is perhaps overly encouraged. It can also have important feedback effects on method and theory in the discipline, as have the incorporation of gender perspectives, multiethnic perspectives, and innovative combinations of quantitative and qualitative methodologies.

Both engaged research and academic formulations must be prepared to shape and be shaped by each other. The experiences and activities of engagement must be distilled and brought within the purview of anthropology's theoretical discourse. As a complement, theory and thought must be open to the distinctive insights offered by research on real-world problems. True openness entails shifting the location of issue and problem definition from the academy alone to the community of engagement, and this may entail recognizing distinctive methods and modes of presentation. To help create the bridge between an engaged anthropology and anthropology as currently thought and practiced:

1. The contributions made by engaged research to the development of theory should be made explicit continuously. In the service of this objective, the Panel on Disorders of Industrialized Societies should be reconstituted as a continuing committee of the Association.
2. In light of the earlier call for self-criticism, we encourage anthro-

pologists to consider substantive research toward a critical social history and contemporary analysis of anthropology.

3. To assure that the discipline does receive feedback from the experience of engagement, editors of anthropological journals should open their pages to manuscripts that arise from such experience.

4. The annual meeting of the Association should include sessions designed for self-examination of anthropology's role within our society.

5. The profession should encourage people, through research funds and journal articles, to develop an anthropological theory of disorder and corrections.

Conclusion

Social-science theory remains inadequate to the task of conceptualizing the world's problems and how they may be corrected. Needless to say, the conceptualization of *disorder* or *problem* is itself highly problematic because the consequences of problem definition are great: it is in terms of our understanding that we respond to what we perceive to be disorders, and to the extent that we understand them well we either correct them or make them worse. In a highly differentiated world, the question of who has the prerogative to define problems and in whose terms they are analyzed are matters of grave social consequence.

If we are impoverished with respect to theories of disorder, we are in even worse shape with respect to theories of correction. The problem-solving approach favored by troubleshooters tends to rip issues out of context and, therefore, is likely to make more problems than it solves.

Some theories of disorder do exist, of course, but few would argue that they are adequate to comprehend the problems of a culturally diverse world. Furthermore, the corrective actions that they imply are often too general for effective application in particular contexts. Anthropology, we suggest, may be in a position to contribute significantly to both theories of disorder and theories of correction, for its strong ethnographic bias makes it more sensitive to nuance and distinction than other theories currently favored in policy circles, which tend to dissolve all qualitative distinctions into mere quantitative differences, permitting the world and its problems to be reduced to comparisons of bottom lines.

Anthropology, virtually alone among the social sciences in its attempts to comprehend the world, take actors' understandings as seriously as it does the other causal factors that analysts may discover. This proposes, among other things, that definition of the world's problems and the terms in which they are to be analyzed must be, in part at least, those of the communities experiencing them. But definitions of disorders are not exhausted by the understandings of those most directly experiencing them, for the disorders locally manifested do affect and are affected by the wider world. Furthermore, some aspects of any disorder are likely to be uncomprehended by the community suffering it.

In keeping with an understanding of disorder that implicates local, culturally formulated definitions, anthropological theory and practice should also advocate culturally sensitive theories of correction. Such theories of correction would not impose programs formulated in alien terms on communities to correct problems they might not even recognize, but rather would stimulate indigenous institutions to respond to the disorders besetting them in their own terms. Anthropological theory, this is to say, proposes that diverse communities not be preserved by being protected or massively assisted but, to the extent possible, by strengthening indigenous institutions and empowering local communities. A truly engaged anthropology, then, would engage communities in terms meaningful to them and, with them, work toward resolution of problems besetting the society in which we all must live together.

Contributors

Michael L. Blakey is associate professor of anthropology and anatomy and curator of the W. Montague Cobb Skeletal Collection at Howard University, where he is also director of the African Burial Ground Project. He served as president of the Association of Black Anthropologists between 1987 and 1989. His publications include articles on the history and philosophy of science, paleopathology, historical demography, and medical psychophysiology. His publications appear in *American Anthropologist, American Journal of Physical Anthropology, Critique of Anthropology, International Journal of Anthropology,* and others.

Shepard Forman is the director of the International Affairs Program at the Ford Foundation, where he has also served as director of the Human Rights and Governance Programs. Prior to joining the foundation, he taught anthropology at Indiana University, the University of Chicago, and the University of Michigan. He conducted field work in Northeast Brazil and Portuguese Timor. He is the author of *The Raft Fisherman: Tradition and Change in the Brazilian Peasant Economy* and *The Brazilian Peasantry,* as well as many articles on Brazil, Latin America, and East Timor.

Frank A. Dubinskas (1946–93) was the Howard W. Alkire Chair in International Business and Economics at Hamline University in St. Paul and the director of International Studies and associate professor of anthropology there. He wrote numerous articles and several case studies for Digital Equipment Corporation and Harvard Business School and edited books including *Making Time: Ethnographies of High Technology Organizations* (1988) and *Electronic Technologies and Instruction: Tools, Users, and Power* (with J. McDonald, 1993). He died while writing *On the Edge of Chaos: An Ethnographic Study of Manufacturing Engineering Management at Apple Computer.*

Carol MacLennan is associate professor of anthropology at Michigan Technological University. She is currently studying how the sugar industry has affected democratic development in Hawaii. She has written on automotive regulation, administrative law, and political participation and is coeditor of *The State and Democracy: Revitalizing America's Government.*

Katherine S. Newman is professor of anthropology at Columbia University. Her books include *Declining Fortunes* (1993), *Falling From Grace* (1988), and *Law and Economic Organization* (1983). She has also published widely in academic journals and the popular press, including *Newsweek, The New York Times,* and *Mother Jones.*

James L. Peacock is Kenan Professor of Anthropology and chair of the faculty at the University of North Carolina, Chapel Hill, and is president of the American Anthropological Association. His research interests include projects in Indonesia and studies on religion in the American South. Some of his publications are *Purifying the Faith: the Muhammadijah Movement in Indonesian Islam, Pilgrims of Paradox: Calvinism and Experience Among Primitive Baptists of the Blue Ridge* (with Ruel W. Tyson), and *The Anthropological Lens: Harsh Light, Soft Focus.*

Roy A. Rappaport is Walgreen Professor for the Study of Human Understanding at the University of Michigan, where he has been a member of the anthropology faculty since 1965. A past president of the American Anthropological Association, he is the author of *Ecology, Meaning and Religion* (1979) and *Pigs For The Ancestors* (2d ed., 1984). In recent years, he has worked on environmental problems in the United States while also pursuing research interests in religion.

Carlos Vélez-Ibanez is presently a fellow at the Center of Anthropology at the University of Arizona. He previously served as director of the University's Bureau of Applied Research in Anthropology. Selected publications include *Rituals of Marginality* (1983), *Bonds of Mutual Trust* (1983), and *Lazos de Confianza: Los Sistemas Culturales y Economicos de Credito en las Poblaciones del los Estados Unidos y Mexico* (1993). Forthcoming is *Many Visions of One World: The Culture of Mexicans of the Greater Northern Southwest.*